Those
Damned Rebels

Those Damned Rebels

Britain's American Empire in Revolt

MICHAEL PEARSON

HEINEMANN : LONDON

William Heinemann Ltd
15 Queen Street, Mayfair, London W1X 8BE

LONDON   MELBOURNE   TORONTO
JOHANNESBURG   AUCKLAND

To my mother

Printed Offset Litho and bound in Great Britain
by Cox & Wyman Ltd,
London, Fakenham and Reading

CONTENTS

Contemporary Maps

Illustrations

Portraits of George III, Frederick Lord North, General Sir William Howe, Sir Henry Clinton, Vice-Admiral Lord Richard Howe, Lord George Germain, General John Burgoyne, Charles Earl Cornwallis and Colonel Banastre Tarleton follow page 224.

FOREWORD

Those Damned Rebels tells the story of the American Revolution as it was seen through contemporary British eyes. Many of the basic events will, of course, be familiar to American readers, but the attitudes, the behind-the-scenes developments and, in particular, the vital repercussions that victories and defeats produced in London and Versailles will, I hope, provide a fresh perspective.

The prime source material available for a book of this nature is, of course, vast. In addition to the very large number of journals and long descriptive letters written by British officers in the field—I quote more than fifty—there are tens of thousands of pages of often ill-penned government documents, kept in dusty box files, in the Public Record Office in London.

Those readers who are not historians may not fully appreciate the fact that by the second half of the eighteenth century the British had an established military, naval and colonial government organization. It was under great pressure, for the Empire had outgrown it; certainly it had never attempted to conduct overseas operations on the scale deployed in America from 1776. But there was in existence a formal structure, involving correspondence at all levels, much of which still exists.

Governors and commanders reported home regularly. Their staffs were in constant communication with the Colonial Office, the War Office, the Admiralty, the Artillery HQ and the various official supply boards. Civil servants in government departments corresponded with each other daily.

Most of their letters and memos are still on file and form the basic source material for this book, as indeed do those minutes of Cabinet meetings scrawled briefly by one of the ministers after the private dinners during which the meetings so often took place. The idea of Cabinet responsibility was still relatively new, but the minutes, limited though they were, did at least indicate what had been decided.

The fact that there is so much material is both remarkable and exciting. For example, the log—the actual log, written at sea—still exists for every British ship that took part in the Battle of the Chesapeake. So there is a precise record that the "fore topsail yard" of the *Shrewsbury*, the lead ship in the line, was shot down at "45 minutes past 4."

Also, the private papers of almost every leading minister, general and admiral involved in the war have been preserved—and are available—though few of these are in the PRO. Many junior officers too came from influential families and corresponded regularly with the Secretary of State and other important men in London, and their letters are valuable.

One particularly important source for *Those Damned Rebels* has been Lord Stormont, British ambassador at Versailles during the critical period between 1774 and 1778, when the French, without whose support the rebellion would almost certainly have failed, entered the war. Stormont's long and frequent reports to London of his delicate negotiations are fluent, laced with dialogue, and even portray vividly the expressions on the faces of the French ministers. I have, therefore, been able to write descriptions of important meetings in the Palace of Versailles with a high degree of dramatic detail supplied by one of the men who were present.

Much the same applies to such points that might seem suspect as the weather and the exact times when events occurred in the field in America. Even the most tight-lipped of the British tended to give this type of information so that, as an author, I know from a prime source at what time the wind changed during the night before the assault on Long Island.

The picture of the British that emerges from these books and documents and the mass of printed British sources has seemed to me very different from the traditional idea of the "redcoats" or the "bloodybacks."

Judgment after the event, coupled with fiction disseminated originally as rebel propaganda and developed with time into legend, has presented a portrait of royal officers as absurdly foolish men, inept, inefficient, brutal, dulled by the previous night's drinking. The truth, as I began to discover, is that despite the system of commission purchase and complete lack of formal training, many of the British officers, from generals down, were surprisingly competent. They had their mistresses and drank their wine, but in the field their performance was often very high. (Some were incompetent, of course, but today's system does not invariably produce competence.) For example, only a small handful of officers, mostly teen-agers, stopped the panic stampede of British troops on the road from Concord to Lexington. They raced to the front, presented their bayonets (on their small musketlike fusees) and quickly forced nearly 700 terrified men to form ranks under intense rebel fire.

Many of the decisions, which appear in retrospect to be astonishingly stupid—such as Howe's move to Philadelphia in 1777 when Burgoyne advanced from Canada—were not as unreasonable as they seem when the circumstances in which they were made are appreciated. Of all the British commanders, Howe in particular was an enigma; he was unquestionably an able field general, yet he failed sometimes to exploit openings on which he should have acted. Still, even some of these—such as his decision not to storm the American redoubt after the Battle of Long Island—are not as strange as they appear when his explanations in evidence at his investigation are considered.

This book tries to see the war—the decisions that were made and the actions that were fought—in a contemporary setting. It does not set out to whitewash the British or even to argue that Howe was necessarily right to make his drive for Philadelphia in 1777. What it does try to do is to strip away some of the distortions of patriot propaganda, pitched partly on mockery and partly on brutality (so that Americans would fear the British while laughing at them), and to present a realistic picture of a major power attempting to put down a revolt for the very understandable reason that its leaders believed that if they failed, the whole Empire would collapse.

In 1775 most Americans did not want a revolution. They had to be cajoled into it—though admittedly, the British administration was a great help to the revolutionaries. For this reason, virtually all the rebel accounts of the first year's events were wild exaggerations and the propaganda system continued, albeit in a more muted, more sophisticated form, for the rest of the war. For the real conflict was for the somewhat changeable minds of Amer-

icans, as Washington discovered to his cost in New Jersey in 1776
and as Burgoyne found out so painfully in upper New York in
1777.

The sheer professional expertise of Samuel Adams and the more
radical men in the Massachusetts Provincial Congress is deeply
impressive even against a background of today's highly developed
public relations techniques. Their activities developed a whole
mythology.

What does emerge most strongly from the source material is that
the one vital factor that the eighteenth-century commanders and
ministers lacked was information. Generals rarely knew what other
British generals were doing. Advances into battle were often
ordered without any kind of proper knowledge of the enemy's
disposition, partly because so much of America was rugged and
wooded. Almost certainly, had adequate communication techniques been invented by 1777, the Saratoga disaster would never
have happened, for Howe never would have let Burgoyne cross the
Hudson. Nor is it likely that the Yorktown fiasco would have
occurred.

In fact, the appalling communications problem was one aspect
that helped whittle down the advantages of the superior British
strength and resources.

Although Those Damned Rebels sets out to tell the story of the
Revolution, it does not attempt to be a regimental history. If the
reader wants to know that the Seventy-first was on the left wing
and the Forty-third was on the right, this book will not inform
him. Because battles are often confusing enough, British regiments, like most of the rebel units, are mentioned only when
there is a special reason.

Also, it must be emphasized that the book often reveals facts as
they were learned at the time by the British. The information was
not always correct, even though it formed the basis for many of
their actions. Troop figures—and, in particular, casualty statistics
—were almost always subject to dispute between the two sides.
Because the perspective of the book is British, I naturally favor the
British versions. Spellings and even names of places vary a great
deal in contemporary reports and maps and I have tended to use
those that the British commanders employed.

In my notes at the end of the book, I give my main sources for
each chapter, but there are certain works by notable historians
that have served as valuable guides and information sources

throughout the whole project. They are the late Christopher Ward's *War of the Revolution*; Piers Mackesy's *The War for America*; William B. Willcox's *Portrait of a General* and his edition of Sir Henry Clinton's account of the Revolution, *The American Rebellion*; and *The Correspondence of George III*, edited by Sir John Fortescue, as well as his *History of the British Army*.

Finally, I would like to thank the many people who have assisted me in writing the book: Michael Crabbe, for his great and expert help with research; Sylvia Voller for her laborious typing of the book in its various drafts and the pages of notes that were far more voluminous than the manuscript; the staff of the Public Record Office (especially those in the Rolls Room); the staff of the British Museum (especially those serving the dictating and typing room); and, in particular, Joan Bailey, of the London Library, who has taken an enormous amount of trouble to help me trace many of the printed books that have been required, as indeed has Douglas Mathews, deputy librarian.

I am very grateful, too, to Major R. G. Bartelot of the Royal Artillery Association and to A. J. Dalkin, curator of the Rotunda Museum at Woolwich, for their guidance on gunnery systems and weapons. R. J. Hill, secretary of the Lord Chamberlain's Office, and the library staffs of the War Office, of the Royal Maritime Museum at Greenwich and of the Navy Records Society have also been most helpful.

And the greatest thanks of all to my wife and my son, Robert, for their many hours of assistance correcting the manuscript.

1

LONDON, January 13, 1774

The King, wearing the jeweled crown of state, sat on the Great Throne of the House of Lords to open the seventh session of the Thirteenth Parliament of Great Britain.[1] Facing him in tight rows were his peers, in coronets and ermine robes. Crowded behind them, summoned in formal and traditional ceremony by royal command from the lower chamber, were members of his House of Commons.[2]

George III was thirty-five. He was a tall, awkward man with an oval face marked by straight, thick lips and vapid blue eyes set wide apart. Britain had been governed in the past by monarchs who were more handsome and who had more presence, but none of them had ruled so vast a territory.

That day the king of the most powerful imperial nation in the world was in an optimistic, almost buoyant mood, as the "speech from the throne," which laid down the broad design of parliamentary business for the new session, was soon to reveal.

World affairs were running strongly in Britain's favor, for peace always favored a dominant power. There were minor colonial problems to be solved, but no major crises, no disturbing reports from the embassies on the Continent. Relations between the great nations of Europe, always smoldering and so often broken in war, were cordial. Only Russia and Turkey were in conflict, and—although ending any dispute involving so important an empress as Catherine was in Britain's current interest—the battlefields were far away.

"My Lords and Gentlemen. . . ," declared the King, "you will, I am persuaded, agree with me in regretting that the peace . . . is not yet effected between Russia and the Porte; but it is with real satisfaction that I can repeat that other foreign powers continue still to have the same pacific dispositions with myself. . . .

13

"In this state of foreign affairs," he instructed them, "you will have full leisure to attend to the improvement of our internal and domestic situation."

Parliament, which, like Europe, was so often in conflict, was that day as peaceful as the international scene. When the royal procession had retired, the Earl of Northington rose, on behalf of the peers, to express the customary gratitude for the "most gracious speech." They, too, were concerned that "peace, so long expected . . . is not yet concluded between Russia and the Porte" but gave "sincerest thanks" for His Majesty's endeavors to establish and preserve "the public tranquility" in Europe.

In the Commons, Lord Guernsey,[3] proposing the thanks of the lower house, was more dramatic. "His Majesty," he declared, "saw the most glorious sight a monarch can behold," during a recent review of the fleet off Portsmouth, "yet it did not fill him with any vain notions. No rapacious thoughts filled his breast. It was true we keep up a powerful fleet and armament, but it is not to destroy or disturb the peace of weaker powers, but to maintain the honour and dignity of this nation."

The King had already been assured by his Prime Minister that Lord Guernsey would be suitably complimentary. Even so, he was pleased with the reception of the speech. "It is always a pleasant appearance at the opening of a session," he commented happily, "to have the first day conclude without debate."

For although George III was a man of great power, he was not an autocrat like such rival monarchs as Louis XV or Frederick II or Catherine II. He exercised personal executive control of a nation that possessed great expanses of territory thousands of miles away, both to east and west, but he did so only with the cooperation of a careful and often critical parliament.

He had transformed gaining that cooperation into an art, at which he was highly skilled. His pleasure in the reception of his speech was coupled with a sense of professional pride. The machine was operating well.

The headquarters of the British Empire was St. James's, a rambling red-brick Tudor palace half hidden behind high walls. From St. James's Park, which it bordered, all of it that could be seen was a small pointed clock tower and the upper part of a long, low complex of crenellated buildings. Behind it lay fashionable London, where nearly everyone of influence owned houses.

By that January St. James's was no longer a residential palace. It was the King's working office, the formal home of the court, the social and political hub of the British capital. It was here during the next few days that George III, on the advice of his Cabinet, was to make decisions that were to have enormous repercussions. They were to transform the tranquil scene he had described in Parliament, plunge Britain into war once more with his traditional enemies, the Bourbon kings of France and Spain, and, eventually, even cause the birth of a new world power.

Several mornings every week, the King held a levee in the Throne Room on the first floor of the palace where he met ministers, ambassadors and others with access to the court under conditions of rigid court protocol. Under four giant crystal chandeliers, the aristocrats who ran Britain spoke with the King, who was seated under a purple canopy.

The power base was relatively small. A coterie of peers and their families provided the nation's officers of state, its generals and admirals, its parliamentarians, most of its colonial governors—and owned much of its land.

In public the King was unimpressive. He was uneasy in company, and his heavy jokes often lacked taste. The satirists lampooned him for his lack of style, for his domesticity. Certainly, by European standards, his court was uncolorful. There were no royal mistresses, no gambling, few balls.

He was a family man—dull, pedantic, stubborn, precise—who grew impatient sometimes with the panoply of monarchy. To the despair of his staff, he often insisted on driving to St. James's from his riverside country palace at Kew in a simple unostentatious coach.

It was not in the open court he displayed that flair for political strategy, but in the Closet, the oak-paneled apartment behind the Throne Room at St. James's, which was the royal operations center. It was there that he proved he understood completely the subtle forces that, as a monarch of a nation operated on partly democratic lines, he needed to control and influence. Unlike Charles I, who had fought Parliament with such unfortunate results, George III exploited it.

By January, working quietly and methodically with bribery and the prizes of political rewards that were available to a king, he had managed to control 220 votes in the House of Commons. He had gained strong support in the Lords, where the conflict between opposing powerful Whig peers—with their ganglike groups of supporters—had lessened their influence.

In his fat, genial Prime Minister—Frederick, Lord North—the King had a man who was suited ideally to his operational design. For North, who accepted the firm royal guidance, was adept at controlling the parliamentary machine. He could push bills through adroitly and displayed the resilience of a feather mattress when fending off attack.

In fact, the whole technique of manipulating Parliament obsessed the King. He ran his ministers like the manager of a team, pressing them into action, commenting on their performance in debate, warning them where they were open to attack, praising them when they had accomplished a successful maneuver. From the Closet, he scribbled an endless stream of notes—orders, encouragement, criticism—most of them dated to the exact minute of writing.

He worked at being a king with dogged Germanic industry. In the afternoon, if he was not going to Kew, he left the palace by the private sovereign's entrance, just below the Closet, and traveled by sedan chair the short distance across St. James's Park to Queen's House—as Buckingham House was now called since Parliament was giving it to the Queen—where the royal family lived when they were in London. There, until well into the night, he would continue penning his sharp dispatches to his ministers.

The line of command, dominated by his busy quill pen, had barely changed in centuries. There were curbs, such as the Privy Council—the relic of the old Norman King's Council—and Parliament, but essentially orders were still routed from the King through his Secretary of State, though now there was more than one. The staffs of the Secretaries of State had grown bigger over the years, but the machine was in bad need of overhaul. For the explosive expansion of Britain over the past decade had set up heavy strains.

The Seven Years' War, which had ended in 1763, had been the last major clash between the great powers, and Britain had emerged in triumph. Across the Atlantic with the help of its colonists, it had driven Catholic France from Canada and the north. In Europe, it had backed Frederick the Great of Prussia against the combined force of France, Austria, Russia and, subsequently, Spain, which had entered the conflict in the last stages. At the Treaty of Paris, its dominance as an imperial power had been established. Thereafter, it controlled all America, east of the Mississippi, Canada, many islands in the West Indies and large parts of India—an imperial complex that it saw primarily in trading terms. Its colonies bought British goods, and their exports were channeled by law through the London wholesalers. As a result, British merchants traded under protective conditions that were virtually unprecedented—conditions that, by that January day the King opened Parliament, were under direct challenge by a group of militant colonials in Boston in the American province of Massachusetts Bay.

Just how militant these men had become did not become evident until six days later. Early in the morning of January 19 a merchant ship named *The Hayley* had dropped anchor in Dover Harbor after a voyage from Massachusetts. Her captain brought with him a copy of the Boston *Evening Post*, which was rushed to London by express.

That night, in Queen's House, the King read the *Evening Post*'s jubilant report of a riot that had occurred in Boston on December 16: A mob, disguised as Indians, had thrown 340 chests of British tea into the waters of the harbor.

There was no sudden dispatch of messengers to summon council meetings. The King's first thoughts were technical, concerned with distribution of an imperial product. "I am much hurt . . ." he wrote that night, "but I trust by degrees, tea will find its way there; for when Quebec is stocked . . . it will spread southwards."

The reaction of the ministers to the Boston Tea Party, as it came to be known, was much like that of the King. Not until five days after the news reached London did the Earl of Dartmouth, Secretary of State for the Colonies,[4] send for the master of *The Hayley* to hear a firsthand account by an eyewitness. Weeks were to pass before it was even mentioned in the House of Commons.

The press, too, made no great play with the story. The morning after the news reached the capital, the London *Evening Post* ran the Boston news report without comment. During the next few days, most of the other dailies gave it the same kind of treatment. The American Problem—like the Irish Problem—had been a running topic for so long it lacked news value.

The American Problem, of course, centered on taxes. The cost of the Seven Years' War had faced Britain with economic crisis. Since the American colonies were more prosperous than ever, British ministers had reasoned it was only fair to request some contribution for the imperial benefits they received—in particular the security provided by the navy.

Various governments had attempted to levy a range of taxes and duties in America, and a strengthened Customs Service had been ordered to clamp down on the smuggling that was regarded as legitimate practice in the seaports.

Resentment flared through the thirteen American colonies. Jealous and divided on many issues, they shared a common opposition to the whole concept of taxation by a parliament 3,500 miles away in which they had no spokesmen—especially since the main imperial benefit, protection against the Catholic French, no longer seemed needed.

With the colonists rallying around the slogan "No taxation without representation," the first signs of patriotism began to emerge. Progressives in each province formed activist groups under the emotive name the Sons of Liberty and set up committees to coordinate activities.

To strike at the mother country where it was most vulnerable, embargoes were declared on all British goods carrying import duties. And the Sons of Liberty attacked anyone who did not observe the ban by the liberal use of tar and feathers and riding a rail.[5]

The fiercest opposition to Britain's revenue laws was staged in Boston, the principal port of Massachusetts, where a militant group of agitators—led by an ex-tax collector, Samuel Adams, and a local merchant, John Hancock—conducted a campaign that skillfully combined violence with sophisticated legal and political strategy. Radicals were now sitting not only in the elected Massachusetts Assembly, but on the executive Council that governed the colony.

Faced with this pressure by the "liberty" mobs, Britain had reacted with astonishing tolerance. By the fall of 1773 nearly all the taxes had been dropped. Tea was the only product still carrying an import duty, and this was a minimal threepence in the pound. Still, the Sons of Liberty blocked its sale by their embargo.

To overcome this, the government planned to slash the price by changing the law. Parliament granted leave to the East India Company to ignore the imperial trading rules and to bypass the London wholesalers. Stripped of the middle profit, British tea, now sold direct by the EIC, would be far cheaper in America even than the smuggled products from other sources.

The news of this skillful move to market the only product still carrying British duty was greeted with furious outcry by the radical groups in America. Throughout the coastal towns, the Sons of Liberty swore they would stop the landing of EIC tea.

In Boston, however, Governor Thomas Hutchinson decided to make a stand against his local agitators, with whom he had been in bitter conflict for years. He was in a position of some strength. On Castle William, an island in Boston Harbor, he had British troops to support him. Lying at anchor were British men-of-war.

It was against this background that, in early October, the tea ships had sailed from Britain—for Charleston, for Philadelphia, for New York and for Boston. *pass through ports*

The first smell of new trouble across the Atlantic permeated the Colonial Office in Whitehall a few days before Christmas. It took upwards of four weeks for the mail packets to sail the Atlantic, so the dispatches laid on the desk of Lord Dartmouth in December had been written before the tea ships arrived.

He was scarcely surprised to hear that the Sons of Liberty were planning their usual tactics. Even so, he called in the EIC chairman for a preliminary conference to talk over possible action the government might take if the opposition became too violent. There was no question of changing government policy; the EIC's warehouses were bulging with tea for which it had to find a market.

By Monday, January 10, the pattern of the radical colonials' campaign was becoming clear. The EIC agents in New York reported that threats had forced them to seek the protection of the governor. The tea ship lay at a Manhattan wharf under the defensive guns of a British sloop. "Unless the act imposing a duty upon tea imported into the colonies is repealed," wrote the EIC agents, "there is not the least prospect of it being sold in this province."

From Boston, two days later, came news that the Sons of Liberty had demanded that the EIC agents declare at a public meeting that they would return the tea to England. Backed by the governor, the agents had refused, and a noisy crowd attacked a warehouse where they were in conference, but fortunately injury had been avoided.

The ships destined for Boston had not yet arrived, but their appearance in the harbor was certain to spark off a wave of serious rioting. No news had yet come in from Charleston or Philadelphia, but there was little doubt now in London that they would meet similar opposition.

Thus the news report of the riot of "Mohawk Indians" was no great shock, but the destruction of the tea—the property of a major British corporation, operating under royal charter—was an act that went far beyond acceptable limits. It was a blatant insult to the mother country that no imperial power, no matter how tolerant, could ignore.

Even the great Lord Chatham,[6] America's most influential friend in Britain and a bitter opponent of its taxation, believed that the Bostonians had gone much too far. "They manifestly violate the most indispensable ties of a civil society," he wrote to Lord Shelburne.

Reports from newspapers—especially newspapers in colonial towns—were always treated with reserve; they were so often exaggerations. But the next day a letter from Rear Admiral John Montagu, naval commander in American waters, arrived at the Admiralty and left little doubt of the truth of the news of the "tea party."

It had been written before the tea had been actually destroyed, but already the ships, lying alongside the quay in Boston, had been commandeered by the mob. Armed men paced their decks; others paraded their wharves to prevent the tea from being unloaded; the town and country around were in "anarchy and confusion." Such inflammatory speeches had been made against the government and its laws that the admiral could not answer for the consequences.

Very slowly, the wheels of government began to turn in reaction to the events in Massachusetts. At Cabinet meetings that week— normally held over dinner at various ministers' homes—the "American business" was one of the items under discussion. With the new session of Parliament just beginning, pressure of other work on the government was heavy.

Under critical debate in the Commons were the budgets of the army and navy, since Parliament had to approve them. The costs of the imperial forces were still far too high—mainly, as Lord North emphasized, because of the high expense of provisioning the

fleet in the East Indies—but the ships would be home by
Christmas, and he hoped to make substantial cuts the next year. It
was a hope the Boston militants were soon to destroy.

On January 27 the first official report of the incident from
Boston by Governor Thomas Hutchinson reached London, and its
implications were more disturbing almost than the destruction of
the tea. His efforts to organize a meeting of the twenty-six-man
Council that governed Massachusetts had failed; so many councillors had pleaded "indisposition" that he could not produce the
necessary quorum for executive action.

It was a typical Boston maneuver. The radicals on the Council
were staying away deliberately to obstruct the governor; those
who were not radicals were under threat by the Sons of Liberty.

Hutchinson was trying to organize another meeting outside
Boston, where the pressure might be less intense, but he was not
optimistic about the results. The vital prosecution of the ringleaders would be difficult, for the men who had thrown the tea
into the harbor had been disguised in war paint, and a vast crowd
had surrounded the ships during the operation, possibly to obscure
the view of the British authorities.

To the ministers in London on that winter day, the letter
sounded very inadequate for the governor of a colony with troops
at his command. Clearly, Hutchinson had lost his nerve.[7] And it
was obvious from letters that arrived with the governor's report
that the naval and military commanders thought so, too. By
contrast with Hutchinson's vague reference to the problems of
discovering who was involved, a new dispatch from Admiral
Montagu asserted bluntly that the mob had been "encouraged by
Mr. John Hancock and Mr. Samuel Adams" and insisted that he
could have prevented the whole affair if anyone had asked his
assistance—although some innocent lives would have been lost in
firing on the town.

Lieutenant Colonel Alexander Leslie, commanding a regiment in
Castle William, complained angrily that the Council had forbidden
him to march troops on the town. Appalled by the whole official
reaction, he pointed out that John Hancock, who was captain of
the Boston Cadets—traditionally the governor's militia guard of
honor—had used this very unit to take over the tea ships.
"However," he wrote, "it must end in that. Leniency won't do
now with the people here."

This was a view that was fast taking hold in London. The King was convinced that Britain was now paying for its past weakness toward the American campaign against taxes.

Another letter from Hutchinson supported the royal view. He had at last managed to organize a meeting of the Council, but it was divided about how the affair should be handled. A grand jury prosecution seemed unlikely. "I cannot find any persons . . . ," reported the governor, "willing to give an account of the persons who were most active. . . ."

By going to these extremes, the Boston militants had faced the King and his ministers with a constitutional problem. Under the terms of its royal charter, until now Massachusetts had been governed by what was in practice a fairly democratic system. But Samuel Adams and his wild men had undermined it.

For years they had defied the laws of Parliament and thwarted the courts by putting pressure on witnesses and juries. Britain, in turn, had sought mainly to placate them. For example, when customs officers had searched John Hancock's ship for merchandise that was subject to the controversial duties, a seafront mob had thrown them into the harbor and attacked the customshouse. When no witnesses could be found to support a prosecution, the British had put in a regiment of troops in an attempt to keep order. Some of the soldiers had opened fire in error on a menacing, yelling crowd, and five men had died. The government had handed over their officer for civil trial in a Massachusetts court, but the radicals had played up the incident, mourning it dramatically every year as "the Boston Massacre," as though hundreds had been killed.

The British action was typical of the soft policy at the time. Not only did they submit one of their own officers as a sacrifice to the colonials[8]—for if he had committed any offense at all, it was a military crime, subject to trial by a military court—but they also withdrew the offending troops to Castle William on the island in the harbor.

But now it was becoming clear that there had to be a limit to tolerance. The raid on the tea ships had provided proof that Britain's past colonial policy of appeasement had been a complete failure. Control had broken down. Evidently, British property could be destroyed without redress.

The more the ministers considered the incident, the more outrageous and the more dangerous in potential repercussions within the Empire it began to seem.

On Friday, February 4—two weeks after the news first arrived in London—the Cabinet met at the Whitehall office of Lord Rochford, one of the three Secretaries of State responsible for Britain's overseas affairs.

The six aristocrats who sat around that table were probably the most influential men in Britain, apart from the King. Three of them, because of the offices they held, were more closely involved than the others.

Lord North, a heavy man with drooping, jowly cheeks and bulging myopic eyes, was the First Lord of the Treasury⁹—the department that, by controlling finance, lay at the center of the British administration. North would have to mastermind the political aspects of the measures they decided and steer them through Parliament.

One of North's biggest problems was Lord Sandwich, also sitting at the Cabinet table. For as the First Lord at the Admiralty he was by tradition almost a law to himself. Britain was an island that had become a major power on the back of its navy. By contrast, the Secretary of War—the man who controlled the army—was rarely even invited to Cabinet meetings. But the First Lord moved very close at times to ignoring the Cabinet altogether.

Fifty-six years old, tall and broad-shouldered with a long, narrow face dominated by a Roman nose, Sandwich was famed for his taste for women. He lived openly with a mistress and had been an active member of the now-disbanded Hell Fire Club, whose members, it was rumored, held orgies with girls dressed as nuns.

The support of this tough and rakish earl was vital to North, who needed the navy to carry out his American plans. On foreign stations, the admirals—so often obtuse, unsubtle men who believed a few broadsides would solve any problem—were almost always quarreling with the generals and governors with whom they had to work.

By contrast, in the Earl of Dartmouth, the Secretary for the Colonies, North had a man who was his half brother, who had been brought up with him in the same house. A slim, slight man with a small, round face and soft gray eyes, Dartmouth was liberal, intelligent and devoutly religious.

It was all the more surprising, as North told the King, that this mild man had suggested the hard-line proposal that the town of Boston should be punished by closing the port.

What was ingenious about the idea was that it could be done

quickly and easily. The customs and the Massachusetts government would move to another coastal town, and British ships would blockade the harbor. As North said later in the Commons, "Four or five frigates will do the business without any military force."

It had other advantages: It would hurt badly, because most Bostonians earned their living from the port, and it was flexible. As soon as the tea had been paid for and the town shown a proper respect for the mother country, the embargo could be easily lifted.

Meanwhile, it would serve as a searing example to the other American colonies to curb their militants.

Despite their personal conflicts, every man at that Cabinet meeting was in agreement with the King that the situation in Boston could not be allowed to continue. Clearly, a strong policy was now needed. The riots must be stopped and the ringleaders disciplined. The ministers had already discussed Dartmouth's punitive proposal at previous Cabinets. Now they voted formally to recommend it to the King for official action.

Meanwhile, the King had been active at St. James's. He had summoned to the Closet a man who could give him expert advice on how the Boston crisis should be handled: Lieutenant General Thomas Gage, commander in chief of British military forces in America, who was in England on leave.

Gage knew the Americans very well. He had fought with them, lived with them, worked with them, even married one of them—the daughter of an affluent New Jersey family. For ten years now, he had held his appointment as C in C. Clearly he had a wealth of experience, and the King was delighted that the general should share his views so closely. "While we're lambs," Gage told him graphically, "they'll be lions." What was needed now was resolute action.

That night the King wrote to North enthusiastically about his meeting with the general and asked the First Lord to see him.

Now that the decision had been taken, Dartmouth wasted no time. The next day, Saturday, he briefed the government's law officers—the Attorney and Solicitor Generals—who had to confirm that the Cabinet's proposals were legal and to suggest the best way of bringing Adams and Hancock to trial.

Insisting that the King wanted a "speedy decision," he sent the two lawyers a string of questions: Did Britain have the right to close the port? What was needed from Parliament? Had the crime of high treason been committed? If so, how should they go about prosecuting?

At last, on Friday, the law officers gave their formal reply that, in their view, the Cabinet's plans were practical but needed the approval of Parliament. High treason, they said, had been committed—although three weeks later, to the King's exasperation, they changed their minds and decided, after all, that it had not.

Meanwhile, their go-ahead freed Dartmouth for action. In the King's name he instructed the five Lords of the Treasury to issue the necessary orders to move the customs and other officers out of Boston, and to make sure they did so quickly, he avoided the usual channels. He had John Pownall, his Undersecretary, send the order over to Sir Grey Cooper, who held a similar post at the Treasury, with a special request for immediate action.

Pressure was clearly vital. If the creaking bureaucratic Treasury machine proceeded at its normal pace, months would pass before anything happened. For one thing, the Treasury staff would have to draft the parliamentary bills.

At the same time, Dartmouth was trying diplomatic back-door methods to soften the attitude of the militant leaders of the Massachusetts Assembly. Writing to a correspondent who had friends among them, he urged him to "set before them how fatally and effectually they have now shut the door against any possibility of present relief for any of the things they complain of and how utterly vain it must be to expect that Parliament will ever give it to them until there appears to be a change in their temper and conduct."

Inevitably, the British plans began to broaden. If no jury in Massachusetts would convict the patriot leaders who were brought to trial, something would have to be done about the courts. If the governor could not persuade the Council to take necessary action, then this body, too, needed attention. So new acts of Parliament were drafted to bring Massachusetts under control.

The timing of the Boston militants' spectacular "Mohawk raid" —with its demonstration of the extremes to which these unruly men would go—could not have been worse. For years, the London agent of the Massachusetts Assembly, the province's elected house of representatives, had been Benjamin Franklin.

Sixty-eight years old, bespectacled, with a high bald head ringed with silver hair, Franklin held a position in London that, for a colonial, was exceptional. He was highly revered as a man of science, as a publisher, as a diplomat and even as a kind of philosopher. The ambassadors at the Court of St. James's treated him as an equal, although since he was merely representing British colonies (he also acted for Pennsylvania and Georgia), his technical status was far below theirs. In addition, he had many friends among the British power elite.

Suddenly, the previous autumn his reputation in London had been shattered by a scandal. Private letters written from Boston by Hutchinson and by his lieutenant governor, Andrew Oliver, to a London friend had been sent to Franklin. They were frustrated, hard-line letters stating that if Massachusetts was to be controlled, drastic changes were necessary—the kinds of changes that the government was now considering. "There must be an abridgement of what is called English liberty," Hutchinson had written in one.

Franklin had sent the letters to the leaders of the Massachusetts Assembly. He had advised discretion, but the local fury at the idea of new controls had blasted aside his urge for caution. Formally, the Assembly had petitioned the King to replace both Hutchinson and Oliver.

On Saturday, January 29—when the Cabinet was already considering methods of punishing Boston—the Lords of the Plantations Committee of the Privy Council assembled at the Cockpit, a large oval building between Whitehall and St. James's Park, to consider the application. As official representative of Massachusetts, Franklin attended the hearing.

The "letters" scandal that had so enraged the colonials in Boston had also appalled London's top social circles in which Franklin had previously been accepted so warmly. For the correspondence was private. By sending the letters to America, Franklin had broken the code of gentlemen even if he did act for Massachusetts. In 1773 this had appeared heinous. But now that the sense of outrage about the destroyed tea was growing, the dishonor seemed far worse.

Because of this, Alexander Wedderburn, the Solicitor General, who was appearing before the Privy Council on behalf of the royal appointees, transformed the hearing into a slashing attack on Franklin. "I hope, My Lords," he demanded, "you will mark and brand the man for . . . he has forfeited all the respect of societies . . ." Drawing a quick picture of Franklin's future in social

London, he asked: "Into what companies will he hereafter go with an unembarrassed face . . . ? Men will watch him with a jealous eye, they will hide their papers from him and lock up their escritoires.

"He will henceforth esteem it a libel," Wedderburn quipped, playing on Franklin's formerly respected role in the literary sphere, "to be called a 'man of letters.' "

The Lords of the Privy Council, already tittering, howled with laughter. Only Lord North, recalled a witness, did not appear to find the situation funny.

Under this gibe, Franklin in a dress suit of Manchester velvet, stood impassively before the rows of the peers of the Council. His calm must have irritated Wedderburn, for he now made a feature of it.

"I ask, My Lords," he said, "whether the revengeful temper, attributed by poetic fiction to the bloody African, is not surpassed by the coolness and apathy of the wily American."

It was a shameful episode—for Franklin was not the subject of the investigation—and it was sharply criticized in the London press, one paper describing Wedderburn's attack as "decked with the choicest flowers of Billingsgate [fish market]." It was, however, a clear indication of the anger, the sense of trampled royal dignity, that now gripped official London.

Inevitably, the Privy Council advised the King to reject the petition from Massachusetts. Franklin was fired from the sinecure crown post he held as deputy postmaster of America and resigned his appointment as agent in London for the Massachusetts Assembly.

At last, on March 7, in a crowded House of Commons, Lord North rose heavily to his feet and read a message to Parliament from the King. It was the first technical move in the promotion of several bills designed to punish Boston and to establish a close grip on Massachusetts—"to secure," as the royal message put it, "the execution of the laws and the just dependence of the Colonies upon the Crown and Parliament of Great Britain."

A week later the Prime Minister formally introduced the Boston Port Bill.

During the two weeks it took to pass through the Commons, the bill was not opposed very violently. The tea party now seemed shocking to everyone, including most of the royal critics. There were a few speeches questioning Parliament's right to tax Americans, criticizing the effect on British trade, suggesting other methods of punishing Boston, but the big guns of the opposition were comparatively muted.

When a petition was presented on behalf of Massachusetts, claiming that it was unlawful to punish Boston without informing the town of the charges or hearing its defense, it was ordered to "lie on the table." Tolerance and magnanimity had been tried for years—and had failed abysmally.

At the last moment before voting, Edmund Burke, the opposition leader[10] in the Commons, made a critical speech arguing that the idea of singling out Boston was wrong. "The distemper is general," he declared, "but the punishment is local," and he forecast serious repercussions. "Have you considered," he asked, "whether you have troops and ships sufficient to enforce a universal proscription to the trade of the whole continent of America?"

The bill, however, was easily passed, to the somewhat smug satisfaction of the King. "The feebleness and futility of the opposition," he noted at 8:35 p.m. that night, with his quaint passion for precision, "shows the rectitude of the measure."

Three days later the Port Bill was passed by the House of Lords and merely awaited the King's signature to become law. As a last desperate effort, Benjamin Franklin, despite his disgrace, moved back into the London political arena. Together with other prominent Americans in England, he begged the King by petition not to sign.

But it was a futile effort. The political machine that Lord North controlled under direction of the King was gaining speed. Now that the formalities for punishing Boston were completed, two more acts designed to achieve the other objects of the new policy were being promoted in Parliament.

The purpose of the new bills was to bring Massachusetts under direct British control. Since the democratic aspects of the province's charter were being exploited by the militants, these were to be suspended. The executive government and the courts were to come under the unfettered direction of the King and his governor. There was to be an end of flagrant crimes for which evidence could not be found and on which juries would not convict. Those sharp lawyers in Boston, with their clever arguments and their violent rabble, were to be trimmed down to size until they displayed a proper sense of respect to the mother country.

The opposition, deeply concerned by the principles involved, fought the new bills much more tenaciously than they had opposed the Port Bill, but North's well-organized political machine was running smoothly. Each reading of the bills in both houses of Parliament was cannonaded through by the King's supporters. The names of any waverers were reported the same night to the King, so that appropriate pressures could be levered.

In April, as the new bills were being pounded through the slow parliamentary machinery, the King took the action for which Massachusetts had petitioned. He replaced Hutchinson as governor of Massachusetts Bay—though he did so for his own reasons. Gage, who had urged "resolute action" in the Closet, was appointed to take his place—and to retain his existing appointment as captain general of all British troops in America.

Despite the autocratic powers Parliament was in the process of giving the general, Dartmouth cautioned him "to use every endeavour to . . . quiet the minds of the people . . . and by mild and gentle persuasion to induce . . . submission." The troops would enable him to meet any opposition should they be necessary, but "the King trusts that such necessity will not occur. . . ."

He was ordered to arrest and try the tea party ringleaders—unless he considered there was no hope of obtaining a conviction. He was also to veto the election to the Council of those men who had caused trouble in the past session.

And so, on April 16, the new governor-elect of Massachusetts sailed from Plymouth in a 20-gun frigate named HMS *Lively*.

2

BOSTON, May 17, 1774

Rain driven by a sharp sea wind lashed the warehouses on Boston's crowded Long Wharf as the *Lively*, with lines slung ashore from her bows and stern, was eased gently alongside the crowded quay.[1]

It was exactly five months to the day since Admiral Montagu had growled to a group of Bostonians:[2] "Well, boys, you've had your Indian caper, haven't you? But mind, you've got to pay the fiddler yet."

That wet May morning was the day of reckoning.

With drums rolling and bosun's pipes shrilling, Lieutenant General Thomas Gage, the man entrusted with the task of punishing Boston and placing an iron grip on Massachusetts, stepped on deck.

The scene before him bore no signs of the turbulent background that lay behind his arrival in the port. The people and officials of Boston had assembled to greet him with the formal ceremony that they always gave to a new royal governor. The wharf and streets through which the procession would pass were crowded with Bostonians. Massachusetts provincial troops lined the route.

On the wharf itself the reception was marked with irony. For standing stiffly at attention in front of Gage was the Independent Corps of Cadets, the governor's guard of honor who, to the disgust of Colonel Leslie in Castle William, had taken possession of the tea ships.

There, too, in front of the crowd was a VIP committee waiting to greet the general. They included representatives of the Council and of the General Assembly—both of which, in the session that was just about to end, had openly defied the King's governor.

The general, in his long scarlet coat decorated lavishly with gold, descended the gangplank. The crowd yelled; the guns of the warships anchored in the harbor thundered in salute; the church bells of Boston pealed.

At the statehouse, Gage presented his commission and was sworn in by the president of the Council. From the balcony, the high sheriff read the proclamation as cheers came from the people jammed in the streets below. There was a roar from three brass cannon manned by the local Ancient and Honorable Artillery Company. It was a day of truce, a day of forgetting, a day of lip service to the British crown whose rule was now more than a century old. But as Gage and the Massachusetts leaders knew, it did not alter anything. It did not even signify anything.

The *Lively* had, in fact, sailed into the harbor four days before. Since then, Gage had been in the island fortress of Castle William in briefing sessions—with Hutchinson, with the naval and military commanders, with the commissioners of customs—planning the closing of the port. By now more regiments of troops, destined for Massachusetts, were boarding transports in British ports. Unlike the soldiers at Hutchinson's disposal, these men would not be kept discreetly out of sight in Castle William, they would be in Boston itself, a constant reminder to the citizens of the port that the King and Parliament meant business.

Meanwhile, as Gage was in conference on the island, the reaction in the town was crystallizing. The Committee of Correspondence was promoting a campaign to combat the new British policy; Gage was quickly informed, for it was no secret.

The Committees of Correspondence existed now in many towns in every American province and had been set up years back to coordinate united resistance against Britain's colonial tax laws. By 1774 the committees with their communication link system of express riders had become well established and hardened into a practical working structure.

Boston's committee, probably the most active in the whole of America, was led by the man whom Governor Hutchinson referred to in his letters home as "the Chief Incendiary"—Samuel Adams, a tough, cunning, full-time professional politician of the Assembly.[3]

Rugged, stern, puritanical, as were most of Boston's leaders, fifty-one-year-old Adams was the first of the new school of eighteenth-century revolutionaries, the man who drew the blueprint for the French holocaust twenty-five years later. Though he had not grown up in a poor family—his father had left him some capital which he had quickly spent—material possessions seemed to have little meaning for him. His suits were old and stained. His little house in Purchase Street needed repair. Often, there was not enough cash even for food, a fact that did not seem to worry this strange dedicated ascetic.

"Samuel Adams eats little, drinks little, sleeps little," commented Joseph Galloway, a political contemporary, "and is . . . indefatigable in the pursuit of his objects."

Politics consumed all his energies. He was head of the radical political Caucus Club. For years he had written scathing bitter articles in the Boston press, castigating the Massachusetts power structure and warning the people of a secret conspiracy to enslave them.

As clerk to the General Assembly, he had ample opportunity for antiadministration maneuvering on the floor of the house, but his most important flair lay in his skill at exploiting public opinion through campaigning newspaper articles and in his "operations."

Adams controlled two Boston mobs, and he could organize a riot whenever he chose, as he had on the day of the tea party. Then, having created the news, he could spread it fast—in a form that was often untrue and always emotionally loaded—through his correspondence network.

But he seemed to know his limitations. In John Hancock, a rich young Boston merchant, Adams had a front man and a standing answer to his critics, who were always accusing him of rabble-rousing. For since the death of his father, Hancock was head of one of the top families in the town. Socially, he could not be challenged.

Boston's two chief revolutionaries were a strange and even comic couple. Thirty-seven-year-old Hancock was vain and immaculate with a taste for beautifully tailored and elaborate clothes. He was quite a contrast with Adams, with his stained cloak, who was a main influence on his policies and speeches.

The British saw Adams as a fortune hunter, exploiting the militant patriot movement for personal gain, a motive with which they could at least sympathize. His "political existence," Captain William Evelyn was to write a few months later, "depends on the continuance of the present dispute and [he] must sink into insignificance and beggary the moment it ceases."

Even though Adams pretended that he did not seek a formal break with the King, aiming only to change British policy, his aims were nothing less than outright revolution; he was far more extreme than most members of the Massachusetts Assembly, which, elected democratically, reflected all shades of political view. But Parliament's strong reaction to the tea party had swayed many of the moderate representatives at least some of the way toward supporting Adams.

By the time Gage arrived in America Adams had already made his initial plans for the confrontation he knew would come after the tea party he had organized; at his urging, the Assembly had ordered the commissary general to buy 500 barrels of gunpowder to be stored in Boston and Charlestown just across the mouth of the Charles River to the north of the port. Ostensibly the purpose was for "His Majesty's safety in the service of the Province." But the British knew the real reason. Throughout Massachusetts, as a result of Adam's rebellious activities, the people in the country towns had been learning to use firearms. Military companies were being organized.

The Boston Port Bill, which the town press had published on May 10, flared the crisis. Even Adams was said to be astonished by the severity of the act and its effective potential for punishment. Many of the city's inhabitants were clearly going to starve unless he could develop some kind of emergency plan.

Watched carefully by the administration, the politician moved fast. As soon as he heard the news, he summoned meetings of the selectmen, the elected officials who ran Boston, and the Committees of Correspondence of eight nearby towns to consider how they could retaliate against the "injustice and cruelty" of the Port Act.

On Friday, May 13, the day that *Lively* sailed into the harbor to anchor off Castle William, Adams took the chair at two meetings held one after the other in a public building named Faneuil Hall.

Plans materialized fast, but Adams did not have everything his own way. He was challenged by a group of Tories.

Both in politics and in religion, America was divided—as Britain was divided, in a slightly different way—into Whigs and Tories. The divisions were subtle, and the nature of each party varied greatly in different colonies. The distinction, already the cause of bitter enmity that was soon to grow into impassioned and vicious hatred, was more a matter of philosophy, an attitude of mind, than basic policy.

For there was remarkably little disagreement at this time between the two on the fundamental colonial political issues. Virtually all Americans were both loyal to the Crown—their quarrel being with Parliament rather than the King—and opposed to British taxation in the colonies. The dispute arose not so much in the argument itself as in the way it should be handled.

By and large, the Tories were conservative in their views and worshiped in the Anglican churches that were run by an organized hierarchy of bishops with loose links to the Church of England. Many Tories were wealthy; many held Crown appointments. They were not all rich. But intellectually and emotionally they supported the colonial government. There was a tendency for them to fashion their lives around a British pattern.

The Whigs, on the other hand, were progressives. Because they favored change, they inevitably attracted the less affluent, who would be likely to benefit from such change. But they also had many wealthy men among their supporters—such as the powerful Livingston family in New York and John Hancock in Boston. And not by chance were most Whigs nonconformist Presbyterians who, unlike the centralized near-British Anglican system, ran their own houses of worship through local elders.

From the start, when the Sons of Liberty, the radical extremist end of the Whigs, began to promote trade embargoes to make Britain to· change its policies, it was the Tories who had to be "persuaded" to cooperate. As a result, they had learned by painful practical experience that in any plans to oppose the views of the Sons of Liberty it was wise to move with caution. The political situation in Boston, however, was changing fast. The British had clearly decided to act at last against the Faction, as Adams' revolutionary group was known. Shiploads of British troops were on the Atlantic. The Tories could now afford to be bolder.

On that emotional Friday the thirteenth, however, they did not get far with their move to oppose Adams at the meetings in Boston. Their proposal that the town should solve the whole problem by paying the EIC for the destroyed tea—which conformed with the views of quite a number of "patriotic" Americans, including Benjamin Franklin—was soundly rejected. "It was," according to a resolve, "unworthy even to notice the humiliating offer."

Instead, the meetings decided that the tactics which had been successful in the past should be employed once more, though this time on a much wider scale: a combined ban by the colonies of *all* trade with Britain.

Riders rode off to the Committees of Correspondence in all the provinces from New Hampshire in the north to Pennsylvania to the south. The letters they carried asked for aggressive cooperation in the ban on commerce.

That night, while Adams' messengers were hurrying to the other colonies, General Gage at Castle William was still considering his plans. He was not the best candidate for the appointment that the King could have chosen. With his tall military figure and a round face featured by a small weak mouth, he was a good-natured, unimaginative professional soldier. Everybody liked him. Even most of the Faction liked him. But he lacked the subtlety and the strength and the sense of fast maneuver that the situation would soon demand. Worse, in crises he vacillated, and Boston at this time needed firm and careful control.

When he arrived, he had been in some doubt about the way he should interpret his instructions. But his advisers, who had now been enduring insults from the Boston mob for years, were all hard-liners. They urged him to execute his orders to the letter, and this is what he did.

By royal command, he announced that Massachusetts' two legislative houses would meet until further notice outside Boston, at Salem, a town near the sea about 10 miles up the coast. He employed his power as royal governor of the province to veto no fewer than thirteen members of the Council, the executive body that ruled the colony. Since Council appointments were drawn in the main from the elected Massachusetts Assembly, with this one autocratic stroke he removed all the troublesome members of Adams' Faction from the government.

Then he ordered the real punishment for the audacious raid on the tea ships in December, the measures that would really bite on the people of Boston: At noon on June 1, with the bells of the town tolling protest, the port was closed formally. The commissioners of customs moved to Salem. The warships took up their stations. No vessels were allowed to enter the harbor, and those there already were given two weeks' notice to leave.

Boston Harbor, serving as an estuary for several rivers, was a large bay, protected to the north and to the south by curling promontories of land. For centuries, the shores had been beaten by Atlantic seas and eroded by rivers flooding down from the hills of New Hampshire and Vermont. Now it was rugged and broken, scarred with inlets, splintered away into islands and near islands. The town itself was on a small peninsula connected to the

mainland only by a narrow neck of land. So, too, was Charlestown.

Gage ruled that the act applied to all traffic within the harbor.
No boats, except the ferry, could operate between Charlestown
and Boston. No goods could be transported to the islands.

Boston became a ghost port. "Our wharfs," wrote Bostonian
John Andrews a few days later, "are entirely deserted; not a
topsail to be seen, save the ships of war. . . ."

Against this show of sheer force, there was little the angry
Samuel Adams could do for the time being. "The violent party
seems to break and people fall off from them . . . ," Gage had
written jauntily to Dartmouth two days earlier. "Many are
impatient for the arrival of the troops and I am told that people
will then speak and act openly, which they dare not do now."

The request for cooperation carried by Adams' messengers to the
other provinces had not been entirely successful. There had been
plenty of sympathy, but, as Gage reported home happily, the
trade embargo, which would, of course, hurt American merchants,
too, had met opposition. Philadelphia had declared a day of
mourning on June 1, with a stoppage of business and a muffled
tolling of bells. But it had sent back Adams' messenger, a man
named Paul Revere; why not pay for the tea? suggested the
Committee of Correspondence. New York, too, decided not to go
along with the radical suggestions from Boston.

However, the response to the starvation threat resulting from the
closing of the port was universal. Food and money were dispatched to Boston from all over the American colonies to help the
thousands who were now unemployed. Hundreds of wagons
lumbered into the town. Sheep, cattle, rice, corn, flour and
potatoes arrived in the port to be distributed by the Faction-con-
trolled Committee of Ways and Means that sat daily at Faneuil
Hall.

Meanwhile, Adams, as clerk to the Assembly, won a big move.
He lulled Gage into believing that he was conceding that the power
of the King was too great for him; then, when the governor was
least expecting it, he had the door of the house locked, so that no
member could leave, and proposed a motion that all the American
provinces should be invited to join Massachusetts in a general
congress.

Gage, receiving an urgent warning while the Assembly was still in
session, promptly sent his secretary to dissolve it. But the locked

door kept him out, and the motion was passed and five delegates were appointed to represent the province. Among them were Samuel Adams and his distant cousin John Adams, an affluent Boston attorney who was destined to become a leader of the revolutionary movement.

On June 14 the first of the troop convoys from Britain sailed into the harbor. Under the sullen stares of Boston's unemployed, scarlet-coated British soldiers, with their standards fluttering in the wind and their bands playing, marched once more through the streets of the town. Their tents were pitched in lines on Boston Common. Teams of horses hauled artillery and ammunition wagons over the cobbled roads of the port.

Other transports were not far away. British soldiers were converging on Boston from New York, from Canada and from Britain. Almost every week new lines of tents were pegged out on Boston Common.

Early in July, Hugh, Earl Percy, son of the powerful Duke of Northumberland, arrived at the port to act as second-in-command of the troops under General Gage. A new admiral came, too. Samuel Graves, bombastic, touchy, blinkered, sailed into the bay in a big new flagship, HMS *Preston*, to replace John Montagu.

Inevitably, there were incidents between the British troops, strolling through the streets of the town in their off-duty hours, and the Bostonians. The town citizens taunted the "bloodybacks," and the soldiers sneered back. Fights were frequent.

Gage and his commanders, who believed that most of the people of Massachusetts were loyal to the King but frightened of the Faction, did their utmost to damp down the sparks in a situation that was clearly inflammable. Complaints were received with courtesy; soldiers were punished when they seemed at fault.

Despite these placatory efforts, the tension in Boston rose. Cautiously, Gage ordered all transports to stay in the harbor instead of returning to England and warned General Frederick Haldimand, British C in C in New York, that he might send them down to him for more reinforcements.

At the same time, Admiral Graves had all the small boats collected from the Boston shores and kept them moored around his flagship.

As the numbers of troops encamped on the Common were growing, the rumors that the governor would soon order the arrest

of Adams and Hancock spread. Defiantly, the Committee of
Correspondence announced that it would continue to attend to
business unless "prevented by brute force." Gage was indeed
considering arresting them, but the chief justice advised that the
time was not yet suitable. In the taut climate of Boston, it would
be certain to spark off a massive riot that could well spread
beyond the town. There were still only 3,000 troops in the port,
relatively few to handle trouble on any scale.

Since arrests seemed inadvisable, Gage tried to bribe Adams.
Hutchinson had already attempted this and explained incredulous-
ly to friends in London, where political horse trading was not
unusual, that "such is the obstinacy and inflexible disposition of
the man that he never would be conciliated by any office or gift
whatever."

Gage had no better response. When the colonel he sent offered
Adams anything "that would be satisfactory to him"—and warned
that his conduct made him liable to transportation to England to
stand trial—the demagogue snarled at him that the governor should
cease insulting "the feelings of an exasperated people."[4]

Gage was forced to resort to more regular measures to control
the situation that was fast deteriorating. For Adams was pressing
ahead fast with his plans to enforce the embargo on British trade
throughout Massachusetts and had developed a highly emotive
way of so doing. Throughout the province, bands of men directed
by the Committees of Correspondence were demanding that
everyone should sign a "solemn League and Covenant" not to buy
or consume any merchandise imported from Britain—or to allow
anyone else to. It took a brave man to refuse.

The moment the governor heard about Adams' tactics, he rushed
out a proclamation condemning the covenant as criminal and
ordered all magistrates to bring to trial anyone who signed it. But
by then the magistrates were already having enough difficulty in
conducting the normal business of the courts, without the added
burden of organizing what would inevitably be thousands of
arrests.

On August 6 the warship HMS *Scarborough* had sailed into
Boston Harbor from England. Its captain carried formal instruc-
tions to the Governor designed to bring Massachusetts under direct
British control.

Under the new acts of Parliament, the province was to be ruled
under a new system. The Assembly was still to be elected by vote,

but its powers, already curbed by the sharp use of the governor's veto, had been emasculated. The Council, appointed heretofore by the Assembly, would now be nominated directly by the King. Rioters would be sent back to England for trial. Town meetings, which were essential to Adams, were banned unless prior permission had been given by the governor.

Among the documents brought to Gage by the captain of the *Scarborough* was the list of the members of the new Council appointed by the throne.

Promptly, the Committee of Correspondence took action. As soon as the governor's messengers had ridden off to inform the new councillors of the honor the King had done them, large groups of angry men marched on their homes to persuade them it would be healthy to reject the new commissions.

Immediately, eleven of the men on the King's list explained to the governor why they could not accept seats on the Council. During the next few weeks, the rest were forced to do the same—or to accept round-the-clock protection of British troops.

In the lawcourts the situation was no better. Mobs moved into the courtrooms. Trials were stopped. Judges and sheriffs were forced to sign documents agreeing to conduct no business. At Great Barrington, angry men hurled the judges from the bench. Even in Boston, where British soldiers ensured there was no violence, the jurors at the High Court refused to be sworn.

Propaganda against the British and the new acts was poured out constantly. Cartoons lampooned "Tom Gage." "Rule Britannia" was rewritten with patriot verses. The Whig press maintained a running harangue. Even the Presbyterian pulpits were exploited in the cause, some ministers threatening damnation to those of their congregation who did not sign the Solemn League and Covenant.

Meanwhile, on August 10, in full view of the regiments on Boston Common, the five delegates of the Massachusetts Assembly to the General Congress that Samuel Adams had proposed climbed into an elegant coach they had been lent for the trip. With four armed outriders and two black servants in livery traveling on the back of the coach, they clattered along the mall that skirted the Common on their way toward the mainland—and Philadelphia, which had been selected as the meeting place. The Congress was, of course, illegal, but Gage took no action to stop the coach from leaving; it would have been almost as provocative as arresting Samuel Adams himself.

* * *

Massachusetts was in a state of anarchy. There was no effective Council and few courts. Everyone was waiting for the inevitable clash. Gage continued to carry out his instructions as well as he could. He tried to replace those Council members who had been forced to refuse their seats; he made a determined attempt to stop the now-illegal town meetings. The day before leaving for Philadelphia, Samuel Adams had presided at a town meeting in Faneuil Hall. Gage sent for the selectmen and warned them this had been against the law. They argued that it was not a new meeting, but an old one—started but not adjourned before the act was effective.

This was typical Adams—and far too technical for the governor. He bought time and referred the matter to his law officers. When a meeting was held right under his nose at Danvers, his countryseat near Salem, and kept sitting long after its business was completed in the hope he would break it up, Gage is reported to have said, "Damn them, I won't do anything about it until His Majesty sends me some more troops."

Meanwhile, other meetings were taking place throughout Massachusetts at every level from the villages to the country towns, all planning resistance to the new acts. Express riders were constantly on the move across the province with messages from one committee to another.

Gradually, the local meetings escalated toward a central assembly of delegates from all Massachusetts. On August 26 the Committees of Correspondence of four counties met in Faneuil Hall in Boston. They decreed that "since no power on earth had the right, without the consent of this province, to alter the minutest tittle of its charter," Parliament's new laws were unconstitutional. For this reason, it was resolved, a provincial congress should take over the government of the colony. Until then, the courts should be opposed, and any officer attempting to hold them, or anyone attempting to execute the new acts, should be declared a traitor and ostracized. Finally, "to secure the rights of the people . . . the military arts should be attentively practiced."

If there were any doubts that the country was on the verge of revolution, these resolves removed them. Throughout Massachusetts, they came to be regarded as a basis for action.

Wearily, Gage reported home to Lord Dartmouth about his impossible situation. His early buoyant optimism had vanished. "It is agreed," he wrote, "that popular fury has never been greater in this province than at this time, and it has taken its rise from the old source at Boston. . . . Those demagogues trust their safety in the long forbearance of Government. . . . They chicane, elude, openly violate, or passively resist the laws as opportunities serve. . . ."

He also warned that "commotions" had spread to Connecticut and emphasized that if matters became any worse, they would be faced with the problem of controlling two colonies, not just Massachusetts.

The confrontation came faster than even he expected—within days, in fact, of his letter home. On the last day in August he was tipped off by a Tory in Cambridge that powder stored in Charlestown, and owned by the people of Massachusetts, was being distributed through the country.

At dawn the next morning 260 British soldiers marched from the common, down Queen Street and King Street, to the Long Wharf and onto thirteen landing barges. The boats headed north for Charlestown. By that afternoon the soldiers had loaded them with 250 barrels of powder—all that remained in the magazine on Charlestown's Quarry Hill. Meanwhile, troops had marched to Cambridge, taken possession of two cannon that had just arrived in the town and returned to Boston.

Both operations had been quietly and efficiently conducted. There had been no resistance. No shots had been fired. By that night, however, to the surprise of the governor, signal bonfires were burning on the hilltops. He soon heard of the rumors outside the town. The troops' little expeditions had been exaggerated wildly into something far more serious: Boston had been bombarded by the warships in the harbor.

And he knew that the beacons on the hills would be signaling the alert—ahead of the express riders—through a Connecticut that was already turbulent and on to New York and New Jersey and Pennsylvania, where the delegates were gathering from all over America for the General Congress.

A crowd was collecting at Cambridge as the alarm, based on the false information, spread through the county. By the next morning there were 3,000 men on the common, and an additional 10,000 were reported to be on their way from the backcountry of Massachusetts.

Restless and tense, keen for action, the growing mob waited on the common uncertain what to do. Two judges, nominated by the

King for the Council, were spotted passing by and surrounded—but released when they insisted that they had resigned their posts on the Council.

The crowd surged on the nearby home of Peter Oliver,[5] chief justice and the new lieutenant governor. Oliver saw the danger and dispatched a rider at full speed to the governor, urging him on no account to send any troops to Cambridge. The mob was big and impatient. Any kind of military move against it would spark off a violent conflict.

Then he did what they asked. He signed a paper resigning from the Council. He even offered to give up his lieutenant governorship if they wanted him to. But this was declined. "We don't want a better man than you," mocked one of them.

Benjamin Hallowell, a commissioner of customs, was passing in his chaise, accompanied by a mounted black servant, on his way from Salem to his home in Roxbury, a Boston suburb, and made a derogatory comment about the rabble.

His remark was heard, and promptly a group was after him. Seeing the danger, Hallowell yelled to his servant to dismount, leaped on the horse and galloped desperately for Boston. When one of his pursuers drew level, he drew a pistol and fired. He missed, but as always, the incident was exaggerated as the story spread through that enormous crowd. A shot had been fired.

Meanwhile, anxious selectmen from both Boston and Charlestown were hurrying to Cambridge to quell the rumor that had started it all—that Boston had been bombarded. Already the crowd was far bigger than it had been in the morning; by night, according to advance reports of marching men, it would have grown to 50,000. Crude plans were developing to advance on Boston "like locusts and rid the town of every soldier."

The selectmen calmed the crowd, but they did not disperse immediately. They sought out the local sheriffs and made them sign documents agreeing to serve no writs and call no juries. The idea, born in the meeting a week before in Faneuil Hall when the first plan of action was resolved, spread as at last they all went home. In other towns, too, the sheriffs were forced to sign undertakings that they would do no business.

But the men who had massed at Cambridge were only part of a total call to arms that was enveloping New England. The news of Boston's bombardment was still being rushed south, uncorrected.

Men, as Gage was fully aware, were marching north—reacting to the false news in exactly the same way as those who had assembled on Cambridge Common.

The governor of Massachusetts and the captain general of British forces in North America faced the facts. "The disease," Gage was soon to write to Dartmouth, "was believed to have been confined to the town of Boston . . . but now it's so universal there is no knowing where to apply a remedy." He had been disturbed, too, by Oliver's report that the men who massed at Cambridge were not all rabble but included farmers and property owners.

The last remnants of Gage's civil administration were fast disappearing. His problems now were primarily military: how best to use his 3,000 soldiers. He decided on retrenchment. By concentrating his forces, he stood a good chance of defending Boston until, as he urged in a letter home, the King "resolved to stem the torrent" and put "a very respectable force" in the field.

So the government and the commissioners of customs moved back to Boston. So, too, did many of the leading Tories.

There Gage prepared for war. British guards were placed on all ammunition and guns of the Boston militia in the town. Teams of horses dragged cannon noisily through the cobbled streets to the narrow neck that joined Boston to the mainland—two big 24-pounders and eight 9-pounders that the gunners set up in a battery, so that they could fight off any advance on the town from the mainland. A regiment marched from the common to camp near the battery, and 200 soldiers began to erect fortifications. At night, military patrols toured the streets.

The warships were hauled in close to the town on all sides where depth permitted. Lines were run through their stern ports to the forward anchor cables, so that they could fast be swung around for the guns to bear.

The governor dispatched a message to New York: Nearly all regiments based there were to sail for Boston. Then he asked Governor Sir Guy Carleton in Quebec to send two regiments down from the St. Lawrence, which, with the natural protection of the hard Canadian winter about to set in, he should now be able to spare.

Meanwhile, alarming reports were flowing into the port from the South. In Connecticut,[6] 100,000 men were reported to be marching on Boston. Colonel Israel Putnam, one of the most celebrated soldiers in America, was riding at the head of 15,000. Among them were two sons of the colony's governor.

Two days later, as a sense of crisis gripped the town, two soldiers from the Connecticut Light Horse rode slowly and dramatically across the neck, passed unchallenged by the battery, eyed the British soldiers on guard, and walked their horses through the town. They were reconnoitering for a cavalry regiment of 500. After satisfying themselves that there had been no bombardment, they rode quietly back to the mainland to report the news to their units.

Gradually, the news spread through the advancing men from Connecticut that they had been alerted by a false alarm, and they returned home. Even so, conflict had only just been avoided, and nothing in New England was ever the same again. It had been a kind of dress rehearsal. Men had mobilized in thousands against the British. The militant patriot movement had progressed beyond riots and impassioned speeches. It had created an army.

Psychologically, the alarm and the enormous response to it had produced a new situation. It had proved it could happen. Now resistance to the British became more aggressive.

This was true especially in Boston. For the next few days, the tension was so great that the smallest incident could have flared into fighting. Every time British soldiers marched away from the common, express messengers on round-the-clock intelligence duty rode the news into the country.

When Boston's Honorable and Ancient Artillery Company marched innocently down Copp's Hill near the *Lively* on her moorings close inshore, it caused a sudden flurry of alarm aboard the frigate. The crew went to battle stations. The gunports opened. The marines lined the upper deck with loaded muskets.

In a long and alarmed dispatch sent to London on board the *Scarborough* on September 9 Gage reported his new situation to Dartmouth. It would be months before he could receive any new orders or even any more troops. Meanwhile, he tried to retain what little control he still had by playing a waiting game. He was excessively cordial to the Boston selectmen and even the Faction members who came to see him, although he continued accusing them in his letters home of every kind of trickery to maintain anti-British resentment among the public.

Writing home to his friend Lord Barrington, the Secretary for

War, Gage urged him to press the government to repeal the new acts—not because this would remove the cause of the revolt but because it would provide time to raise the big army he was convinced was necessary.

For all the governor's efforts to be pleasant to them, the selectmen pressed him angrily to remove the battery and fortifications on Boston Neck. He was, they complained, turning the port into a garrison, and they appealed to Philadelphia, where delegates to the General Congress from all the American provinces except Georgia were still in secret session, for support in their quarrel with the governor. In October, Randolph Peyton, president of the Congress, wrote to Gage. Boston's inhabitants, he said, suspected him of planning to "overthrow the liberties of America." If he would remove the fortifications on the neck, it would "quiet the minds . . . and reasonable jealousies of the people."

Gage realized that as usual the situation had been exaggerated by the skilled publicists of the Faction. Peyton's complaint was phrased in a way that suggested that the guns on the neck were threatening the Boston citizens. He sent back a spirited reply, colored by poetic touches. Insisting that "there is not a single gun planted against the town," he attacked the Faction. "I ardently hope . . . ," he said, "that the common enemies to both countries may see to their disappointment that these disputes between the mother country and the colonies have terminated like the quarrels of lovers. . . ."

As a hope, it was as romantic as its language. The General Congress passed his letter to the very men he was attacking.

As it had planned in August, the Massachusetts Assembly had turned itself into a Provincial Congress and had moved from Salem to Concord, 18 miles inland from Boston. Its president was the elegant revolutionary, John Hancock.

In a furious answer to the governor's letter to Randolph Peyton, Hancock accused him of "imprisoning the many thousands of inhabitants of Boston" and of perverting his powers as governor "to ruin and enslave the Province."

It was all pure Adams, designed to keep public emotions roused when it was published in the press and to justify the actions of the Congress. For they were now concerned with far more spectacular matters—such as reorganizing the militia, raising funds to set up magazines to supply it and mounting emergency plans: One-quarter of the force, the Minutemen, was to be ready to mobilize within hours of the call to arms.

A Committee of Safety was formed to take fast executive action if there was no time to summon a meeting of Congress.

This was the most organized challenge that Gage had yet encountered, and he was impotent to meet it. He sent out a proclamation ordering all "His Majesty's liege subjects" to disobey the resolves of the "unlawful assembly," but nobody took any notice. The drilling continued on village greens throughout Massachusetts—*and* Connecticut and Rhode Island.

Under this new surge of militancy, the new danger of a military clash grew far more imminent. Regularly, regiments of British troops marched across the neck and into the country, then turned about and marched right back again. Gage wanted the presence of British soldiers to be a normal sight in the villages. Then if ever he had to send them out for a specific purpose, at least it would not seem unusual.

And every time the troops moved out of Boston on these innocent forays, they were shadowed constantly. Expresses rode ahead of them—just in case the time had come.

Meanwhile, news of trouble from other New England colonies came streaming into Province House. The governor of New Hampshire reported that, following the arrival of a messenger named Paul Revere from Boston, 400 men had assaulted Castle William and Mary, the royal fortress at Portsmouth. All the ammunition, cannon and small arms were seized. Another raid at New Castle on the Piscataqua River was stopped only by the arrival of a British ship; even so, some of the cannon were taken. From Rhode Island came a report of an attack on Fort Island at Newport and the capture of its guns.

At the same time, in Boston, so Admiral Graves reported to London, the Sons of Liberty were making open plans to assault Castle William as soon as the water froze between the island and mainland, and to take it by sheer numbers. He suspected that attempts might also be made on the King's ships.

It was December. The cold Massachusetts winter was setting in. There was nothing Gage could do but wait—and take action as the crisis flared. It was obvious that the whole of New England was on the verge of armed revolt. He had already reported the worsening situation to London in a series of urgent letters.

A schooner, named the *St. Lawrence*, was at that moment battling through the Atlantic gales carrying to England the rebellious resolves of the Provincial Congress and a dispatch from the governor that put the issue very clearly: If the King wanted to stop the revolt, then Gage needed an army of 20,000 men.

3

LONDON, October 3, 1774

London lay damp and heavy under low clouds as the Cabinet met in a large room at 10 Downing Street to consider the latest dispatches from America.[1] The *Scarborough* had made a fast crossing.[2] It was less than a month since it had sailed from Massachusetts Bay on September 9 with the long reports, scrawled in Gage's sharp pointed handwriting, that "civil Government is near its end," that he would "avoid any bloody crisis as long as possible," that "conciliating, moderating, reasoning is over. Nothing can be done but by forceable means."

And the men at that Cabinet table knew that "forceable means" were out of the question for the time being. Because of the winter gales, it was too late in the year for transports to sail, even if any troops had been ready for them to carry.

It was eight months less a day since the King's ministers had made the decision in Lord Rochford's office to act against Boston and Massachusetts. Since then, the picture in both America and Europe had changed out of all recognition.

At that moment, as their lordships in London discussed the news from Gage, the General Congress in Philadelphia was planning joint action against Britain. At any time this illegal combined movement by colonies in a subcontinent would have caused great concern in Whitehall, but a new situation had just emerged in Europe that framed it in a setting of enormous national danger.

In May, Louis XV had died at Versailles. The sixty-four-year-old French autocrat, with his famous mistresses and his spectacular court, had pursued a policy of maintaining peace with Britain. France had been badly savaged in the Seven Years' War, and Louis had firmly opposed any moves to resume the conflict.

However, the war had now been over for more than ten years. France had recovered. The trauma of a new king had gripped Paris and Versailles. Anything could happen. Governments all over Europe were transfixed as they studied the changing power structure with intense care. Louis was only twenty-one—a dull, plain, slow-witted young man, allegedly impotent, with little political acumen and a single-minded obsession for hunting. Marie Antoinette, his beautiful young wife, daughter of the Empress of Austria, was frivolous, irresponsible and wayward.

The young couple had absolute power, and their preferences had been reflected very fast at Versailles. Old favorites had been banned from court, ministers stripped of influence. Madame du Barry, the old King's favorite mistress and previously a woman of enormous stature in the court, had been ordered to a convent soon before the dying monarch expired. In the tense mood at the French palace, Marie Antoinette had only to be a little cool to the wife of a member of the old regime for the news to be reported that day to the capitals of Europe—as, indeed, it was in one note to London.

Every week Lord Stormont, British ambassador in Paris, wrote long letters to Lord Rochford, Secretary of State for the Southern Department, speculating on the changes as they occurred, reporting every rumor. On the new King's attitude to Britain, he was reassuring but uncertain. "I should not think it impossible," he wrote, "that he [the new King] may have censured as pusillanimous the conduct of this court for some years past . . . but his passion for economy and his dread of expense give room to hope that he will not wantonly and hastily plunge into a war with England."

All the same, a revolt in America—an old and sensitive territory of conflict between the two traditional enemy powers—would clearly expose a vulnerable underside of the British Empire that could be tempting to a France humiliated ten years before. As Dartmouth had written to Gage, "Everything depends on what ministers the young king will choose to put his confidence in."

In May, another factor emerged that was closely linked to France. Parliament processed the final stages of a bill on the future of Canada. The Quebec Act, which had, in fact, been on the drawing board long before Samuel Adams organized the Boston Tea Party, restructured the government of Canada, altered its borders, and gave formal recognition to the Roman Catholic Church in Canada.

This was an enormous concession to the many Catholics who,

following the years of French control, now lived in the colony. But it created a fierce wave of resentment both in England and in anti-Papist America.

When the King drove by coach to Parliament to sign his royal assent to the bill, angry crowds in Parliament Square mobbed him. "No Popery," they yelled. "Remember Charles the First!" The King was not likely to forget Charles I. Every year, on January 30, St. James's Palace went into mourning for a day to commemorate the royal execution.

Whig sophisticates in London, however, viewed the religious clauses in the bill cynically as a clever move to keep Canada clear of the American agitators. "It was evident," commented the waspish diarist Horace Walpole, "that the Court was preparing a Catholic Army to keep the colonies in as great subjection as they had been when Canada was in the hands of the French."

This, too, was the interpretation seen by many Americans. In a petition to the King the General Congress made a big and emotional highlight of it. And it figured prominently as an important extra grievance in the stream of reports that, through the late summer and early autumn, had been flowing into Dartmouth's office in Whitehall. All the governors of the colonies —even Sir James Wright in Georgia, the only one of the thirteen American provinces which had not sent delegates to the Congress in Philadelphia—had warned of the universal support of Boston and Massachusetts and a violent opposition to Parliament's measures.

Most of them were very gloomy about the future. "The cloud to the eastward," commented William Tryon, governor of New York, where the Tories were very strong, "seems to thicken and will, it is probable, break in thunder and lightning."

At that October Cabinet meeting in Downing Street, the ministers considered the possible action that was open to them—and hoped the problem would go away. "This . . . is a state that cannot have long duration," Dartmouth wrote cheerfully to Gage a few days later. "The discontinuance of the courts of justice must produce the greatest anarchy and confusion."

Time would be needed to raise more troops, and it would be the spring before they could arrive. Meanwhile, as a gesture, the Cabinet decided to send out three big ships of the line to augment Graves' fleet—provided they could make the winter voyage without too much risk. The touchy Lord Sandwich was not present at the Cabinet meeting, and when Dartmouth suggested the possibility of hazard in his note to the Admiralty, the First Lord bristled. "English men of war," he retorted, "are likely to make the passage at any time of year."

And so the *Boyne*, the *Somerset* and the *Asia*, together with nearly 600 marines, headed through the Atlantic storms for Boston. This meant that by Christmas Gage would have a fighting force that, in addition to his ships, amounted to nearly 4,000 men.

Meanwhile, from Holland came a report that a ship from Rhode Island was loading with small arms, ammunition and cannon in Amsterdam. Immediately, Lord Suffolk, Secretary of State for Northern Europe, ordered the British ambassador in Holland to urge the Prince of Orange to intervene. And the Admiralty sent a fast cutter to stand off the port and seize the ship if it was permitted to sail.

From Hamburg in Germany came news that a ship named the *Flora* was also loading with firearms. The destination was unknown, but Dartmouth did not have any doubts about the course it would be steering. By then Lord Barrington, the War Secretary, was anxious about similar trouble on home ground. At Plymouth lay a vessel loaded with gunpowder, waiting to leave for America. "I do not know," he wrote to Dartmouth, "by what authority it can be stopped."

Repeatedly, the British administration, in great need of overhaul to meet the worldwide imperial problems that it now had to cope with, was caught unawares by sudden situations it had not anticipated. Now it rushed out an order of the King in Council—a technical emergency device—banning the export of arms and ammunition from Britain for a limited period of six months, while Parliament processed legislation to put the embargo on a more permanent basis.

During these weeks of crisis, Britain was in the throes of a general election. Because of the bad news brought by the *Scarborough* and the political ammunition it gave the opposition, the King had dissolved Parliament. He was busy buying his power in the new Commons with the Secret Service Fund, normally reserved for the payment of spies. Skillfully managing the royal campaign, he scribbled note after note to Lord North with his election instructions. No less than £70,000 was spent in bribes. The cunning Lord Falmouth, who controlled six seats in the

House, exploited the King's critical need for voting power and forced up his price of £7,500 to guineas.

By the middle of November the King could relax. The voting was over. From his palace at Kew, he wrote to North: "I am much pleased at the state of the supposed numbers in the new Parliament." And he had good reason, for he had stepped up his control.

Now, with a Parliament he could rely on to support his policies, he could concentrate once more on America. In fact, he was spoiling for a fight. "I am not sorry," he wrote to North from Queen's House at precisely 12:48 a.m. on November 18, "that the line of conduct seems chalked out . . . the New England Governments are in a state of rebellion, blows must decide whether they are to be subject to this country or independent."

On November 29, attended by the household cavalry, he drove in the state coach to Parliament to open the new session, and made a fighting speech about "the daring spirit of disobedience to the law . . . in Massachusetts Bay.

"These proceedings," he declared to the Lords and the new members of the House of Commons, crowded together listening to him, "have been . . . encouraged in other of my colonies and unwarrantable attempts have been made to obstruct the commerce of this kingdom by unlawful combinations."

The King's message was a battle cry—a public declaration that, come what may, Britain would curb its colonies. It served to heighten the crisis. For throughout the remaining weeks of 1774, the news from the governors in America, arriving with every ship that crossed the Atlantic, grew steadily worse.

The General Congress had announced from Philadelphia its full approval of the resistance of the people of Massachusetts and urged that "if Britain tried to use force, all America ought to support them in their opposition."

Privately, Joseph Reed, a Congressional delegate for Pennsylvania who for some time had corresponded with Dartmouth in a series of rational letters in which both men displayed great tolerance, warned of the imminent dangers of "a civil war not to be equalled in history."

Tea was no longer discussed on either side of the Atlantic. The dispute was now about "slavery," as the issue was being canvassed in Philadelphia, and "sovereignty," which was the prime concern of the men in London who had to cope with the repercussions of American events throughout the Empire.

"The question,"[3] Dartmouth pointed out to Reed, was whether the laws of "the mother country . . . are to be submitted to. . . . If the people of America say no, they say in effect they will no longer be a part of the British Empire; they change the whole ground of the controversy. . . ."

Despite the aggressive attitude implied by the King in Parliament and in his private letters, conciliation was in the wind. The policy that was emerging gradually from the Cabinet meetings and the King's conferences in St. James's aimed at combining peace offers with even more repressive measures—power accompanied by benevolence—but the government's presentation was poor. It could have used a Samuel Adams. For in Parliament, various bills often seemed to be in direct conflict and bore the impression of having been devised hurriedly, almost on impulse the night before, depending on whether the strong men like Sandwich or the moderates like Dartmouth had been most persuasive in the Cabinet.

Strangely, in view of his former disgrace, Benjamin Franklin was pressed diplomatically to play the key role in an important unofficial peace move, during a series of chess games with the attractive sister of the Howe brothers. Vice Admiral Richard, Lord Howe and his younger brother, Major General William Howe, were celebrated more for their talents as fighting commanders than in politics. But they had some influence at court, and the general was even rumored to be the illegitimate son of George II.

Lord Howe had plans to lead a British commission to America to settle the dispute before events reached a point from which they could not be reversed—a move which, if successful, would carry a great deal of recognition.

He used his sister, Mrs. Caroline Howe, who was a skillful chess player, to act as intermediary. Friends the Howes had in common with Franklin, who was known to be especially fond of the game, extended the invitation.

She did not mention the subject until their second game. Then casually, according to Franklin, in the course of play, she asked: "What is to be done with this dispute between Great Britain and her colonies? I hope we are not to have a civil war."

"They should kiss and make friends," Franklin said with a smile.

"I have often said," she answered carefully, "that I wished Government would employ you to settle the dispute for them. . . ."

Apparently, Franklin's answers encouraged her to go further, for on Christmas Eve, she introduced him to her elder brother. Lord Howe asked him if he would use his personal contacts to join him in seeking a peace formula.

Franklin agreed, though he was not optimistic, and even prepared a memorandum that was discussed with Dartmouth. But the King was not keen on the idea of a peace commission because "this looks like the Mother Country being more afraid of the continuance of the dispute than the colonies and I cannot think it likely to make them more reasonable."

From the start, the basic attitude of George III was consistent. He demanded submission—nothing less. He was prepared on occasions to consider and even to go along with the idea of concessions, but his correspondence suggests a skepticism about this as a technique. Military force was the way to curb rebellion. "I entirely place my security in the protection of the Divine Dispenser of all things," he told Lord North, implying complacently that God was on the side of kings, "and shall never look to the right or left but steadily pursue the track which my conscience dictates to be the right one."

On January 2 the *St. Lawrence* reached England with Gage's latest dispatches and news of extreme crisis. Now the government knew the worst. The Massachusetts Provincial Congress, aided and abetted from Philadelphia, had taken over the government of the province and was actively preparing for armed revolt. The angry mobs of September, uncertain and leaderless, were now being organized. Crude, perhaps, un-uniformed, barely armed, but an army for all that.

From then on, the government hard-liners dominated the Cabinet meetings. Dartmouth wrote to Gage ordering him that "now force was to be repelled with force." In the early spring, when the weather permitted, big reinforcements, including a cavalry regiment, would be shipped to him.

The long-term plan was to give Gage a strength of 10,000 men—exactly half what he had asked for, but more than double what he already had—and he was ordered "to take a more active and determined part" than the defensive policy he had operated so far. And "the first essential step" was "to arrest and imprison the principal actors . . . in the Provincial Congress [Adams and Hancock]."

Meanwhile, across the park at St. James's, the King was planning to strengthen the military command in Boston. To support Gage,[4] who no longer seemed as tough as he had, the King planned to send out to Boston three major generals: William Howe, who had led the assault up the Plains of Abraham when Wolfe had stormed Quebec; "Gentleman Johnny" Burgoyne, a flashy but competent cavalry commander who had eloped as a young officer with the daughter of the powerful Earl of Derby; and Sir Henry Clinton, a quiet somber man with a tendency to brood about the injustice of his superiors. "As you know," Clinton wrote to a friend about his voyage with the other two generals, "I'm a shy bitch."

All were to play vital leading roles in America, but the prickly Clinton, complaining all the time, was to be at the center of the conflict for virtually the entire period.

Howe went through the motions of resisting the appointment— because, as a Whig Member of Parliament, he had told his electors that he would. But when Dartmouth sounded him out through a joint friend, the report to the Colonial Office suggested that he was open to offers. "Is this a request or an order?" he asked when told of the appointment. All the signs indicated a sense of relief when he was told firmly that it was an order.

By then the opposition in Parliament to the British policy in America had hardened. Because of the King's voting control, government critics could achieve little that was practical, but they were angrily persistent. In the Commons, Edmund Burke and Charles Fox, two of the most brilliant orators ever to speak in Parliament, lashed repeatedly into Lord North, attacking him for the crass failure of his policies and threatening him with a move to impeach him. In the Lords, the Marquess of Rockingham and the Duke of Richmond led a sustained attack on the government's plans.

"We were promised," taunted Fox, "that on the very appearance of troops, all was to be tranquility at Boston, yet so far from reducing the spirit of that people, these troops were . . . reduced to the most shameful situation. . . ."

"Your army," sneered Burke, "is turned out to be a mere army of observation."

The aim of the British Whigs was similar to that of the

Americans, but their reasoning was different. The war, they declared, was one that could never be won. "It is obvious," insisted Lord Camden in the House of Lords, "that you cannot furnish armies or treasure competent to the mighty purpose of subduing America."

"What are your armies?" challenged the rakish John Wilkes, once expelled from the Commons but now back in full voice. "And how are they to be kept up and recruited? Do you recollect that the single province of Massachusetts Bay has at this moment 30,000 men well trained and disciplined? Do you not know that they can bring near 90,000 men into the field?" This was an exaggeration, but he had made his point.

Whig after Whig in both houses attacked the government for persisting so stubbornly with its tax rights in America. They argued that the benefit of trade, not tax, was the key to the situation. Estimating that there were already 2,000,000 European Americans, Burke insisted volubly that they were multiplying daily at an incredible rate. "Whilst we spend our time deliberating on the mode of governing two millions, we shall find we have millions more to manage. Your children do not grow faster from infancy to manhood than *they* spread from families to communities, and from villages to nations."

The trade figures supported Burke's argument. In 1704 Britain's exports to North America and the West Indies had been less than £500,000. By 1772 they had soared to nearly £5,000,000. "The trade with America alone," declared Burke, "is now nearly equal to what this great commercial nation, England, carried on at the beginning of this century with the whole world!"

British merchants were suffering under the American trade bans, and petitions were pouring into Parliament and St. James's Palace from men who saw their profits diving. Burke himself sat for Bristol, a big port and commercial center. Wilkes was lord mayor of London, as well as one of the city's MP's. "Who can tell," he forecast, ". . . should success attend them, whether in a few years the independent Americans may not celebrate the glorious era of the Revolution of 1775, as we do that of 1688?"

It was, however, the great Lord Chatham—who, as William Pitt, had directed British victorious wars against France and Spain—who made the biggest impact. Now old and crippled with gout, he hobbled into the upper chamber in black fur boots and submitted a peace plan. It had much in common with the proposal the

Howes and Franklin had been working on: the dropping of taxation, the removal of troops and, of course, the repeal of the punitive acts that gripped Boston.

Tactfully, Dartmouth—speaking for the government—suggested that Chatham's proposal should "lie on the table" for study. But immediately, his Cabinet colleague Sandwich was on his feet in strident protest. "I could never believe this bill to be the production of any British peer," he snarled and turned to look at the "bar" of the House of Lords, where Benjamin Franklin, who had come as Chatham's guest, was standing. "I fancy," continued the First Lord, "I have in my eye the person who drew it up—one of the bitterest and most mischievous enemies this country has ever known."[5]

Inevitably, Chatham's bill was thrown out by a big majority, and for all the oratory in favor of the Americans, the voting during those early weeks of 1775 was overwhelmingly in favor of the government that was now pursuing the King's tough policy. All the American governors had already been ordered to take every step they could to stop delegates from attending the second General Congress, scheduled for May. And, at home, North was doing what he did superbly—manipulating Parliament.

Through weeks of debate, bill after bill was steered through with big majority votes. Opposition amendments were stamped on. Petitions that urged peace negotiations were overridden. Massachusetts was declared to be in a state of rebellion. Parliament approved an increase in the size of the army.

Again and again the opposition attacked, but the government ministers stood their ground with a wooden stubbornness. When Lord Camden in the Lords insisted that the bill must involve a war that Britain could not win, Lord Sandwich was incredulous. "Suppose the colonies do abound in men, what does that signify?" he asked. "They are raw undisciplined cowardly men. . . . Believe me, my Lords, the very sound of a cannon would carry them off . . . as fast as their feet could carry them."

The Commons, too, had been reassured about the frail courage of the Americans. Colonel James Grant, who had served across the Atlantic, insisted that "they would never dare to face an English Army." Richard Rigby sneered at the whole opposition notion that the Americans might be goaded into bravery by despair, describing it as "an idea thrown out to frighten women and children."

On April 5, after General Henry Conway had warned of "the horrors of a civil war," Rigby still persisted in his confident belief in the deterrent of British troops in Boston. "The Americans," he declared stoutly, "will not fight. They will never oppose General Gage with force of arms."

It was an opinion that within days—twelve days to be exact—was to be challenged.

4

BOSTON, April 19, 1775

1

It was 7:30 a.m.[1] There was a chill in the morning air; but the sky was clear, and the early sun was striking shadows from the steeples of the Boston meetinghouses.

On the parade ground, formed of Scollay Square and the streets on either side of it, Brigadier Hugh, Earl Percy sat on a white horse, scanning the three regiments of infantry formed in ranks before him—the First Brigade of some 1,200 men that he commanded.[2]

The young earl, with his gently slanting eyes and his thin bony nose, was an aristocrat of one of the oldest and most famous families in British history. William de Percy had invaded England with William the Conqueror in 1066. Since then, his descendants had played key roles in every major conflict in which Britain had been involved. Hugh Percy was tough, confident and very cool—as he was just about to prove.

His soldiers, like all the British army, were a rough lot of men, underpaid, disciplined by the terror of awful punishment, dragged into the service by press gangs, enlisted drunk in English pubs or tempted into joining up as a way of getting out of jail.

Their officers regarded them as very close to animals—one reason why they trained them to operate, like packs of hounds, in tight ranks in which they were easy to control—and their needs were catered to in much the same way as those of their horses. Drunkenness was tolerated as a necessary way of letting off steam, although in the recent inactive months within the confines of Boston it had required a strict curbing. Women—wives and prostitutes—accompanied the troops in numbers that were laid down by the commander in chief who had the same absolute control over

Massachusetts: Boston Harbor, Concord and Lexington.

The British Museu

them as he had over the men. In Boston the allocation was seven women to a company.

Normally, the army lived on looting to compensate for the soldiers' low wages—and the women played an accepted and skillful role in plundering operations—but in America this was strictly forbidden. The commanders, relying on the fact that many of the colonials were loyal, wanted to offend them as little as possible. None of the generals, however, ever succeeded in stopping looting despite the employment of every kind of punishment, from death to terrible floggings.

The men ranged in the long ranks in Scollay Square before Lord Percy were not, in fact, as resplendent as they would have been a few years back. Then the sartorial demands made on British troops had been excessive, and saluting had been introduced because the old custom of doffing hats played such havoc with coiffured wigs. All the same, the soldiers looked impressive enough in their black tricorns over hair that was greased and clubbed at the back, with their white breeches and the long scarlet coats crossed by two broad belts.

As company after company was called to attention by the sergeants, there was the continuing crash on the parade ground of the butts of the firelocks—the heavy smoothbore brown Bess muskets that were not as accurate as rifles but could do a lot of damage when their solid shot, weighing more than an ounce, was fired in barrage by a line of advancing men.

The officers, in their high black boots, some on horses and some on foot, waited near their divisions. Like their men, they wore cocked hats and long scarlet coats, but their shoulders were decorated lavishly with gold epaulets. Instead of heavy firelocks, they carried light fusil muskets, fitted with bayonets. Across their bodies, they wore yellow sashes, made broad enough to act as sling stretchers if they were wounded.

By that night many of them would need their sashes.

At one end of the parade ground were two 6-pound cannon, each behind six horses,[3] traced in pairs and held by the civilian drivers the Army employed. Near them, formed in squads, were the gun teams—eleven to a cannon—in the blue uniform coats of the Royal Artillery.

There was also an ammunition wagon on the parade ground, but, as Artillery Colonel Samuel Cleaveland later reported to London, "Lord Percy refused to take it saying it might retard their march and that he did not imagine that there would be any occasion for more than was in the side boxes." This meant that he was taking only twenty-four rounds for each gun.

At dawn a young officer had galloped across Boston Neck from the mainland with the news that reinforcements were needed for British troops who were already out in the country. Against this possibility, Gage had issued orders the previous night that the brigade was to be awake and ready at 4 a.m., but the order had been mislaid. As a result, the assembly on parade was already behind schedule.

It was 8:45, nearly four hours after the alert had reached General Gage in Province House, that Lord Percy and the First Brigade started marching across the neck—the advance guard first, followed by the artillery in front of the regiments. The drum and fife band was thumping out "Yankee Doodle Dandy," an English soldiers' song of the Seven Years' War that mocked the straw-in-hair American provincials who were their allies. British bands always blared the long note of "Dandy" in derision, making it sound like a raspberry. That morning it was appropriate enough as a marching tune, for they were on their way out of Boston to help their comrades deal with the same provincial yokels who had inspired it.

The long months of waiting since the crisis in September had suddenly ended. Inevitable though the clash had always been, it had taken a surprisingly long time in coming. The winter had, in fact, passed without much in the way of alarms.

But Gage's new hopes were soon to be cooled. Early in March, the situation in Massachusetts began to acquire a new intensity. On the fourth one of Gage's agents reported that the Provincial Congress had appointed a committee to watch the British army. If it went out of Boston into the country, it was to summon the Minutemen to oppose the troops. "The Minutemen amount to 7,500,"[4] reported the agent, "and are the picked men of the whole body of the militia and are properly armed." Their whole magazine of powder, consisting of 90 to 100 barrels, was at Concord, 18 miles inland from Boston.

Five days later Gage had another intelligence note, this time in French, informing him that food supplies and arms for the militia were also being stored at Concord. This report was highly detailed, naming the exact location of the various dumps. The main magazine, in fact, was at the farm of James Barrett, who had just been appointed colonel of the local militia. Among the arms were cannon.

Cannon carried a special significance, albeit largely symbolic, for both the Americans and the British, and Gage was convinced that, limited though his military forces were, he could not just allow the Americans to build ever-growing arms dumps. He began making plans to raid the magazines at Concord.

Toward the end of March he sent out two young officers in disguise to reconnoiter the route to the town and to map the houses featured in his secret intelligence. A few days later he received news that placed the Concord dumps in a far more dangerous setting.

Among his spies, Gage had one superagent in the inner ring of the Provincial Congress—Dr. Benjamin Church, a leading member of the Faction and close associate of Samuel Adams and John Hancock. As a result,[5] he soon learned that new developments were emerging in the Congress that was then meeting secretly at Cambridge. If he was going to act, it became clear, he needed to act quickly.

Samuel Adams and the aggressive groups in the Provincial Congress were promoting a confrontation with British troops. In March some of the soldiers of Lord Percy's First Brigade, who had marched out of Boston on one of the routine excursions that had been part of British policy since the fall, had done some damage, and a string of protests had been sent in to the Congress. A new resolve had been passed, despite opposition from moderates who feared British retaliation: If the troops should march out of Boston again with artillery and baggage, "the country should be instantly alarmed . . . to oppose the march to the last extremity."

The Congress had voted to raise immediately an army of 18,000 men—8,000 to come from Massachusetts and the remainder from other colonies. Already top men from the Committees of Correspondence in New Hampshire and Rhode Island had arrived in the province for discussions.

Gage was facing a big new crisis. Two days later news from London reached the Congress that more troops were on their way to Gage and that Parliament had voted for a tougher policy in America. Although Gage had not yet heard from Whitehall officially, the Congress was alarmed. Plans to raise the army were accelerated.

"A recess at this time could easily be brought about," Gage's spy in Congress suggested to him, ". . . it would prevent their taking hasty steps until he [the general] received his dispatches [from London] . . . a sudden blow struck now would overset all their plans." Much of Gage's organization was poor, but it would be hard to fault the quality of his information service.

Four days later, on April 15—presumably because Gage agreed to his spy's suggestion—the Congress went into recess for two weeks.

Gage grabbed his opportunity. For psychological as well as practical reasons, the new crisis demanded a military gesture—demanded it, what is more, before the plans of the Provincial Congress could be finally formed. So Gage made plans for a raid on Concord and scheduled it for the night of April 18.

Against the background of growing tension, with the militia keen for a chance of putting into practice their training of the past few months, secrecy was vital. The raid would have to be sudden—and completed, if possible, before the Minutemen had time to organize in opposition.

At the same time, some kind of preparation was necessary, and the troops were soon aware that a military operation was imminent—as indeed, ultrasensitive as the port was to every change of mood, were the people of Boston. On Saturday, April 15, the day he knew that Congress had gone into recess, the general issued orders that the grenadiers and the light infantry[6]—Britain's crack troops in Boston—should be relieved of normal duties. The cover story was that they were to learn new evolutions, but it was a thin one. "I dare say," Lieutenant John Barker of the light infantry mused in his diary, "they have something for them to do."

When that night the admiral ordered all the boats of the navy's ships in Boston to tether under the stern of the *Boyne*, the big 70-gun man-of-war lying anchored off the port, the cover story seemed even more suspect.

On Tuesday, Gage activated the plan, still doing all he could to maintain secrecy. He summoned to Province House Lieutenant Colonel Francis Smith, a ruddy, corpulent regimental commander now nearing retirement age, and handed him sealed orders that were not to be opened until he started marching that evening.

At 8 p.m. the officers of the grenadiers and the light infantry were briefed: They were to have their men on the beach of Back Bay, where the Boston Common reached down to the water, in two hours' time at 10. The soldiers were to be told nothing until the very last minute. They were to leave their barracks by the back entrances and to move to the beach in small groups as silently as possible.

If it had not been for the awkward jigsaw position of Boston, the Charles River would have streamed down from the town of Cambridge straight out into the harbor. As it was, because of the port on its peninsula, the waters of the river were diverted sharply north at its mouth before mingling with the tidal flow around Boston that went out on the ebb through the narrow channel that separated it from Charlestown. This stretch between the mouth of the Charles on the mainland and the west coast of Boston was called Back Bay.

By ten o'clock the 700 soldiers selected for the raid had slipped quietly across the common in small parties and were waiting by the water. When a dog had suddenly started to bark at one group, it had been silenced with a bayonet. The boats that had been assembled at HMS *Boyne* on Saturday had been rowed around to Back Bay and were waiting at the shore.

The moon was already high in a cloudless sky. Across the bay, the soldiers could see clearly the low hills and shoreline of the mainland.

Slowly, the ferrying operation began. The boats were loaded; then their crews rowed them, against a cross tide that had just started flooding to a beach a mile and a quarter away on the mainland.

The landing point was on a farm that was out of sight of any houses because of a nearby hill.

The boats grounded in shallow water. The troops waded ashore and moved through soft marshy land to a cart track where they waited for the craft to return with the rest of the force.

On the beach, the provisions and ammunition were issued: food supply for twenty-four hours and thirty-six rounds of ammunition per man.

Colonel Smith whispered the order to advance, and the mass of men moved carefully in broken column along the dirt road that curved upward around a hill.

For four hours now, the tide had been coming in, washing over the marshes and flooding a small creek that the cart track crossed at a small timber bridge. But Smith was afraid that the noise of 700 men and the horses clattering over the wooden planks would be so loud it might destroy the secrecy of his mission. On his orders, the troops waded the waist-high waters of the creek.

The dirt track led to a little village that was joined to Cambridge by a lane.

Quietly, the troops passed the darkened houses and, as the road widened, formed the proper ranks for marching.

Smith had ordered six companies of the light infantry—some 200 men—to go ahead under his second-in-command, fifty-two-year-old Major John Pitcairn of the marines.

While Smith's troops were in motion, British officers sat quietly on their horses under the trees at intervals along the roads out of Boston and Charlestown to Concord. They had ridden out from the port the previous afternoon in pairs, as though they were taking a leisurely ride in the country, as they often did. Now that it was dark, they were waiting for any express riders who, despite Gage's precautions, might have learned of the raid.

That night, soon after eleven, while the troops were being ferried across Back Bay, two officers stationed on the road from Charlestown to Cambridge had seen a horseman galloping toward them. As they moved out from their cover to intercept him, he immediately reined back hard, swung his horse around and rode fast back the way he had come.

The two British realized what he was intending to do. He had just passed the junction where a road branched off to Medford. He could get to Concord via Medford, even though he would have to travel farther than on the Cambridge route.

Promptly, one of them rode across the triangle of land formed by the two roads to head him off. But the rider, unlike the British, knew the country. The officer's horse sank deep to his haunches in what remained of an old drained pond.

The other officer, however, stayed on the road, riding hard after the horseman. But he was not as well mounted. The distance between them lengthened, and knowing that there were other British stationed on the road ahead of him, he checked his horse.

On Gage's orders, other men, too, had moved with apparent innocence during daylight across the Boston Neck to the mainland: blue-coated troops of the royal artillery in light chaises, filled with the equipment for destroying cannon. Now they were waiting in the woods to join the troops on the road to Concord.

Smith's long column of men, headed by the six light infantry companies under Major Pitcairn, was marching along the road between Cambridge and the small township of Menotomy[7] through flat open country that was clearly visible in the moonlight. At Cambridge, they had met three men driving toward them on a milk wagon from Lexington and ordered them to turn their wagon and travel back with the troops the way they had come. Pitcairn was not taking any chances. They could have alerted all Cambridge as soon as the troops had passed up the road.

They had been marching for an hour when they passed through the town of Menotomy—the only sounds the regular thud of their feet in time on the hard mud of the road and the slight rattle of the bayonets in the holders on the muskets.

Pitcairn was riding at the rear of his six companies. Junior officers were at the head of the column. Two of them, Lieutenants William Sutherland and Adair, were acting as scouts, moving along unmounted on each side of the road well ahead of the troops. With them were a couple of young Tories who had come with them as guides.

Once through Menotomy, the road became a steep hill, bordered by rough stone walls, winding up through woods. In the predawn dampness, the smell of the bark of the trees hung thickly in the air.

The officers ahead of the column heard the hooves of horses approaching fast. Then Lieutenant Adair, who was ahead of the others, saw them. "There are two fellows galloping express,"[8] he called out.

Sutherland—as he recorded in his report—drew his pistol and ran into the middle of the road with the guides. As the riders came down on them, he leaped for the bridle of one horse. One of the Tory guides hung on the reins of the other.

Like the men with the milk wagon, the riders were ordered to stay with the soldiers as they continued on their march, toward Lexington, the next town on the way to Concord.

An hour earlier, way ahead of the troops on the road to Concord beyond Lexington, a group of British officers on lookout duty had captured Paul Revere. His name was well known to them, and under questioning he had made no effort to conceal his identity.

In fact, he taunted them. It was then two in the morning; Revere, so he told his interrogators, had left Boston at ten.

"There'll be five hundred Americans here in a short time," he declared, "for I've alarmed the country all the way up."

This worried the interrogating officer and he rode off to report to Major Edward Mitchell, his senior, who was in a wood nearby. The major came back with him at full gallop. He dismounted, drew his pistol and held it at Revere's head. "I'm going to ask you some questions," he said, according to Revere's deposition, "and if you don't give me true answers, I'll blow your brains out."

With obvious pleasure, Revere repeated what he had said before: The country was alarmed.

So was the major. Clearly, Colonel Smith and the column that was then marching on the Lexington Road should be warned.

He ordered Revere to mount his horse. A sergeant took his reins, and with the other officers, they rode back along the road.

They were two miles from Lexington when they heard the musket shots. If Revere's story was correct, these were almost certainly signal guns.

Anxiously, Mitchell ordered Revere off his horse, and leaving him to walk to the village on foot, the British cantered off down the road toward Lexington.

Lieutenants Sutherland and Adair, scouting ahead of the advance companies of the column as it progressed up the hill road, heard the signal guns, too.

A few minutes later they saw an officer riding toward them through the woods. It was Lieutenant William Grant of the Royal Artillery, who had gone out from Boston in daylight with the gunners in the chaises.[9] He told the two lieutenants that the woods were filled with armed men, and rode back down the column to report to Pitcairn.

Soon afterward they met Major Mitchell and the officers who had taken Paul Revere. They supported what Lieutenant Grant had said. The raid was no longer a secret.

As Sutherland and Adair marched on, they stopped several American express riders. All spoke openly and triumphantly of men massing ahead of the troops on the village green at Lexington.

The numbers varied. A well-dressed American driving a sulky carriage put the figure at 600. Another said there were 1,000 men waiting in ranks on the green.

It was dawn, and a pallid light was streaking the sky. Sutherland had mounted the horse of one of the men he had intercepted. Adair was riding in an artillery chaise.

At one moment they realized that now they were more mobile they had gone too far ahead of the column. They turned and rode back along the road. On the way, in the woods in the dawnlight, they saw men moving over the hill in the direction of Lexington.

When the two young officers reached the British advance companies, they found that the column had been halted. Pitcairn, now at the head of his men, was issuing his instructions for the march through Lexington. An officer had been sent to Colonel Smith with the grenadiers farther back on the road, warning that some kind of opposition was likely. Smith, too, had heard the signal guns and, in his turn, had sent a message back to Boston.

Meanwhile, the sergeants had ordered the troops to load their muskets.[10] Each soldier took a paper cartridge, containing powder and ball, from the cartridge box on his belt, tipped a little powder into the flashpan above the trigger and, holding the musket butt down on the road, poured the remainder of the contents of the cartridge down the barrel. Then, taking the ramrod from its holder on the gun, he rammed the powder tight.

It was a cumbersome operation, but British troops were well drilled in the use of muskets. All of them could fire three rounds a minute, and the brighter men could nearly double that rate.

Pitcairn re-formed the column in case of ambush: a small advance guard to go ahead, flankers in the woods on each side. Then, riding at the head of the main body, he gave the order to march the remaining half mile to Lexington.

As the British swung down the hill, Lexington's tall three-story timber meetinghouse came in sight. It stood dominating the opening formed by the trees at the end of the road, on the near corner of the triangular green at the fork of two roads—one that led on to Bedford and another that veered left to Concord.

The advance company, with Sutherland and Adair leading, neared the meetinghouse. Beyond it on the green they could see the ranks of men waiting for them. They wore no uniforms—just the leather jerkins and broad-brimmed hats that country people always wore—but they were armed, and a militia officer stood alone in front of them. At the edge of the green, also waiting, was a large crowd, watching tensely.

Although the road to Concord lay to the left, the advance

company marched straight on past the meetinghouse and halted beside the green. Suddenly, a man moved out from the crowd, aimed a gun at Sutherland and fired—but the musket merely clicked as the powder flashed in the pan.[11]

The lieutenant swore at him, but conscious of the explosive situation, he did not retaliate—just turned his horse and cantered back to report to Pitcairn, riding at the head of the approaching column.

Pitcairn was now near enough to assess the situation, and he decided how to handle it. He could hardly march on to Concord leaving armed men formed up for conflict in his rear. On the other hand, if he acted carefully, he could possibly avoid any shooting.

"Don't let the soldiers open fire," he ordered his officers. "Have them form—and surround them."[12]

The British wheeled onto the green past the meetinghouse, moving parallel with the ranks of militia who stood waiting for them. Then they halted and turned to face the Americans.

Pitcairn rode around the other side of the meetinghouse and stationed himself at the end of the space between the two big bodies of men, eyeing each other tautly.

"Lay down your arms, you damned rebels," he ordered the militia, "and disperse!"

For a moment, nothing happened. Then slowly and reluctantly the men of the militia broke ranks and began to amble toward the outbuildings of the Buckman Tavern—an old inn with two crooked chimneys across the road. But none of them dropped his gun.

Pitcairn rode closer to the retreating men. "Lay down your arms!" he repeated. "Damn you, lay down your arms!"

It was at this moment that the first shot in the American Revolution was fired. No one knows for sure who fired it. According to most British eyewitnesses, it came from the direction of the Buckman Tavern. Whoever fired from whatever direction, it started a war.

The soldiers reacted to it as though it were a signal. For months they had been forced to endure insults from provincials in Boston. Now their frustration seemed to erupt. Without any orders[13] they raised their muskets to their shoulders and fired; then they charged, yelling as they went.

By this time most of the American militia were on the edge of the green. Some of them swung around and started shooting at the charging soldiers. Others made for the tavern. A few leaped behind the cover of a stone wall near the inn and fired from there.

Furiously, Pitcairn yelled at the troops to stop firing and re-form their ranks. But none of them obeyed him. "The men were so wild," recorded Lieutenant John Barker later, "that they could hear no orders."

The major spurred his horse in among his men, shouting at them to fall back and jabbing his sword downward in the cease-fire signal. But it had no effect. The troops were intent on slaughter.

Farther back toward Menotomy, burly Colonel Smith, riding at the rear of his grenadiers, heard the shooting and drove his panting horse down the side of the road, past the column of marching men, onto Lexington Green. By now some of the British were trying to break down the tavern door. If they succeeded, as their officers knew only too well, there would be a bayonet massacre in the crowded inn.

Smith was horrified by the chaos he saw. "Where's a drummer?" he snapped at Sutherland.[14]

The lieutenant rode through the yelling soldiers and found a drummer boy. It was only then, as they heard the pounding orders of the drum, that the troops at last began to obey their angry officers and formed up again in ranks on the green.

By then there was not an American in sight . . . except for eight dead men lying awkwardly on the grass. The only British casualty was a soldier wounded in the leg—and a horse, nicked in the flank.

One by one, the companies filed off the green onto the Concord road and, now that there was no need for silence, marched to the music of a drum and fife band.

As before, Pitcairn and the light infantry led the column. The grenadiers, in tall bearskin hats, followed. They were all big, broad-shouldered men, for the grenades that they had once been trained to hurl were heavy. And although grenades were no longer in current use in the army, the tradition for enlisting husky recruits had lingered on. They were an elite corps, normally employed on the flanks in battle formations.

The road was deserted. For an hour, as they marched, they passed nobody—no wagons, no farmers. There was no sign of anyone in the fields, not even any women by the houses. After the confrontation on the crowded green at Lexington, the quiet was ominous. A horseman was spotted on a nearby hill. He sat still, watching them, then galloped away.

They marched past Lincoln—the road skirted the edge of the town—and on down the long wooded hill toward the groups of clapboard houses, ranged on each side of a curving river, that formed the township of Concord.

It was then they saw the militia—several hundred men moving toward them up the road in a long column that was still curling out of the town.

For a few minutes, the two columns continued to approach each other. At last, the militia halted, then turned about and moved back into the town ahead of the advancing British.

The purpose of this little show of strength was not clear to Smith or Pitcairn, but it warned them that there was an organized opposition in Concord of some size.

Concord was cradled under steep hills, and a high ridge overlooked the road where it joined the outskirts of the town. On these heights, groups of men with guns were clearly visible. From here, they could fire from cover onto the British on the road.

Smith ordered some of the light infantry up onto the hills to clear them. There was no conflict. As soon as the provincials saw the red-coated soldiers coming up toward them, they retreated and moved down through the town.

Gage's plan was running several hours behind schedule, but he had worked it out carefully. When the column halted in Concord, Colonel Smith ordered contingents of troops onto the bridges to the north and south of the town to hold off any Americans who might converge on Concord from the neighboring country, as they had in an incident at Cambridge during the fall.

Then the grenadiers, directed by officers using the intelligence map that Smith had brought with him, began their search for supplies. Cannon were dug up from their burial place in the courtyard of the jail and broken into uselessness. Gun carriages were burned. Ammunition and flour, stored for the militia, were thrown into the town pond.

Meanwhile, a crisis was growing at the North Bridge. There Captain Lawrence Parsons had been put in command of seven companies. His orders were to hold the bridge, and also to lead a party two miles farther along the road to raid the farm of the militia Colonel James Barrett. Gage's spy had reported it as the site of one of the biggest arms dumps in the area.

But as soon as the British troops approached the bridge, they saw across the river on a hill to their left the entire militia force of several hundred men that had marched out earlier toward them along the road from the town.

On the hills stretching miles behind them were many groups of approaching men—called out presumably from neighboring towns.

Carefully, Parsons posted two companies, between sixty and seventy men, on a hill to his right to cover the road, left one company to hold the bridge, and marched off to the Barrett farm with the rest of his men.

His troops were still in sight, with the dust swirling behind them, when the militia began to move in a long column from their position on the hill down the half mile of country lane that joined the road about 200 yards from the bridge.

There were, in fact, 400 of them, and their steady progress, to the thumping of a band, was watched uneasily by the 38 British soldiers at the river who were there to stop them. After a few moments, Captain Walter Laurie, who was in charge at the bridge, sent an officer galloping back into the town to ask the colonel for reinforcements.

On the hillside opposite, the officers of the two companies stationed there to cover the road also eyed the long orderly column of farming men as it snaked slowly down the country lane and wondered what they ought to do. Over to their left, in the town, they could see smoke curling skyward from the fires that the grenadiers had made of the gun carriages.

At last, Lieutenant Waldron Kelly, in command of the covering party, decided to move his men back to the river ahead of the approaching militia. This would give Laurie about 100 soldiers at the bridge—enough to stand a fair chance of holding it, despite the fact that they were heavily outnumbered. There was plenty of cover provided by the stone walls that bordered the fields near the river.

At the bridge, Captain Laurie decided that despite his orders to hold the position, his little force was too small to challenge so large a number of men if they made a serious attempt to cross the river. So he formed his soldiers in column, hoping presumably that the sight of them would be enough to cause the Americans to halt.

If not, he had given orders for tactical withdrawal—slowly, backwards, with each rank at the front firing before doubling to the rear.

The plan did not work. The American column did not halt. As it neared the bridge, someone started shooting—although, as at Lexington, no one knows exactly who first pulled the trigger. Within seconds, everyone was firing. Two British soldiers died, and several fell wounded in the first volley.

The troops, conscious of their exposed position, turned and fled "despite," as Laurie reported later, "of all that could be done to prevent them." As they reached the nearest houses, they met the reinforcements that Laurie had sent for.

But the Americans, having taken the bridge, were not pressing them. The British formed in ranks and marched to the town square.

When Captain Parsons and his men returned from the Barrett farm, the militiamen had dispersed. All that remained at the bridge were the bodies of the British soldiers. The head of one of them had been bared bloodily to the skull—apparent evidence to his horrified comrades that he had been scalped.[15]

By now Lord Percy, with his relief column of the First Brigade and his two cannon, had been marching from Boston on the road to Lexington for an hour. At Cambridge, he had been checked because the planks of the bridge over the Charles River had been taken up. But since the timbers were piled nearby, the halt was not too long. Only the heavy supply wagons at the rear of his column were held up while the bridge was fully repaired, and Percy did not wait for them.

In Concord, at noon, Colonel Smith gave the orders for his troops to start the 18-mile march home. Some of the more seriously wounded were left with local doctors in the town. The rest limped along with the troops or hung on the stirrup leathers of horses. Lieutenant Sutherland, shot in the shoulder during the action at the North Bridge, traveled in a chaise.

As the column moved out of the town, Smith sent out flankers of the light infantry up onto the ridge of hills, now on his left, which he had cleared of provincials on his way into Concord that morning, and also onto the far side of a meadow on his right. The flanking troops met no Americans.

A few hundred yards along the Lexington road, the hill sloped down to a small bridge over a stream. The road beyond climbed gently toward Lincoln half a mile away. On either side fields, with scattered clumps of trees and stone walls, sloped upward from the road.

As the column approached the little bridge, the flankers moved back onto the highway to cross the stream with the main column. It was then that they saw the provincials who were waiting for them on the hillside on their right—"a vast number of armed men," as Sutherland described it graphically, "drawn out in battalia order, I dare say near a thousand were approaching through the trees. . . ."

He saw "a much larger body drawn up to my left. . . ." The column of red-coated soldiers bunched to cross the little bridge. Then the shots cracked out in sharp irregular succession like the noise of burning wood. Within seconds several men in the forward companies lay dead and wounded on the road, and the men who followed in the long column had to step over the bodies or drag them to the side so that the chaises could get across the bridge.

The troops, shocked and surprised, stopped and fired back, but by then their targets had taken cover behind stone walls and trees and were not exposed, except at very long distance.

The officers urged the men on so that they could get the flankers over the bridge and out into the fields to force the nearest Americans to give ground near the roadway and lengthen their range and enable the column, pinched tight at the bridge, to open ranks and make themselves harder to hit.

This, as the soldiers were soon to discover, was not an isolated attack at the bridge. Along the road Americans were taking up station, hiding waiting for them. Almost invariably clumps of trees or houses or boulders near the road meant bursts of fire from men concealed behind them, infuriating the troops, for this was dirty conflict. These were methods of men who were afraid to stand up and fight, who thought nothing of shooting soldiers in the back. The troops who suffered worst were in the rear. Unlike the men at the front, who soon moved farther up the road into longer range than their marching comrades behind them, these remained as a focus of marksmen, who, as soon as the British had passed, left their cover and pursued, shooting as they came.

The progress of the column, under continuing fire from the unseen gunmen, was slow. Repeatedly, the angry men had to stop to load their muskets—fifteen to twenty seconds when they were not moving forward, when they were easy standing targets.

As they neared the top of the hill toward Lincoln, the trees fringed the highway, and all along, on both sides, the muskets cracked.

The flanking parties did their best, vaulting the stone walls, coming up behind the provincials, lurking behind trees; but the numbers of Americans who had swarmed toward Concord from the neighboring towns was now in the thousands, and the flankers themselves were often closer targets than the battered column moving painfully along the road, under fire from all sides.

The front companies reached the top of the hill on the edge of Lincoln Township. The hilltops were favored by the Americans. Here, the staccato noise of the firing grew as the soldiers moved into range of more waiting men.

There were two more hilltops for the troops to brave before they even reached Lexington, where, after the killing of that morning, they could expect to face very heavy pressure.

On the column went, leaving its trail of supine figures, enclosing its wounded in the middle of its ranks, jerking like a giant red caterpillar as companies stopped to fire and load before moving forward once again. Down to the bottom of the hill, across another stream and along the curving road toward a point where thick forest land edged the highway on both sides.

It was an obvious place for concentrated force, ideal for the sneak fighting techniques the provincials were using. The front companies were checked while the flankers went ahead to clear it. They only partly succeeded, and as the column entered the shadows thrown across the road by the dense trees on either side, a hail of bullets spattered into the column. Again, they stopped and fired, but again they were firing at opponents they could not see, for their attackers lay down to load.

Still the soldiers held their ranks, but they were more ragged now. They were tired, too. They had had no sleep the night before. They had marched more than 20 miles since two o'clock the previous morning. They were in no fit state to fight any kind of action—let alone endure a buffeting as punishing as they were now suffering.

Then they were clear of the stretch of forest. For a wonderful mile, they marched through open country with few trees and no walls to provide cover for the local musketmen. For a few minutes, they had a breathing space while they were not under attack, and the officers had their first real chance to attempt to mold disciplined order on the tattered ranks.

It was their last respite. The country ahead of them was full of natural danger—a roadside farmhouse, which, they had now learned, always concealed several gunmen and, on the hillside, large boulders big enough to provide ample cover for a group of aiming men.

The shots rang out again. The house and the boulders concealed all the guns they had feared. More men died. More were left wounded in the road. More clung to horses—some of them relinquished by officers who had now discovered that they made prominent targets on horseback—or lay slouched on the animals' backs, held in place by their comrades.

Past another house—and another shattering blast of fire. Over another hilltop. Then worse, under a high rocky ledge from which the provincials poured down an incessant cannonade.

The troops were near breaking point. Most of them had now fired the last of the thirty-six rounds of ammunition they had been issued on the moonlight night that seemed so long ago. They quickened their pace. Then some of them began to run. The ranks broke. They ceased being even a ragged column. They were a mob, gripped by panic.

Frantically, the officers ordered them to check and form in two ranks, but they were ignored. Major Pitcairn, seeing what was happening in the forward companies, galloped his horse to the head of the column. Suddenly, it shied at a musket shot and reared up. The major lost his balance and toppled from his saddle onto the road.

And the men ran on—up over the last hill to Lexington, still under heavy fire. The flankers, exhausted from climbing walls and moving through the rough country off the road, had virtually ceased to have any effect, and the American gunmen were moving closer to the roadside.

Still, the officers were trying to stop the running men and force them into some kind of order; but fear was now the main motivation, and they barely heard the orders. At last, a group of officers raced ahead of their troops, turned to threaten them with their bayonets, and forced them to halt. "We told them," reported Ensign Henry de Berniere, "that if they advanced they should die. . . . Upon this they began to form under very heavy fire."

* * *

Lexington was now less than a mile away, and the leading companies could see the village some 80 feet below them as they moved down the hill toward it.

The wounded Sutherland in his chaise was at the rear of the column. Suddenly, he heard "the soldiers call out that there was a vast number in their rear." Looking behind, he saw "about 2,000 men" marching down the hill after them, firing as they came.

At last, beyond Lexington Village, the forward ranks saw three firm lines of waiting red-coated soldiers, formed across the Boston road. It was Lord Percy's First Brigade. The sight to the worn and harassed men was overwhelming. A burst of cheering broke out at the front of the column and rippled back through the long lines of desperate soldiers.

As the first of Smith's men reached Percy's waiting troops, the ranks opened to allow them through. The weary men sprawled on the grass near an inn called Munroe's Tavern that Percy had commandeered as his headquarters.

He had ranged his troops, facing outward, in a large rectangle, enclosing a stretch of the road, the tavern and several houses near it, so that they were prepared to fight off attacks from any direction.

On each of the small hills on each side of the road, overlooking Lexington, he had mounted his cannon. As the pursuers of Smith's column followed the harassed British down the road from Concord, they had joined other waiting Americans on the green. It was a big crowd of elated men, and Percy decided that a gesture was needed. One of the cannon flashed with a loud explosion—and a 6-pound ball smashed through the wall of the meetinghouse. Instantly, the crowd cleared; men ran for the sides of the green, taking cover by the buildings and the stone walls.

Percy allowed the tired soldiers from Concord half an hour to recover. The wounded were tended in the tavern. In another room, the earl talked over plans for the march to Boston with Smith and Pitcairn and his officers. When he learned of the way the Americans had used roadside homes as concentrated shooting posts, he ordered the burning of the houses near the tavern.

At three forty-five the 1,800 men began their march to Boston. Smith had emphasized that the biggest casualties they had suffered on the way from Concord had been at the rear and middle of the column. So his weary divisions were positioned at the front. The fresher troops, who had come out from Boston that morning, were used on the flanks and to form the rear guard, which was changed regularly.

"Before the column had advanced a mile along the road," wrote Lieutenant Mackenzie, who was with the first troops to be assigned to the rear guard, "we were fired at from all quarters, but particularly from houses at the roadside and the adjacent stone walls. . . ."

It was the same story as before, but this time the Americans were using their Indian-fighting techniques that would have been branded as dishonorable in any European battle against fresh troops who were appalled at the slaughter of their comrades. As a result, these angry soldiers rushed house after house, killing everyone they could find inside.

The flankers, too, once they realized the pattern, were moving ahead of the column clearing the houses of snipers. In one house they shot to death seven men who were waiting with guns.

Whenever the army of provincials who were following pressed too close on the rear guards, as they did on the steep woodland hill that led down to Menotomy, Percy ordered his cannon to be galloped onto the nearest piece of high ground and opened fire. Always, this forced the Americans to keep their distance.

As the long day wore on, the number of British wounded grew. They rode on the gun carriages when they were not in action, then flopped off onto the road whenever the cannon were ordered into action. The wounded Ensign Jeremy Lister had acquired a horse, which he was using as cover, walking on the side that was farthest from the shooting. Nearby, another horse, with a wounded man on its back and three others clinging to its leathers, was shot, and all collapsed in the road in a heap. They begged Lister for his mount, and he agreed willingly.*

As the long column approached Cambridge, the fighting grew hotter. The new flanking troops were tiring, and owing to the rough nature of the country, they were being forced to work nearer to the road than before; this meant that the provincials could shoot at shorter range. At the same time the Americans, who had been streaming into Cambridge all day, were assembling ahead in greater numbers than the British had yet encountered.

---

*It is almost incredible that under such pressure the British soldiers still made time to plunder. Several men were killed in the act of stealing.

Cambridge was a key point. For there Lord Percy, miraculously unhurt on his white horse, could choose two routes back to Boston. Either he could march back the way he had come out that morning—crossing the Charles River by the bridge that his men had repaired—or he could fork left for Charlestown and, relying on the navy to cover his retreat, send his troops over the water to Boston by boat.

For the first time since the confrontation that morning at Lexington, the British approaching the Charlestown crossroads found the Americans facing them openly in ranks. They were formed across the Charlestown road, and Percy realized that their purpose was to force him to return to Boston by the same route he had taken that morning—and this time clearly the bridge would have been completely demolished. So it was obvious to him that they had to go to Charlestown.

He checked the column. Once more, the wounded slid off the gun carriages, and the cannon were driven forward past the ranks of waiting soldiers to the front.

As usual, the crash of the guns had its daunting effect. The Americans broke ranks, and the British marched on down the Charlestown road under constant heavy attack from the rear by crowds of men chanting, "Hancock! Hancock! Hancock forever!"

By the time they were approaching the narrow neck that connected the mainland to the Charlestown peninsula it was dusk. But shooting was still coming from the few houses that lay ahead. Wearily, a party of soldiers went into the buildings to clear them of the snipers. The last man they killed, according to British records, was a Negro.

Then they marched across the neck, and for the first time since they had left Lexington, they were no longer under fire. Their pursuers stayed on the mainland.

Percy, however, was not taking any chances. They could always make a rush attack. Also, he did not know what he might expect from the inhabitants of Charlestown. So he gave orders for the column to march on up the easy slope of Bunker Hill and prepare to defend the high position. It was a strong one, for from there he could overlook both the Charlestown Neck and the town.

At Province House, Gage had known the full story by four o'clock, when his aide-de-camp, who had ridden out with Percy and turned back at Lexington, managed at last to get to Boston by a cross-country route after repeated stops to avoid the assembling Americans. Promptly the general had sent a curt warning to the Boston selectmen that if any more armed men left Boston to oppose the King's troops, the most disagreeable consequences could be expected. Then Admiral Graves was alerted to have his boats ready for a ferrying operation if Percy marched to Charlestown.

With the 74-gun *Somerset* at anchor with its gunports open only a quarter of a mile off the little town, the British did not anticipate much trouble from its inhabitants. And as soon as Percy arrived on the peninsula, the Charlestown selectmen delivered an urgent message to him assuring him that his soldiers could march through the town unharmed on their way to Boston.

Gage sent over new troops to man the defense posts that Percy's hard-pressed force had set up on the northern slopes of Bunker Hill facing the mainland. Engineers began to strengthen the fortifications that the tired and battered men had begun.

Meanwhile, now that they were safe from the persistent American gunning and covered by fresh troops, what remained of their organized discipline collapsed. The hillside became a scene of chaos. Hundreds of soldiers milled around in the darkness. Some units were ordered to the town hall to wait for evacuation. Others stayed, uncertain what to do, in the fields on the outskirts of Charlestown.

A sergeant approached the wounded Ensign Lister, explained that he had twelve men, and could not find any other officer. Lister told him "that he would have to do the best he could because, since I was wounded, it was not in my power to be the smallest use." The ensign went on down to the waterfront, where he found Captain Parsons, who had been in charge of the British companies at Concord's North Bridge, "in a worse situation" than himself and young Sutherland complaining he was in violent pain.

Slowly, the British were evacuated, the wounded being given priority in the boats, across the water to Boston. It was after midnight when the last of the troops who had marched out on what had been designed as a simple raid, had returned wearily to their barracks.

In twenty-four hours, the situation in Massachusetts had changed out of all recognition. The clash that had been expected so long had been traumatically different from what anyone in the army would have forecast. For the British it had been a disastrous day: 273 casualties, many of them wounded, but as always, many of the maimed would soon die in hospital.

Even though it indicated that much of the American shooting had been wide, it was an appalling total, considering the quality of the soldiers—most of them from the best fighting units in the British army—and the nature of their attackers: farm men, largely ungeneraled and uncoordinated.

Although the shame became blurred and excused by time, the action produced a sharp change in the British attitude to the Americans. "Whoever looks upon them as an irregular mob will be much mistaken," Lord Percy wrote privately to London. "They have men amongst them who know very well what they are about, having been employed as rangers among the Indians. . . . Nor are several of the men void of a spirit of enthusiasm . . . for many of them . . . advanced within ten yards to fire at me and other officers, though they were mortally certain of being put to death themselves in an instant."

His new and grudging admiration, however, was tempered by his disgust, expressed in his official report, "at the cruelty and barbarity of the rebels who scalped and cut off the ears of the wounded men that fell into their hands."[16]

2

That night, while the rescue operation was in progress between Charlestown and Boston, Gage was in conference at Province House with Admiral Graves.

The admiral urged the immediate burning of Roxbury and Charlestown and the fortifying of the two hills that overlooked Boston—Bunker Hill to the north and Nook's Hill near Dorchester on the mainland to the south. But Gage, conscious of his mauled and limited forces, decided as always to play for time. He persuaded his belligerent admiral to confine himself to threats.

The next day the selectmen at Charlestown and Marblehead, which acted as a port for Salem, were warned by naval captains that if they allowed rebel forces to occupy them, they would be set on fire immediately.

Meanwhile, the British prepared for siege. The rebels, who had pursued Percy's column from Concord, had stayed where they stopped at Prospect Hill on the mainland across the causeway from Charlestown. Others had occupied Roxbury, the suburb on the other side of the neck from Boston. Several thousand were at Cambridge, which was the headquarters of the army that was now in the process of formal organization, soon to be sanctioned once again by a resolve of the Massachusetts Provincial Congress.

Gage ordered the lines closed by the battery at the neck and intensive fortification. The men-of-war were hauled in close on all sides of town so that their guns could be used for defense against an attack from Roxbury. In Back Bay, where the water was too shallow for ships, flatboats, each with a 6-pound cannon fitted in the bows, were on constant patrol. Admiral Graves landed four big 24-pounders from his ships and employed his sailors to set up a battery on Copp's Hill, which dominated the water, and some of his anchorage between Boston and Charlestown.

By this time Gage, pursuing a policy of concentrating his force, had called back the troops who had relieved Percy's men on Bunker Hill. Although the exposed detachment could have found itself in a vulnerable position, this was a decision that Gage was to regret.

Formal news of the battle of April 19 was rushed to all the colonies by rebel express riders and by a fast ship to England. Signed by Dr. Joseph Warren, a Boston physician who was now president of the Provincial Congress, the account described the British actions during the day in lurid terms, mixing facts with fiction and providing little suggestion of British soldiers in full retreat. "Women in childbed were driven by the soldiery naked into the streets, old men peaceably in their houses were shot dead, and such scenes exhibited as would disgrace the annals of the most uncivilised nations."

Appealing to all Americans, Warren asserted: "The barbarous murders committed on our innocent brethren on Wednesday the 19th instant have made it absolutely necessary that we immediately raise an army to defend our wives and children from the butchering hands of an inhuman soldiery. . . ."

It was a deliberate, provocative, false report of what had happened, almost certainly drafted by Samuel Adams, but its impact on an appalled America was traumatic. It was the call to arms—a challenge to every colonist to rally around Massachusetts in its stand against tyranny. The years of talking about resistance

to slavery, of "no taxation without representation" were over.
Now the issue was to be fought out in the battlefield.

Although Gage was besieged in Boston, reports of the developing
situation reached him very fast. Volunteers were soon marching to
Massachusetts from all over America to enlist for 40 shillings a
month in the full-time army that was temporarily under the
control of the Provincial Congress until the Continental Congress,
due to meet in Philadelphia on May 10, made other arrangements.
The Provincial Congress, then sitting at Concord, was proceeding
with plans to issue its own currency.

Gage, alarmed by Joseph Warren's highly colored allegations of
the battle, sent a circular to all the governors of the American
colonies with a more sober account of the day. But as always, the
Faction's presentation and its speedy action had made a big
impact. In fact, one of the governors was as rebellious as the
subjects he ruled in the name of the King.

From Connecticut came an angry letter from Governor Jonathan
Trumbull accusing Gage of a "most unprovoked attack upon the
lives and property of His Majesty's subjects" and of "such outrages
. . . as would disgrace barbarians." Gage denied this sharply, but
his arguments did not convince Trumbull. The government of
Connecticut put an embargo on any provisions, destined for
Boston, in the colony's ports. So too, Gage soon learned, did the
government of Rhode Island.

In New York and Pennsylvania the Committees of Correspondence ordered similar bans on supplies for the troops. They were
not supported officially, but it no longer made much practical
difference. After Warren's shock report on Lexington and Concord, the effective power of the committees had grown much
greater. Their edicts produced the same result.

Even in New York, whose governor, in common with many of its
inhabitants, was strongly Tory, the first news of the battle had
sparked off a riot.

A dispatch reached Boston from Governor Josiah Martin of
North Carolina. The people of the province had put his home
under day and night surveillance while he was "not supported by a
single man." From Williamsburg came a panic call from Virginia's
governor, Lord Dunmore; he was in refuge with his family in HMS
Fowey, anchored in the harbor.

In Massachusetts, at the eye of the crisis, the conflict was focused temporarily on the issue of food supplies for Boston. For the newly enlisted rebel army—now some 15,000 strong under the command of General Artemas Ward—had taken over from the militia and was entrenched in a semicircular blockade of the causeways of both Boston and Charlestown.

By now all the thirteen colonies—either by government decree or through the action of their revolutionaries—were closed as sources of supply.

Apart from Europe, Canada was the only province available to the provision ships, and all along the New England coast, American privateers were lying in wait, hoping to seize them before the British frigates, sent out by Admiral Graves in response to this new threat, could provide protection.

Within the harbor itself, the islands were a scene of regular skirmishes between troops sent out on foraging missions and rebel forces who moved to stop them.

The British in Boston, waiting tensely for the big reinforcements promised by Dartmouth, were forced onto emergency rations. There was not even hay for the horses, which were being fed on Indian corn.

Then, halfway through May, Gage received news so bad that he could hardly credit it, in a letter from Dr. Joseph Warren that a British agent had intercepted. American forces had stormed the British fort at Ticonderoga.

Ticonderoga, on Lake Champlain, was the key defense bastion on the northern border of the province of New York. It controlled the main waterway to America from Canada. Worse, the fortress had fallen without a single gun's being fired in its defense.

General Gage was unprepared for almost every event that overtook him, but he *had* foreseen this particular danger. The fort had been repaired and regarrisoned but, it now seemed, poorly officered.

The rebels had advanced up Lake Champlain, attacked another fort at Crown Point, and sent raiding parties into the little town of St. Johns on the Richelieu River at the northern end of the lake. In this one fast coup, the Americans had completely wiped out their extreme shortage of artillery, for they had captured no less than 200 British field guns.

Clearly, in retrospect, Gage should now have taken the hills that dominated the Boston peninsula both to the north and the south before the rebels could bring down their captured guns from Ticonderoga. But as British generals often were, he was obsessed by the need to concentrate his limited forces.

Soon they were not quite so limited. The three major generals the King had appointed to support him arrived at the port with a reinforcement of 1,500 men.

The generals were all able men, even though they each had their faults. Howe had gained most of his experience in America in the Seven Years' War. Burgoyne had won his campaign accolades in Portugal. But Clinton, the youngest of the three, had fought alongside Frederick the Great's Prussians against the coalition of France, Austria and Russia. It was the same war that Howe had been fighting across the Atlantic, but the officers of the "German school" considered themselves the elite of the army. "Oh my dear boy," exclaimed Clinton's close and ebullient friend William Phillips, who was to serve later with Burgoyne in the famous march to Saratoga, "the last war made men! But it was only in one part of the world, Germany. . . ."

So Clinton, fair-haired with a vaguely boyish look about him despite his forty-five years, regarded his two superior generals with a slightly superior attitude that soon developed into harping criticism. In contrast with the amiable and popular Burgoyne, he was at best a remote man, who drank sparingly and did not socialize easily in the mess. Howe, too, though quiet with a tendency to brood, enjoyed high living: cards, women, drinking.

At Province House in Boston, Gage discussed plans to attack their besiegers with his three new generals, but three weeks passed after their arrival before a scheme was settled. The army—so Howe reported on June 12—was planning to attack Dorchester, to the south of Boston, and then to strike fast at the rebel positions at Roxbury and Cambridge.

The British commanders were confident that their attack would be decisive. There was little doubt that, under formal battle conditions, professional British troops, who had proved themselves superior to the French and the Austrian armies, could rout an untrained opposition of New England farmers, even though numerically superior.

Lexington and Concord were not forgotten, but the conditions of the day—and the need to retreat under such sudden assault for so long a distance through country so suited to the sneak rebel techniques—were regarded as exceptional. It seemed unlikely to most of the senior officers in Boston that anything similar could happen again during a planned attack. Lord Percy was not quite so confident, though now that there were so many generals in the port, he was fairly junior in the rank hierarchy. Clinton, too, did not share the general attitude of easy optimism, but then Clinton was a worrier.

Clinton[17] was worrying as usual on the night of June 16. The British attack on Dorchester was scheduled for two days later.

Although he wrote fully about what he heard on that warm summer evening, he did not record his exact movements. Probably he took a walk along the harbor or strolled up Copp's Hill, where Admiral Graves, nervous of the heights across the water behind Charlestown, had set up his battery of big naval guns.

From there, Clinton would have seen the warships, dark masted silhouettes marked by their riding lights, swinging gently on their cables in the harbor below him: *Lively, Falcon, Cerebus, Glasgow, Symmetry* and the big *Somerset*, with its three tiers of guns, which that day had been moved into deeper water because Graves was nervous about the limited maneuverability in the shallow channel off Charlestown.

Either from the hill or the wharves, Clinton heard in the night stillness the sounds across the water, as the rebels with spades and picks fortified the peak of Breed's Hill, which loomed just behind Charlestown.

Clinton walked back to his quarters and told Howe, the most senior of the three major generals who had just arrived, of his suspicions. But Howe was enjoying his evening and felt disinclined to follow Clinton's suggestion that they should make a dawn attack.

Even Gage, whom Clinton then called on with the news, did not react warmly. Clinton recorded: "I have given in a proposal in writing. If we were of active disposition, we should be landed tomorrow at daybreak. As it is, I fear it must be postponed until two." Two o'clock the following afternoon was the next high tide.

So the generals went to bed.

They were awakened early—by the repeated explosions echoing and reechoing between the hills around Boston Harbor, as the ten port guns of the *Lively* opened up on the hilltop works that had been revealed by the morning sun. The achievement of the rebels during the few hours of darkness was fantastic. They had built a redoubt—an ultrastrong defense position made of thick walls of earth and stone, standing 6 feet high. The front of the fortification, as the *Lively*'s captain could see through his glass, was some 50 yards long.

The teams of rebel diggers were still working hard, and the redoubt was only partly finished. The exact form it was planned to take finally was not yet clear from that distance, but obviously it would be big enough to hold several hundred men who would dominate the steep slopes on all sides up which any assault on the position would have to be mounted.

Admiral Graves, in his house near the seafront, was also roused by the repeated salvos of the *Lively*. Angrily, he sent off a boat with irritated instructions to the *Lively* to cease firing without orders. But when he, too, peered through his glass at the redoubt that had appeared on the hill, he issued new orders: All ships within range were to bombard the rebel position.

Slowly, as the crews ran springs through the stern ports to the anchor cables, the warships swung around and steadied broadside to the hill. Within half an hour more than 100 guns were firing at the redoubt. Soon, too, the big 24-pounders in the battery on Copp's Hill had opened up at a range of nearly half a mile.

In fact, the ship's gunners, unlike the teams on Copp's Hill, could not elevate their cannon high enough to strike the hilltop, but the psychological effect of the heavy bombardment on the rebels, working desperately to complete the fortification before the British attacked, was clearly daunting. Several rebel officers were seen standing bravely on the walls—presumably to give courage by example to the men striving with the entrenching tools.

At Province House, Gage held a council of war. Clinton—zealous, touchy, disliked by the others—had foreseen the danger and had studied the terrain. Inevitably, as he always did, he had a plan. They should land a few hundred men immediately in Charlestown and take the lower part of Bunker Hill by the causeway to the mainland. Ships could be brought up on either side to ensure at close range that no more rebels crossed the narrow strip of land.

They could then either attack the redoubt from the rear before it was completed or starve the men on the hill at their leisure.

Promptly, Gage objected on military principles: British troops would be between two enemy forces, one of which was numerous and the other in a strong strategic position.

Howe was the key figure at that meeting. As the senior of the three major generals, he would command the attack. He was a strange man—very tall, dark, brooding with thick eyebrows, ample black hair and a rather wide nose that gave a coarseness to features that were otherwise handsome. He was a skilled commander, as he had demonstrated in the ascent of the Plains of Abraham in Wolfe's attack on Quebec. And he was brave. But always he was unhurried.

Howe sided with Gage against Clinton's suggestion. Apart from military principle—which all British generals had to observe, for the shadow of a court of inquiry was everpresent—the plan was unspectacular and untidy. It could take time to complete.

Instead, a formal attack was planned: a slow approach from the front to concentrate the rebels' attention, backed up by a fast sudden assault from the flank which would do the real damage.

The orders were issued: Fifteen hundred men were to be landed by the navy at high tide on Moulton Point on the east corner of the Charlestown peninsula. Eight field guns and four howitzers were to accompany the troops.

Clinton was deeply disturbed by the plan. "The general idea," he recorded, "was that . . . it would easily be carried." He did not believe that the others had bothered to study the facts. The hill was steeper than they appeared to think. The redoubt would not be open at the rear as they seemed to expect—at least not by the time of the attack, when the rebels would have put in several more hours of work—and behind it was a lane buttressed by stone walls, excellent additional cover for men who had already shown they could shoot.

But the doubts of the gloomy general were discounted by Howe and his staff officers present at the conference. In fact, they planned to make the assault the first stage of the original attack designed to take the country surrounding Boston, only to take Charlestown first instead of last, as they had intended before the rebels' night operation. The soldiers were ordered to take blankets and provisions.

Truly, it was not Clinton's concern; he was there by courtesy, as

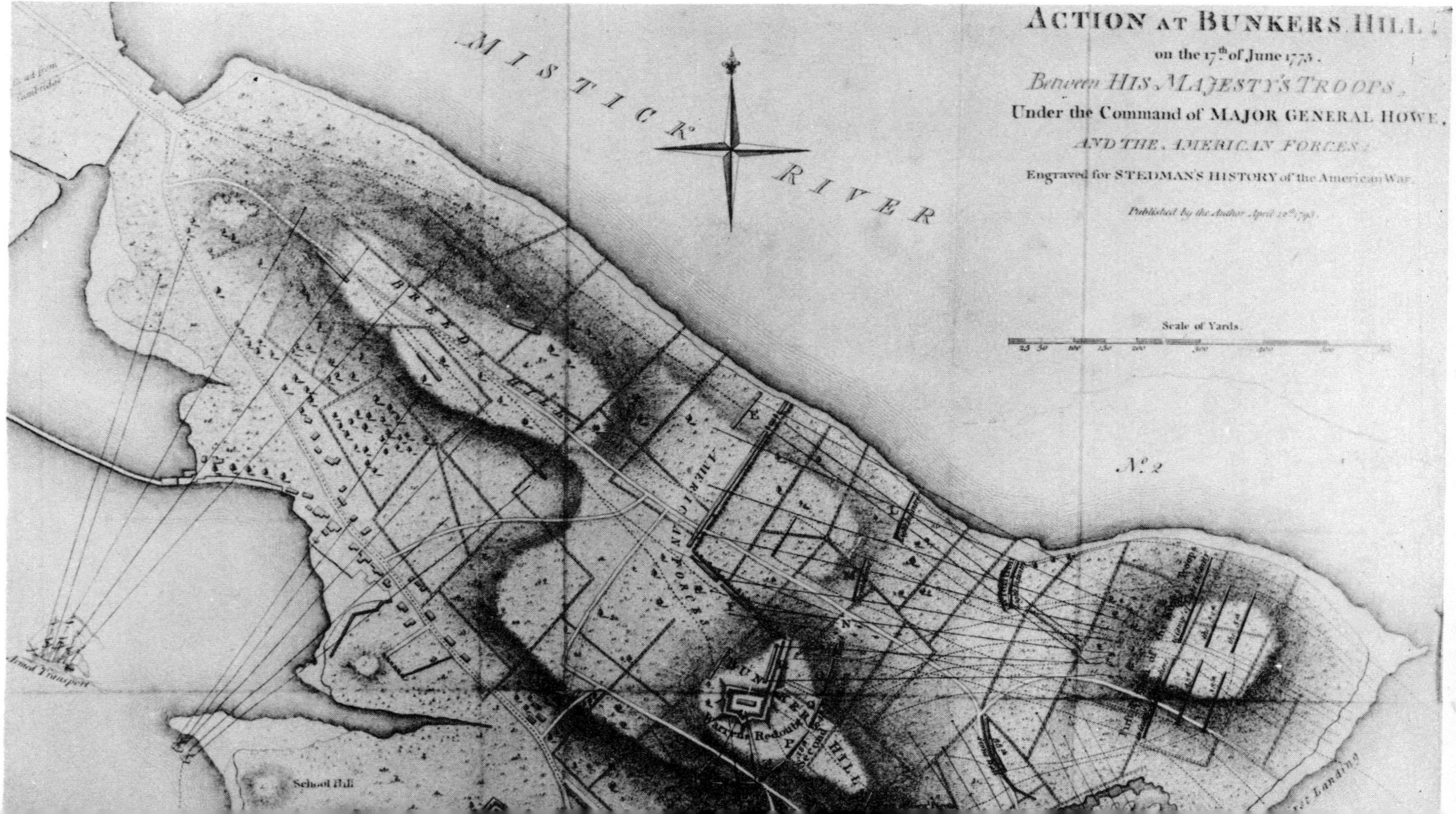

ACTION AT BUNKERS HILL,
on the 17th of June 1775.
Between HIS MAJESTY'S TROOPS,
Under the Command of MAJOR GENERAL HOWE,
AND THE AMERICAN FORCES;
Engraved for STEDMAN'S HISTORY of the American War.
Published by the Author April 12th 1793.
Scale of Yards.
No. 2
MISTICK RIVER
BREEDS HILL
AMERICAN FORCES
BUNKERS HILL
Warren's Redoubt
School Hill
Armed Transport

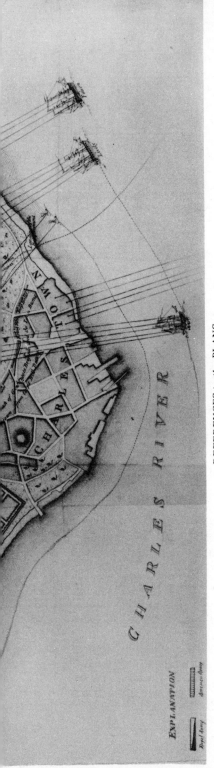

EXPLANATION

CHARLES RIVER

REFERENCES to the PLANS

No. 1

A 10 Companies of Grenadiers, 10 Detachments of Light Infantry, 2 Battalions in 3 Lines
B 1st Detachment behind a Stone Wall
C Light Infantry moved forward covered by a break in the Ground
D The Battalion moved forward from the Stone Wall, and joined by another from the line being covered by the rising of the Hill from the Fire of the Redoubt
E.F A Hedge being part of the Enemy's Defences only Musket proof
G Redoubt & Intrenchment proof against our Field Pieces
H 1st Situation of our Field Pieces with the direction of their Fire
I.F Fire of the Artillery against the Hedge F. to cover the Attack upon their Left
K The Order our Troops would probably have Attacked in, had our Light Infantry been able to penetrate

No. 2

L Light Infantry advancing to the Attack of the Point
M.M Grenadiers taking Ground to the Left of the Light Infantry which had not been able to force the Enemy
N The principal Fire of the Artillery was directed from this Point against the Hedge F.
O.O The 43d and 52d Regiments after having inclined to the Left to leave an Interval for the Artillery
P.P The 5th & 38th Regiments
Q.Q The 47th Regiment & Battalion of Marines disembarked near the Right of Charles Town, after it was Evacuated & assisted in the Reduction of the Redoubt.
Note: The part R was first forced by the Grenadiers & Regiments immediately opposite to it, which had for some time formed one Line in order to return the Enemy's Fire.

The Battle of Bunker Hill, June 17, 1775. Note the artist has confused Breed's Hill with Bunker Hill.

The History of the Origins of the American War by Charles Stedman, 1794 an adviser since he and Burgoyne were not needed. It was suggested they might care to occupy their time by directing the guns on Copp's Hill.

3

At eleven thirty, with the guns still thundering a barrage, twenty-eight boats filled with British soldiers left Boston's Long Wharf and moved slowly south in two long lines toward Moulton Point. It was a hot brilliant day. The sun flashed from the bayonets and highlighted the vivid scarlet of the uniforms against the deep blue of the harbor water. Thousands of spectators on the rooftops and hills of Boston and from the high ground of Charlestown were watching that double column of craft as, oars jerking in unison, it moved steadily westward.

The noise of the cannon grew to a new intensity as another battery added to the noise: Under the command of Lord Percy, the big guns on Boston Neck, which Gage had set up the previous summer against so much opposition from the selectmen, started a heavy bombardment on Roxbury on the mainland. This would require the rebels to keep troops there in some strength, just in case it was the softening barrage before a secondary British attack.

Meanwhile, farther north, two frigates and a couple of gunboats were raking the Charlestown causeway to keep rebel reinforcements from crossing from the mainland.

The guns on Copp's Hill and the cannon on the *Somerset*, more than thirty fired per salvo, were still pounding heavy cannonballs at the rebel redoubt.

To the southeast of Charlestown, two more frigates—*Lively* and *Falcon*—and *Spitfire*, a sloop, were hurling shot in salvo after salvo onto the lower slopes of Breed's Hill and the ground behind the landing beaches to curb any challenge to the approaching boats.

The leading barges in the flotilla were level with Moulton Point. A blue signal flag fluttered from a leading boat. The helmsmen pushed over the tillers, and the twenty-eight craft deployed in two long lines abreast moving steadily toward the beach.

The guns on the three covering ships flashed as their broadsides crashed cannonballs and the smaller antipersonnel grapeshot onto the ground ahead of the barges. Great clouds of smoke mush-roomed over the water.

The boats grated on the beach, and the soldiers leaped over the sides, splashed ashore, and ran up the 100-yard slope of Moulton's Hill, and formed in ranks. The sailors pushed the boats off the beach, and the flotilla, which could carry only 1,100 men, returned to Boston for the remainder of the attack force, the artillery and the commanding officers.

The rebels did not fire a single gun in opposition to the landing. They waited on Breed's Hill.

Howe landed with his second-in-command, short, stocky Brig-adier General Robert Pigot, and the bellicose Admiral Graves. From Moulton's Hill he studied the country through which he would have to mount his attack.

His officers had already set up strong outposts to bear the first impact if the rebels attacked before they were ready to mount their assault. Each consisted of several companies—one, to Howe's left, not far from Charlestown, the other away over to his right not far from the banks of the Mystic River, which flowed down the north side of the peninsula.

As the general considered his plans, the guns that had come over from Boston with him were being moved forward into the area between the two outposts. They were heavy. Each needed up-wards of fifteen men, heaving on ropes and handholds on the carriages, to get them into position. The cannon—12-pounders and 6-pounders—were for long shooting; the fat, short-barreled howit-zers, though less accurate, were for high-angle lobbing.

Each cannon had a firing crew of five, trained to work in careful and deliberate drill that would never vary even under the most urgent battle conditions. The gunners lived in constant danger from the material they were handling. Cannon often blew up—just a few smoldering sparks in the barrel unextinguished in the sponging that followed firing were enough to set off the next charge as it was rammed home.

Even the ammunition wagons often exploded, as friction, set up by movement, set off loose powder. That day there were no ammunition wagons, for there were no horses. The thick car-tridges, powder packed in paper, and the shot that was not carried in the side boxes on the gun carriages were being manhandled in boxes and set up in dumps well to the rear of the guns. The recoil was a constant working problem of the gunners; every time the cannon fired they leaped back and had to be hauled forward again with ropes by the six-man nonfiring team. Even so, it was not uncommon for a battery of guns to end a session of heavy firing at least 100 yards behind their starting position.

The guns were set up in line between the two outposts under Moulton's Hill. In the rear at the side stood the senior artillery officer with the linstock—a small pike, held point upward. Entwined around the crossbar was the smoldering ropelike slow match from which the lead gunners lit their matches. Holding their bodies well clear of the gun carriages so that they would not be knocked over by the recoil, they would reach forward to the touchholes.

Together, Howe and Pigot studied the country before them. The Charlestown peninsula was a triangle. In the corners were three hills, each smaller than the last so that the contour resembled a curving switchback. The biggest, to the northwest, was Bunker Hill, which looped south to Breed's Hill, whose lower eastern slopes curved up to Moulton's Hill, where the British force was now waiting and which was the smallest of the three. The countryside was farmland—featured by apple trees and meadows divided by wooden fences. A small lane, lined by rough stone walls, encircled the lower slopes of Breed's and Bunker hills curving through the valley to the north.

From where Howe was standing, he could see Breed's Hill to his left with Charlestown at its foot. Farther to the right, he looked directly at the more distant heights of Bunker Hill.

The rebel positions were very different from what he had expected. Apart from those rebels who were concealed in the redoubt, the Americans were in force on the hillsides—especially Bunker Hill, which was probably designed as a fallback position if they were forced off Breed's.

The redoubt, too, was more substantial than he had anticipated—as Clinton had warned. It was now completely enclosed with thick 6-foot-high walls on all sides. Basically a rough square, 50 yards across, the front wall was angled so that it jutted into a point. To the west, a breastwork—a bare wall constructed like those of the redoubt itself—reached down the hill to check an attack on the flanks.

The rebels were clearly aware of the potential danger to their flanks. The breastwork stretched only down part of the hill; the British could still march along the lower country to the north near the Mystic River. To cover this ground, the rebels had set up a lighter fortified position behind an old rail fence. This, though parallel with it, was about 200 yards behind the breastwork, but it reached all the way down to the banks of the river.

As Howe was studying the rail fence through his eyeglass, he saw several hundred rebels moving down from Bunker Hill to take up positions behind it.

His force was not adequate, he decided, and he sent back to Boston for reinforcements. To cut delay to the minimum, they were ordered to land near Charlestown—instead of traveling all the way to Moulton Point—and join up with his left wing that would attack up the hill from his western outpost near Charlestown.

Meanwhile, this post was under fire from snipers on the rooftops of the town. Admiral Graves, always eager to set fire to anything, offered to burn it; that morning he had given instructions for cannonballs to be heated in the forge on the *Somerset*.

Orders were sent back by boat both to the *Somerset* and to Burgoyne and Clinton on Copp's Hill. By the time the flotilla was streaming across the channel with Howe's reserves, red-hot shot was dropping on Charlestown's fragile houses. The Boston battery was shooting carcasses—hollow iron shells, filled with burning materials that licked flames through holes in the casing.

Within minutes, fire was sweeping through the little town. "The church steeples, being timber, were great pyramids of fire above the rest . . . ," the watching Burgoyne reported later, "a crash of churches, ships upon the stocks and whole streets falling together, filled the ear. . . . All sending up columns of smoke and flame. . . ."

At two o'clock, when he had seen his reinforcements approaching, Howe ordered the advance.

Pigot was in command of the left wing, with orders to march straight up Breed's Hill toward the rough rebel fort at its peak. The reserves that would soon be landing near the burning town would join him on the slopes. This would give him 1,000 men for an attack that, because it was really a feint, would be slow and showy.

Howe, who also had 1,000 men, but with more crack troops

than Pigot, would advance along the edge of the peninsula near the Mystic River, leaving the redoubt and its defense breastwork well over to his left, and storm the rail fence. Then he would wheel sharply and attack hard up the hill.

But Howe was planning a double flank assault. The banks of the Mystic River—to which the rail fence reached—were eight feet high; even though the tide was now in full flood, there was just room on the beach below for a column of men to make a fast advance out of sight of the defenders above and to leap on them from the rear at the same time that Howe's main force attacked from the front.

The field guns opened up to support the advances of the two forces moving slowly in their different directions through knee-high summer grass.

Howe's regiments were already formed abreast in the three ranks that were traditional for the British army: In the front line were the light infantry, followed by the tall, broad-shouldered grena-diers, while in the third rank were the ordinary foot soldiers from line infantry regiments of lesser renown. Behind them they heard the booming explosions as their field cannon and howitzers fired in unison. The balls whistled over their heads toward the rebel positions.

Then they were halted while the guns were hauled closer to the enemy by the sweating pioneer teams.

Again, they were ordered to advance. The long ranks of red-coated soldiers curved and broke as they clambered over the timber posts and rails between the meadows. Their faces glistened with the heat. With their blankets and packs and heavy muskets, they were each carrying 125 pounds into battle. Despite the full glare of the afternoon sun, they were wearing the same thick coats they wore in the winter.

On the lower slopes of Breed's Hill, Pigot's columns, working their way, like Howe's men, through tall grass and fences, were moving toward the rebel redoubt. The soldiers could see the enemy above the high walls—heads in the familiar deep-crowned country hats with floppy brims. Shot from the guns behind them were striking the redoubt; but it was strongly constructed, and the artillery was not making much impact on the thick walls.

Pigot ordered his drummer[18] to beat to deploy, and the columns swung slowly around to form long, wavy ranks, two deep, moving up the hill closing on the little fort of earth and stone.

Howe's division advanced into a hollow from which they were hidden temporarily from the rebels waiting at the rail fence. The general gave an order. The front rank, the light infantry, suddenly filed off to the right toward the river, clambered down the bank and formed in ranks of four on the narrow strip of beach beside the swirling water. Then they moved forward fast.[19]

On the ground above them, the rest of Howe's divisions—now only two ranks with the grenadiers, in their tall black fur caps, in the front line—continued with their slow unhurried advance toward the rail fence. Ahead of them lay a brick kiln and, near it, two small ponds. Again the long ranks broke as they moved around the obstruction and stopped on the other side to re-form. They were not too far from the rebels now. Meadows stretched ahead of them—wide grassy fields broken by apple trees and more wooden fences. To their left was the breastwork jutting down the hill toward them. That, too, was lined with the heads of watching men. Circling above them, frightened by the noise of the cannon, was a thick flock of swallows.

The British guns behind them had stopped firing, and Howe sent back an aide to find out why. The young officer was horrified by what he saw. For the cannon were bogged down in ground that was deceptive.[20] The carriages had sunk to the axles. The pioneer teams were heaving on the ropes; other men were dragging on the wheel spokes, pushing from behind, hauling on the carriage handholds. Sweating, red-faced soldiers were slipping in the wet ground as they flung their weight forward in response to the sergeants' urging.

Given time, the artillerymen would be able to get the guns onto firmer ground. There was a road nearby—the same country lane Howe would have noted in his anxious survey from Moulton's Hill—that led to the west of Bunker Hill between the rebel breastwork on the left and the fortified rail fence on the right.

If necessary, the gunners could take the guns off the carriages and transport them separately, then reassemble them on the roadway.

But Howe, with his light infantry already advancing along the beach, with Pigot's 1,000 men strung out, moving upward on the hillside, did not have the time to wait. He had no alternative but to press on with the attack without the support of his guns.

The column of light infantry—some 300 men—was progressing fast along the shore. The rebels had realized that the beach was a vulnerable point, and they had constructed a rough defense position—a pile of stones taken from nearby walls. Behind this, the British could see the men crouched waiting.

To the advancing soldiers, the obstacle did not seem very great; their orders were not to fire their muskets but to attack fast with the bayonet—15 inches of three-sided steel that they were well drilled to use.

On they swung toward the pile of stones—tight in their ranks, four men to a row. High on their left was the riverbank; close on their right was the water.

In retrospect, it is hard to see how the attack could ever have been successful. It depended solely on enough soldiers reaching the defense work of stone to attack with the bayonet, which the rebels did not possess. It depended on bad shooting. It depended, most of all, on every rebel's firing his gun in the first volley, enabling the British to be over the parapet of stones in the time taken to reload.

All the Americans did not fire in the first volley; they shot in groups in rotation.

The first volley, fired when the troops were barely 100 yards from the pile of stones, was lethal enough. Nearly all the men in the leading ranks staggered as the metal struck them, then collapsed on the beach. The next volley did just as much damage as the following soldiers charged, leaping over the bodies of their comrades to become sprawled bodies themselves.

The column stopped, bunched as the men in the rear ranks still advanced, then, under the urging of the officers, advanced again. Once more, the rebel muskets fired, and again men fell in heaps on the narrow strip of shore.

It was impossible to go on. The column checked. The officers urged their men to attack, but the objective was impossible. The soldiers turned and ran, leaving ninety-six men, a third of the column, in the writhing human heaps on the narrow strip of beach beside the waters of the river.

Reluctantly, Howe accepted the fact that the beach position was too strongly held. He ordered a frontal assault on the rebel position behind the fortified rail fence—a much more formidable operation now that there would be no surprise attack from the rear but still practical. The line was 250 yards long; there would be no bunching as there had been on the beach.

The British advanced. Cannon shot were falling from the rebel artillery positioned on Bunker Hill but did little damage. There was some fire from the men behind the enemy position, but it was sparse. Almost certainly, those men shooting were doing so prematurely.

As usual, Howe had given orders that the grenadiers in their long ranks were not to fire. They were to get to the enemy as fast as possible and attack with the bayonet.

He ordered the charge, but there was a fence in the way—a fence he later blamed as the cause of his whole disaster. As the grenadiers clambered over it, checked sitting targets, the rebels opened up. Again, the shooting was close-range and lethally accurate. Right along the extended line, the tall men toppled into the thick grass. Instinctively, the men who remained on their feet stopped and, instead of rushing the fence as they had been ordered, "began firing," as Howe wrote later, "and by crowding fell into disorder and in this state the second line mixed with them."

Horrified by the sight of his broken ranks so soon after the repulse of his light infantry, "there was a moment," as Howe conceded later, "that I have never felt before."

The fire from behind the barricade at the fence was incessant—a continuous crackling of gunshot, carving gaps in the confused mass of men in front of the post and rails they had just clambered over. Soldiers on the ground were screaming from their wounds, their cries piercing the staccato rattle of the muskets.

The grenadiers broke. They turned their backs, vaulted the fence that had proved such an obstacle and ran out of range.

Nearly all the staff officers with Howe were killed or wounded. At one moment, too, a British Major John Small stood alone, deserted by the retreating grenadiers.[21] He saw three men raise their muskets and aim at him—when General Putnam rode up and knocked the guns up with his sword. Putnam was one of America's most famous veteran soldiers; in the French and Indian War he had fought beside many of the men he was now fighting, among them Major Small. The rebel general saved his life.

·At last, Howe's officers checked their fleeing men and, pricking the frightened soldiers with their swords, forced them to re-form in their ranks. Again they advanced, "stepping over the bodies of their comrades," as one watching American described it later, "as if they were logs."

And again a storm of carefully aimed lead flayed the lines of charging men and broke them with terrible casualties. The assault became impractical. For the second time, the troops turned and fled out of range.

Meanwhile, high up on the hill, Pigot's division was attacking the redoubt and the breastwork wall, even though the planned drive from the west had not yet materialized.

The pattern of the rebel defense was similar to what Howe's men had already experienced down below, on the banks of the Mystic. As the long lines of soldiers moved up the hill, closing on the redoubt, there was little firing from the fort, just a few badly aimed impatient long shots. But the closer they moved, the better they could see the rebels—faces under the country hats bent to the stocks of their weapons—lined along the muddy walls, waiting for them to come close.

The troops were only 50 yards from the fort when the first blast of fire came—and continued with the same catastrophic effect that had reduced Howe's force below.

Each of the Americans' best shots, as the British learned later, was using several guns, served by loaders. There was no respite for reloading that normally followed the first volley—the pause when the charge was always ordered. Many of the guns were rifles,[22] more accurate than smoothbore muskets but slower to load.

Pigot's left wing was under the heaviest fire of all in that long devastated line.

In addition to the deadly close-range shooting from the east side of the redoubt, the troops were under heavy fire from rebels in a group of farm buildings on the hillside. Many officers were killed. One of them, Major John Pitcairn, who had led the advance guard at Lexington, fell dead into the arms of his son.

Pigot, in the center of his extended line, realized that he could not sustain his attack and ordered the retreat. When the soldiers heard the drumming, they fell back so fast that it was nearly a rout.

From the redoubt they heard the jubilant cheering of the rebels.

* * *

On every front, Howe's attack had failed. His troops had been mown down by precision shooting at close range. Throughout the whole length of the rebel lines, British dead lay in heaps. The wounded, in their hundreds, were trailing slowly toward the beaches. According to some reports, a group of officers begged Howe to abandon the battle, but this would have been inconceivable to the general.

Defeated military leaders were always roughly handled in London. In this case, when Howe's force was heavy with Britain's top troops against an enemy of untrained farmers, there could be no defense. It would have been the end of his career.

Howe was not finished yet. He replanned his attack with his bruised and battered regiments. He had already sent back to Boston for yet more reinforcements and asked the admiral for some naval gunpower in the Mystic behind the rebel lines. He never got his cannon in the river because the tide was flowing in the wrong direction, but his own field guns had now been extricated from the marsh and were waiting on the road with their firing crews, together with their teams of pioneers.

This time Howe changed the strategy. As before there would be an attack on the rail fence, to be mounted by the light infantry, but it would be a feint designed to keep the rebel force there occupied. The main assault would be a combined operation on the main rebel position on the top of the hill by the rest of the British regiments in the divisions of both Howe and Pigot.

He had also learned by savage experience that the battle would be tough enough without any unnecessary hindrances. The troops were ordered to take off their heavy packs. Some of them, according to American sources, even removed their scarlet coats.

Pigot, still commanding the left, held back his main force and sent forward his marines and one infantry regiment to storm the farm buildings on the hillside from which the rebel snipers had poured such accurate fire on his left in the previous attack. He waited until he saw his troops swarm through the buildings; then, once more, he ordered his division to advance in the long, crooked scarlet lines up the hill toward the redoubt. This time Pigot was not concerned with the breastwork wall, for it was at this point that Howe was going to concentrate the whole of his attack. Pigot's men had to rush the walls of the fort itself.

* * *

The train of cannon began to move up the country lane that reached around the base of the hill between the breastwork on its left and, 200 yards farther on, the rail fence position on its right. As the huge teams of hot and grimy men hauled on the ropes, the iron-rimmed wheels stirred up a cloud of dust. Behind them, more men lugged the boxes of reserve ammunition.

Meanwhile, Howe's grenadiers moved slowly through the long grass, this time in columns toward the breastwork. The cannon continued along the road until they were past the breastwork; then they were swung around and set up so that they could fire from the rear on the rebels behind the wall waiting for the assault of the grenadiers.

The cannon opened up. Howe, with his men still formed in columns, watched the flash from his guns as they dropped shot along the wall. Then, as the smoke from the salvo drifted toward him, he ordered the attack. Yelling, the grenadiers charged in column. The leading men clawed their way up the wall to meet a hail of bullets from the side crossfire from the redoubt and from three small isolated enemy positions on the right. The defense was too deadly. The men dropped back off the breastwork.

Howe rallied them as his repeated explosions of smoking guns echoed through the hills and metal rained on the rebels behind the wall. Once more the grenadiers charged and swarmed the breastwork. This time the rebels did not remain to meet them. Short of ammunition, they ran for the shelter of the fort.

The British cannon lengthened their range, aiming now at the six-foot walls of the redoubt itself to force the men defending to take cover. The grenadiers advanced, then checked before the barrage of cannon shot falling ahead of them.

The rebels crouched behind the wall of the redoubt for shelter were firing in the intervals as the field pieces loaded. So close at last to the enemy, the waiting soldiers "grew impatient"—so Lord Francis Rawdon reported—and shouted, "Push on! push on!"

The cannon held their fire as the grenadiers charged the redoubt, and the Americans could then raise their heads above the parapet to pour "in so heavy a fire upon us that the oldest officers say they never saw a sharper action. They kept up this fire until we were within ten yards of them . . . they even knocked down my captain close beside me, after we got into the ditch of the entrenchment."

The ditch was immediately under the redoubt—designed to make the walls higher to climb. Temporarily, it provided good cover because it was hard for the rebels to aim without leaning right over the parapet and making themselves easy targets.

Meanwhile, as Howe's grenadiers, some of them waiting in the ditch, were preparing for a final assault on the northern side of the redoubt, Pigot's men were closing in on the southeast.

Farther down the hill, Clinton was at the head of an approaching column of British troops. From his position with Burgoyne on Copp's Hill, he had seen the British left wing crumple in the earlier assault; he had watched the two reserve battalions that Howe had summoned as they landed from the boats. The troops had seemed uncertain where to join the battle.

At last, he could bear it no longer. Although he had no orders, he decided that Howe could clearly use another general. He had hurried down the hill, crossed the channel in a boat and landed under sniping from rebel marksmen still concealed in smoldering Charlestown. There he had taken command of the reserves "and such wounded men as could follow, which to their honor were many, and advanced in column with as much parade as possible to impress the enemy."

It also impressed the British. Again the left wing was under terrible pressure. The marines were edging forward, but they were held back by a stream of heavy fire from the eastern wall of the redoubt. "We did not retreat an inch," insisted Marine Adjutant Waller, though he conceded that "we were now in confusion, after being broke several times in getting over the rails. . . ."

Desperately, Waller did all he could to form his troops in ranks for a charge, but all the time men were dropping as the rebel muskets cracked out. "Had we stopped there much longer," reported Waller after the battle, "the enemy would have picked us all off."

Waller knew that they would either have to make a fast run for the walls or have to drop back. Urgently, he asked the commander of some of the new infantry Clinton had brought up to form with his marines for a charge. "I ran from left to right while this was doing and, when we had got in tolerable order, we rushed, leaped the ditch and climbed the parapet."

When the British appeared on the wall, the rebels retreated to the far side of the redoubt so that they were far enough back to shoot—and out of immediate reach of the bayonets.

* * *

On the north side, a grenadier company also stormed the walls. The company's captain had already died. His lieutenant leaped onto the parapet. "The day is ours," he yelled and dropped dead off the wall. The sergeant scrambled into his place. "Conquer or die," he bawled, and jumped into the redoubt with his men streaming over after him.

On the east wall, Pigot, short and tubby as he was, led the charge himself, grabbing a branch of an apple tree and swinging himself onto the wall.

The British were now swarming over the parapet in several places. At last, after all the slaughter in their own ranks, they were able to use the bayonets which their commanders always favored. Waller, who had led the charge of the British left, was appalled. "Nothing could be more shocking than the carnage . . ." he wrote. "We tumbled over the dead to get at the living who were crowding out of the redoubt. . . ."

The soldiers, thrusting and twisting their bayonets, went wild in an orgy of killing of an enemy that, until now, had always been hidden. "All was confusion," wrote Clinton. "Officers told me that they could not command their men and I never saw so great a want of order."

Major Small, whose life had been saved by Putnam, jumped from the wall to the floor of the redoubt and saw Dr. Joseph Warren, president of the Provincial Congress, among the Americans breaking their way out of the northern side of the fort. "For God's sake stop," Small yelled to him, "and save your life.

"Warren looked and seemed to recognise me, but kept on," Small recounted.

Warren was shot in the head during the retreat a few minutes later. Marine Lieutenant John Clarke saw him lying in a trench, a soldier standing over him, bayonet poised. Warren pleaded for his life, "for he was much wounded and could not live a great while longer; however the soldier swore that . . . he had done more mischief than anyone else and immediately ran him through the body." The soldier stripped Warren of his light-colored coat, white satin waistcoat and white breeches with silver loops and left him sprawling half-naked, dead on the ground.

Howe himself was wounded in the foot but remained in command, leaning against a support. He accepted Clinton's offer to take charge of the soldiers who were pursuing the rebels down the hill toward the causeway. The Americans were retreating slowly, fighting all the way.

Clinton formed up the British in ranks and marched down the road that stretched down the hill in the middle of the peninsula toward the Charlestown Neck. From there, using the cover of the stone walls, they could fire on the rebels on either side.

The Americans set up a cannon at the causeway to cover their retreat. By six o'clock that evening the last of the rebels who could walk had crossed to the mainland. The British were in control of the peninsula.

It had been one of the most costly victories in British history. Out of an estimated assault force of 2,200, there were 1,054 casualties, nearly half the men engaged.

As the dusk fell, the British began to clear the battlefield. Dead private soldiers were buried where they lay. Officers were carried in their sashes to the boats for transport to Boston for "decent burial" in churchyards.

Many of the wounded British privates, like all the rebels that lay still alive on the battlefield, had to remain where they were all night until the next morning, when those who had survived were finally shipped to the Boston hospital, now so overcrowded that even its yard was full of moaning soldiers.

Many would die or lose their maimed limbs in amputation. The rebel muskets, wrote one British hospital doctor later, "were charged with old nails and angular pieces of iron; and for most of our men being wounded in the legs, we are inclined to believe it was their design, not wishing to kill the men, but leave them as burdens on us to exhaust our provisions and . . . intimidate the soldiery."

That night, while the wounded still lay on the hillside, below the redoubt—now occupied by 100 British soldiers—the wounded Howe lay propped against some straw on the north side of the fort where he could watch the rebels build a fortification on a hill on the mainland. His attendants had orders to wake him if he fell asleep.

Early the following morning he wrote his daily orders as if nothing exceptional had happened though he noted "the bravery and intrepidity he [the general] with the greatest satisfaction observed they [the troops] displayed yesterday."

As always after a battle, the women came into their own. The following day Howe ordered each corps to send two women to attend the hospital where army surgeons worked without sleep for forty-eight hours to help with the casualties. To comfort the troops on Bunker Hill, four women were to cross the water to Charlestown for each company camped there. This order was clearly exceeded, for two days later Howe repeated his limit of four women per company and insisted "that these be the best behaved and bring no children with them."

It was all very unemotional and practical. In his formal report to Gage, Howe was brief and to the point—a masterpiece of understatement that omitted any direct reference to the repeated repulses his men had suffered.

Gage, too, was coolly factual in his official letter to Lord Dartmouth, commenting that the "orders were executed with perseverance under a heavy fire with vast numbers of rebels. . . ."

He knew this would be published in the London *Gazette*, so he was cautious. But, in a private letter to Dartmouth, he elaborated about "the success" and wished "most sincerely that it had not cost us so dear. . . .

"The trials we have had show that the rebels are not the despicable rabble too many supposed them to be. . . ."

By the time Gage's letters arrived London had long been shocked into action by the news of Lexington and Concord. Britain was already preparing for a full-scale war.

5

LONDON, June 1, 1775

"Will any man endued with common sense," jeered the London *Gazetteer*, "believe that a hundred and fifty[1] New England militia, defeated eight or nine hundred regular troops and drove them like sheep through the country for six miles? . . . The brutal violence, the savage barbarity . . . are all words designed to exasperate more the people of New England against the King's troops. . . ."[2]

It was two days since the first report of the Lexington-Concord conflict had exploded in London—as usual in the form of a reprint from a Massachusetts newspaper, this time the *Essex Gazette* of Salem. The news story charged British troops with "commencing hostilities," with being pursued by "our victorious militia" and with "cruelty not less brutal than our venerable ancestors received from the vilest savages of the wilderness. . . ." It attacked the troops for "shooting down the unarmed, the aged and infirm" and for "killing the wounded" and "mangling their bodies in a most shocking manner."

The whole presentation bore the expert stamp of Samuel Adams. The Massachusetts Provincial Congress had commissioned Captain John Derby to bring the news to London in a fast light packet, sailing in ballast for speed. The ship slipped out of Salem four days after HMS *Sukey* had left Boston for England with Gage's official report of the action. But it easily overtook the slower royal naval vessel and anchored at Southampton on Sunday, May 29.

The London press on Monday merely ran the bare story that had been printed in the *Essex Gazette*. Then, the next day, just as the public was absorbing the shock and beginning to discount the news as a fabrication, depositions of eyewitnesses, including one by a captured British officer, were released.

The same papers carried an appeal to the people of Britain from Joseph Warren, as president of the Provincial Congress, angled carefully to fan popular feeling against the government. "These, brethren," he declared of the alleged British atrocities, "are marks of ministerial vengeance against this colony for refusing, with her sister colonies, a submission to slavery."

Carefully, the document avoided criticism of the King, implying strangely that he had nothing to do with the acts of his ministers, who were the truly guilty men. "We profess," said Warren, "to be his loyal and dutiful subjects; and, so hardly dealt with as we have been, are still ready with our lives and fortunes to defend . . . his crown and dignity; nevertheless, to the persecution and tyranny of his cruel ministry, [we] will not tamely submit. . . ."

The Colonial Office still had no information. Hurriedly, Dartmouth issued a statement through the official London *Gazette* intended to calm the tremors created by the rebels' brilliant publicity tactics: "It is proper to inform the public that no advices have yet been received of any such event [the skirmish]."

Promptly, Arthur Lee, one of the Massachusetts agents in London, sent a note around to the newspaper offices "as doubt of authenticity of the account from Salem . . . may arise from a paragraph of the Gazette of this evening." The originals of the published eyewitness affidavits were, he said, available for inspection at the office of the lord mayor of London, who was, of course, the violently prorebel John Wilkes.

The impact on London was tremendous. Every paper ran the news as its main story with big editorials [3] written, as was the custom, by writers using pen names. Apart from those such as "Politicus" in the *Gazetteer,* who refused to credit the truth of the reports at all, the commentators used the account of the conflict to show that their own political viewpoint was right: proof of the need for tougher hard-line measures by the government or as evidence of the constant Whig reiteration that the war was unwinnable. "A country two thousand miles long," asserted "Crito" in the *Morning Post,* ". . . intersected by rivers, passes, mountains, forests and marshes, where the conquest is . . . over the people, their affections, their hearts and their prejudices. . . . If conquest gives us the command of America we cannot keep it by force; the only possible plan is to burn and destroy it from one end to the other. . . ."

"The sword alone," insisted a Tory in the *Morning Chronicle,* "can decide this dispute . . . to prevent the ruin of the British Empire, which will inevitably take place if we are defeated."

In Lloyd's and Garraway's, the city coffeehouses, the news dominated all discussion and created a mood of caution. Prices on the stock market dropped.

The City of London, whose merchants had been badly savaged by the loss of American trade, was a focal point of resistance to the government. Within days, members of the Constitutional Society meeting at the Kings Arms Tavern on Cornhill launched a subscription for the "relief of widows [and] orphans . . . of our beloved American fellow subjects . . . unhumanely murdered by the King's Troops at or near Lexington and Concord."

Criticism of the administration in the press was well tolerated, but this was going too far. When the appeal was advertised in the press, the government mounted a prosecution for seditious libel.

Meanwhile, in Whitehall no report had yet been received from Gage, and Dartmouth tried desperately to obtain more information. He sent for Captain Derby, who had brought the news, but the American refused stubbornly to see the Secretary of State.

The King was at Kew Palace when the news was rushed to him on May 29, the day before the press covered it. As always, his reaction was cool.

"I am far from thinking that the General has reason to be displeased," he wrote. "The object of sending the detatchment was to spike cannon and destroy military stores; this has been effected . . . but with the loss of an equal number of men on both sides—the die is cast. I therefore hope you will not see in this a stronger light than it deserves. . . ."

It was not until June 9, eleven days after the rebel news had reached London, that the *Sukey* lay off Portland, waiting for a favorable wind. The navy's Lieutenant Nunn, stalking the deck impatiently with Gage's dispatches to Dartmouth, hired a passing scow to take him ashore and rushed to London.

In essence Gage confirmed the truth of the rebel account, except that he claimed the Americans fired first at Lexington. The allegations of rebel scalping and ear lopping in Lord Percy's report, which Gage enclosed, provided a gruesome retort to the American brutality charges.

The government published the official report as fast as it could, holding up the presses of the London *Gazette* until midnight of the Saturday it was received. Like the rebel version, it caused a spate of publicity and critical press comment.

"Congratulations, Your Lordship," mocked one writer, recalling Sandwich's speech in the Lords about American cowardice, "upon the complete triumph you have recently gained over your enemies."

More serious commentators, however, pointed to the real danger of the crisis. "The French and Spanish," said a correspondent of the *Morning Chronicle*, ". . . only wait for a general engagement between the King's troops and the Provincials. . . ."

The news of a general engagement came fast enough, preceded by a report passed between two becalmed vessels in the Channel that the British under Howe had been defeated in a battle near Boston. On July 25, Gage's account of Bunker Hill, with its appalling list of casualties, shocked a London that had not yet fully absorbed the impact of the narrow escape from Concord.

In Whitehall and St. James's, the news precipitated urgent action. Messengers were dispatched to summon a meeting the next day of the Privy Council.

Since the report of Lexington and Concord, the government had been moving in its usual leisurely way toward building up its force in America. The King had written to Hanover, of which he was prince, for 2,000 German troops for garrison duty in the Mediterranean, thus freeing British soldiers for American service. Sir Guy Carleton in Quebec had been told to raise an army of 2,000 Canadians, and money and equipment were already authorized to supply it. A ship with 2,000 stand of arms had been ordered to join Lord Dunmore, still in refuge aboard HMS *Fowey* in Virginia's York River, to arm, as Dartmouth put it, "such faithful adherents as shall stand forth in his defense against the lawless rabble. . . ."

Still British ministers saw the militant Americans as "rabble." Despite Concord, the conflict was still regarded in Whitehall as a series of Adams-organized riots.

The news of Bunker Hill came like a flash revelation, stripping the riot mentality from government thinking. It stopped abruptly the idea that it could stamp out the trouble with a little rearrangement of the peacetime military establishment, bolstered up with some outside help.

Britain was engaged in a full-scale war that it must win fast before France and Spain, now allies, took advantage of it. Already, the *Daily Advertiser* had pointed out ominously that the French had a "large body of horse and foot within a day's march of

Dunkirk." Rumors were spreading through London that the Spanish ambassador had been recalled to Madrid for consultation.

On July 26, the day after the news of Bunker Hill reached London, the Cabinet met at 10 Downing Street and, according to a minute roughly scrawled on a page and a half of notepaper, voted to urge the King to establish an army in America of 20,000 men.

The next day the elderly Lord Rochford, Secretary of State for the Southern Department, sent for the French ambassador, the Comte de Guines. In a careful discussion—consisting, so De Guines reported later, of insinuations rather than statements—Rochford warned him against exploiting the Revolution. A strong body of opinion in Britain, indicated the Secretary of State, thought that the easiest way of ending the revolt was to fight France now—*and* Spain, if it joined the conflict.

These were brave insinuations, for at that moment in the crisis, as the French well knew, Britain was very short of troops. It was now clear that much of the proposed army of 20,000 men, needed to put down the American rebellion, would have to be raised from foreign sources.

The first place the King decided to seek help was Russia. Catherine had indicated to Sir Robert Gunning, British envoy extraordinary in Moscow, that she might be prepared to lend troops. But by the time the royal request to "Sister Kitty" for 20,000 Russian soldiers arrived she had changed her mind—as a result, according to the British ambassador in Berlin, of pressure from Frederick of Prussia.[5] She advised Gunning to urge his king to settle the American dispute by peaceful means. "There are moments when we must not be too rigorous," commented the autocrat of all the Russias. It would, she said, be an ill compliment to him if she consented to a course of action that suggested he was one of those monarchs who could not put down their own rebellions.

By then the London press had already reported on the visit to London in September of the Prince of Hesse-Cassel, one of the German mini-states. Hesse-Cassel had troops that the prince was happy to rent, and although George III also hired men from Hanover and Brunswick, the little state became his main source of troops to support British soldiers in America.

Meanwhile, a lone negotiator had arrived in England from the

American Congress at Philadelphia. Just three weeks after the
news of Bunker Hill had reached London, Richard Penn, grandson
of the celebrated William Penn of Pennsylvania, rode a stagecoach
from Bristol to London with a petition begging the King to
interpose his authority to assuage mutual fears and jealousies and
to negotiate a reconciliation with "his faithful colonists." Because
the Americans knew that the Congress was regarded at St. James's
as an illegal body, the petition was signed on behalf of His
Majesty's subjects in the individual colonies.

Penn had come a long way on his mission, but in London that
summer the humble tone of the petition seemed in striking
contrast with the "faithful colonists" who had gunned down
British troops on the Concord road and Breed's Hill. It came from
a group of men who were now directing the army that was at that
minute holding the British under siege in Boston. In fact, news had
just arrived that they had appointed the prestigious George
Washington to command it.

In view of the background, the petition was asking a great deal
of a reactionary monarch who had very firm ideas about the divine
right of kings. Penn was wasting his time, and this was soon made
very clear. Dartmouth refused to see him, and eventually the
American was informed frigidly that since the King did not receive
the petition "on the throne," no answer would be given.

George III was the formal head of the army, and he now took
over firm control of the policing operation that had escalated into
a war. "I am clear as to one point . . ." he told his Premier as soon
as he heard of Bunker Hill, "we must persist and not be dismayed
by any difficulties that may arise on either side of the Atlantic. I
know I am doing my duty and therefore can never wish to
retract."

He recalled Gage, who he now saw was far too mild a man to be
commander in chief, and appointed Howe in his place. Since he
knew he could not get enough troops to America for a major
campaign until the spring, he began planning a minor operation in
the mild winter climate of the South. The governors of Virginia
and both Carolinas, temporarily in refuge from the revolutionaries,
had written to London insisting that there was a large potential of
Loyalists just waiting for a chance to fight for the King. What was
needed was a Southern landing by a small force of regulars to

provide a rallying point, and the army would be augmented by thousands of Americans.

This sounded like good sense, and the King gave orders for the operation to be initiated at once. Meanwhile, he urged Howe to consider moving his army to New York, whose strategic position at the mouth of the Hudson made it a preferable base to Boston, before the winter. But Howe could not act on the royal suggestion because he did not yet have enough ships.

The war in America was by far the biggest overseas operation that Britain had ever mounted, and the whole system of administration and supply was completely inadequate for the task. Patronage and graft were an accepted integral aspect of the whole structure, as indeed they were in politics; military contracts were used to siphon off enormous fortunes.

The navy's ships were rotten, as Graves complained constantly to the Admiralty, and much of the military equipment was in the same state. The letters from Boston by the artillery Colonel Samuel Cleaveland about the state of his gun carriages make it seem astonishing that he succeeded in getting his cannon into action at all at Bunker Hill.

Even more important, the King's rigid faith that British troops would quickly put down the rebellion was not shared by his military chiefs. Lord Barrington, the War Secretary, had long insisted that the use of land forces was hopeless, that the only effective action open to them was to use the navy to blockade American ports.

Even as recently as June, Adjutant General Harvey, the most senior staff officer in Whitehall, had declared that "to conquer it [America] by our land forces is as wild an idea as ever contraverted common sense."

General Jeffrey Amherst, the most respected military figure in the country, took roughly the same view. But the King was determined. The whole principle of his sovereignty was at issue. Britain had to win because it was in the right. He was unmoved by the advice of his military chiefs and refused to accept Barrington's resignation. His attitude to the whole situation was almost religious.

Few wars in history have been launched deliberately in the face of such violent opposition at home.

The City of London, with John Wilkes as its lord mayor, took its passionate objection to British policy in America to lengths that were almost treasonable. When the royal proclamation declaring that anyone aiding the rebels would be prosecuted as traitors was read by the heralds at the Royal Exchange Building, it was hissed by City men.

In Parliament, which assembled in October for the first time since the news of Concord had reached London, the angry Whig opposition moved into the attack once more, lambasting the ministers with the same arguments that they had used so forcefully over the past eighteen months. In the Commons, burly, ruddy Charles James Fox, who could stay up all night gambling with thousands of pounds at Almack's Club and still speak brilliantly for hours, led the main assault: "I cannot consent to the bloody consequences of so silly a contest about so silly an object, conducted in the silliest manner that history . . . has ever furnished an instance of; and from which we are likely to derive nothing but poverty, misery, disgrace, defeat and ruin."

Flaying the Premier sitting on the other side of the house, fat, jowly, watching his attacker good-naturedly with his big, bulging eyes, Fox declared scathingly: "Lord Chatham, the King of Prussia, nay Alexander the Great never gained more in one campaign than the noble Lord has lost. He has lost a whole continent."

But his violent opposition did not deter the King. It was ineffective where it mattered—in the voting at the divisions. The royal political party machine was well geared to secure the majorities needed to approve the King's proposals for the war in America.

The King realized that against this rising barrage of oratorical brilliance Lord North needed support in the House of Commons, where Dartmouth, being a peer, could not speak. In addition, the new scale of the crisis in America now demanded a strong man to direct it. The moderate Dartmouth, fighting every foot of the way, was forced out of his post as Secretary for the colonies to make way for the hard-line Lord George Germain.[6]

Cold and austere, Germain was exceptionally tall, with broad, muscular shoulders, and he imparted an impression of supercilious arrogance that offended many people. "By contrast with Lord

North who was liked even by his political enemies," commented Alan Valentine, Germain's biographer, "Lord George was disliked even by his political allies."

He was a rather sinister, solitary man, reported by gossipy London to be a homosexual. Later his relationship with the young American Loyalist Benjamin Thompson, who lived in his house and even became his undersecretary, added substance to the rumors. In his office, however, he was briskly efficient and extremely punctual. A striking contrast, noted one of his secretaries, to the amiable, easygoing Dartmouth.

Germain's appointment was an astonishing lesson in sheer survival, for he had been the focus of a sensational scandal that, by its nature, should have ruined him completely. At the Battle of Minden, he had commanded the cavalry. Ordered to advance under conditions that contraverted basic military principles, Germain sent his troops forward slowly while he checked the orders personally with the commander in chief. By the time his horsemen arrived on the battlefield the enemy was already in flight.

Germain was court-martialed for cowardice and dismissed from the army in disgrace. George II, who hated him because of his friendship with his rebellious grandson, Prince George, ordered the verdict to be read to every unit in the army; he even stripped the privileges from every officer who testified in his support at the hearing.

Ever since, Germain had been taunted by satirists in the press and by his political opponents in the House of Commons. But the rebellious prince had now become King and very gradually, with the royal assistance, Lord George had staged a comeback, topping it with this spectacular leap into one of the senior posts in government. Ironically, he now directed an army in which he was forbidden to serve.

It was an example of the reward of patience, of being in the right place at the right time—and having the right opinions. For Germain was as rigid in his views on the American rebellion as the King.

Scarred by bitter experience, this competent, haughty, calculating man had developed into a fighter the hard way. Immediately, on taking office he demanded equal status with the other two Secretaries of State[7]—which Dartmouth had been prepared to forgo—and got it. Then he launched a frontal attack on the appalling inefficiency of the Admiralty, bringing him up squarely against Lord Sandwich.

The two men would never have got on under any circumstances. Sandwich, with his immense influence and his traditional rakish tastes, was "one of the boys," solidly entrenched in the Establishment. Germain was a loner. Now that they were in conflict at the source of power, the natural acrimony was intensified.

So the direction of a major military-naval war across 3,500 miles of ocean was now to be shared, in effect, between two aristocrats in constant bitter combat.

The news that had been flowing into London during the autumn and early winter could have given nothing but anxiety to either of them. British ships had been captured by rebel privateers. In New York Harbor, HMS *Asia*, the big 64-gun ship of the line, was serving as a kind of floating home for royal sympathizers, such as the publisher of the Tory *Rivington's Gazette*, who dared not stay ashore.

In Boston the rebels had captured the lighthouse at the harbor entrance, even though it was garrisoned and regarded as virtually impregnable. In Philadelphia, John Hancock, one of the two archrebels Gage had formally outlawed, had been appointed president of Congress.

From sources right up the eastern seaboard came reports of persecution of people who were still loyal to the King. "Daily," reported one correspondent from Pennsylvania, "there are examinations before the Committees of His Majesty's faithful servants branded with the name of Tory."

It was from Canada, however, that the most serious news was coming. For in August, the rebels, who had withdrawn after garrisoning the forts at Ticonderoga and Crown Point in May, had blazed their way in force across America's northern border.

6

QUEBEC, September 7, 1775

From the west, the direction from which the express rider approached the city, most of Quebec lay hidden. For it was built on the side of a cliff facing east at the narrow points where the St. Charles River flowed down from the north to mingle with the waters of the great St. Lawrence. It peered, as it were, over the high plateau called the Plains of Abraham while the body of the town was covered by the rock face.[1]

High walls encircled the Upper Town protectively, reaching from the lofty crag of Cape Diamond, which overlooked the St. Lawrence on the south, to the bank of the St. Charles, near Quebec's little port to the north.

It was a fortress city—gaunt, cold, but brilliantly sited for defense. It was from here that Britain ruled Canada, the vast province that, with the help of its American colonists, it had wrested from the French a decade and a half ago.

Dominating the upper part of the city was the formal residence of the royal governor, Sir Guy Carleton, the Chateau St. Louis, a magnificent building featuring the tall, pointed towers favored by French architects.

To the chateau news was rushed that day that the rebels had invaded Canada in force, sweeping along the Richelieu River from Lake Champlain to the little town of St. Johns. St. Johns was the northernmost point ships could reach, for from there the river fell sharply in rapids and waterfalls for 10 miles to Chambly before flowing on into the St. Lawrence.

It was no surprise to Carleton. He had been doing what he could to prepare for it for months—ever since the morning in May when, after the fall of Ticonderoga, two big American raiding parties had swooped on the Richelieu. They had been led, so Carleton had reported disdainfully to London, by Benedict Arnold, "said to be

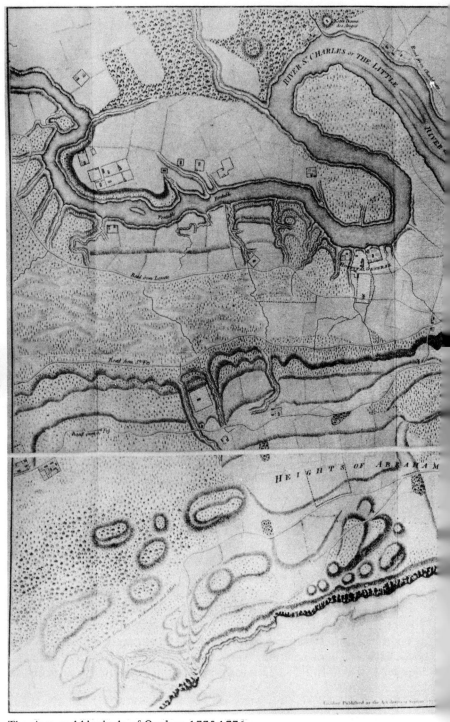

The siege and blockade of Quebec, 1775-1776.

PLAN
of the
CITY AND ENVIRONS
OF
QUEBEC,
with
ITS SIEGE and BLOCKADE
by
THE AMERICANS,
from the 8th of December 1775 to the 13th of May 1776.

References.

A. Bastion of Cap Diamant
B. ____ of la Glacière
C. ____ of St Louis
D. ____ of St Ursule
E. ____ of St John
F. ____ of la Potasse
G. Porte du Palais
H. Governor's House
I. Lower Town Church
K. Nuns of the Congregation
L. The Place where Genl Montgomery began his Attack on the 31st of December between 4 and 5 in the Morning

M. le Saut du Matelot where Colo Arnold made his attack on the 31st of December and was wounded

Engraved by Wm FADEN.
Scale of 600 Yards.

POINTE DES PERES

RIVER St LAURENCE

CAP DIAMANT

The British Museum

a native of Connecticut and a horse jockey," and Ethan Allen, "said to be outlawed in New York."

They had stayed only to raid some British stores in the town and to capture two vessels, moored on the river; then they had dropped back along Lake Champlain to Crown Point. Arnold had warned the local inhabitants that they would soon return with 5,000 men, and Carleton, who had just heard of the thousands of men who had massed to attack the British troops on the Concord road, did not disbelieve him.

Carleton, a tubby, buoyant, energetic general, was virtually helpless. He was the royal governor of one of the most powerful nations in the world, yet from the start he had known there was little he could do to challenge a major strike by the rebels. For to protect the whole vastness of Canada, he had barely 600 soldiers fit for duty.

Truly, his only hope lay in the Canadians and possibly, as a very small fringe extra, in the Indians for whom Carleton had little regard. In London the Canadians were seen as a potential force of some size, a militia that merely awaited the call. When the first searing reports of the conflict in Massachusetts had reached Whitehall, Dartmouth had sent out prompt orders for 2,000 men to be raised and dispatched the equipment for them by ship. Later he increased the figure to 3,000. It was a typical piece of London planning designed around men who were just not there—at least not there willing to take up arms.

During the previous year, as Carleton discovered very quickly, Samuel Adams' agents had been moving through the towns on the St. Lawrence, urging the Canadians to form Committees of Correspondence and to send delegates to Congress. They had some ready-made ground support, for the Old Subjects, as the Protestant families of British origin were known, had greatly resented the Quebec Act with its concessions to the Catholics. In January, Carleton had written to Dartmouth that some of the Old Subjects were, with their "cabals and intrigues . . . exerting their utmost endeavours to kindle in the Canadians the spirit that reigns in the province of Massachusetts. . . ." But Canada sent no delegates to Philadelphia.

In theory, the colony seemed a fertile ground for revolution. It was controlled on completely undemocratic lines, with no form of elected assembly in the sense that there was in all the American provinces. But the Catholic Canadians, especially the numerous priest-controlled peasant *habitants*, were not eager to join forces with a congress of Americans who, in an impassioned letter to the King about the Quebec Act, described their faith as "a religion that has deluged your island with blood and dispersed . . . persecution, murder and rebellion through every part of the world."

As the tension rose in Boston during the spring, the American agents changed their tactics to combat the stony apathy they encountered in the north. John Brown, a representative of the Massachusetts Provincial Congress, on a visit from Massachusetts, warned merchants in a Montreal coffeehouse that "if a man of them dared to take up arms and act against the Bostonians, thirty thousand of them would march into Canada and lay waste the whole country."

Canada was vital strategically. Under British control, it would form a constant threat to the Revolution, for at any time an army could be thrust quickly down the Richelieu River-Lake Champlain waterway that reached south almost to the Hudson; that was why the British considered it essential for Carleton to hold the province against attack.

Through the summer the governor had done his best. He had fortified the strategic towns where he could. He had tried to rally the Canadians and had succeeded in raising 500 men, though they were not very reliable. He had rushed the construction of a couple of armed schooners at St. Johns—racing with the rebels who he knew were busy on a similar high-speed program along the lake at Crown Point—and dragged up some flatboats, each mounted with one cannon, through the rapids from Chambly.

With some misgivings, he had presided at a conference with the Indians of the Six Nations, for he knew that when Ethan Allen had led his raiding party into the Canadian forest in May, he had contacted the Indians. "George our former King," Allen had written in a letter that had been duly sent on to the Chateau St. Louis, "has made war . . . and sent his army and they have killed some of your good friends and brothers who lived at Boston. . . . I want your warriors to join with me and my warriors, like brothers, and ambush the regulars. If you will, I will give you money, blankets, tomahawks, knives. . . ."[2]

Clearly, Carleton had to keep the sympathy of the "savages," and the British were well placed to do so. Their Indian Department had been dealing with the tribes for years. Thayendanegea, one of the Mohawk chiefs, had even been brought up in the home of the Johnson family, who had run the department for years. Traditionally, Britain had helped the Six Nations of the Iroquois League, whose lands were south of the St. Lawrence, against their enemies.

At the June conference, organized in Montreal by Colonel Guy Johnson, the present department head, each of the assembled tribes was given a war belt. War songs were chanted, and Johnson invited the Indians "to feast on a Bostonian and drink his blood." The symbolism sounded more bloodthirsty than it was. Carleton refused to exploit this source of savage killers and rejected their offer to lay waste the New England frontier. All he wanted, he said, was to keep a party of forty or fifty braves at St. Johns for scouting, in which role they were unsurpassed. "The Indians," recorded Colonel Daniel Claus, who was present, "were somewhat disgusted at their offer being rejected," but they agreed to do what Carleton asked.

The first news of the September invasion to reach the Chateau St. Louis was that a group, consisting mainly of these Indians, had thrown back the first rebel thrust at St. Johns.

With its undertone mockery of the rebel fighting abilities this news made a dramatic highlight for the letter to London, but Carleton knew that he had no resources for anything more than a holding operation.

Leaving Hector Cramahe, the lieutenant governor, in charge of the siege preparations at Quebec, he hurried to Montreal to command his slender defense forces. Within only a short while both the Richelieu towns—St. Johns and Chambly—were under siege, their meager garrisons hopelessly outnumbered. Advance rebel parties under Ethan Allen were at Laprairie, just across the St. Lawrence from Montreal.

The senior rebel commander was Brigadier General Richard Montgomery, a tall competent Irishman, known to Carleton because he had spent most of his life in the British army. In fact, as a boy, Montgomery had taken part in Wolfe's siege of Quebec.

Carleton had been there, too, and, as he well knew, he would soon be there again, this time on the inside. For his only hope now of retaining any part of Canada was to hold Quebec.

By the third week in September Carleton's position in Montreal was precarious. Apart from a few Canadians he had persuaded to help, he had only fifty soldiers remaining from other garrisons, to hold a town whose extensive walls were completely inadequate for defense against sustained attack. The Indians had deserted him and made peace with the rebels. Many of the residents of Montreal, while not necessarily favoring the Americans, were sullenly anti-British. When the rebels first appeared at Laprairie, there was a move in the town to offer immediate surrender "to prevent their being pillaged, but," reported the governor, "they were laughed out of it temporarily."

Carleton had sent an urgent summons to Boston for troops, but he knew that even if Gage could spare them, the chances of reinforcements arriving in time were slim.

On September 24 there was a rumor that Allen was going to attack that night. Carleton issued orders that surburban residents who owned ladders should lodge them within the walls, but he was flagrantly disobeyed.

Early the next morning an advance guard of the rebels crossed the river. In the town, the drums hammered out the alarm. "All the old gentlemen and better sort of citizens . . . turned out under arms," reported Carleton.

A polyglot force of 200 marched out of the town to attack the marauders. To their surprise, they captured Allen with 35 of his men.

For Carleton, desperate for any kind of victory to rally the Canadians, Ethan Allen was an important prize. He sent him down the river to Quebec to be shipped to England as soon as possible. But basically it did not alter the situation of the British. The only checks on the rebels were the besieged posts on the Richelieu.

On October 19, after a couple of American flatboats had made a perilous descent through the rapids from St. Johns with some 9-pound cannon, the rebels opened fire on Chambly. The walls were not strong enough to withstand cannon shot, and the end came fast.

St. Johns was now completely isolated. In one last wild emergency move, Carleton tried to launch a big enough force onto the south bank of the St. Lawrence to make a push south to relieve the town. He ordered Colonel Allan Maclean, who had raised a small force of loyal Scottish immigrants, to approach from Quebec and advance up the Richelieu. Simultaneously he himself led an assault across the water to Laprairie.

The rebels fought back fiercely. Their guns bombarded the assault craft and forced the flotilla to turn back to Montreal.

Maclean, too, was badly savaged. Canadians he had pressed into service refused to fight. He fell back to his boats and retreated down the St. Lawrence.

St. Johns held out for a few more days until, on November 2, the garrison surrendered.

Now that there was nothing to divert the rebels from Montreal, Carleton knew he could not hold the town. "It is obvious that as soon as the rebels appear outside the town in force," he wrote home, "the townspeople will give it up on the best terms they can procure. I shall try to retire the evil hour . . . though all my hopes of succour now begin to vanish."

Hurriedly, he made plans to escape with his soldiers and supplies to his last post in Canada—Quebec. Anchored in the St. Lawrence, off Montreal, he had eleven ships[3] of varying sizes. Their captains were ordered to prepare for the run down the river that was certain to be strongly challenged.

Meanwhile, at Quebec, Lieutenant Governor Hector Cramahe, an anxious civil servant with no experience as a soldier, was supervising the final preparations for the defense of the town that had been in progress for several weeks now. The walls had been repaired. Lanterns, attached to long poles, lay ready on the ramparts to illuminate the approaches in case of night attack. Four merchant ships had been fitted out with cannon. During the past few days, two royal naval vessels, the sloop *Hunter* and the *Lizard* frigate,[4] had arrived at Quebec, and Cramahe had eagerly taken the *Lizard*'s thirty-five marines to supplement his tiny defense force.

Since Maclean had gone up the river to help Carleton with his last-minute attempt to relieve St. Johns, there were no British soldiers in the town at all. The defense of the walls was in the hands of volunteer Irish fishermen and a highly suspect militia. In addition, many of the citizens of Quebec were openly favorable to the rebel cause.

The prospects for Quebec were never good. But on November 3, while Carleton was in Montreal planning his evacuation, they grew drastically worse. News reached the Chateau St. Louis of an enormous threat from a new and entirely unexpected direction. Cramahe was handed a letter taken from an Indian messenger addressed to a Quebec merchant named John Mercier.[5] It was from Benedict Arnold and revealed, to the lieutenant governor's appalled astonishment, that at the time he wrote the letter the American colonel was at Dead River on his way north with a force of "2,000 men . . . to restore liberty to our brethren of Canada."

Dead River was south of Quebec in the vast rugged wilderness of present-day Maine. The implications of the news were almost incredible. For they meant that Arnold and his army would be advancing on Quebec from country that in November, when Canada and northern New England were already snowbound, the British regarded as impassable.

In fact, as Cramahe must have realized when he studied his maps and consulted his Canadian advisers, Arnold had traveled by an old Indian route—up the Kennebec, a long river whose churning waters tumbled down to the Atlantic from the forested highlands of Maine over endless falls and rapids and every kind of human obstacle. High up the river they had carried their boats and equipment 12 miles to Dead River, along which they could move north for 30 miles before they again had to lug their transport and baggage overland to a stream that flowed into Lake Megantic and linked with the Chaudière River.

The waters of the Chaudière streamed into the St. Lawrence only four miles from Quebec. For Indians in the summer with light canoes, the route was not too difficult; but for an army of nonwoodsmen, laden with equipment, in the late fall, it was a fantastic journey to attempt.

Fantastic or not, reports from the villages on the Chaudière soon confirmed the truth. It was an incredible achievement in leadership by a man who soon became something very close to a legend. Every war produces its blood-and-guts commanders, but thirty-four-year-old Arnold, as the British were soon to learn and eventually exploit, combined an impassioned personal dynamism with great intelligence. Thickset, swarthy, with immense physical strength, he was a superb and daring tactician.

Brought up in one of Connecticut's richest families, he was an entrepreneur businessman who, in addition to other ventures, had made a great deal of money out of shipping horses from Canada to the West Indian sugar plantations.

By that winter the British in Canada knew very little about him except for his vague connection with horses. But the news of his advance out of the rugged backcountry of Maine at a time when they were so vulnerable was enough for Cramahe to order all canoes and small craft across the St. Lawrence from the south bank. On November 9, just six days after the rebel leader's letter had arrived in the chateau, American advance troops appeared at Point Lévis across the river from Quebec.

By then Colonel Maclean was on his way back along the 120-mile stretch of river from the Richelieu to Quebec with the eighty men he had been able to extricate from the force he had taken down to join Carleton. On the journey downriver, he was approached by a boat moving upstream; on board, with dispatches from Arnold, was an Indian who assumed that the returning British were advancing Americans.[6]

From Arnold's own letter to Montgomery, Maclean learned the story of his incredible journey. "We have hauled our bateaux over falls, up rapid streams . . . and marched through morasses, thick woods and over mountains about 320 miles. . . ."

Arnold had been warned by his scouts that Cramahe had stripped the south shore of the river of small craft, but Indians had joined him with twenty canoes that could be used as transports. "I think the city must fall into our hands," he had written.

Maclean hurried on toward Quebec into a gale-force easterly wind that churned the broad waters of the river. It was far too rough for canoes, and when Maclean's boats heaved and wallowed their way into Quebec's little harbor on the night of the eleventh, Arnold's men still waited on the south bank.

Gratefully Cramahe, the civilian, handed over the military command of the town to Maclean, who formed immediate plans to attack Arnold as soon as he tried to make the three-mile river crossing. Armed naval vessels sailed out of the harbor into the open choppy waters and took up station: three of them along the north shore to head off the rebels as they tried to land; one, the *Gaspe* brigantine, scanning the south bank for signs of their departure.

On November 13 the gale blew itself out. That night, despite the British ships and the small craft that patrolled between them, Arnold and his men slipped across the river, landed at Wolfe's Cove and climbed the cliffs—now made easier with a path—up which Howe had led the celebrated assault sixteen years before onto the Plains of Abraham. By the time one of the patrol boats detected them they had almost completed landing on the north shore. As the boat approached to investigate, the rebels opened fire, and it veered away sharply to carry the alarm to the *Lizard*, the frigate anchored off the town.

That morning the rebels advanced to within 800 yards of the city and gave three great cheers. They were a ragged lot. Bearded, with their tow-cloth hunting shirts torn, many of them had no hats and, instead of boots, wore moccasins made from raw skins. As one of them, Abner Stocking, recorded later: "We much resembled the animals which inhabit New Spain, called the Ourang-Outang."

However, to the men at the guns watching them from the walls they seemed formidable enough. They put their matches to the touchholes of the 24-pounders, loaded with antipersonnel grape and canister shot, the guns flashed, the explosions following each other loudly in quick uneven succession. For a few seconds smoke obscured the view from the ramparts; then, as it cleared, the artillerymen saw the rebels dropping back.

Later in the day, Arnold sent a letter to the town under a flag of truce demanding surrender "in the name of the united colonies." He warned: "If I am obliged to carry the town by storm, you may expect every severity practised on such occasions and the merchants who may now save their property will probably be involved in the general ruin."

During those critical hours, as they waited for Arnold to attack, the situation of Quebec seemed very grave. There was now little hope of reinforcements. Howe had refused a second urgent call for help to Boston because of the dangers to relief ships at that time of year. Although vessels could still just get through, very soon the thick ice would block the sea approach to the St. Lawrence and the town would be sealed off from England until the spring.

Arnold, however, would soon be strongly supported. With Montreal on the point of surrender, before long Montgomery's army with its guns would be advancing up the river to join the besiegers. In addition, the rebels had many sympathizers in the town; an internal attack was a strong possibility.

Cramahe summoned a council of war in the Chateau St. Louis to decide policy—Maclean, the captains of the naval ships, the masters of some of the cargo vessels, the colonels of the militia and the town mayor.

The anxious men in the big room in the gloomy chateau must

have been only too conscious that General Montcalm had presided over a similar conference sixteen years before. But then it was the British who were outside the walls. The French, however, had been in Quebec in some strength; Montcalm had regular soldiers to defend the town. Now Maclean had only a handful of trained men: thirty-five marines, one or two gunners and a few fusiliers. In addition, he had his Royal Highland Emigrant Regiment, which he had recruited in Nova Scotia and Newfoundland in the summer, but they had been under arms only a few weeks.

The truth was that if the town was to be held, the main brunt was going to fall on civilians—merchants, civil servants, sailors and fishermen. The walls were long, and though they had guns to fight off attack, they had very few experienced gunners. Crudely tutored civilians would have to handle the big cannon—highly dangerous to the gun teams, unless handled with precise care.

On the other hand, Quebec was a fortress that had never been taken by storm. Montcalm's fatal error had been to march out from behind his strong protection and fight the British in straight combat. There was enough food in the city to last until the spring and adequate ammunition—if the amateur garrison could only succeed in firing it.

The war council decided to fight, to hold Quebec to "the last extremity." All surburban houses that were close outside the walls and could provide cover to the besiegers were to be destroyed.

An embargo had already been placed on all vessels in the port—except for the ships bound for Britain with the valuable cargoes of furs—and the crews recruited for defense.

There was still just time for a ship to get through to the Atlantic before the ice closed in. It was decided that a naval officer would be sent to Britain to describe the exact situation; pilots would go with him to bring in the relief forces on the off chance, which seemed remote at the moment, that the garrison could hold out until the ice melted. A secret signal—a blue pennant over a Union Jack and the firing of five guns—would inform an approaching fleet that the ships that remained and the city itself were still in British hands.

For four days after they paraded in front of the walls on the Plains of Abraham, Arnold's tattered army quartered in nearby houses besieged the town. Then, on the eighteenth, the men on duty on the walls saw them trailing west across the snow in a long and ragged column. Reports came in that they had withdrawn to Pointe aux Trembles, 20 miles up the St. Lawrence, to wait for Montgomery.

Arnold, so the British learned too late, had been warned that Maclean was planning an attack from the town to coincide with an assault on his rear from two armed ships that were rumored to be on their way down the St. Lawrence with 200 British troops. He was retreating, according to reports that streamed into the town, only to wait until Montgomery joined him with cannon; then the combined rebel force would storm the town.

The rebels were better informed about the crisis situation in Montreal than the British. By the nineteenth there was still no news of Carleton in Montreal, but reports *had* arrived in Quebec of American plans to stop his escape. At Sorel, where the Berthier Islands split the waters of the St. Lawrence into narrow rocky streams, the rebels had set up batteries of guns.

Eight days earlier, on November 11, Carleton had been warned that Montgomery's main force was approaching Laprairie on the far side of the river. He ordered the planned evacuation. At dusk, his eleven ships, loaded with ammunition, supplies and more than 100 fighting men, weighed anchor and moved down the St. Lawrence under fire from rebel guns on the south shore.

The next day one of the ships ran aground, and the little fleet had to heave to until it could be cleared. Then that night the easterly gale that had held Arnold down opposite Quebec roared up the river past Sorel. The British vessels had no alternative but to drop anchor and ride out the storm. But Carleton's luck was out. On the sixteenth, five days after they had left Montreal, the wind was still in the east. Until it veered west, they would have no hope of making their gauntlet run through the long narrows at Sorel—with rebel guns pounding them at close range from both sides.

At last, Carleton decided he should go on ahead and try to escape past the rebels so that he could take command in Quebec. He sought the help of Captain Bouchette, master of one of the merchant ships in his flotilla, who was nicknamed *La Tourte* (the pigeon), owing to his reputation for fast sailing.

That night Carleton, disguised in the clothes of a Canadian peasant *habitant*, clambered down into a whaler[7] commanded by the captain. The oars were muffled to hide the noise of wood on wood in the rowlocks; signals to be passed by touch from man to man had been agreed on so that complete silence could be maintained.

The whaler pushed off quietly down the river. It was a dark night under a clouded sky, and by staying in the middle of the broad river, they were in little danger until they reached the narrows of the Berthier Islands where the rebels had set up their gun batteries.

As they approached the dark bulk of the islands, with the oars slipping quietly in and out of the water, they could see the American bivouacs along the bank. Blazing fires lit up whole areas of the stream. As they passed into the flickering pools of illumination cast by the flames, the oarsmen stopped rowing and crouched down, drifting with the current, which on the St. Lawrence ran very fast, so that the boat resembled one of the big hunks of rotten timber that were always floating down toward the sea.

For nine miles they went on through the narrows, holding their position in the stream by paddling with their hands. All the way down, they could hear the routine challenges of the sentries and the barking of the camp dogs.

Then, at last, they were through the islands—and out in the wide waters of Lake St. Peter, which balloons the St. Lawrence at that point.

The town of Three Rivers lay near the head of the 30-mile lake. Not far beyond it, they found at anchor a British armed brig which took them the rest of the way to Quebec.[8]

At Quebec, Carleton still seemed to hope that there was just a chance that some of his ships, at least, might get through the narrows of the Berthier Islands when the wind changed. "The seamen tell me that the wind was fair for passing by Sorel last night, yesterday and the night before," he wrote to London on the twentieth with an optimism that must have been forced.

By then the fleet had been surrendered to the rebels. More than 100 fighting men—among them British regulars, needed vitally in Quebec—had been taken prisoner.

One of Carleton's first actions in assuming command of Quebec was to do what the war council had not dared for fear of causing resentful reaction: By proclamation he ordered every man in the city to enroll in the militia or to quit the town; otherwise they would be prosecuted as spies. By the end of November his garrison of sailors and civilians, supported by his few precious regulars, amounted to 1,800 men.

Tensely the garrison waited for the return of the rebels. Snow fell heavily; ice swirled down the river; rumors abounded. On December 1 a report came in of a party of rebels at Menut's Tavern, a mile to the west. Carleton, taking no chances, ordered the cannon to open up on the inn. They shot the head off a horse standing outside and smashed the cariole behind. Later it was rumored that Montgomery had just stepped out of it.

The next day a man was reported for making alarmist speeches to the superstitious and highly credulous *habitants*. They had already been astonished by the light clothing worn by Arnold's men after their miraculous journey. The provocateur had played on the French word *toile* (linen) and suggested it should be *tolle* (ironplate). The belief that the Americans were clad in vests of musketproof sheet iron spread fast, so on Carleton's orders, one of Quebec's huge gates was hauled open, and to the noise of rolling drums, the man was made to walk out of the town.

The next day reports filtered through the city that Montgomery had joined Arnold at Pointe aux Trembles with "many cannon" and "4,500 men."

As usual it turned out to be a wild exaggeration, but on December 5 the sentries on the wall saw in the distance the long American column—the combined forces of Montgomery and Arnold—approaching across the snows of the Plains of Abraham. Not long afterward the bateaux carrying the guns and ammunition were spotted on the river by a naval patrol boat.

The two American forces surrounded the town. Arnold's men, who had now abandoned their awesome *tolle* shirts for captured British winter clothing brought up by Montgomery, occupied the suburbs of St. Roch to the north. Montgomery's troops camped on the plain to the west.

For two days little happened. There was a report that Arnold's men were building a battery behind a house in St. Roch within a mile of the walls and, according to Thomas Ainslie, a collector of customs serving as a militia captain, "we sent several shots through the house."

On December 7 Montgomery made an attempt to demand surrender, but since Arnold's surrender demand under a flag of truce had been rejected, he tried another tactic.

A woman approached the Palace Gate and said she had an important communication for General Carleton. Surprisingly, Carleton agreed to see her, but when she revealed that she had a letter from Montgomery, he ordered a drummer to burn it unread. He held her captive for a few days then had her drummed out of the town with a message to Montgomery that he would receive no communication from a rebel.

Determined to have his letter read, Montgomery had copies fired into the town attached to arrows—with some apparent success, for Carleton sent it home to London. "I am well acquainted with your situation . . ." it warned, taunting that the walls were "incapable of defense, manned with a motley crew of sailors the greatest part our friends, of citizens who wish to see us within the walls. . . . The impossibility of relief . . . point out that absurdity of resistance. . . ."

Carleton did not rate his chances of holding Quebec very highly. "I think our fate extremely doubtful, to say nothing worse," he had written to London in November. But he himself had besieged Quebec, and he had learned from Montcalm's error. There was going to be no sallying forth to battle on the plains. He knew that the classic assault tactic—of approaching the walls in trenches—was impractical in the frozen ground; even with his amateur garrison he could ensure that Quebec was a hard place to storm.

At 2 a.m. on December 10 a battery of Arnold's mortars, set up behind a building in St. Roch, began firing shells—hollow cannonballs, filled with explosives, slow fused to detonate after hitting the ground. Quebec's 5,000 citizens had long been terrified about the prospect of bombardment by the rebel artillery; in the same way that they respected Arnold's bulletproof *tolle* shirts, they had anticipated wholesale disaster. "But," recorded Ainslie, "after they saw their 'bombettes,' as they called them, did no harm, women and children walked the streets laughing at their former fears."

At daylight the following morning, however, the sentries saw something not so funny: Up on the Cape Diamond heights to the west were the beginnings of an artillery battery, built in thick ice; Montgomery's men were installing guns ranging up to 12-pounders in size—by no means heavy enough to pierce the walls but more than adequate to cause a lot of damage, overlooking the town as they did.

Four days later the artillery in the new battery opened up.

Quebec's big cannon were trained on the rebel guns; 32-pound and 24-pound solid shot and 13-inch shells splintered the ice protection. "A great pillar of smoke rose . . . on their work," wrote Ainslie in his journal.

But although the battery was put out of action, it was not against Montgomery's cannon that the town was mainly tensed. It was against the assault that they knew must come on the night when the rebels stormed the gates.

At four in the morning of the sixteenth, the guards on the walls near the Palace Gate sounded the alarm. Carleton, sleeping in his clothes, was awakened with the news that 600 men were approaching from St. Roch. The drummers pounded out the beat to arms; the cathedral bells pealed urgently. Throughout the town, the garrison hurried to its posts and peered through a heavy snowstorm into the blackness beyond the light cast by the lanterns jutting out from the ramparts. But the attackers never materialized.

Four days later Ainslie wrote in his journal: "Montgomery is reported to have said that he would dine in Quebec or in Hell at Christmas. We are determined that he shall not dine in town and be his own master. . . . The weather is very severe indeed. No man, after having been exposed to the air about 10 minutes, could handle his arms to do execution. One's senses are benumbed. Whenever they attack us, it will be in mild weather. . . . Ice and snow, now heaped up in places [against the walls] where we have reckoned the weakest, are exceeding strong."

Two days later it was still bitterly cold. Late that night Joshua Wolfe, a clerk who had been taken prisoner by the rebels, escaped by getting his jailer drunk. Wolfe reported that the rebels planned to storm the town the following night—the twenty-third. Montgomery, he said, was having trouble persuading his men "to undertake a step so desperate." He had promised them £200 each in plunder. They had 500 scaling ladders made "in a very clumsy manner."

"Can these men pretend that there is a possibility of approaching our walls laden with ladders, sinking to the middle every step in the snow?" mused Ainslie.

Carleton was not so skeptical. That night 1,000 men were posted on the walls, waiting, staring across the snow, until the sun rose.

It was a wise precaution. For the following day a rebel deserter ran up to the St. Johns Gate on the west of the Upper Town, fired

his musket into the air, clubbed it to indicate surrender and asked
for admission. Because the guards had orders not to open the
gates, they hauled him onto the wall by ropes. He reported that
the attack had indeed been planned but Montgomery had postponed it when he realized that Wolfe's escape would raise the
alarm. They would surely attack that night, the deserter warned,
unless his own escape deterred them.

But nothing happened, although the guards "saw many lights all
around us which we took for signals." The weather, however,
turned milder[9]—which, so Ainslie conjectured, would make attack more likely. However, as it later appeared, Montgomery
planned to attack under cover of bad weather.

On the thirtieth another man deserted from the rebels and
reported, wrongly it later turned out, that the Americans were
"now three thousand strong having been reinforced from Montreal" and "expressed much impatience to be led to the attack."[10]

The next day, New Year's Eve, it started to snow again in the
late afternoon. The wind blew up from the northeast, streaming
cold across the icy wastes of upper Canada. By midnight the
sentries on the walls were huddling against the battlements for
protection against a blizzard.

At 4 a.m. the officer of the guard, Captain Malcolm Fraser of the
Emigrants, trudged along the wall on his routine rounds, his body
bent before the gale. As he approached the posts at the southern
end of the walls, he saw what looked like musket flashes on the
heights, but he was puzzled because he could not hear any shots.
He questioned the sentries facing Cape Diamond, and they said
they had seen the flashes for some time. He moved back along the
wall and asked the guards at the next post about the lights. "Like
lamps in the street," was how one man described them.

Fraser guessed that they were lanterns, that the rebels were
forming for attack. He ordered the alarm.

Again the drummers pounded out the call to arms. Once again
the bells of the city clanged out an insistent warning through the
noise of the storm. Officers ran through the streets, bawling to the
militia to turn out. Men tumbled from beds on which they were
lying in their clothes, grabbed their guns and hurried to their
posts.

At parts of the walls, the howling of the wind drowned the
alarm. "At some posts," Captain Patrick Daly recorded later,
"neither bells nor drums were heard." But the guards were soon

aware that the assault they had been expecting so long had come at last.

Two rockets whooshed skyward in quick succession from Cape Diamond by the St. Lawrence. Then the firing started. Rebels shooting from the cover of rocks on high ground by Cape Diamond were only 80 yards from the post on the ramparts and at a level that was almost as high.

But by firing, the rebels exposed their positions. "The flashes from their muskets made their heads visible," recorded Ainslie, "we briskly returned the fire."

Farther north, on the wall by the St. Johns Gate, the gunners had fired flaming shot to illuminate the approaches beyond the circles of light thrown by the lanterns thrust out from the ramparts on long poles. Anxiously they stared through the snowstorm toward the suburbs of St. Johns that were a good starting point for an assault.

The attack came fast—men running from the far blackness of the houses toward the gate, the flickering fireballs turning them into dark giant moving shadows.

The big guns crashed out, the muzzles flaring white flame, jerking back on their carriages until they strained the retaining ropes. Hundreds of leaden grapeshot flayed into the ranks of the advancing men. Between the guns, the militiamen lined the walls, shooting volley after volley of musket balls at their attackers.

Again and again the cannon fired—the explosions blocking the stinging ears of their unaccustomed crews.

Still the rebels came on until they were almost at the big gates. Then suddenly they broke and ran. It was, so the British discovered later, only a diversion with no intention to follow through, but, to the men on the walls, it had looked determined enough.

Meanwhile, the men posted above the Palace Gate, on the north of the city, facing the St. Roch suburb, were suddenly alerted. There the walls merged into tall buildings, the backs of which overlooked the St. Charles River far below. At the foot of the buildings, above the wave-washed rocks, was a path that led down around the eastern edge of the town to the port.

Shells from the rebel mortars in St. Roch had been falling for some time. Now suddenly the guards over the gate—their attention diverted until then by the noise of attack on the west—noticed in the dim light a long column of men in single file passing silently from the direction of St. Roch down the rock path to the harbor. The column, already going by below them, was too close for cannon. The militiamen opened up with their muskets.

Seamen from the ships in the port were manning the eastern windows of the Hôtel Dieu. As the rebel file passed below them, so Ainslie reported, "they were exposed to a dreadful fire of small arms which the sailors poured down on them." As one of the Americans, John Henry, recorded later: "They were even sightless to us. We could see nothing but the blaze from the muzzles of their muskets."

The pathway was rough, heaped with rugged piles of ice and soft snow. Fireballs, lobbed from the town, illuminated the long line of slipping, sliding men, some of them carrying scaling ladders, as they worked their way down toward the harbor. To the defenders above they made easy targets; gaps were ripped in the file by the musket shot; men jerked and toppled into the snow.

But despite the heavy shooting from above them, the rebel column still went on, stepping over dead and wounded comrades, toward the Lower Town.

The Lower Town, the underbelly of the fortress city, was, as Carleton had fully realized, where Quebec's true weakness lay. Log palisades and barriers supported by guns and men with muskets blocked the streets that led from the wharves and from paths such as the one to the east that Arnold's men were now descending under heavy fire.

There was another route that stretched out of the Lower Town—this one to the west, along the rock face of the towering Cape Diamond to Wolfe's Cove. Narrow, cluttered with snow and ice, bordered on one side by bare cliff, it dropped sheerly to the St. Lawrence below.

The main defense of this entrance to the Lower Town was a blockhouse formed out of an old brewery building that commanded the upward curving roadway from behind a log barrier. There a small battery of 3-pounder guns had been set up with their barrels jutting out of the windows. To man and support it with small arms were some fifty men, most of them Quebec residents, but they were backed up by eight seamen from the ships in the port and a Royal Artillery sergeant, the only professional among them. In command of the post was Captain Barnsfare, master of a merchantman, and John Coffin, a Boston Loyalist who had refused a militia commission but, in view of the crisis situation, took on "the authority of an officer."

From the windows of the blockhouse, Barnsfare and his men stared out toward the bend in the road—only faintly visible in the dawn light and falling snow. The gunners had lighted matches waiting ready.

Then they saw them, at first just a suspicion, a sense that there was movement out there in the gray storm, followed by the certainty: a group of shadowy figures with the snow swirling around them. They appeared to be an advance unit, for they stopped as soon as they saw the blockhouse as though waiting for the main body to catch up.

Tensely the men in the blockhouse watched the attackers. "We shall not fire," Barnsfare warned, "until we can be sure of doing execution." Coffin had taken charge of a party of British Canadians who stood at the open windows with muskets at the ready.

At last, the rebels began to advance slowly. The gunners in the blockhouse waited for Barnsfare's order. As they walked, the Americans scuffed the snow with their feet, looking almost unreal in the half-light. When they were about 50 yards away, they stopped again "as though in consultation." Then one of them moved forward alone, peered at the barricade and the blockhouse for a moment and returned to the others.

Again, for a few minutes they seemed to be discussing what to do. Suddenly, as a group they made a dash—all of them running fast to storm the barricade. Barnsfare still waited, watching the rebels advancing swiftly. Then at last, as the nearest men were almost at the barricade, he gave the harsh order: "Fire!"

The explosions as the guns went off in those close confines were deafening. The musketmen squeezed their triggers and swiftly reloaded. "Our musketry and guns," Ainsley wrote, "continued to sweep the avenue leading to the battery for some minutes. When the smoke cleared there was not a soul to be seen."

Not on their feet—but thirteen bodies[11] lay in the snow, and two of them were groaning.

The slaughter of the close-range firing seemed to have convinced the rebels that the post was held too strongly, for they did not attack again.

Carleton was directing the defense of the city from the Upper

Town in the Place d'Armes, where the mobile reserve was held waiting. He knew now that the attacks on the walls at Cape Diamond and St. Johns had been feints, designed to divert the defenders' attention from the real target—the Lower Town, now under assault from both east and west. He had already ordered an artillery officer to hurry down with a militia company to support Barnsfare, who had been reported under heavy attack.

Now he received news of the assault from the east side of the Lower Town that was far more serious. Some schoolboys, according to one report,[12] hurried into the Place d'Armes, shouting, "The enemy's in possession of the Sault-aux-Matelot."

The Sault-aux-Matelot was a very narrow street that led from the waterside into the Lower Town. It was the route for any attack around the outside of the city from the direction of the St. Charles. For this reason, it was strongly defended at the point where the rebels would enter—a high log barricade, well manned and armed with two cannon.

Since it should have been able to withstand a sustained attack, at least until a message could have been got to Carleton asking for support, the information that the enemy had broken through so quickly was very surprising—a breakthrough that was due, it was later charged, to the fact that the officer in command of the ports was a rebel spy.

But the critical aspect was that the Sault-aux-Matelot led directly into the main part of the Lower Town, and once the rebels gained control of that, they would have a very strong base from which to assault the Upper Town.

At first Carleton did not believe it. He sent Maclean down to check. Carleton was an experienced fighter. When the colonel returned with confirmation, he swiftly planned his strategy. The Sault-aux-Matelot had cannon-supported barricades at each end; although the rebels had broken through the first, they had, according to Maclean's report, paused in the street before the second barricade.

Why they had not yet attacked this was not clear, but it was obvious that the assault would soon come. And it was vital to Carleton's defense planning that when it did, they should be held at this point.

Now Carleton sent the militia Colonel Henry Caldwell down to reinforce the defense at the vital barricade at the end of the Sault-aux-Matelot. With him the colonel took Carleton's handful

QUEBEC, September 7, 1775

of fusiliers—virtually the only regulars in Quebec—and a substantial force of militia and sailors.

At the same time the general ordered another strong detachment to march out of the Palace Gate in the north wall of the city and down the same rock path above the St. Charles which the rebels had traversed earlier under fire to attack from the rear.

The plan to trap the rebels in the narrow Sault-aux-Matelot was brilliant, but it depended completely on Caldwell's holding the barricade.

He arrived only just in time. The rebels were just about to assault the high log stockade that blocked the Sault-aux-Matelot. Scaling ladders were already propped against the barrier.

Caldwell had more room in which to deploy his forces than the rebels had in the narrow street only 20 feet wide. The road curved upward away from the Sault-aux-Matelot, then split into two branches. Swiftly he ordered the fusiliers into line, backs against the houses, facing the barricade with fixed bayonets. From there they could fire at the rebels as they mounted the tops of their ladders and charge with the bayonet if any of them succeeded in getting over the stockade.

Some of the militiamen, on Caldwell's instructions, hurried into the nearby houses so that they could fire from the upper windows both at the barricade and over it into the men crowded in the narrow street behind.

As part of the planned defense of the post there was a cannon mounted on a platform, positioned so that it could fire over the stockade.

The rebels charged, clambering up the ladders onto the barricade, and the fire from the defenders mowed them down. Again and again they attacked as musket shot and grape from the barking cannon raked the top of the log barrier.

It soon became obvious that no one could get over the 20-foot summit of the barricade alive against Caldwell's murderous density of shot. The rebels' only course was to weaken the defense, holding it down with heavy fire, while they stormed again. So they swarmed into the houses on either side of the Sault-aux-Matelot and opened fire from the upper windows, concentrating their shooting from the cover of the stone walls on the cannon crew who were well exposed on their platform.

As an assault tactic it succeeded. The gunners leaped from the platform to take cover. On Caldwell's orders another gun was set up farther back along the curving hill road. This was out of sight of the rebel marksmen, but because of its high position, it could fire on the houses that were sheltering them. Solid shot began to drop through the roofs, smashing the floors and stone walls.

Because of the narrow area on which Caldwell could concentrate his musket fire, none of the Americans had yet got over the barricade, but at one point they came close. They swung a ladder over onto the defenders' side of the stockade, but a burly French Canadian named Charland rushed to the barricade, exposing himself to point-blank fire through the loopholes and wrenched the ladder away.

Almost immediately the colonel was faced with new danger. The rebels had entered a house on one side of the barricade whose doorway was in the Sault-aux-Matelot, but some of whose side windows overlooked Caldwell's main defense position. From there they would be able to shoot down at close range on the fusiliers and militia in the street below them.

It was a critical moment. A Highland officer grabbed the captured ladder, placed it against the side of the house, then leaped up it, followed by the others. They met the rebels coming into the room and fought them back down the stairs.

"I called out to Nairne in their hearing," Caldwell reported later, "that he should let me know when he heard firing on the other side"—from the lay party, in other words, that Carleton had sent outside the city to attack the rebels from the rear.

The general's design to trap the Americans in the Sault-aux-Matelot worked exactly as he planned. His men swarmed over the barricade at the other end of the street and demanded surrender from the rebels, now hemmed in from both sides.

The first prisoners, each with a label pinned to his hat worded "Liberty or Death," were passed through the window and down the ladder from the house that Nairne had taken. Then Caldwell had the gate in the barricade opened for the remainder.

Arnold had been wounded and carried from the town, leaving in command Daniel Morgan—a man who, together with his unit of expert Virginian riflemen, was to become one of the rebel field officers most respected by the British army. Morgan, who had once been flogged for striking an officer in the French and Indian War, hated the British; now defiantly, with his back against a wall, he refused to hand over his sword to his captors. They threatened to shoot him, and his own men begged him not to risk his life. He saw a priest among the watching crowd. "Are you a priest?" he snapped.[13] The priest said he was. "Then I give my sword to you," he conceded, angrily. "But not a scoundrel of these cowards shall take it out of my hands."

In all, 426 rebels were taken prisoner. Carleton took advantage of the demoralized American forces and sent out a raiding party to capture Arnold's mortars in St. Roch.

Among the bodies lying in the snow outside the blockhouse on the western side of the Lower Town was the corpse of the rebel General Montgomery. Carleton, who was often magnanimous, ordered a burial with full military honors.

Carleton had held Quebec. He had badly mauled the rebel force. He had left Arnold, now commanding from a hospital bed in St. Roch, with barely 600 men, but the British were still under siege. There could be no relief until the spring. Arnold, on the other hand, could be reinforced and could then storm the city again. Although the morale of Quebec's defenders had received a big boost, their prospects of holding out were in truth no better than they had been before.

By that blizzard-bound New Year's morning of 1776 the colonial revolt had left Britain with only two slender toeholds[14] in the enormous territory that it had once controlled through its network of governors: Quebec, under total siege; and Boston, hemmed in from the land side by a vastly superior force in numbers, now commanded by George Washington.

And compared with Quebec, which, even though facing the threat of another attack, had adequate supplies for months, conditions in the Massachusetts port were serious.

7

BOSTON, January 3, 1776

So far it had been a very hard winter.[1] The troops were desperately short of both food and fuel; rebel privateers, using the shallow coast inlets into which the bigger British ships could not pursue them, were attacking forage and supply vessels. Urgently Howe warned the Colonial Office in London to route all single vessels bound for Boston via Halifax to enable them to make the last dangerous leg of the journey in groups under the escort of Graves' frigates.

Worse, a big supply convoy from Britain did not arrive. "Presumably," Howe wrote gloomily, "northerly winds have forced them far from the coast." Because of the dearth of fuel, he gave orders for some of the wharves to be taken up "which must be our only source if fresh supplies do not arrive. . . ."

The troops, underfed and freezing in their barracks, embarked on a rampage of plundering. The military authorities tried to stop them with repressive measures; the general orders warned the soldiers that the executioner would attend the provost marshal on his rounds and "hang upon the spot the first man he should detect in the fact without waiting for further proof by trial."

No summary execution is recorded, but the punishments for plundering became increasingly harsh. "Robberies and housebreaking," Howe was soon to write to London, "have got to such a height in this town that some examples had to be made."

And they were. On January 3 a court-martial sentenced two men to death and ordered a woman, Isabella McMahon, to be given 100 lashes on the bare back at the cart's tail in different sections of the town. Women, like anyone else who traveled with the army, were subject to its discipline.

The same court sentenced seven men to severe floggings. Among them was Isabella's husband who was condemned to 1,000 lashes.

For flogging, soldiers were bound to a whipping post of crossed halberds. Because 1,000 lashes would probably kill a man, the sentence was usually spread over four sessions of 250 strokes at weekly intervals, administered by the drummers, each man wielding the cat-o'-nine-tails twenty-five times. At the end of the flogging, buckets of salt water were sloshed over the bleeding lacerations to guard against infection.

The punishments were savage, deliberately so, because most officers believed fear was the only way to control the rough raw material that formed the army. They may have been right. The progressive John Burgoyne tried to lead his troops without corporal punishment, but once his army faced crisis he was forced to become just as harsh as other commanders, as, indeed, was Washington, for all the rebel scoffing at the British as "bloody-backs."

Many of the generals, however, understood fully the weapon they were handling. Howe's letters to London reveal a clear sympathy for the men under sentence of punishment, especially the young soldiers. Commanders in chief could order the execution of court-martial sentences of death, but only the King could reprieve. On many occasions, Howe pleaded for the royal mercy for his condemned men; often, too, he exercised his authority to reduce flogging sentences.

That January mercy was not very evident. Every week, often several times, the army was forced to watch floggings that reached such a pitch that on one occasion a drummer flung his cat-o'-nine-tails to the ground and refused to continue the punishment. He was arrested but freed the next day.

Yet despite the brutal sentences, the plundering continued as it always would, though in Boston it was greatly provoked by the shortages.

In an independent attempt to alleviate conditions in the port by deterring the rebel privateers, Admiral Samuel Graves sent a ship up to the seaport town of Falmouth, and burned it. Only with great difficulty did Howe who, as military commander in chief, had no control over the navy, persuade him not to repeat the operation elsewhere: This was hardly the way to impress the loyal Americans Howe was trying to rally to the cause of the King. It was the final operation of the belligerent admiral. He was soon replaced by Admiral Molyneux Shuldham. Certainly, the burning of Falmouth had not worked as a deterrent; the raids of the privateers went right on.

Howe's one consolation was that the besiegers were also suffering from severe shortage. "I am informed," he had reported home hopefully the previous month, "that the troops [rebels] are in great want of clothing and much dissatisfied on other accounts. Their agreement to serve will expire for the most part by the last of December."

The army of rebels was indeed in trouble, as was always the case at the turn of the year when service agreements ended. That year the problems were more marked, for the new revolutionaries found discipline hard to accept. When the Massachusetts Provincial Congress had reorganized the militia, which formed the early skeleton of the Continental Army, it had set up a system under which the men elected their own officers. This was very democratic and conformed with the principles of liberty that were being aired so freely, but it did not result in a very high standard of soldiering. Also, Congress's early attempts to set up supply systems were completely inadequate.

While Howe was trying to survive the winter and curb the plundering of his men, George Washington was still attempting to carve some kind of order out of the chaos of his new army. Forty-three years old, tall and elegant, Washington had now been commander in chief of the rebels for eight months since arriving at Cambridge in May just after the Battle of Bunker Hill.

John Adams' proposal that he should be appointed had been unopposed in Congress, mainly because his military background was clearly outstanding. Like most of the senior men in the rebel army, Washington had fought with the British, displaying a spectacular ability for leadership in the French and Indian War. At only twenty-three, he had been appointed commander of Virginia's forces to repel the attacks by the Indians who were then sweeping across the border of the province every few weeks. By the time of the Revolution, Washington was not only the South's most famous soldier, but also, through his own inheritance and his marriage to a wealthy widow, one of Virginia's biggest landowners with a keen interest in the province's politics.

He was a natural choice as a delegate to Congress as he was for political as well as military reasons for the post of commander in chief. Samuel Adams and the New England delegates, who had sparked off the rebellion and who were therefore suspect in some quarters as extremists, favored the appointment of a Southerner in the cause of colonial unity.

To the British commanders, Washington was a bit of an enigma. As a rebel he merited little respect, but unlike Carleton in his dealings with Montgomery at Quebec, they negotiated with him on the assumption that he was a gentleman who observed the same rules of war that they did. Gage and Howe corresponded with him regularly—usually on the twin issues of treatment of prisoners and unacceptable fighting practices (both accused the other of using musket balls with nails driven through them), and their letters were phrased with elaborate courtesy marked by a kind of unspoken regret that a man of Washington's caliber could have allied himself with an illegal movement led by such riffraff as Samuel Adams. And they distrusted him with good reason on the running negotiations on prisoner exchanges, for obviously he considered every British soldier held a far greater loss to the British army than were the untrained Americans in Howe's custody to the rebel force.

Through that winter, despite the rebel problems, Howe knew that Washington was actively planning attack. From New York Governor Tryon warned Howe that there was a scheme under discussion to kidnap him and hold him as hostage. Other plans included many kinds of new secret weapons—some futuristic—for use against British ships. Yet throughout those hard months, though he had kept Bunker Hill on his north fully manned, Howe had left the Dorchester peninsula, only just across the narrow strip of water to the south of Boston, completely unprotected.

This omission is hard to explain. On the hills of Dorchester the rebels could repeat exactly the operation they had started on Bunker Hill. They could set up cannon and make Boston untenable. The American army was better equipped with guns than it had been in June, better generaled and, though Washington was facing enormous difficulties, far better organized.[2]

Some of the reason for Howe's neglect of this obvious precaution may have been rooted in his character. He was an interesting, complex man, an intelligent and shrewd military tactician; as he had proved at Bunker Hill and on other battlefields, he had great courage and determination in action, and his men and most of his officers held him in high respect. But he was withdrawn and taciturn. He could be very difficult to deal with, as Clinton, who was prickly himself, often experienced. Despite this, he enjoyed social life. He gambled at faro until late at night and had a blond mistress, the wife of Joshua Loring, who on the strength of his wife's relationship with the general was appointed commissary of prisons, a post that through graft provided ample financial pickings.

Howe's great basic fault was a strange apathy that seemed to cloud his judgment. Very often he was slow to go to battle. Sometimes this was due to the fact that he was waiting for men or supplies, but he seemed to have an instinctive tendency to delay aggressive campaigning. There was a weariness about him, as though the slightest effort required strength of will. His dispatches dealing with the postponement of attack through lack of stores or equipment carry little of the impatience that would have nagged many other commanders. On the contrary, there is almost a sense of relief. For "Billie" Howe, there was always time.

In February the British general was informed by his agents that the Americans were making preparations to fortify Dorchester. But he still did not take the hint. He sent over a raiding party which burned some vacant houses and captured some rebel sentries but took no further action.

On the night of March 2 Washington's battery of heavy guns at Roxbury opened up on Boston. The British cannon responded. All night long the cannonballs were whistling in both directions. The following night the rebel barrage started again.

The bombardment, as Howe soon discovered, was a diversion to focus British attention. But at ten o'clock that Sunday night somebody noticed at last that there was activity across the water to the south. Brigadier General Smith, promoted from lieutenant colonel since he had led the British to Concord, was informed that the Americans "were at work on Dorchester Heights." Incredibly, history repeated itself. Howe apparently refused to be hurried from his game of faro or Mrs. Loring. It is hard to believe that after the savaging he had endured at Bunker Hill he could have happily left the matter until the morning. But that is what he did.

The next day he viewed fortifications on the heights far more elaborate than those the Americans had erected on Bunker Hill. Astonished, he commented: "The rebels have done more in one night than my whole army could have done in months."

Howe ordered his cannon to open fire, but the forts were too high for the guns to elevate adequately. The admiral warned him that once Washington brought up his artillery, the British ships would be hopelessly exposed; the fleet would have to vacate its anchorage.

Howe ordered a night attack by a force of more than 2,000 men. During the day the soldiers were shipped down to Castle William since it was a better springboard from which to launch the assault, but that evening a violent storm blew up making the crossing impractical. In any event, Howe's heart was not in it. Plans had already been agreed to evacuate Boston and take New York.

At seven o'clock that night a council of war was in session in Province House. Lord Percy, according to engineer Archibald Robertson, advised strongly against persisting with an attack that was likely to be expensive in casualties and could at best result only in controlling a position they were about to abandon.

"Those have been my own sentiments from the first," said Howe with a sigh, "but I thought the honour of the troops was concerned."

It seemed a pretty poor reason for a possible replay of the slaughter of Bunker Hill, and so it evidently appeared to the men sitting at that council table. For the next morning the evacuation was ordered. The transports were brought up to the wharves, and the loading of equipment and stores was begun.

Boston became a town of turmoil. The Tories, who would have been fiercely persecuted if they had fallen into the hands of the rebels, were packing to leave with the troops. Wagons, piled high with stores, jammed the streets on their way to the wharves.

The Boston selectmen approached Howe with entreaties not to burn the town, and he agreed, provided Washington did not attack. So they sent an urgent message to the rebel commander, who, suspiciously, would agree to nothing—though, in fact, he made no move.

On the morning of March 16 the British fleet of nearly 100 ships carrying more than 10,000 people, including 1,100 Tories, sailed from Massachusetts Bay and set course for the British naval base at Halifax.

It was the last movement in the British defense against the initial onslaught of the Revolution. But as Howe's ships were sailing north for Nova Scotia, plans in London were far advanced for a massive new offensive to stamp out the revolt. The decisions

following the shock news of Bunker Hill were now being transformed into action by an administration machine not equipped for
such major ventures.

Troops were being recruited and trained. Arrangements had been
completed to hire mercenaries from the mini-states of Germany,
to be known, though not all were from Hesse, as Hessians.

In fact, no less than three campaigns, all to be launched more or
less concurrently in the late spring, were being prepared: (1) 9,000
soldiers for Carleton—if, in fact, he still held Quebec—to drive the
rebels out of Canada and to assault from Lake Champlain down
the Hudson; (2) 25,000 men to join Howe for an attack from the
sea on New York to annihilate Washington and the new American
army; and (3) a small force of 2,500 troops to sail to the South to
form a nucleus of an army of Loyalists from Virginia and the
Carolinas. This should have left in the autumn but had been
delayed by the overburdened supply departments.

It was against the supply departments, the graft-ridden, dilatory
bureaucracy of Whitehall, that Lord George Germain, desperately
anxious to retrieve a reputation tarnished at the Battle of Minden,
was battling with determined vigor. The new armies, by far the
largest force Britain had ever sent overseas, needed tents, kettles,
uniforms, blankets, food, muskets, cannon, ammunition, wagons.
An enormous fleet of hundreds of transports and warships would
have to be ready by the spring.

Germain knew that the only hope of the fleet's sailing anywhere
near the required time lay in the pressure he could apply in the
name of the King. And he applied it with enormous energy—demanding in pert, cold notes to know the situation regarding
schedules and delays and completion dates, always undertoned
with the implied threat that he would refer the matter to the King.

Even the Prime Minister was not beyond Germain's insistent
probing. Two days before Christmas the appalling news of the
rebel sweep through Canada and the siege of Quebec was placed
on the Colonial Secretary's desk. Immediately he stalked to the
Admiralty to demand relief ships, but everyone had gone home for
Christmas except Admiral Sir Hugh Palliser, whose authority was
limited. Promptly Germain hurried the admiral to 10 Downing
Street, where Lord North was just about to drive in his coach to
his country house at Bushey, and insisted that the Premier should
wait and deal with the emergency. Reluctantly, North agreed, and
the three men hammered out the plans for the relief of Carleton.

No ships could get through until the early spring, but Germain knew that unless the machinery was put in motion immediately, they would not be there then—and the garrison only had food enough to last until mid-May.

The dictatorial methods of this haughty aristocrat were often criticized—and with reason, for later he tried impractically to apply them across 3,500 miles of ocean—but without them on this occasion it is highly doubtful if the three relief vessels would have sailed in time. As it was, on March 11, while the fleet carrying Carleton's main reinforcement was still forming, the little squadron of three fighting ships, carrying 200 soldiers, headed out into the Atlantic on course for the St. Lawrence.

8

AT SEA, the Northwest Atlantic, April 12, 1776

That morning[1] Captain Charles Douglas stood on the upper deck of his 50-gun ship, *Isis*, and stared across the wastes of sea ice that lay between his squadron and Canada. It was 10 to 12 feet thick, as an initial survey had already revealed, but the question occupying the captain was: How strong was it? Could they break through it? Courageously, for it was the type of operation that could be costly to a career officer in the navy should he be wrong, he planned to test it.

He ordered canvas, and as the sails filled, the *Isis* moved forward at 5 knots. The helmsman steered straight for the thick edge of the ice field. The bows of the ship struck the frozen wall; for a few moments the ship checked, shuddering; then the ice split, cracking loudly, and the *Isis* began to plow a channel.

"Encouraged by this experiment," crowed Douglas, "we thought it . . . an effort due to the gallant defenders of Quebec to make the attempt of pressing her by force of sail through the thick, broad and closely connected fields of ice, to which we saw no bounds towards the western part of our horizon."

Signaling the other two ships to follow, he plowed on through the ice, and by night, when a snow blizzard was howling over the ice, they had progressed some 20 miles through the field, "describing our path all the way with bits of sheathing of the ship's bottom. . . ."

The little squadron moved slowly on through the ice for nine days until at last it cleared near Anticosti Island in the wide Gulf of St. Lawrence. Then they were checked by fog and later by the wind veering to the west. It was not until May 6 that the *Surprise* frigate, sailing ahead of the others, came in sight of the gaunt towers of the besieged city. Fluttering at the head of the flagpole was a blue pennant over a Union Jack—the agreed signal that the town was still in British hands—and five guns roared a welcome from the walls. The captain of the *Surprise* ordered his gunners to acknowledge, and, as planned at that crisis council of war in the Chateau St. Louis in November, seven of the frigate's cannon fired in reply.

The rebel army was still camped outside the town. It had been reinforced substantially, but the morale of the troops, ravaged by smallpox, was low. They had tried to fire the town with red-hot ball, shot from batteries set up on the far banks of both the St. Lawrence and the St. Charles. Later there had been an attempt to sail into the port a flaming fire ship, but it had burned out before it could damage any of the shipping.

By May Arnold, now a brigadier general, was in charge of Montreal. General David Wooster had taken personal command of the besiegers, but as the three British warships sailed into Quebec Harbor, he was about to be replaced by General John Thomas.

Until then Carleton had stubbornly resisted any temptation to attack from Quebec, but now that he had 200 more regulars and knew that thousands of reinforcements were on their way, he switched to the offensive. British troops marched out of the western gates onto the Plains of Abraham to "see what those mighty boasters were about," as he reported scathingly to London. "They were found very busy in their preparations for retreat . . . the plains were soon cleared of those plunderers; all their artillery, military stores, etc., were abandoned. . . ."

Carleton led the pursuit, advancing down the bank of the St. Lawrence to Three Rivers, where he set up his temporary headquarters, sending on a small detachment to probe the rebels at Montreal. On both sides of the St. Lawrence the Americans were retreating.

On May 27 the first of the troop convoys arrived off Quebec, from Ireland. Six days later another, which had set off from Portsmouth, sailed up the river; on board one of the ships was Major General "Gentleman Johnny" Burgoyne, who had arrived to serve as second-in-command of the army under Carleton.

Captain Charles Douglas on the *Isis* was well prepared for the convoys. Pilots were sent aboard the ships at Quebec, and they passed on up the river to the assembly point off Three Rivers. A frigate was already standing by just below the narrows at the Berthier Islands, through which Carleton had made his night

escape in November, to guide the transports through the dangerous rocky channel when the commander ordered them forward.

By then Carleton, who had returned to Quebec, had learned
from a New York newspaper that Brigadier General John Sullivan
was marching with six regiments to rally the rebels and mount an
opposition to the British advance in Canada.

At three o'clock in the morning of June 8, Captain Henry
Harvey on the *Martin* sloop, anchored at the entrance to Lake St.
Peter, was awakened with news brought by a Canadian canoe that a
large force of rebels had crossed the river in bateaux, had landed at
Pointe-du-lac on the north shore and was now advancing through
the woods to attack Three Rivers.

Most of the newly arrived British troops were still on board the
transports anchored in the river near the town, so hurriedly, they
were rushed ashore. The soldiers in the town had already been
alarmed. Men were forming in their units; guns were being
manhandled into position.

The clash in the woods was brief. At five o'clock in the morning
the rebels advanced in three columns along the woodland paths—
into the fire of the waiting British cannon. They broke and made
for their boats. While 1,200 soldiers under Brigadier Simon Fraser
tried to cut them off by marching up the riverbank, the *Martin*
sailed ahead, firing on the retreating men. But the wind dropped;
the frigate was checked, and the rebels escaped. Twenty-four
hours later the British captured General William Thompson hiding
in a swamp.

It was the last halt to the British advance. The transports sailed
through the narrows between the Berthier Islands, and while one
small force moved on up the St. Lawrence to recover Montreal,
the main army under General Burgoyne advanced up the Richelieu
River to Chambly, where the rebel schooners at the foot of the
rapids were burning, and on to a flaming St. Johns, set alight by
the retreating Americans just before the British entered.

The rebels fell back to the Isle aux Noix at the entrance to the
Richelieu, and then sailed south along Lake Champlain, from
which, just over a year before, Benedict Arnold and Ethan Allen
had led the first raids into Canada.

For the time being, Burgoyne could not follow, for while the
rebels had armed vessels on the lake, all the British ships were
below the rapids at Chambly.

Carleton had anticipated this and saw it only as a temporary check. The wealth of Britain and the sheer logistics of war that, given time, it could deploy were now available to him. There were more than eighty British ships on the St. Lawrence above Three Rivers, an enormous source of manpower and equipment.

Even so, assembling enough vessels at the water level of Lake Champlain to transport the army and fight the rebels was a mammoth operation. No fewer than 560 bateaux and 25 long-boats were hauled up as far as possible through the rapids, then heaved through the forest on rollers by teams of horses. Elaborate plans were formed to drag two 12-gun schooners from the water at Chambly up the rugged 12-mile forest hill track, broken at many points by slender bridge crossings over waterfalls, to St. Johns. It was an ambitious project, and it failed. The road began to crumble under the great weight of the *Maria*, the first schooner they tried to move.

Captain Douglas, who was in charge of the operation, accepted his engineers' advice and ordered the schooners to be broken down into sections and reassembled on the stocks at St. Johns, where two other vessels were already under construction. At Quebec, the captain had discovered a 180-ton ship was being built. He commandeered this, had it broken down in sections like the others and sent it down in a convoy of longboats taken from the transports.

Throughout the summer, in addition to the drivers of hundreds of horses, more than 700 sailors, as well as chain gangs of Canadian prisoners working in shackles, took part in this gigantic transport operation. At the end, the British had a fleet of five major vessels—one an 18-gun sloop—and twenty-four gunboats, backed up by a supply flotilla.

By then the rebels had also been busy preparing for the inevitable confrontation on the lake. They did not have the resources of the British, but they had plenty of timber. And they had Arnold driving them on. They, too, were constructing a fleet to challenge the passage of the British on the lake.

It was October before the British were ready to sail from the Richelieu. By then Howe had launched a major offensive with an army of 35,000 men against Washington in New York.

9

NEW YORK HARBOR, July 12, 1776

It was nearly seven o'clock on one of those pristine pink-skied evenings that were a feature of the New York summer when the big 64-gun flagship *Eagle*, with its sails full and the slim white admiral's pennant snaking from the top foremast, progressed slowly down the line of anchored ships, each firing its guns in salute as she approached and passed.[1]

For two weeks 138 British vessels had lain in the harbor, swinging on their cables near the flat shore of Staten Island, where Howe's army, evacuated from Boston via Halifax, was camped in long, neat rows of round white tents. Now on this brilliant July day, the general's elder brother was joining him with yet another army in a huge armada of 150 ships that were streaming through the Narrows between Staten and Long islands that formed the entrance to New York. And even this was not all: Two more fleets were on the way.

From the *Eagle*'s quarterdeck—as the warship moved steadily through the fleet, cheered on, according to an eyewitness, by the sailors in the ships and the soldiers on the beach—the admiral could see the immediate objective of the biggest military force that Britain had ever sent overseas: the town of New York, a dense cluster of houses and churches cramped on the tip of the hilly, wooded Manhattan Island, the new headquarters of George Washington and the rebel army.

He could survey, too, the magnificent Hudson[2] River. Streaming along the west bank of Manhattan, it reached up straight and wide through eastern America toward Lake Champlain and Canada, where Carleton's teams of sweating sailors were dragging his ships in sections around the rapids of St. Johns. Soon, it was planned, Carleton would strike south with his force of 10,000 soldiers as

154

the Howe brothers swept north to meet him with their big army that would then total nearly 35,000 men.

The cable rattled noisily as the *Eagle*'s anchor splashed into the water and checked the way of the big ship. From the Staten Island beach, a longboat carrying William Howe pushed off and headed for the warship. The general had much to report to his brother.

Only the previous day, a Declaration of Independence, issued by the Congress in Philadelphia on July 4, had been announced in New York. From the ships and the camp on Staten Island, the British had seen the bonfires and heard the celebratory booming of the rebel cannon.

Now, so far as the delegates to Congress were concerned, the thirteen provinces were no longer colonies in protest against the treatment of the mother country; they were self-governing states. The rebellion had been transformed into a war. In their eyes, any claim that King George III may have once had to American territory was gone. His role, or at least the nearest role to a royal sovereign possible in a loose federation of states that had just been established, had been assumed by the flamboyant John Hancock, the president of the Congress—advised, of course, by the Machiavellian Samuel Adams.

To the British the Declaration of Independence was one more act of treason by rebels. "It proclaims the villainy and madness of these deluded people," sniffed Ambrose Serle, the admiral's secretary, as he wrote his journal on board the *Eagle* that night. But the Howes were Whigs, and even though they were heading up a massive military machine, they were sympathetic to the American grievances.

They had come to New York not only to stamp out a revolt but as peacemakers, with the King's commission to restore the Anglo-American relationship to what it once had been. Their powers were limited, and it is highly doubtful if their peace mission could ever have been successful; but the new action by Congress had produced an enormous obstacle. After that, how could anything be quite the same again? By definition the Howes' brief was now impossible.

Also, the Declaration of Independence altered drastically the position of those Americans who were still loyal to the King. For if the Congressional edict had any relevance at all, it meant that the Tories were no longer merely men who did not happen to agree with the patriots; they were traitors. If they cooperated with the British, they would be aiding the enemies of their country. The period of the tar and feathers was over; their punishment would be death. As William Howe had now seen clearly, there were a large number of Loyalists—or traitors, as Washington and his army would now regard them—in the province of New York. And never had they been so ardent in their enthusiasm to support the King of England.

Before the Declaration of Independence, the rebels had stopped short of actually executing Loyalists. But the news of Britain's preparation for the big summer push, with the inevitable invasion of New York, had sparked an active campaign against them. In a series of punitive edicts, Congress had declared it a crime, punishable by jail and fines, to help the British in any way or even to dissuade people from uniting against Parliament.

The wave of arrests that resulted was so large that special committees had to be set up to administer what was inevitably very rough justice. "Tory baiting" by the New York mobs became far more prevalent as the rebel authorities, though deprecating it officially, carefully averted their eyes and even on occasions encouraged summary action. Angry crowds pillaged Tory homes and plunged into an orgy of rail riding.

And the Loyalists, only too aware of the armies on their way across the Atlantic, waited eagerly for the chance of revenge that now seemed imminent.

When General Howe put his troops ashore on Staten Island, there was no sign of an enemy; Washington had decided not to contest the landing but to hold his army for a conflict nearer Manhattan.

The beach was crowded with hundreds of welcoming Americans. By contrast with the months of blockade in Boston, there were many willing suppliers of food, horses and the army's other needs. "The fresh meat our men have got here," Lord Rawdon was soon to write home, "has made them as riotous as satyrs. A girl cannot step into the bushes to pluck a rose without running the most imminent risk of being ravished, and they are so little accustomed to these vigorous methods that they don't bear them with the proper resignation, and of consequence we have most entertaining courts martial every day. . . ."

One girl, reported Rawdon, complained to Lord Percy that she had been deflowered by some grenadiers. The earl asked her how she knew they were grenadiers, since it was dark at the time. "Oh, good God," she answered, referring presumably to their size, "they could be nothing else and, if your Lordship will examine, I am sure you will find it so."

Despite the dangers to their women, so many Loyalists streamed into the British camp eager to enlist that Howe established a special American unit. Almost as important, they provided him with a large source of expert guides with detailed knowledge of the rugged country through which his army would have to fight. And by contrast with the farmhouse snipers who had savaged the British so badly on the Concord road, this time there would be sympathizers in many of the homesteads as the army advanced.

Howe had toyed with the idea of an immediate attack on Long Island, but its timbered hills, broken by narrow passes easy to defend and already fortified by Washington, had deterred him. He set up his base on Staten Island, planning to wait for the reinforcements that were on their way and, in particular, for camp equipment and wheeled transport which his army badly needed. As always with Howe, there was plenty of time—and, of course, Mrs. Loring[3] and the faro table, where, according to one report, she lost 300 guineas in one evening's play.

In fact, he made his first remotely militant move only a few hours before his brother sailed through the Narrows. At noon two frigates, the *Phoenix* and the *Rose*, made a run up the Hudson under heavy fire from rebel batteries to the Tappan Bay (Zee) on the north of Manhattan. There they were able to control the river supply route to the rebel army and to arm local Loyalists.

Two days later Lord Howe made his first move to negotiate in his role as a peacemaker with Washington. He sent a lieutenant over to the town in a longboat under a flag of truce, but the rebel commander refused to receive the letter the officer carried because it was addressed to George Washington Esq. with no reference to his status as general. Two days later, delivery was rejected even of an answer to a letter of his own because it was not properly addressed.

Ambrose Serle, the admiral's secretary, was incensed. "We strove as far as decency and honour could permit . . . to avert all bloodshed . . . ," he scribbled angrily in his journal. "And yet it seems to be beneath a little paltry colonel of militia at the head of a banditti of rebels to treat with a representative of his lawful sovereign because it is impossible to give all the titles which the poor creature requires."

The Howes knew that Washington was not being petty-minded any more than they were. "Esq." was the normal way of addressing untitled senior officers in correspondence, but by making an issue of his rank, Washington was trying to force the British commanders to acknowledge the existence of the Congress which had granted it to him. Indeed when William Howe eventually did address him as general, Washington promptly asserted that this constituted recognition of the illegal rebel government and, as a logical consequence, of American independence.

Also, the issue was significant from a military viewpoint. Legally a rebel captured in the field could be hanged. The prisoner of an acknowledged enemy army could not. Although the British do not seem to have executed any captured men, their attitudes to the Americans were certainly colored by their revolutionary status. They were, after all, only "damned rebels."

In any event, Howe achieved nothing by his concession. When Washington received the British Lieutenant Colonel Patterson, he asserted that he was not empowered to negotiate peace terms, and so far as he understood, Lord Howe himself could do no more than grant pardons, which the Americans did not seek.

The elegant general offered the colonel a drink, which he refused politely, and introduced him to his staff officers. "Has Your Excellency no particular commands," asked Patterson before leaving, "with which you would please to honor me to Lord and General Howe?"

"Nothing," answered Washington airily, "but my particular compliments to both."

For four weeks the British waited. Meetings took place constantly on board the *Eagle* with a stream of visitors—refugee governors, Tories, military and naval officers—as slowly the plans for attack developed. Boatbuilding for the assault across the water was in progress, mostly of the round fronted flatboats for the troops, but the program included some big shallow-draft barges with a novel construction:[4] They had flat bows that could be let down to form a ramp so that guns could be hauled aboard.

Meanwhile, according to Serle, a report arrived on the *Eagle* that Carleton's army from the north would soon be at Albany on the upper reaches of the Hudson. Fortunately it made no difference to the Howes' plans, for the truth was that Carleton was still shipbuilding at St. Johns.

On August 1, Serle recorded, "between forty and fifty sail appeared in sight." It was the ill-fated Southern expedition that had been planned to encourage the Loyalists.

A Tory force scheduled to rendezvous with the newly arrived British troops had been attacked and defeated on its way to the meeting point. Despite this, the British attempted to establish a bridgehead at Charleston, South Carolina, to serve as a rallying area. As a first stage of a hurriedly replanned operation, they attacked Sullivan's Island, whose batteries dominated the narrow approaches to the port. It was an utter disaster. Ships ran aground; there was conflict between the naval and military commanders and confusion among the assaulting troops. The rebels fought off the attack. The British lost 170 men and a frigate; several other vessels were severely damaged.

Clinton had been sent down from Boston before the evacuation to rendezvous with the fleet and take military command. He had never been keen on the operation, and its failure, which he blamed bitterly on the navy, made a deep impression on him. The unhappy memory would still be with him when he returned to attack the port three years later with a degree of caution that was highly pedestrian but extremely successful.

Clinton had brought Howe 2,000 more troops. Twelve days later another big fleet sailed through the Narrows and moved into the anchorage to the welcome of the shouting sailors and the booming of the saluting guns. The Hessians—mustachioed, precision-drilled, rented fighters in gaudy uniforms—had arrived.

The army considerably outnumbered the American force and was far superior in equipment and fighting experience. Staten Island was a mass of tents, artillery parks and supply depots. There were now nearly 400 British ships anchored in the harbor.

New York was highly vulnerable to attack from the water. The East River, which flowed down the east side of Manhattan Island into the Hudson at its southern tip, was navigable to the biggest ships. Though the rebels had set up gun batteries to challenge entry into the river, if these could be silenced, the town could be bombarded from all sides.

Howe planned to leapfrog his army onto Manhattan by landing first on Long Island. Then, supported by ships and batteries on the north shore of Long Island, the British would attack across the East River and take New York. The main military obstacle would be the ridge of hills, the Heights of Guana, that rose abruptly from the plainland and reached east from the Narrows for some 10 miles. The hills were not high, but they were thickly wooded, and dominating the surrounding country as they did, they provided a strong defense barrier.

The arrival of the Hessians removed Howe's last excuse for delay. A week later he completed the final preparations for the attack, and in the leisurely timetable he favored, the buildup began. On the evening of August 19 the German troops, whose camp was in a different part of Staten Island from the British, loaded their equipment into little red pony carts and marched to the beach that faced Long Island across the Narrows. There they pitched their tents in two lines, ready for embarkation at short notice.

The next morning the commanders held their briefing conferences—the naval captains assembling on board the *Eagle* and the senior military officers attending General Howe's headquarters in a house on shore. There was little element of surprise. From New York and Long Island, even though they did not know the exact landing point, the rebels could see exactly what was happening. For the whole of the following day the biggest British army that had ever invaded enemy-held territory prepared for embarkation. Horse teams hauled the forty field guns—which were to cross the Narrows with the troops—into parks near the water where they could be loaded into boats constructed for the operation. Wagons for ammunition and baggage were lined up ready.

That evening 5,000 troops, mainly Hessians, were put aboard troopships. These would anchor near the landing beaches as a springboard for the support infantry, cutting down the distance the assault boats—which would take the first wave across the Narrows from Staten Island—would have to go to collect troops for the second wave. The remainder of the 15,000 men who were to take part in the first stage of the invasion were camped near the embarkation beaches, waiting only for the final order.

On the evening of August 21 General Howe, to be close to the all-important amphibious control, went aboard the *Eagle* and ordered his staff to join him there early the following morning.

Then the storm came up. Again and again, great peals of thunder shook the New York islands. Lightning forked across the sky, brilliantly exposing their target town to the two brother commanders who were waiting on the heaving, creaking flagship. Tugging at their cables, the transports and the frigates wallowed in the big sea built up by the howling northeast wind. On the Staten Island shore, the screaming gale lashed solid sheets of rain into the thousands of tents.

It was one of the worst storms in the history of New York—"more terrible," according to the contemporary Pastor Shewkirk, than the one that had "struck into Trinity Church" twenty years before.

On Long Island's wooded hills, the waiting rebel troops suffered even worse than Howe's army. Four of them, it was learned later, were killed by lightning.

The storm died almost as abruptly as it had blown up. Soon after midnight the wind had veered to the west and subsided to a mild breeze; the water in the Narrows was calming.

Aboard the *Eagle*, between one and two in the morning, Lord Howe's flag captain, Henry Duncan, according to his journal, awoke the admiral and told him he was ordering the transports under way. By the time the troopships had weighed anchor on Duncan's signal the *Phoenix* and the *Rose*, which four days before had run the gauntlet of the rebel batteries on a fast return dash down the Hudson, had moved quietly down the harbor to take up station off the landing beach in Gravesend Bay on Long Island. With them to cover the assault were three other ships. One of them, the *Rainbow*, dropped anchor off Denice's Point on the west of the main attack shore, where the ferry which plied across the Narrows always docked. By the ferry stage was a large stone building that Tory informers had warned was a fortified blockhouse.

By four o'clock the transports had anchored near the warships at Gravesend, and the assault flotilla was waiting at the Staten Island embarkation beach: seventy-five red and white flatboats for the infantry, and bigger craft, eleven barges and two galleys, to transport the horses and the cannon and the wagons.[5] All the craft were designed purely for transport—rafts, in effect, fitted with gunwales. They were broad and unwieldy boats whose shallow draft, necessary for beaching, left little bulk below water level to hold them steady against a crosswind.

* * *

In the dawn light apparent chaos marked the long sandy embarkation beach—thousands of scarlet-coated men marching in different directions as they moved to the takeoff areas intermingled with cannon and wagons being hauled through the soft sand by the horse teams to the water's edge.

The assault units—the first wave would carry 4,000 men—were formed up in ranks on the shore. As usual, Britain's crack troops—the light infantry with their familiar tricorn hats and the tall grenadiers in black bearskin caps—were to storm the rebel beach and establish the bridgehead for the landing of the cannon, the cavalry and the followup infantry.

By companies the assault troops marched down to the water's edge to board the flatboats, held steady by the sailors. Each craft was big enough to accommodate fifty men. Farther along the beach plank ramps had been fitted to the bigger craft. As the sky lightened, cannon were being manhandled up the ramps with the help, in the case of the bigger guns, of the tall tripod pulleys always carried by the artillery. In other boats, horses were being led and lashed up the planking into the craft for the crossing.

By eight o'clock the sun was up behind Long Island and the assault troops were embarked. By then the Howe brothers had crossed to Gravesend Bay by boat and had gone aboard the *Phoenix*, which was to be the headquarters ship for the operation. On Lord Howe's orders a signal cannon on the *Phoenix* barked; a blue-and-white-striped flag was hauled up to the mizzen top mast.

The coxswains in the crowded boats off Staten Island rasped their commands. Hundreds of oarsmen dropped their blades into the water and heaved. The boats formed in ten lines, bows to stern, and headed across the Narrows. The soldiers—their muskets, with bayonets fixed, held butt down on the deck between their knees—sat cramped together in the heart of the boats as the sailors, sitting near the gunwales, hauled on their oars.

Slowly, the flotilla passed the transports and on through the lines of warships, lying at anchor with springs on their cables, gunports open, gun crews waiting with lighted matches.[6]

The country behind the long white sandy landing beaches was flat plainland with little cover for defending troops—pastureland mainly, with a few farmhouses farther inland. All the indications suggested that Washington was not planning to contest the landing; from the *Phoenix* the commanders could see a few scattered rebel units, but they were moving inland. Smoke spiraled from several points where they had fired cattle fodder to keep it from falling into British hands. Threatened by the *Rainbow*'s guns, the rebels in the blockhouse at Denice's Point had evacuated the building.

As the flotilla neared Long Island, Commodore William Hotham in a leading boat displayed a red flag; the craft deployed in line abreast, moving steadily toward the shore. There was no sign of opposition and no apparent need for storming tactics. "In ten minutes, or thereabouts," recorded Captain Duncan, "four thousand men were on the beach, formed and moved forward."

The flatboats pushed off from the beach and headed for the transports anchored offshore to collect the Hessian grenadiers and the sharpshooting jaegers. Unlike the British, the German troops did not travel the short distance across the water sitting down; they remained standing rigidly to attention in the boats with their arms sloped.[7] Their martinet officers were never happy unless their men were formed in tight ranks.

Certainly, the visual effect was striking—the grenadiers, in their blue uniforms with turned-back tails and the tall metal-faced high caps resembling bishop's miters, and the tricorned jaegers in green uniforms with scarlet cuffs. Like the rebel backwoodsmen, the jaegers, who were recruited from the German forests, were armed with rifles, as opposed to the smoothbore muskets, and they handled them with expert accuracy.

By midday the heavy bateaux and galleys had brought over the cannon and the wagons. The horses of the dragoons had been landed at the ferry quay at Denice's Point, and 15,000 soldiers disembarked. General Howe had landed and set up temporary headquarters in a house in New Utrecht, a mile from the coast. The troops were pitching their tents, forming a vast encampment stretching some four miles along the coast from the Narrows to the town of Flatlands.

That afternoon a brigade of the light infantry and Hessians probed forward. In command was thirty-nine-year-old Charles, Earl Cornwallis who had crossed the Atlantic with the force that attacked Charleston. Like Clinton, he had fought in the school of officers who considered themselves an elite because they had served in Germany, as opposed to America, in the Seven Years' War. He was a heavy, awkward man with a cast in one eye, and although he was now comparatively junior in the hierarchy of senior officers, he was to play a critical central role in the British operations in America.

Cornwallis' brigade advanced toward the hills under orders to capture the little village of Flatbush, which lay immediately below one of the three passes through the Heights of Guana. As they marched along the road to Gravesend, the first village in the route, they could see the rebels ahead of them across the plain slaughtering the cattle they had not yet been able to drive off and firing the hayricks.

At Gravesend Cornwallis checked his main force and sent on the advance guard of Hessians with six cannon to take Flatbush. The rebels were in possession of the village. Colonel Carl von Donop, the German commander, called up his guns, and the Americans fell back toward the Flatbush Pass in the hills, where they had built a strong redoubt. The Hessians entrenched just outside the village.

Howe had given Cornwallis specific orders not to press on through the pass if it was defended; having tested the strength of the rebels at that access through the hills, he was required merely to hold Flatbush Village. For the next few days, while the main British force remained immobile in its vast camp along the coast, the rebels raided the Hessian lines several times; but the assaults were minor, and the Germans held their position until they were finally ordered to drop back.

Meanwhile, in his usual unhurried way, Howe was considering his plans for the attack through the hills. And Clinton, in *his* usual anxious way, was worrying about Howe's relaxed approach to generalship. Just as he had done on the night before Bunker Hill, he carried out a little private reconnaissance.

Clinton was second-in-command of the British army, yet incredibly he had no informal access to his general. He appears to have seen Howe only when he was summoned, and even then there seems to have been little discussion. Clinton conveyed most of his thoughts on strategy in a series of rather petulant memorandums, which Howe obviously found so irritating that he rarely commented on them. Most of Clinton's contact was with the staff officers at HQ.

It is not hard to sympathize with Howe. His second-in-command had many qualities as a general—he was industrious, brave and intelligent—but he seems to have been utterly humorless and to have nursed a constantly burning sense of grievance. Like Lord

George Germain, he was a solitary man. A picture emerges of him carrying out his lone reconnaissances, only just veiling his poor view of his chief in his memorandums, working late into the night in his tent on independent schemes that induced weary sighs of bored exasperation from the planning staffs at HQ. There is a Clinton in every military community—clever but so pernickety and dogmatic and lacking in charm that the impact of the talent is greatly blunted. This time, however, Clinton's suggestions were noted, albeit reluctantly, and finally acted on.

Howe had a whole range of alternatives open to him. The rebel army had fortified Brookland, on the northern tip of Long Island just across the East River from New York, with a line of forts, linked by thick walls. But before any attack could be launched on the big rebel redoubt, Howe had to get his army through the hills —either, so it seemed at first, by the Gowanus coast road which reached around the western edge of the hills alongside the Narrows or by the two passes which broke through the hills from Flatbush. Like the Gowanus road, both led to Brookland, but one detoured west through the hill village of Bedford.

Whether Howe took one route or attacked on all three at once, the conflict was clearly going to be bloody. For the rebels would be entrenched high above the roads under the cover of trees and boulders—just the kind of country suited to the Indian fighting tactics at which they excelled, as they had demonstrated so vividly on the Concord road.

Clinton worried away at the problem even though nobody had invited him to do so. He reconnoitered the three passes—presumably from a distance by horse, for he decided to go far farther west than Howe appears to have considered and discovered "a gorge about six miles from us" from which the rebel position "may be turned."

The main highway that led from the ferry at Brookland to the town of Jamaica and from there on along the middle of Long Island passed the Heights of Guana through Bedford. For some miles it lay just to the north of the hills, then broke through a small pass and reached for the rest of the way under the south side of the heights. This pass was the "gorge" that Clinton had found. Eagerly pointing out that the terrain suited the use of cavalry in the advance units, he urged a secret push in force through the pass. If the movement were successful, it would mean that the British could attack the rebels from the rear while the other units assaulted from the front. At the same time—"as the tide will then suit"—a squadron of warships could blaze their way up the East River and bombard the rebel lines at Brookland.

To concentrate the enemy's attention away from the Jamaica gorge, Clinton urged, the British should mount initial attacks at the other passes that "were not too obstinately persisted in" until the big flanking column was through the hills and behind the rebel positions.

It was, without question, a beautiful plan. Howe's chief staff officer, Sir William Erskine, agreed to "carry it to headquarters, where, however," as Clinton recorded sardonically, "it did not seem to be much relished."

Howe's reaction can be seen clearly in Clinton's writings. This irritating, dry and overzealous officer, who was always bothering him with pompous self-opinionated suggestions, had come up with an idea that was truly sound. For two or three days Clinton heard nothing. Then Howe sent for him. The commander in chief was not enthusiastic. "In all the opinions he ever gave to me, [Howe] did not expect any good from the move." But stony-faced, he agreed to the plan. Clinton would be in charge of the avant-garde, the traditional role for the second-in-command; he was to seize the pass and wait for Howe, who would follow with the main part of the army.

Meanwhile, 5,000 British under Major General James Grant would be attacking along the Gowanus road near the Narrows. The Hessians, now reinforced by another 5,000 men under General Philip von Heister, would make an assault from Flatbush.

Neither of these movements would be pressed through until the flanking column fired a signal cannon to indicate that they were behind the rebels at Bedford and ready to launch their attack.

The afternoon of August 26 was hot. The sun, still high over the Atlantic, glared on the dry plain. Heat simmered from the dusty ground, distorting the vision, oppressing Howe's soldiers in their heavy all-season uniforms.

Outside Flatbush, the Hessians were fighting off the biggest attack the rebels had yet directed at their lines. Because the conflict had no significance in the new operation, Cornwallis ordered them to drop back on the village. Later that day he withdrew the British units that were with them.

General Sullivan, in command of the rebel units at the Flatbush and Bedford passes,[8] must have watched the long scarlet column snaking slowly across the plain toward the village of Flatlands near the coast and pondered on the British purpose. Howe intended that he should be kept in doubt. Camp was usually struck immediately before an operation. But on the commander's orders, the British tents were still there, pegged out in their long lines, stretching along the coast.

Soon after seven o'clock that evening the flanking force paraded on the village green at Flatlands. For all of Howe's lack of enthusiasm, it was big. Ten thousand British troops would attempt to march undetected along the coast road toward Jamaica before breaking across country to drive through the pass.

Even Clinton's avant-garde, paraded that evening by the village, was substantial: nearly 1,000 mounted dragoons, more than 2,000 foot soldiers, most of them grenadiers and light infantry, and fourteen cannon.

The dragoons, with feathered black helmets, scarlet coats and thigh boots, were light mobile cavalry, trained for the new type of flexible warfare that was developing. They were armed with long swords, pistols and fusils which they were taught to fire from the horse, sometimes at the gallop, taking care, as one military manual urged, to avoid shooting directly ahead, if possible, because this would put the barrel unpleasantly close to the horse's ears.

But unlike the heavy cavalry, the dragoons would often fight on foot if the situation demanded it, using their horses merely as a way of moving fast from one position to another. They were invaluable in the type of war Howe was now fighting.

At eight o'clock, so Clinton recalled, he gave the order for the avant-garde to march. A small advance unit, under Lieutenant William Evelyn, went on ahead. Clinton followed at the head of the cavalry. Then came 1,000 light infantry. Behind them was Lord Cornwallis, riding at the head of his brigade made up of grenadiers and a couple of ordinary line regiments. Last of all were the cannon, with the blue-coated artillerymen riding on the carriages and civilian drivers walking beside the horses. Howe and Lord Percy were to follow later that night with the main part of the force.

It was the noise of the cannon wheels "over the stones" that caused Clinton his main anxiety. Already, before the column had

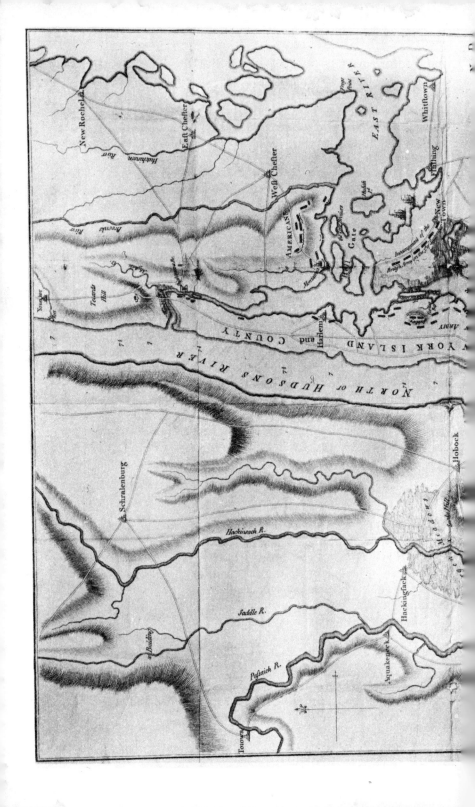

A PLAN of NEW YORK ISLAND, with part of LONG ISLAND, STATEN ISLAND & EAST NEW JERSEY, with a particular Description of the ENGAGEMENT on the Woody Heights of Long Island, between FLATBUSH and BROOKLYN, on the 27th of August 1776. between General HOWE and the AMERICANS under Major General PUTNAM, with the subsequent Disposition of both ARMIES.

Engraved & Publish'd according to Act of Parliament Oct. 19th 1776, by Wm. Faden, Geographer to the King, Charing Cross, LONDON.

Presented by Capt H.M. M'Cance
10·x·1927

The British Museum. A Royal United Services Institution map

The Battle of Long Island.

started off, he had sent out a regiment of Highlanders to scour the country within earshot of the road and gather up anyone they found who could possibly hear his column and warn the rebels.

The road they were now marching along on this fine, warm, darkening evening cut through the hills—the Heights of Guana— toward the village of Flushing, way up the East River, crossing the main Brookland-Jamaica highway at the Jamaica Pass.

The long column did not stay long on the road. It wheeled onto a less conspicuous wagon track that curled northward, then, just before midnight, struck across country aiming to join the Brook-land-Jamaica highway, a hundred yards below the gorge, by an inn called Howard's Halfway House.

When the leading troops were a quarter of a mile from Howard's, a Tory guide warned Clinton they were getting close. The general ordered the column to halt while Lieutenant Evelyn pushed on carefully with the advance patrol.

Cautiously, the patrol approached the inn, which was in dark-ness, and, passing it, moved onto the highway. There was little sign of the enemy's presence until suddenly the British spotted five riders farther up the road to the east. The story of how Evelyn's men captured the horsemen is not recorded in detail.[9] It was carried out "without noise," suggesting that the British surround-ed them and had them covered before Evelyn rode out of the shadows and challenged them.

They were sent back under guard to Clinton, who interrogated them personally. Under questioning—to which they seemed initial-ly to be astonishingly amenable—they revealed that the rebels were not occupying the pass. But as Clinton persisted with his questions about the numbers and disposition of the rebel forces, one of them complained angrily that the general was taking advantage of their situation and insulting them. "You're an impudent rebel," Clinton flashed back, warning that he would have them all hanged if they were not very careful.

Anyway, Clinton had got all he needed. Incredibly, there seemed to be nothing to stop 10,000 British soldiers with a large number of cannon from marching straight through the gorge and on down the road to the rear of the rebels.

In fact, the American generals had not overlooked the Jamaica Pass, but because it was so far from the lines at Brookland, they had decided to maintain mounted scouts to alert them quickly if the British approached.

But the British had captured the scouts. Clinton acted quickly—and with very great caution. On his orders, a battalion of light infantry moved forward past Howard's Halfway House and occupied the east end of the pass. But he was not going to risk marching straight through the gorge into a possible ambush baited by five scouts who had purposely allowed themselves to be captured.

He ordered more troops to advance around the pass through the woods on the rocky hillside so that they could approach the gorge from the other side and from various vulnerable points above. Because the guides—three American Tories who lived in Flatbush—were not too sure of the way through the hills, the innkeeper was awakened and forced at pistol point to lead them along the steep woodland track known as Rockaway Path.

According to one report,[10] Clinton also ordered some cannon to advance to the high ground by the same route. Trees had to be felled to make a wide enough passage for the guns. On the general's orders, the timber was dropped with saws, not axes, to avoid the familiar noise of chopping. Then the guns and the six-horse teams were driven hard up the hill.

Meanwhile, Clinton waited with the rest of the avant-garde for daylight when he could march through the pass along the road, confident in the knowledge that the heights that overlooked it were occupied by his own troops. By that time he had sent a message back to Howe, and the rest of the big flanking column was following close behind him. By that time, too, the feint assaults at the other two points on the hills had already started.

Before midnight the column of 5,000 men, under Major General James Grant, was marching north along the coast road near the invasion beach where they had landed four days before. Among them was a regiment of American Loyalists recruited from the welcoming Tories on Staten Island.

It was Grant who during the angry parliamentary debates before Concord had assured the House of Commons that the rebels would "never dare to face an English Army." His column was marching toward the enemy in the classical military manner—a small advance party well ahead, with scouts thrown forward and out to the side.

As they approached the Red Lion Tavern, where the Narrows road joined the Gowanus road to Brookland, the scouts came on the first rebel outposts and reported back. Grant sent forward a detachment to take the picket sentries. Unlike Clinton's operation to the east, there was no need for secrecy. The firing would alert the rebel generals, but that was the purpose of Grant's attack.

The column advanced past the Red Lion along the Gowanus road, which skirted close to the coast. It was two o'clock and still dark. There was plenty of time.

Grant could not keep his men on the road, for a little farther it narrowed under Blockje's Burgh—a sheer rocky hill from which the rebels, by concentrating their fire, could annihilate advancing troops. The column turned off the road, moving through the woods onto a hill. There the advance units came under fire from a small rebel position in an orchard and checked.

American reinforcements were moving up. There were several skirmishes in the dawnlight. Several times the British fell back.

By the time Lord Stirling, rebel commander of this sector, had brought forward his troops in force, "an angry red sun," as a rebel described it later, was already rising. The Americans formed their lines in the open on a hillside facing the main British position. Some of them were in hunting shirts, their officers distinguishable only by the ribbons they wore; others were in uniforms with the Delawares especially distinctive in red and blue. Two cannon they had brought forward opened up, and smoke drifted in the morning air into the hills.

The British deployed in a long uneven line, broken only by the gun batteries, now crashing out salvo after salvo. The firing, both the small arms and the cannon, was intense. But it was stylized conflict—the first time in the Revolution that the rebels had faced the British in the kind of formal battle formation that was customary in Europe.

In fact, the mood and character of this morning confrontation reached back centuries with the two opposing forces taunting the other to attack. For a couple of hours, as the sun rose higher, they faced each other. Several times Grant sent forward detachments across the marshy valley between them to attack one sector or another of Stirling's line, but they were always fought back.

The British aim was to keep the Americans tensed, all the time awaiting assault—never quite sure that each forward move by smaller units was not the prelude to an advance along the whole front.

Stirling had no alternative but to stay where he was, stanced for defense; he could not attack, for the British outnumbered his troops by more than three to one. And Grant was waiting for the sound of the signal guns at Bedford.

At Flatbush, the Hessians, too, were listening for the noise of Clinton's cannon. Soon after dawn the German guns had opened a heavy bombardment on the rebel redoubt constructed across the road into the hills. At seven o'clock General von Heister ordered the same kind of showy demonstration that Grant was engaged in to the west. To the pounding of his drums, his troops formed on the plain in tight, rigid ranks as though they were on a parade ground. It had much of the old-fashioned character of Grant's confrontation—a taunting, threatening display of military might.

It was going to be a hot day, and as a special concession, this iron disciplinarian general permitted his soldiers to wear their sabers from shoulder straps instead of the tight belts at their waist, thus permitting them to open their heavy jackets.

They were a strange group of fighters, with their rigid drill formations and their extravagant uniforms. In retrospect, they seem almost Ruritanian in character. Hardly any of the officers had horses; Colonel von Donop rode "an old and solid stallion" that he had brought from Germany. But even he had to get off and relinquish it to his aide every time he wanted to send a message.

Von Donop advanced with the jaeger sharpshooters and Hessian grenadiers to the edge of the woods low on the steep hillside and opened fire on the rebel outposts through the trees. But they did not press forward very far—not yet.

The flanking column—some two miles of marching men, cavalry, cannon and wagons—curled up the steep road through the Jamaica Pass onto the main highway to Brookland and the rebel lines. As they neared the village of Bedford, Clinton was still riding with his cavalry near the head of the avant-garde.

There was a small redoubt in the village, which Clinton sent up some light infantry to capture. Then he ordered the attack signal that Grant, by the Gowanus road, and Von Heister, before Flatbush, were waiting for: two cannon fired one after the other.

Abruptly, the mood of the marching men drastically changed. Until then they had moved cautiously and quietly without urgency. Now the moment they had been building up to had arrived: the pincer movement to surround and squeeze the rebels in the hill positions and to cut them off from their fortified lines at Brookland.

Immediately, Cornwallis advanced fast with the grenadiers down the road to Brookland, intending to join up with Grant as he moved along the Gowanus road on the coast.

The dragoons and light infantry moved swiftly down the Bedford-Flatbush road, fanning out into the woods on either side.

From the other direction, the Hessians, with colors flying and bands playing, started to advance. The massed ranks on the plain, split in rigid parade formation into three columns, marched to the foot of the hill and mounted up through the woods, ignoring so far as they could the trees that interfered with their tight lines. Ahead of them went Von Donop's jaegers, moving from tree to tree, firing constantly with their forest rifles.

The rebels holding the Flatbush Pass were trapped between the advancing Hessians on their front and the British in their rear. Frantically they tried to escape west, but the light infantry were already closing on them. Desperately, a group of Americans swung around three cannon they were dragging away and blasted grape at the scarlet figures approaching through the trees.

It could only be a momentary stand as the British swarmed around them. Behind them the Hessian columns had topped the hill, checked for a moment to redress their ranks under the insistent commands of their officers, who insisted on tight formation even in a woods, and then advanced again, a solid body of drilled killers, harshly disciplined to fight in unison.

The rebels fled, pursued by the British, the jaegers with their deadly firing and the Hessian columns, all bayoneting every rebel they cornered. "The greater part of their riflemen," reported the Hessian Colonel von Heeringen, "were pierced to the trees with bayonets."

One German column swung west to attack the flank of the rebels who were facing Grant near the Gowanus road. The remainder, with their drums still pounding the march step, pushed on through the woods behind the Americans who were fleeing toward their lines at Brookland.

Between the wooded hills and the rebel fortifications was a broad stretch of open country. It was here to one side that the dragoons, called back from the woods, were waiting in line, swords drawn, the breadth of a horse between them. In front of the ranks of cavalrymen sat the colonel. Behind him in the center of the first rank was the standard-bearer, covered by a corporal in the rank behind. Beside the commander sat his trumpeter—his means of communication.

Trumpets were employed by mounted troops to signal commands, as drums beat out orders to the infantry, and their use was rigidly regulated. There were trumpeters attached to other officers, but only the colonel's attendant was permitted to give most calls. Just two of them—the charge and the retreat—could be taken up by the others.

The rebels broke from the trees, harried by the shooting of the jaegers, the fast-advancing Hessian columns and the British light infantry. Men streamed across the plain without formation, just running for their lives toward the fort and its protective walls. The colonel ordered the charge. The trumpet sounded. The cavalrymen moved the tips of their swords from their shoulders, holding their right wrists in the scabbard hard down on the top of their thighs, and spurred their horses.

The dragoons swept down on the fleeing rebels as the pursuing Hessians emerged from the woods behind them. Ahead of the Americans, blocking the escape route to the rebel lines, were Cornwallis and the grenadiers.

It was a massacre—within full and tempting view of their own lines, where the rebel flag of red damask[11] inscribed with the word "Liberty," still fluttered above the fort. Desperately, the fleeing rebels grouped in bunches of fifty or sixty and tried to break their way through the closing enemy lines. But the dragoons charged again and again. The Hessians, still working in ranks like automatons, advanced on them, jabbing and twisting their long bayonets. According to American complaints later, attempts to surrender were often ignored in the carnage, but the Hessians claimed that some of the rebels clubbed their arms to indicate pleas for quarter and then fired as the troops approached to take them prisoner. After that the angry soldiers became more brutal. Despite the slaughter, many prisoners were taken. Among them was General Sullivan, who was found hiding in a cornfield.

Meanwhile, the push continued. Two spearheads were racing for the rebel lines. The jaegers, "stimulated by their eager desire for combat," as one Hessian report put it, "advanced with such vehemence that their captain was not able to keep them back;

they pushed on even into the fortified works of the American camp." These were high walls, armored with outward pointing lances, built behind a long ditch and linked to forts.

At the same time that the jaegers were advancing so fast, a column of British grenadiers was· also attacking under General Sir John Vaughan. Howe had given strict instructions they were not to storm the enemy fortifications without further orders, but Clinton, who was in command of these forward units, ignored them. "I had at that moment but little inclination to check the ardor of our troops when I saw the enemy flying in such a panic before them."

Howe was watching the battle from a different hill and saw what was happening. A staff officer rode at full gallop after the advancing grenadiers with orders to halt. General Vaughan sent back an almost desperate plea to be allowed to advance, insisting that the rebels were entirely within their power, but Howe was adamant. "It required repeated orders," he wrote to Germain later, "to prevail upon them to desist from the attempt."

By eleven o'clock, two hours after the attack had started, Howe's troops lay before the rebel lines. Almost the whole ridge of hills behind them was in their hands; only the western tip, held by Stirling, was still held by the Americans, and their retreat was blocked.

Grant had delayed his attack when he heard the signal guns because he had suddenly found he needed more ammunition. His assault soon after ten o'clock, with the Hessians pressing Stirling from the east and Cornwallis approaching from the north, broke the rebel lines. Many of them tried to escape to the rebel redoubt across the treacherous Gowanus marshes, which were split by a wide creek. In an attempt to cover this desperate retreat, Stirling launched a counterattack; with only 250 men, he struck at Cornwallis' brigade of more than 1,000.

The country was open. From the hills, the British and the Hessians could look right across the marshes to the Hudson, and as Stirling advanced, they could see guns being set up on the slopes by tired teams of American prisoners under the control of Hessian guards. Cornwallis rushed other guns to a farmhouse near the road along which rebel suicide troops were attacking.

Stirling's move was courageous, but all it could do was to buy a little time before the British could concentrate their fire on the men trying to get across the marshes. Many of them died in the showers of grapeshot; others drowned in the creek. Some, however, got through to the rebel lines. Stirling himself was captured and gave up his sword to General von Heister.

On Howe's strict orders, the British still made no move to attack the rebel position. At one stage, according to Clinton, there were only 800 men to hold fortifications that were so long that they would have required 6,000 men for adequate defense. They were completely vulnerable. But by that night, when the escapers had made their way behind the lines and reinforcements had been brought across the river from New York, there were more than 9,000 behind the walls.

Even this was not many, compared with the numbers of royal troops, but Howe, as he later told a parliamentary committee, was not prepared to "risk the loss that might have been sustained in the assault." He believed he could take the position at "a very cheap rate" in casualties by approaching the redoubt carefully by trenches, dug in darkness—the classic way of storming towns under siege—and he probably could have done so if his brother's men-of-war had been in the East River.

The wind, however, was blowing from the wrong direction, and there were no British guns to cut off communications between the redoubt and Manhattan.

While his troops lay before the rebel lines, Howe set up new headquarters in a farmhouse at Newtown, farther up the north coast of Long Island, and reported his victory to London. He claimed that there had been more than 3,000 rebel casualties—a figure that as usual was contested by the Americans, who put it at just more than 1,000. Either way, there was no doubt it was a triumph.

For two days the two armies were drenched by continuous torrential rain. During the night of August 29 the Hessian Colonel von Heeringen pushed some troops onto a hill that overlooked the rebel lines from the south. From his new position, soon after dawn, he realized that the Americans were evacuating and sent a lieutenant at top speed to warn the commander in chief. It was not the only report. The men of a British patrol had sensed that all was not quite normal. Moving closer, they had discovered that the outposts were deserted.

Howe ordered an immediate advance. But as the soldiers

swarmed over the rebel fortifications and hurried toward the
water's edge, the last boatload of rebels was disappearing into the
mists of Manhattan.

For the time being Washington had preserved the rebel army, but
as Howe knew, the Battle of Long Island had made a deep
impression on his troops—undisciplined, ill equipped, many without uniforms. By contrast with the successful rebel operations
during the early months of the revolt, when the British were on
the defensive, this was the first major confrontation with its new
army that had been sent to America to smash the rebellion. The
lesson had been severe. Desertions from Washington's army soared.

Meanwhile, having won a battle, the Howes reverted to their
peacemaking role. On their urging, the captured General Sullivan
had agreed to travel to Philadelphia in an attempt to persuade
Congress to send a committee to discuss peace terms, and he had
succeeded.

On September 11 the admiral's barge approached Amboy, New
Jersey, flying a flag of truce. It brought a committee of three to
the peace table on Staten Island: Benjamin Franklin, John Adams
and another Congressional delegate named Edward Rutledge.
Admiral Howe greeted them, apologized for the absence of his
brother, who was on duty on Long Island, and led them between
the ranks of a grenadier guard of honor to breakfast.

The conference had no chance of success. Howe's terms of
reference were limited, and the men from Congress were bitter and
waspish. Only two months before, Franklin had written to the
admiral in rancor over the British burning of American towns,
exciting "savages to massacre our farmers and our slaves to murder
their masters" which had "extinguished every remaining spark of
affection for that parent country we once held so dear."

Certainly the obstacles were great. Howe explained that he could
not treat with them as a committee of Congress—which the King
did not recognize—but only as "private gentlemen of influence" if
they were prepared to negotiate "in that character."

"Your Lordship," Adams retorted quickly, "may consider me in
what light you please . . . except as a British subject."

Howe was not an aristocrat for nothing. "Mr. Adams," he said
coolly to Franklin and Rutledge, "is a decided character."

Despite the cool response, Howe persisted with the meeting,
mentioning his elder brother, who had died beside General Putnam

at Ticonderoga in the French and Indian War, and saying how much the family appreciated the honor of the monument erected for him by the province of Massachusetts. "Such is my gratitude and affection for this country," he said, "that I feel for America as if for a brother. If it should fall, I'd lament it like the loss of a brother."

Franklin, who had discussed the issues with him so often before, was not moved by his emotion. "My Lord," he said with feigned simplicity, "we will do our utmost endeavours to spare your Lordship that mortification."

Howe knew what was in the old man's mind. "I suppose you'll endeavour to give us employment in Europe," he grunted. The three men did not respond to this oblique reference to France but waited for Howe to continue.

The verbal cut and thrust were amusing, but they achieved nothing. Howe was there with an offer to remove grievances from colonials; the men from Congress had come to negotiate as representatives of independent states. There was no common ground. Howe, for all his gratitude and affection and "feeling for America as a brother," went back to war.

At two o'clock in the morning of September 15, 15,000 troops in camps stretching along the north coast of Long Island struck their tents and began marching to assembly points for embarkation. As the sky lightened, five warships that had run through the fire from the rebel batteries at the mouth of the East River sailed slowly across the water toward Manhattan and anchored, broadside to the shore, off Kip's Bay, the scheduled landing place.

At the council of war Howe had held in his farmhouse a few hours before, he had told his officers he proposed to mount a single hard thrust across the river in strength. He was planning a massive artillery barrage to cover the landing.

As usual, Clinton, who would command the assault units, disagreed with him, urging a diversion. But Howe overruled him sharply. Ruefully, after the council, Clinton assuaged his injured feelings in his notes: "My advice," he scrawled, "has ever been to avoid even the possibility of a check. We live by victory. Are we sure of it this day? J'en doute." His continual lapses into French must have been yet another irritation for his commander.

Soon after dawn Clinton took a boat out to the *Roebuck*, one of the five frigates now anchored on station of Kip's Bay, and through his glass studied the landing point 300 yards away. What he saw did not dispel his pessimism. Unlike the case in the invasion of Long Island, there was no long sandy beach; his troops would have to clamber over large rocks, almost certainly under very heavy fire. Just behind them were rebel breastworks, trenches with earth walls thrown up in front of them, "well lined with men whose countenance appeared respectable and firm."

Behind Kip's Bay lay farmland—cornfields, meadows, orchards, woods. Slightly to the right the terrain moved steeply up to the Inclenberg Height on Murray's farm. This was the first objective of the advance troops. They were to rush the hill and hold it until the followup assault waves were brought in.

To his left, Clinton could see the town of New York some three miles down the Post Road; other landing points had been fortified by the rebels, such as Stuyvesant's Cove between Kip's Bay and the town. As soon as the rebels saw where the assault boats were steering, Clinton surmised, the men stationed at Stuyvesant's Cove would hurry to Kip's Bay.

Gloomily, he returned toward the Long Island shore and met the first wave of the troop-laden assault boats coming out of Newtown Creek. The tide was flooding strongly, and Clinton feared that it would carry them upriver of Kip's Bay, so he urged the commodore in charge of the flotilla to wait at the troopships, anchored on the Long Island side of the river, until the slack.

By eleven o'clock the tide had eased. As Clinton, still studying his target area through his glass, waited to give the order to advance he saw that the rebels had misinterpreted his purpose in holding the assault flotilla at the troopships. Clearly they thought the British were going to use the ebb, not the slack as Clinton planned, to carry them downstream for an assault at Stuyvesant's Cove.[13] Many of the men, stationed behind the breastwork of Kip's Bay, started moving south past the windmill to reinforce the troops at the lower landing point.

The general ordered the advance, and the first wave of assault craft began to move in line abreast across the river. It was a beautiful day, the water glass-calm; the sun beat down from behind Long Island. But to the men in the boats, the sight of the rebels waiting for them on the shore was unnerving. "As we approached," reported Lord Rawdon, who was in the same craft as Clinton, "we saw the breastworks filled with men, and two or three large columns marching down to support them." The rebels who had hurried down to Stuyvesant's Cove had realized their mistake and had started moving back.

The Hessians were terrified at their exposed position in the boats; jammed tightly together, easy targets for the rebel sharpshooters as soon as they moved in range, they mournfully sang hymns.

Then the quiet of the morning was shattered. More than seventy guns began crashing shot into the rocky beach at Kip's Bay; the explosions of the repeated salvos reverberated across the water, deadening the ears of the soldiers in the boats. "The most tremendous peal I ever heard," wrote Rawdon. "The breastwork was blown to pieces in a few minutes . . . and those who were to have defended it were happy to escape. . . . The columns [approaching] broke instantly and betook themselves to the nearest woods for shelter."

As the assault flotilla went through the line of frigates near Manhattan, the boats were hidden by the smoke from the guns. When they emerged from it, there were no longer any defenders.

The craft beached, and the troops clambered over the rocks without a single shot being fired at them. They formed on the shore, crossed the Post Road and charged a group of rebels on the Inclenberg Height. But the American morale had been cracked by the bombardment. They relinquished a brass howitzer and some ammunition wagons and retreated fast. From Inclenberg, Clinton could see the main rebel force drawn up about two miles to their north toward Harlem. Ahead of them, in the middle of Manhattan, were some woods, and in the gaps of the trees, American troops, clearly afraid of being cut off by a British push across the island, were making a dash north on their way from the town.

Clinton realized that they should be checked. But his orders were to hold the hill until the supporting troops had landed, and since he only had the advance troops on Manhattan, this was clearly wise. But the slick timing of the landing on Long Island three weeks before was lacking in this second operation. Hours went by before the next wave of assault craft brought in more troops, and it was 5 p.m. before the whole assault force was landed.

Unperturbed, Howe sent one brigade south to occupy the town of New York. Meanwhile, he led his main force north up the Post Road to McGowan's farmhouse, about two miles below the high rocky heights of Harlem, where Washington had withdrawn his

army. As the British column approached McGowan's, a detachment was ordered to advance along a branch road across the island
to Bloomingdale on the Hudson.

That night, as dusk fell, the British were pitching their tents in a
line right across Manhattan between the two rivers. High above
them, the rebels were digging in along a narrower line between the
Harlem River and the Hudson. From the front they were impregnable; only their outposts at the foot of the heights were on the
same level as Howe's army.

It had been a heady day for the British. The rebels had fled
before them without making any kind of stand. In one leisurely
grab, Howe had taken possession of most of Manhattan. Thus, the
British sentries on duty that night in the wooded hill at Bloomingdale were surprised soon after dawn to see a large rebel patrol of
more than 100 men coming through the trees. Opening fire, they
sent an urgent message to General Alexander Leslie in a nearby
house.

Leslie moved fast, called out the two battalions stationed on that
end of the line and advanced on the rebel unit with 400 men. The
Americans had dropped back to the cover of a stone wall and
started shooting as soon as the British approached within range.
Then they fell back again, stood at new cover and once more
retreated with the British in pursuit. As the rebels slipped for
safety behind their outposts at the foot of Harlem Heights, the
British halted in the open on the side of a hill. Mockingly, a
drummer put a trumpet to his lips and—allegedly—blew the fox
huntsman's call of "Gone to Earth."[14]

It was a musical taunt that was to backlash. For Leslie's troops
were dangerously exposed, a relatively small force far ahead of
their lines and close to the thousands in the rebel camp. Even
when the general saw rebel troops advancing from the heights, he
did not order his men to fall back, probably because the approaching column was not very big. But this fact in itself should have
warned him.

The British moved down the hill to the cover of some bushes,
and the advancing Americans opened fire at long range at the earliest moment they could. This, too, should have served as a warning, for their fighting technique was almost always pitched to
close-range shooting.

Sudden heavy firing from a covert at the side alerted them to their danger: They had been outflanked. The rebels in front had been playing with them, keeping their attention fixed. Washington planned to surround them.

They retreated fast up the rocky hill, re-formed at a fence, shooting all the time, then fell back again to the top of the ridge. Urgently Leslie called for major reinforcements even as more Americans streamed down from the heights and some rebels' cannon opened up.

Again the British were forced to fall back—this time into a buckwheat field—and even more troops were needed. Howe was no longer taking any chances. He sent up Lord Rawdon with a large force of British and Hessians, all running at the double with two cannon. By noon 5,000 men were engaged with the Americans.

At last, as Rawdon described it, "the rebels, finding they lost great numbers of men to no purpose, gave over the business. . . ."

It was to be the last conflict for several weeks. Again Howe stayed inactive, considering his next course of action. And Washington remained cannily on his heights.

Meanwhile, Governor Tryon had returned in triumph to Government House in New York. The Tories had welcomed the British with wild scenes of joy. The rebel flag had been hauled down and ceremoniously stamped on as the Union Jack was once again run up the town's flagpole; Captain Duncan, who had taken a boat in from the *Eagle*, was chaired through the streets. And the Loyalists had enjoyed their revenge. The front doors of rebel houses, now officially declared forfeited, were marked with an *R* and pillaged. "And thus," recorded the Tory Pastor Shewkirk, who believed that the British had been sent by God, "was the City now delivered from those usurpers who had oppressed it for so long."

If God sent the British, he also sent the fire—deliberately started by rebel extremists. It burned for twenty-four hours and destroyed a third of the city before the troops and the sailors sent in from the ships managed at last to bring it under control.

On Manhattan there was a temporary lull in the war, but it was about to flare once more into violent conflict in Canada. Carleton's shipbuilding teams at St. Johns had almost completed his ships. The enormous operation of hauling the vessels in sections past the rapids from Chambly was over.

At Crown Point, too, under Arnold's dynamic urging, American construction teams with far fewer resources than the British had been building the vessels that were to oppose Carleton when he attacked. They could hardly hope to beat the British, whose ships were bigger and better gunned, but they could delay them. It was nearly fall. Winter would soon be gripping the St. Lawrence, making long communications impractical.

In fact, less than a week after Howe sprang at Kip's Bay from Long Island Carleton's homemade fleet began moving, one vessel at a time, from St. Johns up the Richelieu River to Lake Champlain.

10

LAKE CHAMPLAIN, October 11, 1776

The early-morning air was raw, and the mist still shrouded the British vessels as they weighed anchor under the protective lee of Champlain's Long Island.[1] The wind was blowing strongly from the northeast, chopping the waters of the lake into short white waves.

It was a quaint little fleet that was sallying forth on that chill day—a masterpiece of improvisation and engineering. Most of the craft had been dragged up past the rapids in pieces and reassembled on the stocks at St. Johns. Others had been fabricated from original designs that were packed with experimental ideas, such as the movable keel that could be raised through the bottom boards of a flatboat in shallow water.

The senior vessel in the motley squadron that was slipping out from the anchorage between Grand Island and Long Island into the short turbulence of the lake water was the *Inflexible*, a full-rigged three-master that with her eighteen 12-pounders had a battery in her broadsides superior to anything she could possibly meet. Following were her two support schooners,[2] *Carleton* and *Maria*, both bristling with 6-pounders; the *Loyal Convert*, a giant 30-ton flat-bottomed gondola, designed both to be rowed as a galley and sailed with limited canvas; and the *Thunderer*, a massive multidecked floating gun platform with a capacity for 300 men and fourteen guns, six of which were 24-pounders.

But much of Carleton's strategy was geared to his twenty-four little gunboats, each fitted with a single cannon in the bows. On their own they were not formidable, but operated as a flotilla, a highly mobile amphibious machine capable of firing twenty-four guns at a time, they packed as much firepower as a frigate.

In full sail, running free with the wind on the quarter, the fleet was impressive—twenty-nine fighting vessels plowing the small

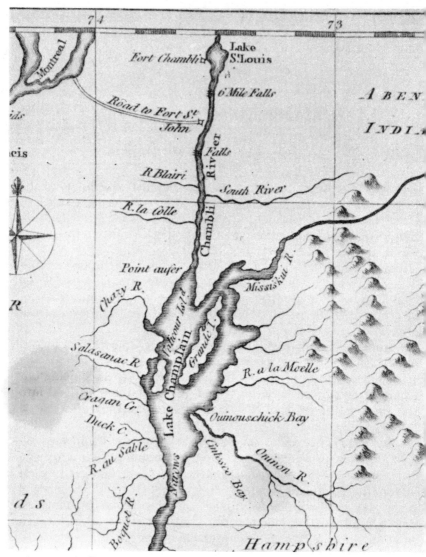

Lake Champlain

slapping waves with a backup force of another twenty-four sailing longboats loaded with provisions and equipment and, behind them, the troop bateaux and the Indian canoes. Looking back from the deck of the *Maria* at the slanting forest of masts and sails behind him, Carleton must have felt a deep satisfaction at the three months' achievement of his engineers and shipbuilders.

Nevertheless, it was three months he could barely afford—three summer months, ideal for campaigning, during which his army, for all its resources, had been held immobile on the Richelieu River. In June the rebels had been in an appalling condition as they fled before Carleton's troops—demoralized, stripped of equipment, riddled with smallpox. But Benedict Arnold, commanding the retreating forces, had held one vital card which he did not even have to play: He possessed three armed schooners the Americans had captured the year before. With these he could dominate the lake and could threaten any forward movement by the troops of General Burgoyne, whom Carleton had placed in local command.

Tactically it was essential that Arnold's schooners should be destroyed or recaptured or at least controlled by British vessels before the army lunged for the fortress of Ticonderoga in the narrow waters at the southern end of the lake.

But while Carleton's shipwrights had been engaged in their crash program at St. Johns, rebel construction gangs at Crown Point, Ticonderoga and Skenesborough had been hard at work building more vessels to challenge the British when they advanced. By October another schooner, four big 10-gun galleys and nine lightly armed gondolas had been completed.

Both galleys and the gondolas, though varying greatly in size, were similar in design: flat-bottomed and propelled mainly by oars that might well prove more reliable in the mercurial winds of the lake than total reliance on sail.

With winter closing in time was vital to Carleton. Through the last days of September, as the carpenters had finished his vessels, he had sent them one by one up the Richelieu to assemble in the lake near the river entrance. On scouting duty on the lake with its many islands that could provide cover for sneak attacks were 400 Indians under the command of the general's younger brother.

Although Carleton had never favored employing the Indians and deeply resented their desertion the previous year, he had accepted their new offer of help. They were uncomfortable allies, often wandering through the camp, smilingly demanding rum in the cause of friendship. Their war dances were unnerving spectacles, for the British were only too conscious how easily they could switch their allegiance.

Tall, beautifully built men, with rings in their ears, they danced completely naked except for "the head of some handsome bird," as Lieutenant James Hadden put it, that each wore fixed to his penis. Smeared artistically with war paint of vermilion and other vivid colors, they leaped into the air with wild howls as the tomtoms pounded. Hair was distasteful to them, and all of it was pulled out by the roots from their bodies, faces and scalps, except for a small tuft at the back of their heads to which they attached a feather for every man they had killed.

In their canoes made of tree bark fixed to cedar wood frames, they could travel fast and in complete silence, usually kneeling on the bottom of their craft as they slipped their six-foot maple paddles noiselessly into the water. They had already brought Carleton warning of the approach of the rebel squadron, but the general knew Arnold was aware that he had not yet been ready to fight him. When the Americans had anchored defiantly close, Burgoyne had sent forward guns to the banks of the lake to force them to keep their distance.

At last, by October 7, the British prepared to attack. For several days, as the last of the vessels had traveled up the river,[3] it had rained heavily, cold fall rain that had chilled the waiting troops. Then as they were on the point of sailing, the weather blew up, pinning them in their anchorage while, noted Digby, enormous flocks of wild pigeons circled cawing above them. The rebels were not far away. The British could hear the explosions as they fired small charges to scale their guns of rust.

At noon on the tenth, when the winds had eased, the flotilla weighed anchor and sailed with their decks cleared for action in search of Arnold. By nightfall, when they anchored, they had not found him, but there were many islands in that part of the lake; he had plenty of cover if he chose to bide his time.

Assessing the latest intelligence reports of Arnold's movements, Carleton guessed that he would confront him near Grand Island, a large G-shaped piece of land in the middle of the lake, for below the island the waters were very wide and the cover was more limited.

The next morning the little fleet, led by the *Inflexible* and the two schooners, sailed south under the brisk northeasterly between Grand Island and the western shore of the lake. High up the rigging the British lookouts searched the rugged coastline of the island for a glimpse of Arnold's masts, but by the time they detected the fifteen vessels of the rebel squadron they were downwind and in the worst possible position to start a battle. They had many more guns than the Americans, but their problem was now to get them into range.

The crafty Arnold was not at Grand Island to the east of the British. He was waiting on their west—concealed in a narrow half-mile strip of water between another island, Valcour, and Champlain's New York bank.

Valcour Island rose steeply from the lake, a high two-mile slab of rock shaped like a hog's back, thick with tall pines. Well up the inside shore of the island, backed closely against a small bay facing south, Arnold's squadron was waiting, ranged defensively in a crescent line.

Not until about eleven o'clock when the fleet had already passed Valcour did a call from the *Maria*'s masthead alert Carleton to a schooner two miles astern of them lying between the southern tip of the island and the mainland. The lone waiting ship was like a signpost pointing to the rebel vessels still concealed from the British by the bulk of Valcour Island.

A signal flag shook out from the *Maria*'s mast. The coxswains put their helms over. Sails flapped as the fifty-three vessels heeled over with their bows swinging around into the wind.

It was a long, long haul as they zigzagged their way slowly northward against the breeze. There was no formal formation now. The *Inflexible* and the two black schooners, previously the leaders, now lay farthest south of the whole squadron; in fact the gunboats, equipped with four long oars as well as sails, were best suited to cross that stretch of choppy water against the force of the northeasterly.

Carleton's little fleet had been improvised with many ideas. But as a tactical concept the gunboat flotilla was inspired. Each carried a gun team of seven, mostly Hessian artillerists, and a sailing crew of eleven. Their cannon, ranging up to 24-pounders, were major weapons that caused lethal damage when they were on target; by contrast Arnold's biggest guns were 18-pounders, and he had only three of these. Most of his top armament was in the 9- to 12-pound range.

*   *   *

The *Inflexible* was heeling over—every foot of her three layers of sail straining for the wind, water swirling by under her larboard gunwales—as she raced for the New York shore. She was far south, but once her officers were able to see up the channel between the island and the mainland, she would be able to open up at long range.

Of the bigger vessels the *Carleton* had been in the best position for making up to Valcour. Now the slim black schooner was running for the shore, leaning over under the wind pressure on her canvas on a parallel course to the *Inflexible*. But she was farther north.

Higher up toward the island were the gunboats, their oars working steadily, their cannon in the bows resembling the head and beak of some giant bird. Beyond them, far out toward Grand Island, were the support boats—and, of course, the Indians in their canoes.

It soon became clear that Arnold first planned to attack the British as they came up the channel. Lieutenant James Dacres, commander of the *Carleton*, saw the four big rebel galleys and a schooner, the captured *Royal Savage* the British had used to defend St. Johns the previous year, advancing south toward him in line. None of the vessels looked quite like ships; spruce branches pointing upward had been lashed all around the bulwarks—a stockade protection, the British learned later, against the muskets Arnold guessed soon would be firing down on his gun crews from the tall trees on the island.

But as the rebels cleared the island and could see the size of the British force, they swung abruptly about, their cannon booming as they went and headed back to their anchorage, where with the others they could concentrate their total firepower over a limited area. The *Carleton* opened up with her bow guns at the four ships that were then broadside on and swathed in smoke. The *Maria* was firing, too, since for a few precious minutes they were not screened by the island. So, too, was the *Inflexible* from farther south. But the range was too wide; none of the shots from British or rebel guns hit their targets.

The uneven contours of the tall island made the wind dangerous, deflecting it in gusts, streaming it suddenly at varying angles, sometimes checking it momentarily altogether. Within the narrow confines between the island and the mainland, the zigzig tacks were shorter and the unreliable sailing conditions demanded high quality seamanship.

Some of the gunboats reached the channel first, but by noon the *Carleton* was moving up the narrows in wide-angled sweeps in pursuit of Arnold's ships, which were making as fast as they could for the other rebel vessels that lay in the small cupped bay of the island. Those uncertain wind conditions favored oars, and Arnold's galleys were running under bare poles, propelled only by their rowers.

But the rebels' *Royal Savage* had no oars. Like the *Carleton*, she was forced to haul up against a tricky wind and so lagged behind the galleys in the race for the anchorage. She was well ahead of the *Carleton*—but not out of range. The bow guns of the British schooner roared: Three solid shots struck the rebel vessel, smashing the woodwork, sending up sprays of splinters, but by that time she had trouble of a different nature.

The galleys had reached the line of rebel ships and dropped their anchors as the *Royal Savage* was running on the starboard tack; then, as she approached the island coast, her captain seemed to wait a moment too long before ordering the helmsman to spin his wheel and go about onto the other tack. Or maybe a spill of wind down the steep hillside affected his judgment.

Her bows swung around. Her sails loosened but did not billow with the wind from the other direction as they should have as the head came about. For a few moments she stayed motionless, her flapping sails giving her no way, as the northerly current bore her closer to the land. Her sails filled—but too late. Suddenly her tall masts shook as her keel scraped the bottom. She shuddered and tilted sideways, stuck fast; she could still fire her guns, but she had no capacity for maneuver.

Slowly but inexorably, the *Carleton* bore down on her, firing with her bow cannon. A longboat with anchor aboard pushed off from the stricken schooner; but Lieutenant Dacres in the *Carleton* anticipated the rebel captain's plan to drag his ship afloat by hauling in the anchor cable, and British guns aimed on the boat and it capsized.

The *Carleton* neared its objective, altered course east to present its guns, and a broadside crashed shot into the *Royal Savage* with a tremendous explosion. Almost immediately the British schooner went about, the starboard guns bearing as she swung onto the other tack until they were on target. Again there was a great detonation and a long white flash along the *Carleton*'s side. Flying metal pounded the *Royal Savage*, ripping her sails to strips, battering holes in her hull. By now several gunboats were also moving up to attack the foundered vessel.

Up to this point the rest of Arnold's ships could not fire on the *Carleton* for fear of hitting their own vessel. But their turn was coming. The British schooner, after firing her second broadside, was running across the front of the anchored rebel vessels in their crescent formation; the range was short and the line of ships hidden by a great bank of smoke as their guns opened up.

By now seventeen of the British gunboats had come up, and they, too, were firing their big cannon. "The cannonade was tremendous," recorded General Friedrich von Riedesel, the Hessian commander. "Close to one o'clock," reported Captain Georg Pausch, who was in one of the gunboats, "this naval battle began to get very serious."

The *Carleton*, heeled over with her canvas hauled taut, should have been past the rebel anchorage. This would have taken her out of the line of fire of most of Arnold's anchored ships, though the crescent formation was carefully chosen to give them a wide shooting arc. But suddenly, owing to the masking of the wind by the island cliffs, her foresail went slack. She swung around out of control "nearly," as naval commander Captain Thomas Pringle on the *Maria* reported later, "into the middle of the rebel half moon."

She could not have been more exposed, head on to Arnold's broadsides and unable to fire her own, and the rebels grabbed their opportunity. Their guns raked the helpless schooner. Grape sprayed her decks; solid shot burst great holes in her superstructure.

Lieutenant Dacres took action as fast as he could. A seaman knocked the shackle off the cable that held the anchor in the hawsepipe. As it splashed into the water, a line attached to it was already being rushed aft under the heavy rebel fire to be paid through the stern bollards. A chain of sailors heaved; the "spring" tautened. Slowly the stern responded and the schooner swung around so that once more she was broadside on. Immediately her guns opened up, shooting as fast as their crews could reload, but with all the rebel ships concentrating their fire on her at close range she endured a terrible battering. Her sails were ribbons. Much of her rigging was shot away. Her longboat was smashed.

Great jagged holes were ripped in her sides. Dacres was knocked unconscious. His second-in-command had an arm shot off. Nineteen-year-old Midshipman Edward Pellew assumed command.

Meanwhile, the gunboats, which had worked up near to Arnold's crescent so they could fire their big cannon at close range, were forced to drop back. Being undecked, as Lieutenant James Hadden reported, they were too exposed to grapeshot if they were closer than 700 yards; this of course meant that they were placed too far off to fire it. But from that distance they could shoot solid shot—and receive it. While the *Carleton*'s crew were fighting fiercely, a ball exploded the powder magazine of one of the boats. Smoke gushed skyward, carrying up on its surface, according to Captain Pausch, a sea chest. Flames leaped up the mast, and she fast filled with water.

The *Carleton*, anchored in front of the rebel lines, was still taking vicious punishment when she was threatened by another crisis. The spring holding her stern tight to the anchor was shot away; the wind streamed her from the cable, once more bow on to the enemy. By now the *Maria* was in sight south of Valcour and signaled the *Carleton* to retire, but the only way she could do this was by getting her sails to draw.

Young Midshipman Pellew ordered an extra jib foresail run up, normally the quickest way to catch the wind, but because they were head on, held by their anchor, the canvas merely flapped. Under the punishment she had received the *Carleton* should have sunk already; now that her sails would not draw, she seemed doomed. Certain she could not last long, the rebels poured shot into the battered schooner; then Pellew climbed along the bowsprit and flung himself against the sail in an effort to scoop wind. Although completely exposed to the hail of metal pounding his schooner, astonishingly he was unhurt.

Still the sail would not draw. Two gunboats approached on the larboard side, and Pellew threw them lines. Slowly, still under very heavy fire, they towed the ailing vessel down the channel.

By late afternoon, when black clouds had obscured the sun and the sea had turned slate gray, the *Inflexible* and the *Maria* had at last made the channel. The big sloop raked the rebel line at point-blank range with her broadsides of nine 12-pounders. She savaged them badly. One galley had twelve holes in her hull, another a shattered mainmast. A gondola had gone down. Two more were so badly damaged that they sank the next day. The *Royal Savage*, still stuck fast, was set on fire.

But darkness came down before the British could complete the destruction. To blockade the rebels until morning the British ships anchored across the southern end of the channel between Valcour and the mainland with the gunboats tied together in a long line between the bigger vessels.

The early-morning mist did not clear until eight o'clock. By then there were no rebel vessels in the little crescent bay. Somehow they had slipped past the British ships during the night.

"The astonishment next morning was great," recorded General von Riedesel, "as was Carleton's rage." Furiously the British commander ordered a pursuit. Arnold could not get far, for the wind had veered southerly; that evening Carleton's scouts informed him that the rebels were at Schuyler's Island, just eight miles south of Valcour.

The next day he resumed the chase, but both flotillas were still heading into the breeze. By the following morning the rebels were 28 miles from Crown Point with the British 5 miles behind them.

Then the wind changed—for the British but not for the rebels. While Arnold and his damaged vessels were still tacking, Carleton had the benefit of a new northeasterly that had not yet reached the rebels. It meant that the end of the strange naval fight was nearly over.

At Split Rock, so named because its tall sheer face looked as though a giant axman had sliced a piece from it, the lake narrowed. It was there near this great cleft of limestone that soon after eleven the British caught up with the stragglers of the rebel flotilla—six vessels out of a total of eleven that remained afloat, slowed by their damage.

The *Inflexible* and the two schooners sailing ahead of the rest of the squadron swooped on them. Since the Valcour battle, the *Carleton* had been repaired and pumped free of the water in her hold; now, together with the *Maria*, she was making for the New York bank to the leeward to cut off any attempt by Arnold to beach his ships.

Meanwhile, the *Inflexible* bore down on the *Washington* galley, which lagged behind the others. The first broadside of the sloop's 12-pounders was fired at some distance, but it was on target and brought the crippled galley lurching around. The second broadside was at close range, and it was the finish. As the smoke cleared and the *Inflexible* went about to attack again, her commander saw the red and white rebel flag moving slowly down the *Washington*'s mast. Her captain had surrendered.

The three British ships moved on to attack the *Congress* galley, now the nearest of the surviving rebel vessels with Arnold aboard. Broadside after broadside exploded into the galley, but they did not sink her. Somehow she went on running south, her guns still firing, her oarsmen still digging the water.

Abruptly the five galleys swung east, their oars holding them almost into the wind; Carleton's sailing ships could only follow slowly, in laborious tacks. Long before they could get near, Arnold had run his flotilla onto the shore and flames were licking up his masts.

It was another British victory. By contrast with Carleton's loss of one gunboat and a damaged schooner, two-thirds of Arnold's squadron had been destroyed. Eighty of his men had died. But as a triumph it was limited. The rebel general had delayed the British advance—not only by fighting, but by being there on the lake.

Carleton took Crown Point and surveyed Ticonderoga with its rebel garrison of 10,000 men. Burgoyne, his second-in-command, urged him to attack the famous fort, but it was mid-October and too late, Carleton decided, for starting what might well be a long siege. Sadly he ordered the army to retreat, to relinquish the lake that he had fought for so hard. The storming of Ticonderoga would have to wait until spring.

The timing had been critically narrow. If Carleton had not waited for the completion of the *Inflexible*, he could have advanced sooner. But British commanders always tended to trade time for strength—perhaps in this case rightly, for without the sloop the general would not have held the fighting superiority. And a defeat by the rebels would have been far worse than his present tactical withdrawal.

Whether Carleton was right or wrong, Arnold had bought the rebels a whole year to prepare their defense against assault from the north.

By now Howe's troops on Manhattan had again gone into action.

Early in the morning following the Battle of Valcour a flotilla of flatboats was fighting its way through the combined turbulence of the East and Harlem rivers at Hell Gate. Four thousand assault troops were heading for a landing point on Westchester—the first stage of a spring onto the country at the rear of Washington's army on Harlem Heights.

11

NEW YORK, October 12, 1776

The fog came down suddenly, damp and blinding, creating crisis.[1] The flotilla of flatboats and transports loaded with men and horses and guns was moving fast on the swift running tide into the turbulence of Hell Gate. At any time, except slack water, the East River was highly dangerous at this point, where it was joined by the rush of Harlem Creek as it reached for Long Island Sound, spinning whirlpools among the rocks around Montresor and Buchanan's islands.

However, now that the fog had turned the early-morning light "into utter darkness," as Clinton put it, the danger was immeasurably increased. It was impossible for the coxswains to see the line of buoys that the fleet pilots had set up earlier to mark the channel through the rocks.

In the admiral's sloop at the head of the flotilla, the Howe brothers considered stopping the convoy and either anchoring or turning back, but the stream was carrying them forward so fast that with such low visibility either operation would be dangerous. So they stayed on their blind course, moving quickly along the curving narrow mile-long strip of water between the hidden bulk of Montresor and Buchanan's islands.

Clinton was in the admiral's sloop—as usual, his memoirs suggest, unconsulted by the Howes. In his normal role as second-in-command of the army, he would lead the avant-garde, the assault troops who would storm the landing beach, *if* the flotilla got safely through Hell Gate.

Even Clinton, despite his dislike of the Howes and the inevitable soldier's disapproval of the navy, was moved to warm praise of the admiral's skill. "By his own excellent management and that of his officers," he recorded, "the whole got through almost miraculously, without any other loss than that of an artillery boat. . . ." In fact, Clinton was slightly in error. Two boats were caught in the whirlpools and shattered on the rocks. From one, all the men escaped alive; from the other, the gunboat Clinton mentioned, only three men out of twenty-five were drowned.

Beyond Hell Gate, the weather was clear. Then, re-formed in the two columns, stern to bows, that the Navy favored, the eighty boats moved on up the river that broadened steadily as it approached the wide waters of the Sound. It was a motley little fleet. Some of the bigger craft had sail, often just one sheet of canvas on a single mast; most of the vessels were flatboats heavy with troops, sitting huddled close together, as the oars worked with mechanically regular movements.

By eight o'clock in the morning they were nearing Throgs Neck, a narrow isthmus of land that thrust south, like a finger, from the Westchester shore. The tip, Throgs Point, had been selected for the landing, and a frigate was already waiting, gunports open, to cover the assault.

The flatboats deployed in line abreast and approached the beach. There were a few rebels on the shore who opened fire with muskets at the first wave of craft. On the frigate, a single cannon cracked out, dropping metal among the handful of defenders. A second gun fired, followed by another, shooting wide to spread the shot, just to clear the landing area; this it did. The Americans turned and hurried toward the mainland.

The troops landed without a single casualty and, as Clinton reported, "pushed for Westchester Bridge in the hopes of securing it, but the enemy had been too quick for us."

Throgs Neck was a poor bridgehead for the Howes to have chosen, for it was divided from the mainland by Westchester Creek, which ran through marshes. There was a single bridge, and by the time the British reached it, the boards were down. Because of the marshland on either side, they could cross the creek only by going through the water in the narrow area where the bridge had been—and where the rebels could concentrate an extremely heavy fire from a redoubt constructed for exactly this purpose.

Possibly, Clinton's advance troops could have made the crossing, but it would not have been worth the heavy casualties. The British could use the isthmus as a forward base, bringing up their supplies and reinforcements from Manhattan, before making the. short jump for another landing point farther up the Westchester shore.

And bottled up though he was for the time being, Howe had

achieved his main object. He had broken the stalemate that had existed for the past month since Washington had dropped back to his impregnable position on Harlem Heights, with his flanks and rear protected by water. Now the British were positioned in strength behind the rebel army—as well, of course, as still being in front of it. Lord Percy had remained on Manhattan in command of the strongly fortified front line that stretched right across the island just below Harlem from the East River to the Hudson.

Washington had no choice left. He must march north, and soon. For Howe merely had to advance across Westchester to the river for the Americans to be hemmed in with their supply routes severed.

Despite the danger, Washington did not start his retreat for six days, even though, as the disenchanted rebels who came through Percy's line every night confirmed, he was fully conscious of the danger. Howe did not move either, for the wind, vital to sailing ships going through Hell Gate, veered to the wrong direction, then dropped altogether, halting all traffic upriver. For two days the transports lay waiting at anchor in the stream below Buchanan's Island.

Meanwhile, the rebels had brought up guns and were bombarding the British on the isthmus. Howe's position was uncomfortable, and at 5 a.m. on October eighteenth, his troops sprang for another bridgehead, three miles to the north.

A battery of six guns on Throgs Neck opened up, and the shot whistled over the water to pound the new landing beaches at Rodman's Neck—another isthmus, but this time with a link to the mainland uncluttered by creeks or marshes.

The two columns of flatboats filled with the avant-garde were led by two frigates, which turned off and opened up with crashing broadside salvos at close range as they approached the shore.

The fields, dotted with trees and patchworked by stone walls, stretched to the water's edge. There was little sign of opposition while the ground was battered with solid shot and spurted into sprays of dirt by the shells. But as soon as the barrage was lifted to allow the troops to land, rebels, who had been crouching behind the cover of the walls, started firing.

Clinton in the command boat tried to assess their numbers and even considered whether he should stop the landing. "But," he recorded, "as I was certain they could not be in any great force, I ordered the debarkation to proceed."

As the assault troops leaped out of the boats and splashed onto the shore, the rebels dropped back fast. The British advanced quickly, making for the main coast road that linked New York with Connecticut—what Clinton called "their great communication." Because the route lay under a hill on their right that was marked with heavy cover, Lord Cornwallis led a detachment into the high ground. While the main column moved forward cautiously below, grenadiers and light infantrymen routed waiting rebels from their positions behind stone walls and farm outbuildings; the sharpshooting jaegers stormed a wood that lay ahead.

Though there were pockets of fierce fighting, by night the British lay in force on each side of the coast road. Cornwallis was on the hillside guarding the lines of communication with the landing beaches, where all day long the boats had been ferrying men and equipment from Throgs Neck.

All day too, 12 miles away on the other side of Westchester near the Hudson, the rebels had been moving north toward White Plains.

Later Howe was criticized because he made little attempt to harry the rebels on the march. Clearly he lost an opportunity, but as always, he hated to make aggressive moves unless he could do so from a firm position of strength. For nearly a week the British prepared carefully, broadened their base, spread out to New Rochelle and set up an outpost a little farther north along the Sound at Mamaroneck.

Meanwhile, although Washington moved most of his army north, he left a large garrison of nearly 3,000 men at Fort Washington, a big redoubt in the seemingly impregnable craggy heights of the northern tip of Manhattan. The fort was a key point in the rebel defense system of the upper part of the Hudson. From the foot of the sheer cliff face beneath the fortification, a line of sunken ships formed a boom across the river to Fort Lee, also set in a fine natural defense position more than 100 feet above the water on the New Jersey shore.

The guns of the two forts could rake any royal ships that moved upriver from the fleet anchorage. Even so, British frigates often ran the gauntlet and early proved that they could break through the boom.

On October 25, twelve days after he had moved his first assault troops north through Hell Gate, Howe ordered Clinton and the avant-garde to advance to Eastchester Heights, just three miles from the rebel lines below the village of White Plains. In the dawnlight they marched from New Rochelle in two long columns of infantry, guns and cavalry: one on the main road that led to White Plains, the other along rough wagon tracks that curled between the fields and through the woods of the hills to the west.

They had to travel only six miles, and when they camped on the timbered slopes, their forward outposts were so close to the American pickets that the sentries on both sides could hear each other.

Washington responded carefully. His army had been waiting on both sides of the Bronx River, which, snaking as it did across the plain and, at one point, turning sharply west, could be a most important factor in battle. Now he moved most of his men to the eastern bank, the side from which the British were most likely to approach. Behind his lines lay the mountains, and in the mountains at Peekskill lay the rebel supply magazines.

Following his usual uninvited custom, Clinton sent his battle proposals to his commander, who was still at New Rochelle with the main part of the army. He favored a reconnaissance in force, since they did "not know the ground about White Plains," followed by a feint retreat, a secret return by night and a dawn attack. Clearly he was hoping to repeat his successful strategy on Long Island.

Howe did not reply for forty-eight hours, and when he did, he merely ordered the reconnaissance. Clinton reported that Washington had chosen his position well. With his main lines just south of White Plains, he had mountains protecting his left flank and the Bronx shielding most of his right wing. Furthermore, any time he chose, he could retreat north into the safety of the pass behind him.

That night Howe gave orders that the whole army would advance to White Plains the next morning. His second-in-command was horrified; apparently it was to be a frontal attack on an enemy who was extremely well positioned. In fact, the evidence suggests that Howe merely planned to get his troops within sight of the enemy and to figure out his tactics from there. At least, on the plain he had room to move.

His strategy may have been a bit vague, but he had a beautiful day in which to execute it. The sun shone brightly from a fine clear sky as Clinton's two columns—one on the road, which he led himself, and one in the country on the left that was advancing along a wagon track so narrow that they had to march in file—moved down the Eastchester Hills, thick with trees nearly bare from the fall, toward the plain. Behind him, the main body of the army was marching from New Rochelle.

Because the road curled downward through hills, Clinton's view of the plain was obscured. But Howe was watching the enemy's movements very carefully; for this reason, he saw the danger that was out of Clinton's line of vision: A large detachment of rebels, alerted presumably by their scouts, was moving fast up the road along which the advance column was approaching.

An aide galloped up to Clinton past the long line of marching men with a warning from Howe that the enemy was forming to attack him as soon as he appeared on the plain. Inevitably, Clinton disagreed with his commander's interpretation. "I was certain," he wrote later, "the instant they discovered my column, they would retire." And he planned that as they did so, he would cut them off from the rest of the rebel army.

On the right of the road was a hill that screened the plain.[2] Clinton halted his column while Cornwallis broke across country around the eastern side of the hill with cannon and some light troops. His orders were to take the rebel advance guard in their rear. Clinton ordered the advance to continue, and the column moved on down the road that skirted the hill onto the plain.

The rebels were waiting in their favorite type of defense position—behind stone walls. And as usual, they held their fire until the Hessians, who were in the lead, came very close.

The clash did not last long, but it was intense. Clinton halted the column, while a detachment of Hessians and jaegers swarmed off the road to attack the rebel positions. The Americans fell back, field by field, firing from each line of walls they came to as they retired. When Cornwallis' cannon opened up from their rear, the conflict ended abruptly. The rebels could not retreat to Washington's main lines, but they had an alternative escape route. Pursued closely by the Hessians, they splashed through a ford across the Bronx and headed for the cover of some woods on the other side of the river.

Meanwhile, the skirmish over, Howe's army descended from the hills and marched in three columns across the plain toward the main rebel lines. "Its appearance was truly magnificent," a watching rebel officer, Otto Hufeland, reported later. "A bright autumnal sun shed its lustre on the polished arms; and the rich array of dress and military equipage gave an imposing grandeur to the scene as they advanced in all the pomp and circumstance of war."

The British halted while Howe held a conference with his senior officers in a wheatfield. Certainly, as Clinton had warned him, he had a problem. Above him, under the mountains, was the wall of beaten earth and stones that marked the rebel front line—reaching from the Bronx on the west to a steeply wooded slope and a lake on the east.[3] Beyond the fortifications, the British general could see the town of White Plains—clapboard houses, gathered around a courthouse and a steepled Presbyterian church.

About half a mile across the river to his left was Chatterton's Hill, a long high ridge of fields thickly timbered at its lower levels. Because it overlooked the town and Washington's lines, it was an obvious place for the British to set up an artillery battery; that was why a big rebel working party was now busy fortifying it.

Howe regarded the hill as the first objective in his tactics—for he could then advance against the main American position under the cover of a very heavy barrage—and gave orders for it to be taken.

While most of his army sat down on the ground in ranks to wait until they were needed, horse teams hauled a dozen guns onto a small hill that faced Chatterton's across the river. The twelve guns opened fire almost simultaneously, terrific explosions echoing back off the mountains like continued peals of thunder. Meanwhile, a mixed British-Hessian detachment of infantry was ordered across the river.

For once, presumably since the scene of action was so limited, Howe and his frosty second-in-command were together as they watched their troops advancing under fire toward the woods that covered Chatterton's lower slopes. It must have brought back memories for Howe, for tactically the situation was not all that different from the conditions that had faced him on Bunker Hill. Two British regiments were moving forward up the hill in line abreast, as indeed they had at Bunker Hill. A wave of rebel fire checked them. Coolly, their commander ordered them to form in column, so as to present a smaller target, and once more they advanced toward the bank of trees. "The instant I saw the move," recorded Clinton, "I declared it decisive." The tactic was carried out confidently and professionally, and the attacking column was soon progressing fast up the hill under very heavy fire. Then suddenly, Clinton saw the whole maneuver collapse.

"When the officer had marched forward about twenty paces, he halted, fired his fuzee [a small musket] and began to reload (his column remaining during the time under the enemy's fire), upon which I pronounced it a 'coup manque,' foretelling at the same time that they would break."

Vital seconds went by while the officer reloaded and the rebels kept firing from the trees at the waiting column. Soldier after soldier dropped in the ranks, which formed promptly to fill the gaps. At last, as Clinton forecast, they broke and ran for cover. "If the battle is lost," he remarked to Howe, "that officer was the occasion of it."

"I had scarcely done speaking," Clinton wrote, "when Lord Cornwallis came up with the same observation."

Clinton's comment was barbed, for he had long urged that officers should not carry fuzees. Their role, as he saw it, was to command, to manipulate the fighting machine—not to take detailed part in it. It was one of Clinton's many theories that Howe did not act on, and indeed it was by presenting bayonets fixed on fuzees that officers had been able to force their men to form as they were running in panic toward Lexington from Concord.

At Chatterton's the setback did not make much difference. It was certainly no repeat of Bunker Hill. The British re-formed and advanced with the Hessians. Another contingent attacked the rebel flank from the other side of the steep slope and quickly took possession of the summit.

Howe had taken his artillery position, but, as Clinton put it, "after this little brush, we paused a while." As well they might, for the problem of how best to attack White Plains was clearly very difficult. For two days, they waited.[5] Howe had called up reinforcements, while at his request Clinton had ridden through the woods on the west side of the Bronx to reconnoiter the possibility of attacking the rebels on their right wing or even their rear. He suggested an attack plan with fairly sophisticated use of the whole front but weighted against the rebel's left wing on the river, but even he was dubious since "the enemy had a very strong position in the gorges of the mountains behind them."

Howe, as almost always, altered Clinton's plan. The attack, which was sure to be costly in British lives, was scheduled for the morning of October 31. The evening before, however, the weather changed for the worse—to torrential rain, followed by snow. The waters of the Bronx, flooding down from the hills, rose higher, breaking over the banks at points. At two in the morning Howe summoned Clinton to his tent to consider if in view of the altered weather, and in particular the swelling river which some troops would have to cross, he should change the attack plans. Clinton, though disapproving of Howe's alterations to his suggestions, did not think the rain was a reason to abandon them. "While the river remains passable to the left," he told his chief with feigned respect, "I shall be ready to obey Your Excellency's commands whenever you think proper to order the attack."

As Howe studied his maps in the candlelight, he must have wished he had another man as his second-in-command—someone a little less cool, less remote, less critical. However, he decided that the attack should proceed as planned.

In the early-morning darkness the troops who were to strike the center of the rebel line were already advancing through the wet when they discovered that the fortifications were no longer manned. The Americans had evacuated their camp and retired into the gorge a mile above White Plains.

Once more there was a stalemate. The rebel flanks were now enclosed by hills. The only attack plan open to Howe was uphill on their front, which would be extremely hazardous, and even if it succeeded, the Americans could easily drop back farther into the hills.

It was, however, a very different stalemate from the situation that had existed only two weeks before, when the rebels had been entrenched on Harlem Heights. Apart from the garrison the American commander had left at Fort Washington, the British now controlled most of Long Island and the whole of Manhattan, Staten Island and Westchester. There was little to stop them from striking across New Jersey, a province in which the Loyalists were particularly numerous. From the north, reports were filtering through that Carleton had defeated Arnold and now controlled Lake Champlain. Accounts of deserters suggested that the morale of Washington's men was appallingly low. "It is a fact," wrote Lieutenant Frederick Mackenzie in his journal, "that many of the rebels who were killed in the late affairs were without shoes or stockings. . . . They are also in great want of blankets. The weather during the former part of the campaign has been so favorable that they did not feel the want of those things, but in less than a month they must suffer extremely if not supplied with them. Under all the disadvantages of want of confidence, clothing and good winter quarters . . . it will be astonishing if they keep together till Christmas." Also, the strain was aggravating the old regional antagonisms that were always simmering below the surface of the rebel forces. "The people from the Southern Colonies," recorded Mackenzie, quoting a deserter, "declare they will not go into New England, and the others that they will not march to the southward. If this account is true in any degree, they must soon go to pieces."

Howe was fully conscious of Washington's difficulties. He knew, too, as he had known twelve months before when the rebel general was blockading him in Boston, that the year's term of service for which many of his ragged men had signed on was due to finish at the end of December. The low morale and the cold early winter nights were hardly likely to encourage reenlistment.

It seemed that the Revolution was almost over, but unlike most of his senior officers, Howe did not believe there was time before the end of the year to strike the final blow. For this reason he gave orders for a force to be prepared to take Rhode Island, which, unlike New York, which often iced up in the cold weather, had a deepwater harbor that would provide the British fleet with a base its ships could use throughout the winter and a springboard for a strike next year through New England, which featured in Howe's planning. In command of the expedition—probably so that he could get a bit of peace—he placed Clinton.

Before daylight on November 5 the main part of Howe's army was on the march south along the coast road near the Hudson that the rebels had used to escape north from Harlem. He had already ordered the newly arrived Hessian General Wilhelm von Knyphausen, who was waiting at New Rochelle, to attack a minor rebel position at Kingsbridge—the link between Manhattan Island and Westchester. Now he was going to storm Fort Washington.

The assault was certain to be formidable, but for once Howe's intelligence, normally a great problem for attacking commanders, was exceptionally good. Three nights before, on November 2, a young rebel officer named William Demont had approached one of Lord Percy's outposts under Harlem Heights and asked to be taken to headquarters. He was, he told the incredulous interrogating officers, adjutant to Colonel Robert Magaw, who commanded Fort Washington and, as a result, knew all the defense arrangements. He had with him maps showing the outposts, the fortifications and the planned disposition of the rebel defenders to withstand attack.

Acting with his usual caution, Clinton took ten days to prepare his attack. By November 15, he was ready. On the Westchester bank of the Harlem River, facing Mount Washington was a battery of twenty guns and howitzers. Gathered near them in the stream was a flotilla of flatboats that had been brought up the Hudson in darkness two nights before under the guns of the fort.

On the bare chance, however, that he could avoid a battle altogether Clinton sent Lieutenant Colonel Patterson, the officer the Howes had sent to parley with Washington before the invasion of Long Island, across Kingsbridge carrying a white flag. With him were three other officers. As they rode slowly up the hill toward the fort, they were met by a rebel officer, to whom Patterson handed a summons to surrender or, under the rules of war, the entire garrison would be slaughtered.

Magaw, the rebel commander, sent back a defiant message refusing the offer. "Give me leave to assure His Excellency that, actuated by the most glorious cause that mankind ever fought for, I am determined to defend this post to the very last extremity." So the battle was on.

The early-morning mist still lay over the Harlem River as, just before seven o'clock, Howe's big battery of guns on the Westchester bank opened fire from the north, supported by broadsides from a frigate anchored in the Hudson. At the same time, Percy's cannon began pounding the lowest rebel line on the southern slopes; then under the cover of the barrage, his troops advanced north along the Kingsbridge road that cut upward through Harlem Heights.

The narrow craggy triangle of Mount Washington was protected on two sides by water, by the Hudson on the west and by the Harlem River on the northeast. Three rows of fortifications, stretching in layers between the rivers, protected the steep approach from the south through which Percy was now advancing.

In fact, the southeast was the obvious direction from which to mount the main weight of attack, for the slopes near the Harlem at this point were easy. But this sector, like the river itself, was dominated by Laurel Hill, on which the rebels were installed in strength. Howe, who had placed himself with Percy's troops, had planned a simultaneous four-pronged strike on the fort. The advance from the south was technical—a breakthrough of the first defense line, which the rebels abandoned quickly, followed by an advantageous placing of the guns. There, the British extended their line to the Hudson and waited, with their artillery firing, for the impact of the main assault: by the Hessians from the north.

The Hessians, too, were waiting. Earlier, under the cover of the artillery barrage, Lieutenant General Baron von Knyphausen had led his force across Kingsbridge from Westchester. Now with their field cannon set up, 3,000 whiskered men, in their tall miterlike caps and their range of colored coats, were poised to attack the fort from the north the moment their commander received the final order from Howe.

But a sophisticated assault plan had been marred by the naval advisers. For another strike force, the light infantry and grenadiers, should have crossed the Harlem farther downstream in flatboats to capture Laurel Hill from the rebels and stop their cannon from threatening yet another landing even lower down the river by the Highlanders.

But the plan, as Engineering Lieutenant Archibald Robertson put it, "did not work immediately, for want of tide not serving, which had not been duly attended to."

The tide did not "serve" until just before noon.[4] Then, as the Westchester guns plastered Laurel Hill with salvo after salvo, the assault force in the boats crossed the Harlem under very heavy fire and charged up through the trees toward the rebel battery that commanded the river.

At the same time, the Hessians swarmed up the rocky, timbered north side of Mount Washington, branching into two columns. The frigate on the Hudson was pounding the outer defense lines above them. Even so, the rebels were fighting desperately, flaying the approaching Germans with musket shot and grape from an outpost, as they clambered up the incline, grabbing bushes to drag themselves over rocks.

It was a short but violent battle. By one o'clock, as their drums pounded, the Hessians on the north side of the mountain were almost at the summit. "Forward!" yelled Colonel Johann Rall, who was leading this attack; cheering, they broke through the rebel line and charged on the fort.

By then the light infantry had taken Laurel Hill. The Highlanders had landed. Percy was attacking hard on the south side. Soon the fort was ringed by Howe's forces, and the rebels had been forced to drop back from the outpost within its walls.

Magaw's position, with more than 2,000 men crowded into what was little more than a big redoubt, was hopeless. If Howe ordered his cannon to shell it, there would be a massacre.

Accompanied by a drummer beating the truce, a Hessian officer approached the fort with a white cloth tied to a musket and demanded surrender. Magaw asked four hours to consider terms— which would have given them almost until darkness with its obvious possibilities of escape—but Von Knyphausen granted them half an hour. Soon afterwards, Howe arrived and promptly sent in a sharp message that if they wished to survive they would surrender immediately, with no terms other than a promise of their lives and their baggage.

At four in the afternoon, Magaw gave up his sword, and 2,300 rebels filed out of the fort under the guard of Howe's soldiers.

It was a spectacular victory, symbolic because it cleared the rebels from their last foothold in New York and dramatic because of the enormous number of prisoners—men Washington was to need very badly.

For once the careful British general did not rest too long on his success. By daylight of November 20 the familiar two lines of boats loaded with men and cannon were moving across the Hudson. Teams of sailors hauled the guns up a steep 600-yard path that reached from the waterside up the high cliffs to New Jersey's Palisades woods.

Four thousand men under the command of Lord Cornwallis advanced on Fort Lee, which lay across the Hudson opposite Mount Washington. They did not have to take it by storm, for the rebels had evacuated it only minutes before Cornwallis' forward troops reached the walls; the Americans' kettles, so Howe reported somewhat jauntily to London, were still simmering over the fires. Cornwallis ordered the pursuit of the fleeing garrison, and more than 100 rebels were killed or taken prisoner before the chase was called off. The capture of the two forts gave the British 146 guns and enormous supplies of rebel ammunition and flour.

The British strike south was an obvious move, but it was *defensive*, not offensive, as it later seemed, designed to secure the rich New Jersey farmlands as a foraging area for the army during its winter on Manhattan. Howe, as he made clear in a letter to

Germain in September, had regarded his campaign of 1776 as over *before* he made his plunge north through Hell Gate. Only the exceptionally fine fall weather influenced his decision to force Washington off Manhattan, where he would have been an uncomfortable neighbor, and, if possible, to tempt him to battle. Events, especially the easy capture of Fort Washington, had gone far better than the British commander had expected, but when he ordered Cornwallis across the Hudson, he certainly had not the slightest intention of driving for Philadelphia.

Clearly Washington completely misinterpreted Howe's thinking and, in so doing, very nearly destroyed the Revolution. So that he could check a British move south, he had crossed the Hudson farther north with 5,000 men and now lay waiting at Hackensack, only a few miles southwest of his abandoned fort. But just in case the British struck north through the hills or west, he had left General Charles Lee with 5,000 troops at North Castle, just above White Plains, and posted yet another smaller force far up in the mountains at Peekskill to guard his magazines.

The rebel commander had made a grave planning error. Obviously, he was thinking in terms of checking any British attacks in any direction, but with the imminent arrival of New York's freezing winter it would have been extraordinarily risky for Howe to have mounted this kind of extensive attack, which would inevitably have involved long and vulnerable communications.

And why should Howe take any risks? The Revolution was already in the death throes, although it would probably take one more campaign in 1777—New England, in particular, needed attention—to settle it completely. Steadily he was extending the territory under British control on a firm and properly governed basis. Most important, as he well knew, Washington was in bad trouble; repeated British victories, capped by the ease with which they had taken the supposedly impregnable mountain fort, were fast sapping the morale of men already distressed by inadequate clothing and equipment. Desertions were soaring.

Now Washington had weakened himself even more by dividing his force, while Howe was free to ship across the river as many troops as he felt the situation demanded. The rebel commander was in no position for a major confrontation with the force of British and Hessians, buoyant with success, that were now advancing on him. Only at this point, as Cornwallis realized the true extent of Washington's predicament, did the idea of striking for Philadelphia begin to be entertained.

For a night after taking Fort Lee, Cornwallis' troops were halted because the rebels had destroyed the bridges over the Hackensack River. But by the next morning his advance corps were across it, and the rebels were in full retreat south toward Newark.

As he ran before the British, Washington's only hope seemed to lie in finding some point where he could make a stand, though this could hardly be successful unless Lee joined him with the troops from North Castle, a rendezvous Cornwallis was now determined to intercept, or unless he could rally sufficient New Jersey militia.

On Manhattan, waiting to leave with his 6,000 men to take Rhode Island, Clinton saw the possibilities that the new situation had opened up.

"Lord Cornwallis' success in striking a panic into and dispersing the affrighted remains of Mr. Washington's army was so great before I left New York," recalled Clinton, "that I had little doubt, and told Sir William Howe so, of His Lordship's overtaking them before they could reach the Delaware. . . . I was much concerned to find his expectations not quite so sanguine."

Howe's plans had not changed. He was still merely intending to take East Jersey for the foraging, holding it with a string of posts until the spring. When he explained this to his peevish second-in-command, Clinton was astonished. "I took the liberty," he wrote, "of cautioning him against the possibility of its [the chain of posts] being broken in upon in the winter, as he knew the Americans were trained to every trick of that country of chicane." Then Clinton suggested that the Rhode Island expedition should be temporarily postponed so that the troops, already embarked on the transports in the harbor, should be pushed up the Raritan River, where they could cut off Washington's retreat.

This was such an obvious move that Howe's failure to act on it, for which he was later attacked bitterly, provided ammunition to his enemies, who were alleging that he was siding secretly with the rebels. But his thinking was fixed firmly on the final blow the next year, and Rhode Island, ideally positioned as it was for attack on the New England mainland, was central to this: He was not being diverted. He rejected Clinton's suggestion, and on December 1 the assault fleet passed by the mouth of the Raritan and headed north into the winter buffeting of the Atlantic.

New York and New Jersey

The British Museum. Drawn by Claude Sauthier, 1779

By then the British pursuit of the rebels in New Jersey had become a chase. From Hackensack Cornwallis marched to Aquakinunk on the Passaic River, then turned south and advanced down the bank toward Newark. Intelligence had come in that the rebels planned to make a stand at Newark, and he moved carefully in the two columns, one advancing through the hills, that the British always employed when they expected trouble. In fact, the rebels stayed in the town for several days, but as soon as Cornwallis' advance guard approached on the morning of November 28, they retreated without even leaving any men to harry them with a few cannon shot.

As Cornwallis learned with satisfaction, Washington had tried to rally the New Jersey militia but had failed abysmally; not one man answered the call. He had no alternative but to continue in full retreat in a desperate attempt to save his small force of demoralized men—at least until Lee could get to him with reinforcements. And Cornwallis' dragoon patrols, who were scouring the routes that Lee might take from North Castle, reported no signs yet of the approach of this force.[5]

Even more encouraging for Cornwallis was the fact that Washington was traveling through country where many Loyalists had long been waiting impatiently for the defeat of the Revolution. Now, like the Long Island Tories three months before, they took their revenge for the persecution they had suffered. Whig homes were plundered and set on fire; Cornwallis got all the information he needed about the movements of the fleeing rebels.

After entering Newark, Cornwallis stepped up the pace. The next day his advance troops were through Elizabethtown and probing the approaches to Rahway, only a few hours behind Washington's men. On December 1 the British marched 20 miles through pouring rain over roads that were thick with mud, and caught up with the rebels at New Brunswick. There the rebel rear guard did open up with their cannon to hold off their pursuers until the bridges over the Raritan had been destroyed. The jaegers in the advance corps attacked the demolition men, but they were just too late.

Despite this, Washington and his column of depressed and bedraggled men now seemed utterly vulnerable. The bridges would be fast repaired by the army's engineers; the rebel commander had not been joined by Lee and the reinforcements; he had not raised the militia. There seemed nothing to stop the British from crossing the river and savaging him—nothing, that is, except Cornwallis' orders to halt at New Brunswick which, positioned as it was on the natural line of the Raritan, had been selected as a key point in Howe's planned chain of posts.

Also, the British needed a pause. Their line of communication was becoming dangerously long for what was still a relatively small strike force. Cornwallis had now had reports that Lee was crossing the Hudson. Because of the swift British advance in the rain through very heavy going, food and fatigue were becoming a problem. "As the troops had been constantly marching ever since their first entry into the Jerseys," he testified later, "they had no time to bake their flour; the artillery horses and the baggage horses of the army were quite tired. . . . We wanted reinforcements, in order to leave troops for the communication between Brunswick and Amboy." Amboy was the nearest Jersey town to Staten Island, which the British already held.

As Cornwallis saw it, there was no need for haste, no "considerable advantage" if it meant taking risks—as it did. For five days the British stayed at New Brunswick while Washington moved on south toward the Delaware. On December 6 Howe arrived at the town with more troops and gave orders for the pursuit to continue.

The next day the British advanced cautiously toward Princeton, their reconnaissance parties probing the Rocky Hill Pass, where they had been warned the rebels were posted in strength. But there was no opposition, and they moved on toward the Delaware River town of Trenton. Again, as the advance guard entered the town, they saw no sign of Washington's men until they fanned out along the banks of the river; then the noisy flashes on the far shore, sending shot screaming over the water, revealed their positions.

The British searched Trenton for boats and sent parties up the Jersey bank of the Delaware to seek them in the other river towns, but the rebels had moved them all across to the Pennsylvania shore. It was not an insuperable obstacle. The army was used to crossing water at short notice. Almost certainly they could have made rafts; the boards of half-completed craft were in the timberyards of Trenton and the other towns. But by the time the Delaware had been scoured for craft it was December 10, only a couple of weeks to Christmas. The nights were cold. Ice was swirling down the river. It was not the weather for campaigning.

The year had ended far more successfully than Howe two months before would have believed possible. He had battered the rebel army to a point of near disintegration. The British now controlled a large area on the eastern seaboard and the whole of Canada. Following the Howes' latest offer of the royal pardon, New Jerseymen were flocking into the towns to sign the oath of allegiance to the King—at the rate, so Cornwallis later testified, of 300 to 400 a day. Congress was so anxious about the presence of British troops on the Delaware that it had left the Pennsylvania capital for safer quarters farther south. As president, John Hancock had issued a desperate panic appeal to Americans to save Philadelphia, justifying Washington's retreat as technical and asserting "that essential services have been already rendered us by foreign states. . . ."

It sounded pretty shrill coming, as it did, on top of other dramatic moves by the rebel leadership to raise men to fight a revolution for which many Americans did not feel much enthusiasm. One province had been forced to introduce compulsory conscription to make its contribution to Washington's army; two others had set up incentive schemes. There were reports that some recruits had been driven into battle at gunpoint. In addition, the weakening resolution in the conflict with the King was revealed in the narrower voting on resistance motions in their provincial congresses.

The Howes were not just waging a military war—which they were clearly winning—they were putting down a revolution inspired by militants. That was why they kept proclaiming the King's offer to redress the grievances of his colonial subjects, and it was fairly obvious that they were winning the political battle as well.

To cap it all, a dragoon patrol had just captured Major General Charles Lee, second-in-command of what was left of the rebel army and, after Washington himself, the most experienced military leader they possessed. To the British Lee was in a very special category, for he was an English soldier who had served with credit in Europe in the British army, in which, as Howe understood it, he was still technically an officer.

If there was any doubt about the punishment that would be meted out to the other revolutionary leaders, there was little speculation in the minds of British High Command about the fate due to Lee. He was a traitor. Even before Lexington, Gage had been instructed to arrest him on the specific orders of the King. The only thing that deterred Howe from ordering his immediate court-martial, which would inevitably sentence him to death for treason, was Lee's insistence that he had formally resigned from the British army. The commander in chief wrote home to Germain for legal guidance, pointing out acidly that his exchange-of-prisoner arrangements with Washington did not extend to deserters.

Meanwhile, he decided to suspend offensive operations until the spring. He gave orders for the chain of posts he had mentioned to Clinton to be set up across New Jersey for the winter, though following the British advance to the Delaware, this reached to Trenton, which was farther south than he had originally intended. Eighty miles long it was, Howe conceded to Germain, "rather too extensive," but he was relying on "the strength of the corps placed in the advanced posts" and on the evident goodwill of the New Jerseymen.

Clearly, under Howe's policy of steadily broadening the territory he controlled, it was advisable to hold Jersey. Also, the Loyalists needed British protection; if he withdrew his army they would be badly persecuted by the rebels, not encouraging the loyal Americans in other areas to declare themselves.

Obviously, Trenton was the most exposed of the posts, but it was protected by a broad river and was manned by a Hessian corps that had proved themselves in battle and that was commanded by an officer who had led the assault on Fort Washington very ably. There were two other posts nearby, at Bordentown and Princeton, which could send quick aid if necessary.

Only one factor must have made the general pause before completing his plans: Even though Washington was across the river in Pennsylvania, New Jersey was by no means settled—a situation that was aggravated, according to disgruntled Loyalists, by the inevitable indiscriminate plundering of Howe's troops, who were not too concerned about the political sympathies of the owners of the homes they pillaged.

Certainly, roving rebel bands were attacking sentries and small bodies of troops that might be on the move between posts. They were raiding British supplies on some scale. On December 11 a militia company swooped on Woodbridge, at the center of the British line, and drove off as many as 400 head of cattle and 200 sheep. Only the next day, because of the hostility of the "peasant canaille," as one Hessian officer called them, Howe issued an order that any un-uniformed men who fired on his soldiers would be "hanged without trial as assassins."

However, he was clearly in a genial mood. It was the end of a campaign. He was on his way to his mistress in New York, which, with Philadelphia, was the nearest the provincials had to a sophisticated town on the European pattern. Christmas on Manhattan would be a welcome change after weeks in the fields.

It was two o'clock on the freezing morning of December 27 when, so recorded Engineering Lieutenant Archibald Robertson, a rider galloped down the darkened main street of Amboy, the New Jersey port that lay just across the mouth of the Raritan from Staten Island. He carried an express from General Grant at the New Jersey regional headquarters at New Brunswick that was alarming: The rebels had crossed the Delaware and attacked Trenton. The commander, Colonel Johann Rall, and his Hessian garrison of more than 1,000 men had all been killed or taken prisoner, except for only 53 men who had escaped.

It was not the attack so much as its total success against experienced troops that was so shocking to the British officers who learned of it as the news was carried north. Rall had broken with traditional defense techniques; he had built no fortifications.

Another messenger left Amboy immediately for New York to alert Howe. For although the rebels had retired across the Delaware, it was obvious they would soon return.

Cornwallis, who hurriedly canceled last-minute plans to return to England, was ordered into New Jersey. On New Year's Day he rode 50 miles to Princeton, which, according to strong rumors, was Washington's next target. By then the Hessians had dropped back there from Bordentown, and big reinforcements had marched south from New Brunswick.

Cornwallis arrived that night to find the town tensed for attack. That morning there had been a skirmish as the rebels, already in Trenton, had approached the pickets. He wasted no time; immediately, in the darkness, he pushed forward his outposts. Before daylight he was marching in heavy rain through the thick mud of the Trenton road with more than 7,000 men and an artillery train of twenty-eight guns. Strong flanking columns made their way through fields on each side.

Behind him in Princeton, he had left a rear guard of 1,200 men.

Now, as they passed through Maidenhead on their way south, he left a garrison to hold the village.

At ten o'clock in the morning, a mile south of Maidenhead, his advance corps came on Washington's outposts. The rebels contested the approach to Trenton very fiercely, and the heavy going slowed up Cornwallis' main body. It was not until late afternoon that the British were in the town, still moving forward slowly under heavy musket fire from the cover of the houses.

Washington had set up his main defense line on a ridge just outside Trenton to the south of the Assumpink Creek, which flowed through the town into the Delaware. By the time the British had fought their way to the creek daylight was fading.

Cornwallis discussed tactics with his senior officers. One of them, Sir William Erskine, according to an unofficial source, favored a night attack across the creek, but the others, arguing that the rebels were trapped against the semifrozen Delaware, advised a morning assault in daylight.

However, the rebels were not trapped. The river and the creek formed two sides of a triangle, and Cornwallis, according to the ever-critical Clinton, who called his failure to act "the most consummate ignorance I have ever heard of [in] any officer above a corporal," should have pushed troops across the creek to form the third which would have boxed in the rebels. Instead, Cornwallis decided to wait until dawn. All night, fires marked the three-mile rebel line on the hill on the other side of the creek. The British pickets could hear the sound of spades as their working parties built more entrenchments.

One young ensign, so Clinton noted with disgust, thought he saw the rebels on the move as "Washington . . . filed off before his fires and not behind them." But if he reported his suspicions, no one took any notice.

By sunrise it was obvious that the rebels were no longer there. And the distant sound of cannon fire from the direction of Princeton indicated very clearly where they were.

There were two roads from Trenton to Princeton: the main route through Maidenhead, along which Cornwallis had advanced the previous day, and a far longer back road through Allentown. It was this that Washington had taken during the night.

Cornwallis ordered an immediate march back to Princeton on the main road. Very soon he learned on the route that his rear guard in the college town, greatly outnumbered by the rebels, had been badly mauled. Taken by surprise, one group had fought their way through the rebels to escape to Maidenhead. Others had fled along the road to New Brunswick. A number had been taken prisoner.

In tactical military terms, Cornwallis faced crisis. As he was only too aware, if the rebels made a quick strike north to New Brunswick, only a few hundred British troops remained to defend the magazines and the military chest that contained £70,000 in cash.

By late morning his advance corps had passed through Maidenhead and had checked on the hill overlooking Stony Brook, which lay in a valley just south of Princeton. A rebel working party was breaking down a bridge over a creek. Guns were rushed forward to disperse the rebels, but Cornwallis would consider no delay while the bridge was repaired. He ordered the infantry to wade the icy chest-deep stream while his engineers reconstructed the crossing for the artillery.

At noon the British forward units entered the Princeton outskirts just as the rebel rear guard was leaving on the road to New Brunswick. The dragoons and the light infantry moved on after them to harry them, but there were not enough of them to fight a battle. It was late afternoon by the time Cornwallis' main column was in the town and formed ready to advance. Anxiously, he pressed on after the rebels along the road to New Brunswick.

But Washington evidently was not aiming for the British regional headquarters, at least not by the main road; he branched north across the Millstone River "into strong country," as the official British report put it. "Lord Cornwallis, seeing it could not answer any purpose to continue his pursuit, returned to Brunswick."

Two days later Cornwallis wrote to London that Washington was at Morristown. "He cannot subsist long where he is," he said optimistically. "I should imagine that he means to repass the Delaware at Alexandria. The season of the year would make it difficult for us to follow him, but the march alone will destroy his army."

This was a big overstatement. The rebels remained in Jersey, raided Elizabethtown and Hackensack, until Howe decided to maintain winter posts only at New Brunswick and Amboy.

Truly, Trenton and Princeton, though Washington had executed them skillfully, were only skirmishes. The push beyond New Brunswick always had been a bonus, and the military situation was now very little different from what Howe had planned at the end of November.

Their main impact was as a morale booster for the rebels, but to the British in New York, this seemed fairly minimal. "The British cause in America," wrote a correspondent to William Eden in London, "certainly does not depend on the conduct of a Hessian Colonel. . . . I saw yesterday a man from Philadelphia who says this affair highly raised a few and but a few. The generality continue dispirited; they see their Congress fled . . . their armies much dispersed . . . their jails full, masters and families and servants forced into the army. . . . The back of the snake is broken. She can never recover to hurt but may hiss a little before she gets to her hole and dies. . . ."

To Howe, it was a minor setback—for which, with some reason, he completely blamed Colonel Rall—"the only disagreeable occurrence that has happened this campaign."

Across the Atlantic, however, it did not seem quite as insignificant—especially in the Palace of Versailles.

12

VERSAILLES, January 28, 1777

The Comte de Vergennes,[1] France's skillful Foreign Minister, "paused for a moment," so British Ambassador Lord Stormont reported to London. "Then he said with a serious and even melancholy tone: 'You cannot conceive what engines are at work, what wheels within wheels!' "

It was a diplomatic tactic to evade Stormont's blunt charge that five ships were at that moment loading in French ports with arms for Britain's American rebels. Vergennes' suggestion that he was enmeshed in a web of court intrigue he could not control was just another move in the highly sophisticated game the two men played very frequently, often several times a week, in the massive Palace of Versailles.

Their conversations, invariably polite, civilized, even witty, were always conducted under the shadow of the threat of major war. The maneuvering was not confined to talking. Many of Stormont's letters home were phrased especially for French spies; that is why two reports to London sent on the same day by different couriers could sometimes contradict each other.

The British were exceptionally well informed of Vergennes' undercover support for the rebels. It was now six months since a onetime schoolteacher named Silas Deane had arrived in Paris, the first agent to be sent to France by the Congress' Committee of Secret Correspondence to negotiate assistance for the rebel cause.

Deane had appointed as his secretary an American, William Bancroft, who had once been his pupil and was now a London-based financial speculator.

Accustomed as he was to living on his wits, Bancroft had quickly perceived the potential in his new association with the Congressional agent and promptly offered his services to the British, which were accepted under an agreement that gave him £500 down and an income of £400 a year. For this he reported regularly on Deane's contacts with the French to the British Secret Service's Paul Wentworth, another American living in London. Using the cover name of "Dr. Edwards," he left his reports in a hollow tree in the Terrace des Tuileries, where Stormont arranged their collection for dispatch to London.

Within days of Deane's first interview with Vergennes at Versailles, the British had full verbatim details of the meeting. The American had told the French minister that news of the Declaration of Independence would arrive shortly in Europe. Congress sought alliance with France. Would the French court recognize the American provinces as independent states?

Vergennes, one of the most experienced and brilliant diplomats in Europe, was not being rushed. The Independence Declaration, he said, was an event "in the womb of time"; at present recognition was out of the question, for it would provoke immediate war with Britain. However, he remarked carefully, "if the Colonies are determined to reject the sovereignty of His Britannic Majesty, it would not be in the interest of France to see them reduced by force."

The American Revolution offered obvious opportunities to a French Foreign Minister who planned revenge for his country's humiliation ten years before. But he was not yet ready for open conflict. He agreed to support the rebels but insisted on great caution. After the first interview in the palace, all future meetings with Deane were arranged secretly in the home of the minister's secretary.

Since the French court could not expose itself to charges that it was aiding Britain's rebels officially, a private company took over the role of secret supplier of arms, cannon and clothing. Its somewhat bizarre president was the dramatist Pierre de Beaumarchais, author of *The Barber of Seville*.

Beaumarchais' ships sailed for America with false papers, which concealed both the cargoes and the destination; usually they were routed technically to Santo Domingo in the Caribbean.

The cover was not very effective since Bancroft informed the British of every detail from the start. Naturally, Stormont had not revealed the extent of his knowledge—he was far too subtle a diplomat—but from time to time in his sparring with Vergennes, he had hinted at the range of information that was being garnered by British agents.

Beaumarchais' company was not the only corporation in Europe supplying the rebels. Despite repeated protests by Britain's ambassadors to the courts of Europe, American vessels were often in Continental ports loading with munitions before making a dash across the Atlantic through the blockade of royal cruisers.

Stormont had often complained before, but this meeting in January between the two diplomats was tenser than usual despite the diplomatic pleasantries. For there was a novel and alarming aspect about the ships that were now taking on board those controversial cargoes: They would not be flying the American striped flag from their mastheads, but sailing under French colors, manned by French crews.

This meant that the French were getting bolder, testing the British closer. Every move that either country made—the repercussions of which were explored in the meetings between Stormont and Vergennes—was performed against the key question: Just how far could France go in helping the rebels without causing a complete and explosive rupture with Britain? And just how aggressively could Britain try to stop traffic without producing the same result?

The European political background was growing continually more critical for Britain. Regularly in Parliament the Whigs flayed ministers with bitter criticism for sending so much of their strength across the Atlantic when the danger of attack from the Continent was so imminent.

This was not merely militant politics; the risk was grave. France, a nation with a population three times that of Britain, was arming and building up its fleet at an alarming rate. Count Pedro Aranda, the Spanish ambassador in Paris, made little secret of his desire for joint attack on the British and hoped, indeed, to command his country's military forces.

Locked in a major war across 3,500 miles of ocean, Britain had no friends left in Europe except Portugal. Facing the rising hostility of the Bourbon Kings of France and Spain, the most it could hope for from the Hapsburg Joseph of Austria, since he was the brother of Marie Antoinette, was to keep his nation out of any conflict that France might initiate.

Catherine of Russia had already refused with blunt rudeness to lend King George any troops. Shortly Frederick of Prussia, who had been unhappy with his rewards at the end of the Seven Years'

George III.
This portrait was painted some seven years before the Boston Tea Party.
(National Portrait Gallery)

Frederick, Lord North.
(National Portrait Gallery)

General William Howe,
created Sir William after the Battle of Long Island.
(National Portrait Gallery)

SIR HENRY CLINTON, K.B.

Commander in Chief of his Majesty's Forces in North America.

London, Publish'd 8th October 1780, for Watson & Dickinson Nº 158, New Bond Street.

Sir Henry Clinton.
(National Portrait Gallery)

Vice-Admiral Lord Richard Howe.
(National Portrait Gallery)

Lord George Germain.
(Captain Nigel Stopford-Sackville and The Courtauld Institute of Art)

General John Burgoyne.
(National Portrait Gallery)

Charles, Earl Cornwallis.
(National Portrait Gallery)

Colonel Banastre Tarleton.

War, was to make his position coldly clear by withholding his permission for Hessian reinforcements to cross his territory on their way to America.

In Paris the idea of war with Britain was welcomed by the public. Benjamin Franklin had recently arrived to add his prestigious support to Silas Deane's negotiating team and had been given an ecstatic reception both by the court at Versailles and by Parisian society. In a few weeks the young Marquis de Lafayette, a member of one of France's top families, was to sail for America with a group of officers to offer his services to Congress.

The mood of the French was dangerous enough without further complications, but poor Stormont had the added difficulty that at Versailles at the center of this ever-changing power complex was a sexually impotent, slow-witted young king and a strong-willed but utterly frivolous queen.

For although Marie Antoinette paid "no great attention" to politics, she was keenly interested in her personal power, which she could use to reward friends by deploying her influence with the King.

One of her protégés was M. de Sartines, the War Minister. "He is a master of little cabal and intrigue . . . ," warned Stormont. "He inclines to hostile measures. . . ."

Against this background of diplomatic brinkmanship, the degree of pressure it was politic for Stormont to lever depended to a large extent on the news of Howe's armies. And on that day in late January when he called on Vergennes at Versailles to complain about the French arms ships the news was particularly favorable.

The latest dispatches from New York had reported the successful and easy storming of Fort Washington and the rapid retreat of the rebels through New Jersey under pursuit by Cornwallis. A letter from Clinton which had just arrived told of taking Rhode Island without a single casualty.

After the string of British victories through the summer, the prospects for the revolutionaries seemed very dim, so Stormont was more aggressive than usual, pressing Vergennes to take action to curb Beaumarchais' activities.

Blandly Vergennes denied all knowledge of the ships and offered to make inquiries of M. de Sartines, the War Minister. But this time the ambassador refused to let him sidestep the issue and virtually accused him of lying. "It's well known in the Palace," he insisted, according to his report, "that Beaumarchais directs the whole of this enterprise and that he . . . has frequent interviews with Franklin and Deane."

He had reason to believe that the arms ships were not bound for Santo Domingo, their usual fictitious destination, but for America. "Suffering the Rebels to be supplied with ammunition," he insisted, "is contrary to the friendship this Court has professed for us. . . ."

Boldly he bared the Santo Domingo cover story. A few weeks back an English man-of-war had stopped a ship that was routed there and on board found nearly 30,000 French-made uniforms. It would be impossible, he argued, to suppose that so many were "designed for the garrison."

"What!" exclaimed the minister, "do they send uniforms ready made up?" But his expression suggested that Sartines and Beaumarchais, with their "engines" and their "wheels within wheels," were going too far. He took the ambassador into his confidence by hinting at his problems in the council. *"Nous avons aussi,"* he said, *"notre opposition."*

But the ships went on loading. Repeatedly Stormont protested, and repeatedly Vergennes, smiling disarmingly, insisting he had difficulties with his colleagues, sympathized, evaded, offered to make further inquiries.

Three weeks later, on February 25, Stormont stalked through the corridors of the palace with even greater cause for complaint: The American privateer *Reprisal* had gone into the French port of L'Orient, taking with her four English ships she had captured. Stormont demanded that the French government hand over the prizes to their British owners and take steps to stop rebel privateers from raiding the sea lanes from French coastal waters.

Vergennes appeared deeply disturbed by the news, of which he was, he said, completely unaware. He would send an immediate instruction to L'Orient that the *Reprisal* and her captures must "instantly put to sea."

By that day, however, news had just arrived from America that was not quite so favorable to British diplomacy. Stormont was angered to see the accounts of Trenton and Princeton greeted rapturously by the French and exploited by Franklin and Deane to seem like great victories instead of skirmishes.

At Versailles, Stormont explained to Vergennes "the utter falsehood of the reports which the Rebel agents had so industri-

ously propagated here and which were so greedily received . . .
speaking to him always upon the supposition of his being pleased
with our successes." Vergennes, Stormont reported, "told me
indeed that he never had given credit to these reports and I know
he has said as much to others. He seemed struck when I told him
that in six weeks our fleets had taken over 200 American ships."

All the same, despite the smooth assurances, there were signs
that the rebels' fast winter raids in New Jersey had caused a new
hardening in the attitude of the French court that had begun to
soften slightly under the British successes of the autumn. Even by
March 18, nearly a month after Stormont's protest, the *Reprisal*
and her prizes were still in port at L'Orient, despite repeated
British complaints and Vergennes' insistence that he had instructed them to sail. Worse, the British ships had been sold and were
now being fitted out to run ammunition under French colors
across the Atlantic. In addition, only a few days before, two other
vessels had left Le Havre, "cleared out for St. Domingo," laden
with cannon.

Stormont demanded repeated audiences with the Foreign Minister, but although he was given the same courteous reception by
Vergennes, he achieved no tangible results.

"Suppose, Sir," the ambassador challenged, "any of our cruisers
meet with these ships carrying French colors and manned with
French sailors?"

"Your cruisers will take them," answered Vergennes lightly as
though the matter were truly simple. Then he added quickly:
"You would restore to us the sailors."

By the end of the month the veneer on the relationship was
wearing thin. "Notwithstanding all the friendly professions of this
court," Stormont wrote home furiously, "the secret succour to
the Rebels not only continues, but increases."

By then the rumors at Versailles were growing more sinister.
Silas Deane began to visit Versailles more often—"he was there no
less than four times this week"—and Stormont was working
desperately hard to discover if there was any truth in the stories
circulating through the palace that the French were about to sign a
formal treaty with Congress. Inevitably this would mean recognition of an independent America—and, of course, war.

The rebel contacts with the Spanish were ominous, too. Arthur
Lee, one of the Congressional agents, was now in Madrid for talks,
according to information at the British embassy. He had written to

Paris that he had had "assurances not only of money but of every other assistance. Let France but begin, say the Spaniards, and we are ready to follow."

"It is certain, My Lord," Stormont warned Secretary of State Lord Weymouth, "that the general animosity against us and the wild enthusiasm in favor of the rebels was never greater than it is at present . . . that M. de Vergennes is hostile in his heart and anxious for the success of the Rebels I have not a shadow of a doubt."

Events were becoming critical, and Franklin and Deane were now exploiting them by indicating to Stormont, through contacts they had in common, that they were open to a peace deal with the British. "Their language," he reported, "is that England should make some fair proposal and make it before they have thrown themselves into the arms of France. I have a strong suspicion that there is much artifice in all this. Perhaps they want to carry in their hands some proposal from us when they get to treat with this Court."

Certainly the French government had suddenly become ultra-nervous about the danger of a British attack coupled with a deal with the rebels. At Versailles, according to Stormont's spies, ministers challenged Deane with double-dealing and "were not satisfied until he denied it in the strongest and most positive terms."

When the news arrived in France that the British had put in commission five more ships of the line, it "spread a great alarm at Versailles; the general cry was that it was now evident that England meant a sudden attack." Promptly the Cabinet reacted to the crisis by ordering the arming of seven men-of-war, although in fact the British move had no anti-French design: The ships were destined for America, where Howe was demanding reinforcements.

The rising tension led once more to some plain speaking by Stormont at the Palace of Versailles—this time with the Comte de Maurepas, the French Prime Minister. It was a significant and important meeting.

France, the Premier warned him carefully, would clearly have to yield soon to heavy pressure from the Spanish government to send a defensive fleet to the Caribbean. Stormont was astonished at the implication. The British had trouble enough on the other side of the Atlantic. "It's impossible," he argued, "that they should believe that either the French or Spanish islands are in the least danger of attack from us."

Maurepas did not think it was so impossible. There were suspicions, he said, that Britain was planning to give the rebels favorable terms "providing [*sic*] they immediately join . . . in an attack upon the French settlement in the West Indies."

Indignantly Stormont refuted the French fears and exploited his chance to complain again about the glowing reception at Versailles of rebel agents who declared openly that they were about to sign a treaty with France. Only one article, he challenged, seemed to be holding it up: French insistence that they should never make peace with England, no matter how favorable the terms might be, without the express permission from Versailles.

" 'It's not true! It's not true,' said M. de Maurepas repeatedly. . . . 'That's not the article that prevents any treaty with them. I will tell you what the article is: It is that of their independency. We have repeatedly told them: You call yourselves an independent state, but you are not so. . . . At present you are at war with your sovereign who by no means admits the independency you assume. If you become a free independent state like Holland, we will then make any treaty of friendship or commerce that shall be for our mutual advantage. . . .

" 'Still, I do not imagine,' he continued with a smile, 'that you will be in haste to grant them that independency.' "

It was an assurance that, even though it came from the French King's principal minister, Stormont could hardly believe. All his other evidence carried a very clear message: Unless Britain stamped out the Revolution before the end of the year, the danger of a French attack would be very acute indeed.

It was April, 1777—the year, as a Whig satirist was to dub it because of the gibbet shape of the 7's, of "the triple gallows." By then Britain's plans to quell the revolt before the end of the year were completed in London and already in motion.

In December Major General John Burgoyne had arrived back in London after serving as second-in-command under Carleton in the operations against Arnold on Lake Champlain. He had not been home more than a few days before his detailed campaign proposals for an advance on America from Canada lay on Germain's desk.

Burgoyne's plan conformed with the overall design that the King and his senior officers had framed from a very early point in the Revolution: two combined movements along the Hudson from Lake Champlain in the north and from New York in the south, thus cutting off New England from the rest of the American provinces.

The general did not specifically propose himself as the commander of the northern army, but the profile he drew of the ideal man to head the expedition fitted him so exactly that no doubt was left that this was what he had in mind.

Burgoyne was an interesting character, combining a flair for living on his wits with more solid talents. He was a good and courageous cavalry commander; he wrote well—in fact one of his plays was attributed to Sheridan—and he was brilliant at cards. At fifty-five he was still strikingly handsome, elegant and popular with everybody—women, men and, particularly, his soldiers. All the areas at which he excelled provided opportunities for personal display; Burgoyne was a performer—which is why he was far more suited to leading cavalry than to commanding an army.

Successful generals needed the panoply of leadership, which Burgoyne certainly had, and the faith of their soldiers that went with it, but essentially they were background figures. They did not charge the enemy; they directed. Victories were won by careful control of such elements as strategy and organization, and it was here that Burgoyne was weak.

It is strange that he did not recognize this, for he was a highly intelligent man. His progressive and humanitarian ideas on leading men, for example, were completely novel. He did his utmost to eliminate flogging and even swearing at the soldiers. He gave formal orders that they should be treated as "thinking beings" and urged his officers to have "the occasional joke" with them.

Burgoyne's meteoric success, though it came comparatively late, was phenomenal, for his background was limited. His overextravagant father was only the second son of a baronet, and in a privileged society dominated by the peerage, this was not exactly ideal as a starting base for an ambitious young man. But "Johnny" Burgoyne had a flair for getting on with influential people and a deep capacity for friendships. Many of his friends remained close to him throughout his somewhat erratic life; one of the first, whom he met at school, was the eldest son of the powerful Earl of Derby. In time this was to prove an enormous advantage, although temporarily it severely hampered his career opportunities, for he fell in love with the earl's daughter as a young dragoon officer and impetuously eloped with her.

He resigned his commission, though reports differ on whether this was forced by his angry father-in-law or by rash play at the card table where he had not yet perfected his skill, and for seven years lived in semidisgrace on the Continent. Eventually, Derby forgave him and deployed his immense influence to help him.

In career terms it was a late start—he was thirty-four when he rejoined the army—but he was ready for his opportunity when it came. He was appointed to organize the newly formed regiment of mobile light dragoons, which the British were to use very successfully in America, and he was ideally equipped to do it.

Burgoyne was highly successful, both with his regiment and at court, where the two kings he served were keen soldiers. George II honored him; George III, as the press regularly announced, was always reviewing his troops. His new ascendancy was sealed when in 1762 he took his dragoons to help Britain's ally Portugal fight the invading Spanish. The performance of his regiment was spectacular. The King of Portugal was delighted with him, gave him honors and a diamond ring. He returned to London a hero.

By the time the American Revolution broke out he was completely established. He had easy access to the King. His relationship with his powerful father-in-law had ripened into a solid friendship. He was a Member of Parliament and on the short list for senior military command.

Furthermore, Carleton's decision not to risk storming Ticonderoga so late in the fall had been a disappointment in Whitehall—especially since Burgoyne, while being careful never to criticize Carleton, made it clear that he himself had recommended an attack. It seemed that a general with just a little more spark and energy was needed to command the combat force.

The time for "Gentleman Johnny," as he was known by his troops, had arrived. On December 13, just after he had landed in England, the King wrote to Lord North that "Burgoyne may command the corps to be sent from Canada." Two months later, after the general had revised his operational plan, it was submitted formally to the Cabinet. By then the ministers also knew Howe's proposals for the coming season—which arrived in the same ship as the dispatches reporting the depressing news of Trenton and Princeton.

Originally, Howe had suggested a strategy similar to Burgoyne's

—two movements north and south along the Hudson—in addition to a secondary attack on Boston from the base he had already set up on Rhode Island. New England would then be ringed by British posts.

But now Howe changed his mind. He had seen Jerseymen pouring into the towns to sign the oath of allegiance to the King and since he was assured that the loyalism of Pennsylvania was even stronger, his new plan was to make a quick strike south across the Delaware for Philadelphia and to use only limited forces on the southern Hudson "to facilitate in some degree the approach of the Army in Canada." From Philadelphia he would be ideally positioned for his followup plan in the fall—a campaign in the mild winter weather to stamp out the last embers of revolt in the Southern provinces.

There was logic in Howe's suggestion. He always thought in terms of carefully spreading the territory he controlled because this enabled him to administer it properly. His plan to absorb Jersey and Pennsylvania fitted this pattern of thinking, especially since their underlying loyalty should make them easy to police.

He was not particularly concerned by the fact that his new proposals provided no big force to move up the Hudson to meet the advance from the north. For he took the view,[2] which was proved correct, that since he commanded the main British army, Washington must move to oppose him wherever he attacked. By driving south for Philadelphia, he would draw the rebel force away from the British strike from Canada.

Clearly the rebel commander would be able to spare only a very limited detachment from the Continental Army to go north, relying mainly on the militia to defend the upper Hudson, and the militia, though they had been effective on the Concord road and Bunker Hill, had since been unimpressive in battle; if their response to an approaching army was anything like that of the New Jerseymen, very few of them would report for duty anyway.

In London, both plans seemed acceptable. But the big problem that the Cabinet faced was not so much Howe's proposal to go south as his demand for reinforcements. He had asked for 20,000 more troops. Germain promised him 7,800 men but was unable to meet even this limited target; fewer than 3,000 men sailed for New York.

Meanwhile, plans for the northern army progressed fast. Burgoyne hammered out the final details with Christian D'Oyly, Deputy Secretary at War, and took them personally to the King, who gave his formal agreement to both operations. The two commanders were each fully informed of what the other was planning to do. Burgoyne's orders specifically required him to proceed down the Hudson to Albany and there to place himself under the command of Howe, but Howe was going to Philadelphia and might not be there to meet him.

This suggests a contradiction in the orders, and unquestionably they were very vague; but almost certainly the key to what appears to be extraordinarily muddled thinking lay primarily in the timing. Howe planned to go south in the spring and intended a "quick" operation. He did not expect the northern army to be at Albany "until September," some four months after the start of the campaigning season. If it *did* prove necessary to support the strike from Canada, there would be plenty of time to send troops north. The important action would be staged in Pennsylvania, for Howe now realized that to extinguish the revolt finally he must annihilate the rebel army in battle. This was now his purpose.

As for Germain, who issued the formal approval of the campaign proposals, he wanted action. He lived in a state of perpetual frustration; events, motivated both by men and by God, were always delaying his bellicose plans. "Do we now need two winds for a ship to sail?" he demanded disgustedly when he heard that a vessel had not left for America despite a favorable breeze. Now, at least, he was being offered aggressive operations on two fronts. His belligerent and energetic effort through the winter had succeeded in forcing some results out of Britain's antiquated supply machine. Recalling his difficulties of the previous year when Quebec lay under siege, he had bludgeoned the Lords of the Admiralty for ships and had levered heavy pressure on the other government departments responsible for equipping and manning the northern army. By the end of March, preparations were nearing completion. Soon troops would be ready to sail, and astonishingly, there would be transports waiting to take them.

Burgoyne wasted no time. At Almack's Club, he had bet Charles James Fox 25 guineas that he would be back in England by Christmas Day. "Be not over-sanguine," cautioned the politician, "I believe when you return to England you will be a prisoner on parole."

Burgoyne had laughed it off. Now with the command of an army of nearly 8,000 men, it seemed an even more groundless warning.

On March 26, only twenty-four hours after Carlton's instructions were signed in the Colonial Office, Burgoyne drove hurriedly to Plymouth to board the ship that would take him to Canada.

13

LAKE CHAMPLAIN, June 30, 1777

The water was mirror-calm, reflecting the trees, now lush green in the rays of the early sun, at the edge of the forest on the shore. The cloudless morning sky, sharply framing the mountains to the east, was brilliant.[1]

Apart from the signs of high summer, the scene was a repeat performance of Carleton's advance up the lake, then roughened by a northeasterly, the previous fall: the same little gunboats manned by the Hessian gunners; the same bateaux filled, as Lieutenant Thomas Anburey pictured it, with "the mass of British scarlet and German dark blue, the green of the Jagers and the light blue of the dragoons"; the same ships that had fought at Valcour.

Ahead lay Ticonderoga, fashioned by nature as a brilliant defense position where the waters of the miles-wide lake suddenly narrowed to only 400 yards as though giant fingers had pinched the land together, and then twisted to form an S bend. As if this were not enough, it was there through a tiny channel that the waters of Lake George tumbled over 3 miles of rocks and falls to join those of Lake Champlain.

The two lakes reached south through the forests in the form of a V toward the Hudson.

These rugged cliff-bordered narrows formed a gateway from New York to Canada and on both sides were dominated by strong fortifications: on the west by a fort constructed in local blue stone by the French twenty years before; on the east by a big star-shaped redoubt on the peak of a hill that the rebels had named Mount Independence. Across the strip of water between them was a bridge boom, made of chain and timber, supported by anchored gunships.

It was this bastion, which Carleton had hesitated to attack in October, that Burgoyne was now leading his army to storm.

235

He had learned caution from the clash with the hidden Arnold at Valcour the previous year. This time, as he moved his army along the lake from St. Johns, he was taking no chances of sudden attack by an enemy skilled at exploiting the forest. The forward corps was advancing a day ahead of the main army, preparing the camps, clearing surrounding brush to give the sentries a view of the approaches and, where necessary, building minor fortifications.

At the Bouquet River, they had been joined by 400 Indians, whom the general had welcomed on behalf of "The Great King, our common Father" with the formal ceremony they enjoyed.

"Etow! Etow! Etow!" they had roared in acknowledgment. Then, after praising the tribes, Burgoyne warned: "I positively forbid bloodshed when you are not opposed in arms. Aged men, women, children and prisoners must be held sacred from the knife or hatchet . . ."—an order which soon earned the mockery of Edmund Burke in the House of Commons, who said this would have the same effect as telling captive wild animals not to hurt anyone, then opening the doors of their cages. Indeed within three days, according to the Hessian General von Riedesel, Indians had ignored Burgoyne's order and scalped ten prisoners from a rebel reconnaissance detachment.

The use of "savages," bitterly criticized by the Whigs in London, even though they had been employed in previous major conflicts in North America, was regarded by Burgoyne and his officers as essential to forest operations. They had a big talent for scouting and could move through thick forest, judging their direction from the tops of the taller trees whose foliage was worn by the prevailing winds from the north. Their highly developed sense of smell could detect the smoke of enemy fires at great distances, and they could read the tracks on a woodland path with an exactness Burgoyne's Loyalist woodsmen could not approach.

However, they were soon to be a great embarrassment to the commander. Their brutality was often impossible to control, and very frequently they were drunk.

At Crown Point, where Arnold had beached and burned his vessels nine months before, Burgoyne assembled his army, waiting for the stragglers who had been delayed in their voyage up the lake by thunderstorms.

Meanwhile, his forward detachments were probing the approaches to Ticonderoga, assessing the defenses, seizing prisoners to discover the size and nature of the garrison, which they soon found out was held by nearly 4,000 men—mostly New Englanders.

As he waited at Crown Point, with the rebel reconnaissance boats on the lake keeping just out of cannon-shot but watching his movements, Burgoyne was optimistic; his army was not as large as he had originally hoped, but it consisted primarily of professional soldiers and was led by competent and experienced senior officers.

In command of the 3,000 Hessians who formed nearly half his army was thirty-nine-year-old Major General von Riedesel, a tubby, cheerful German whose battle record in Europe was outstanding. All winter in Canada Von Riedesel had been training his men in forest fighting and in long-range firing because he "perceived that the American riflemen always shot further than our forces."

The British units were led by Major General William Phillips, a fat veteran artillery officer, now serving as a general officer. Phillips was Clinton's closest friend, and like him, a professional military snob arrogantly proud of the fact that he had acquired his early battle experience in Germany.

From Burgoyne's viewpoint, however, he was a strong asset—a competent, hard-driving, blood-and-guts general. In his enthusiasm as artillery commander at the Battle of Minden, according to one story, he broke fifteen canes over the backs of his horse teams as he galloped the guns onto the field.

At the head of the advance corps, which included the Indians, was forty-eight-year-old Brigadier Simon Fraser, a Scot who had served under Wolfe in the Seven Years' War and taken part in the sieges of Quebec and Louisburg. Burgoyne, who had fought with him before, had specially requested that he should join his army.

But though his combat troops gave him confidence, Burgoyne had substantial problems. Even if in London he had not known about Howe's plans for Philadelphia, he was in no doubt about them now. A letter to Carleton from New York reached Quebec only two days after he did: All he could expect in the way of support from the south was a limited movement against the New York highlands. Not that this appeared to give the new commander in chief much anxiety; later he claimed he assumed Germain would order Howe to revise his strategy, but if this was the case, it was an assumption he kept to himself. And the extrovert Burgoyne was not normally a man to keep silent on so basic an issue.

Far more important than the junction with the army from New York was the critical situation of his supply and transport arrangements—a factor vital to any force operating, as Burgoyne's would be, with very long lines of communication. Yet this appears to have been strangely low down his list of priorities; only after he had been in Canada a month did he suddenly seem to realize that although he had ample trains of cannon and equipment, he had only limited means of moving them, at least overland. Hurriedly he formally demanded that Carleton issue supply contracts for 500 wagons, together with 1,000 horses to pull them, and another 400 animals to make up his gun teams. Even if these were ready i y the start of his campaign in a few weeks' time, which was expecting a lot, he knew they would be inadequate to his needs, but he planned to commandeer more on the march. Finally, he had been unable to raise Canadian labor in anything like the numbers he had expected.

As a result, Burgoyne was about to advance hundreds of miles through rugged country into America without enough carts, horses or men to drive them. He was relying mainly on lakes and rivers to transport most of his equipment; but there were considerable land gaps between the stretches of water, and he did not have enough boats. By now he was only too conscious of the weakness of his supply system and knew that his men would have to live off the land to a greater extent than armies normally did.

As Burgoyne prepared his first big strike against the rebels from Lake Champlain, his subplan was already in motion. A detachment of several hundred men was on its way up the St. Lawrence under Colonel Barry St. Leger to Oswego, on the south bank of Lake Ontario, where it would rendezvous with 1,000 Indians under the famous chief Thayendanegea, as well as two corps of bitter Loyalists, before sweeping down the Mohawk River to approach the Hudson from the west.

It was, in fact, part of a three-pronged attack plan, for Burgoyne intended to send other troops to make a feint at Vermont while his main force advanced south.

The rebels, faced with actual attacks from the west and north *and* a threatened drive east for New England, would be forced to spread their very limited forces and thus weaken themselves on the route to Albany, where Burgoyne would launch his main weight.

On June 30, at Crown Point, Burgoyne's army was ready for the assault on Ticonderoga. In his cabin aboard the *Royal George,* he wrote his general orders with his dramatist's sense of occasion and an eye on posterity: "The Army," he declared, "embarks tomorrow to approach the enemy. . . . During our progress, occasions may occur, in which nor difficulty, nor labor, nor life are to be regarded. This army must not retreat."

At five the next morning[3] the troops boarded the flatboats. The ships weighed anchor. The flotilla progressed slowly along the 10-mile stretch of water, narrowing all the time, toward Ticonderoga. The boats carrying the British under General Phillips hugged the west bank, the shore they would land on to take the old French fort, while the Germans under Von Riedesel, who were to storm Mount Independence, stayed close to the east bank.

The bigger vessels sailed steadily south in the main channel.

The whole expanse of the lake, which was three miles wide at Crown Point, "was covered with boats or bateaux . . . ," recorded Lieutenant James Hadden, "the music and drums of the different regiments were continually playing. . . ."

By noon troops were ashore on both banks, three miles from their objectives. Burgoyne's ships were anchored just out of range of the rebel cannon. A bridge of flatboats was set up across the water so that he could switch his troops easily from bank to bank as the situation demanded.

For three days the general, who from his HQ on the *Royal George* had a clear view of the operations on both wings, ordered little in the way of serious action. Fraser's men of the advance corps, operating with overexcited and drunken Indians, attacked an outpost on the west bank and forced its defenders back to the main rebel lines. They threatened a highly vulnerable rebel outpost on a hill that dominated the approach waters of Lake George. Isolated, the Americans set fire to their blockhouses and evacuated the hill.

Meanwhile, on the east bank, Von Riedesel's Germans were working closer to the three rows of fortifications below the redoubt on Mount Independence. Reconnaissance parties were reaching around the rear of the hill.

Two gunboats, their oars cutting foam in the still waters of the lake, moved out from the anchorage to explore the possibility of shooting a big enough hole in the rebels' bridge boom for the ships to break through—an operation that would put British cannon on the south. But as they moved within range the rebel guns opened up from both sides, the successive crashes of their explosions echoing between the cliffs that bordered the narrows. Shot splashed all around the gunboats. Their commanders decided that their test mission was impossible and put about and made back to the anchorage.

Burgoyne, as the rebels surely realized, was merely setting up the scene, feeling for the weak points in the defense, tidying up the outposts in preparation for the main action. All night on July 3, possibly because they feared an attack in darkness, the rebel cannon bombarded the British lines on both banks.

By then Fraser's reconnaissance parties had crossed the water that gushed into Champlain from Lake George and were probing south to Sugar Loaf Hill—a rugged square-shaped height, 800 feet above the water, with almost sheer, heavily timbered sides. It was not defended, which was surprising because it overlooked the rebel forts on both sides of the narrows. Presumably, Burgoyne concluded when the facts were reported to him, the American general had assumed it was so steep that it was impassable. He ordered Lieutenant William Twiss, his chief engineer, to explore the possibility of manhandling cannon to the summit.

After careful study of the hill, Twiss reported his view that Burgoyne's proposal was practical. Once the battery was established, the guns would look down onto Fort Ticonderoga from a range of 1,400 yards; even the redoubt on the elevated summit of Mount Independence would only be 1,500 yards away *and* 400 feet below them.

The rebels' error was of colossal proportions—so fundamental that it convinced Burgoyne, as he was to write home a few days later, "that they have no men of military science." And he was about to exploit the opening they had left him.

All the next day working parties under the vigorous personal driving of General Phillips cut a track for the gun carriages up the steep mountainside, which was thick with maples and evergreens and obstructed by huge boulders. "Where a goat can go, a man can go," Phillips had declaimed jubilantly when he heard Twiss' report, "and where a man can go he can drag a gun."

This was not quite true. For at parts of the track where

presumably the men could "go," they had to dismantle the cannon and sling them forward from the branches of the trees. By sunset, however, two 12-pounders were being set up on the summit of Sugar Loaf Hill.[4] From their high position, the gun crews could select their targets within the walls of Fort Ticonderoga.

It was over—without a siege, without even a charge. One of the world's supreme natural defense positions, which the rebels had spent a year fortifying and Arnold had given them nine months to strengthen by holding Carleton at Valcour, was no longer defendable. It was about to fall to Gentleman Johnny Burgoyne without his agile gunners even firing a salvo from their new position. And the all-important psychological effect of the news—both on rebel morale and on the complex maneuvering in Paris and Madrid—was to be greater even than that of Trenton.

According to Horace Walpole, George III rushed into the Queen's apartment shouting: "I have beat them, I have beat all the Americans." In the House of Commons, Lord George Germain announced the capture of the famous fort as though it were the deathblow of the revolt.

At Ticonderoga on the afternoon of July 5, with his guns on Sugar Loaf Hill, Burgoyne was planning the climax. Von Riedesel's divisions were trying to work their way around a big swamp to block the garrison's escape route by land—the road that led from Mount Independence to Castleton to the east. But darkness fell before they could gain it.

There was another avenue of retreat for the rebel garrison—by water down the lake. But Burgoyne was relying on his ships to deal with that one.

All that night the rebel cannon were firing, causing the waiting men of Burgoyne's army to wonder whether they were merely taking precautions against a night attack or planning a desperate assault. For flames had suddenly appeared within the old fort, illuminating the blue stone walls, spreading through the log barracks.

As the dawnlight began to streak the sky, three rebel deserters came through the British lines. The garrison, they said, had evacuated both forts. From Mount Independence on the far bank they were retreating down the Castleton road; others from Fort Ticonderoga had already left by boat for Skenesborough, 15 miles south along Lake Champlain.

Carefully, on guard against treachery, the soldiers from the outposts moved through the rebel lines into the old fort, which was now deserted and smoldering. Symbolically they hauled down the striped rebel flag from the masthead and ran up the British colors.

As soon as Burgoyne on the *Royal George* received the news of the evacuation, he ordered Fraser to cross the narrows with his advance corps in pursuit of the retreating rebels on the Castleton road, to the east of Mount Independence. Hurriedly the troops ran across the bridge boom the Americans had constructed across the water, designed to serve also as a barrier to Burgoyne's ships.

The rebel general had anticipated this and had left four men at a gun position to hold the bridge. With grapeshot they could have made it uncrossable, but there was no sign of opposition. The reason soon became clear. "We found them," recorded Lieutenant Anburey, "lying dead drunk by a case of Madeira."

During that hot, sultry day, Fraser's troops, marching light, chased the retreating rebels along a wagon track that curved over a range of short, steep, timbered hills toward Castleton, 20 miles from Ticonderoga. Following more slowly behind him were Von Riedesel and his Hessians, slowed down by their heavy equipment.

Meanwhile, the gunboats had blasted a gap in the bridge boom, and the British vessels were running before a northerly breeze into the southern section of Lake Champlain in close pursuit of those rebels who were attempting escape by water.

By three o'clock in the afternoon the British ships were nearing Skenesborough, a little timbered village near the southern tip of the lake, where the Americans had already landed. From here a narrow road cut south through the forest to Fort Ann and on via Fort Edward to Albany.

The rebels were not far ahead, and cannily hoping to intercept them, Burgoyne landed three regiments a little way up the shore north of Skenesborough with orders to get between the retreating rebels and Fort Ann. Then his ships moved on south along the lake to attack the stockaded village and the American ships that were anchored there.

It was a very short action fought by the American rear guard, merely to delay Burgoyne. The rebels set fire to three of their vessels and to Skenesborough. Flames licked upward from the roofs of the houses on the waterfront and spread fast to the surrounding forest.

Burgoyne wasted no time. He sent a detachment of 200 men up the road to Fort Ann after the rebels, whose retreat, he hoped, would by now be cut off by the regiments he had landed earlier. His plan did not work quite as he had intended. For the country had proved too rugged for the soldiers to reach the Fort Ann road in time to check the Americans. Colonel John Hill, in command of the small unit advancing along the road toward Fort Ann, did not realize he was unsupported—at least not until too late when he was outnumbered by five to one.

Burgoyne managed to rescue the unit, but only just. They were held down on the top of a hill, their ammunition exhausted, when a Tory commanding an advance party of Indians saw the rebels closing on them.

The Indians refused to obey his order to attack. Unable to do anything more aggressive, he fell back on pretense and hollered out a war whoop.

The rebels, believing British reinforcements were close, checked, giving Hill a chance to extricate his men. By the time the Americans realized that they had been fooled reinforcements had in fact come up to cover the retreat.

By then Fraser had caught up with those rebels retreating down the Castleton road. His men, too, had a near escape in a short and violent battle in which they suddenly found themselves severely outnumbered. They were saved only by the precipitate arrival of Von Riedesel's Hessians, advancing in column, with their drums pounding, lustily bellowing a German marching hymn.

It changed the course of the action. The rebels fell back once more into retreat.

Burgoyne, however, needed a breathing space. He allowed the Americans to remain unchallenged at Fort Ann and formed a 10-mile line, stretching from Skenesborough to Castleton, where as part of his feint plan, he ordered Von Riedesel to concentrate his forces in such a way as to suggest he was going to strike into New England.

So far the advance of the northern army, now some 120 miles south of St. Johns in Canada, had been so spectacular that it had exceeded even Burgoyne's optimistic expectations. But the horses and the transport he had ordered in June had not yet arrived at the front. While he had supplies in boats on the lake, he had no way of getting them to his soldiers in the line. "A great part of the troops have wanted provisions for two days," he wrote Germain from his HQ at Skenesborough, "and the whole lot of them have been without tents or baggage."

So Burgoyne was forced to wait. Nòt that the delay was all that unpleasant; like Howe, Burgoyne had taken a mistress, who was the wife of one of his officers. He dined well and even sent several cases of claret and port over to Von Riedesel in Castleton, apologizing both for the quality and the quantity.

Burgoyne was worried that he had been forced to spare from his army, already well below strength, enough men to garrison Ticonderoga. From Skenesborough, he wrote to Carleton requesting him to send down from Canada enough soldiers to defend the fort.

During those few days while **Burgoyne** was waiting, another conflict was being fought beyond the edge of the forest. As he had recognized from the start, the attitude of the inhabitants of the country, many of whom he had been assured were Loyalists, was vital—not only because of the army's need for food and forage but because they were the source of the militia. And the militia had to form the main part of any opposition that the rebels presented to check Burgoyne's advance to Albany.

As Howe had forecast when he planned his strike to the south, Washington had sent up very few troops from the Continental Army to Philip Schuyler, rebel commander in the north; he needed every man he had to shadow the main British force. Howe had not yet activated his secret plan to drive for Philadelphia, but his columns were on the march in Jersey. Schuyler's only hope, therefore, was to rally enough men from upper New York and New England to hold off Burgoyne—just as the Tories became vital to Gentleman Johnny, if he was to stop him.

Burgoyne was very confident, with reason. His army of professionals was more than double the size of the force, mainly amateurs, Schuyler so far had to oppose him. His easy, bloodless capture of the almost impregnable Ticonderoga had made an immense impact on the local Americans; his swift advance had spread terror not only among the farms of upper New York but also in New England. Loyalists were streaming into his camp at Skenesborough with offers to fight; deserters from the rebel army, dazed and demoralized by the fall of the famous fort, were joining him every day. In the towns beyond the forest, Tories were acting as his recruiting agents, as well as his quartermasters.

Schuyler was attempting to counter the efforts of the Tories by demanding a scorched earth policy in the name of revolutionary patriotism. Farmers were being pressured to leave their homes, ordered to take their cattle with them and to destroy all crops and fodder they had to leave behind. By proclamation, the rebel general warned that "to give aid and comfort to the enemy would be punished as treason to the United States."

At Manchester, 30 miles south of Castleton, the rebel Colonel Seth Warner had set up a rallying point, aimed at boosting local morale and calling men to fight from New England. His troops scoured the countryside, ensuring that Schuyler's destruction policy was carried out, threatening farmers to join Warner and attacking Loyalists in bitter, brutal raids.

Von Riedesel soon realized that the 400 men who streamed into Castleton from outlying districts to swear the oath of allegiance to the King were not all ardent Loyalists. They included observers who were taking careful notes. "No sooner had Colonel Warner had the report of these spies," he recorded, "than he at once advanced, plundered the Loyalists, took away their cattle and even carried off the men themselves."

The fight between the Tories and the rebels for the loyalty of local Americans was at a critical stage. The British decision, urged strongly from the distant offices in Whitehall, to use the "savages" had already backlashed. Anyone living near Indian country could not help feeling uneasy about any power that employed them. Even Burgoyne, who had favored their use, wrote Germain that if left to themselves, they would commit "enormities too horrid to think of."

It was now, at this delicate and critical stage in the war for public opinion, that Jane McCrea, the pretty young fiancée of one of Burgoyne's American Tory officers, was murdered. She lived in country occupied by the rebels, and thinking she would be safer with the army, her husband-to-be sent two Indians to fetch her. She was almost at the British camp when, according to Burgoyne, the two men quarreled over which of them should claim the promised reward for her safe-conduct, and one settled the argument promptly by killing her with his hatchet.[5]

The crime appalled the army *and* the rebels and, more significant at the moment, the countryside for miles around. The futile, childish murder underlined only too vividly what could happen and drove many borderline Loyalists into the ranks of the rebels.

Furious, Burgoyne demanded that the tribe should hand over the murderer for trial and execution, but St. Luc Le Corne, the Frenchman in charge of the Indians, warned him that if he insisted, they would go on an angry rampage—a prospect, the general reluctantly was forced to concede, far more evil than leaving the crime unpunished.

The Indians were seething with discontent. Burgoyne maintained this was because he had curbed the cruelties they enjoyed, but Le Corne claimed later that the general's arrogant handling of them was unsubtle and demeaning. "Burgoyne . . . ," he asserted with Gallic scorn, "is as heavy as a German."

Meanwhile, at Castleton, Von Riedesel had realized the necessity of protecting the Loyalists from Warner's brutalities and asked Burgoyne's permission to "attack the traitors." A foraging detachment did force the rebel colonel to drop back from Manchester to Arlington, but Burgoyne refused to authorize a movement in force. For he was about to order the advance of the whole army.

His overwhelming success had placed him in a position on the southern section of Lake Champlain where he had never planned to be. From the start, his intended communication route and the line of advance of his army had been along Lake Champlain to Ticonderoga, by land around the three miles of rapids to Lake George and by water to Fort George at its southern tip. From there the Hudson at Fort Edward was only 14 miles along a fairly easy wagon track.

He had advanced to Skenesborough only because of the unexpected chance to cut off the escaping garrison from the fort. To execute his original plan, he would have to withdraw his troops to Ticonderoga in order to get them on to Lake George, a "retrograde movement" as Burgoyne described it, which at that precise stage in the psychological conflict in the townships of New York and New England, might carry a damaging odor of retreat.

Instead, he now planned to strike south straight through the forest to Fort Edward. It was only 23 miles and had the important strategical advantage of forcing the rebels to abandon Fort George—his vital supply point at the southern tip of Lake George, which they now held in force—if they did not want to risk being cut off from Schuyler's main force.

This was a major change in policy. Although the distance was not great, it meant taking an army of more than 7,000 men along a narrow trail that wound through giant pines and hemlocks growing closely together on hilly ground interlaced with creeks and marshes. Under any circumstances, the march with equipment in the damp heat of high summer would have been extremely arduous; as it was, informed of the plan by their spies, the rebels had done everything they could to harass the operation.

Hundreds of rebel axmen had felled trees to block the trail, dropping them from both sides so they fell across each other. As Sergeant Roger Lamb, a surgeon's mate, recorded, they had destroyed "no less than forty bridges" that crossed the streams and marshes, "one of which was over a morass two miles in extent." They rolled giant boulders into Wood Creek, to prevent Burgoyne from bringing up his equipment along the waterway that covered most of the first leg of the journey to Fort Ann. Every day Philip Schuyler could delay the British army was vital because it gave him more time to rally the militia and to enforce his scorched earth policy on the countryside. If Burgoyne's troops could not live off the country, then he would have to halt—as he had been forced to already—until food and forage could be brought down from the north.

In fact, the blocking of the trail did not delay Burgoyne more than a few days, since he was held up anyway by his supply problems, but clearing it required enormous effort. It took his huge working parties, operating under the orders of his engineers, the best part of two weeks to clear the obstructions and rebuild the bridges. The heat was intense. Swarms of mosquitoes, known as "punkies" by the local inhabitants, attacked the sweating, heaving soldiers. The labor added its toll to men already suffering from the diseases of the swamp. "By now," recorded Von Riedesel, "many of the troops were suffering from Dysentery."

On July 25, nearly three weeks after he had blasted his way into Skenesborough, the northern army began its slow advance through the forest track. It took the men four long days, but by the twenty-ninth they were through the forest and "encamped," as Lieutenant Digby put it, "on a beautiful situation from whence you saw the most romantic prospect of Hudson's River, interspersed with many small islands."

Albany lay before them, only 30 miles away through easy

marching country with a river as a transport route. The rebel force, weighted heavily with untrained farmers and still greatly inferior to the British army, had dropped back to Saratoga, 20 miles down the Hudson. It could hardly have withstood an attack, but it could retreat. And Burgoyne dared not order an advance— not yet, not until supplies had been brought up to the river along the track from Fort George on the lake.

By now there was encouraging news from St. Leger in the west. On August 3, four days after Burgoyne's army broke through the forest by the Hudson, the Mohawk River detachment that had advanced from Oswego on Lake Ontario arrived at Fort Stanwix, an old ruined fortification that the rebels had hurriedly repaired and garrisoned.

St. Leger's force now totaled 1,700 men, including the Royal Greens, a corps of tough and bitter Loyalists under the command of Colonel John Butler, and 1,000 Indians led by Thayendanegea, the Mohawk chief.

The fort had to be taken before St. Leger could proceed down the river valley to the Hudson to cooperate with Burgoyne. So far the post was still under siege, but in a dramatic ambush in the rugged Oriskany Gorge a few miles from Stanwix, St. Leger's Loyalists and Indians had attacked a rebel relief column on its way from Fort Dayton to the south. According to the British colonel, his men had killed 400 rebels and captured another 200. What remained of the relief column had fled.

The victory had been marked by only one minor adverse fact. During the battle, while their besiegers were reduced by detachments to Oriskany, the Stanwix garrison had sallied out of the fort and raided St. Leger's baggage. More significant, they had taken the Indians' blankets. When compared with the stark figures of the rebel casualties, the raid did not seem to be of much moment at the time. Later, however, it was to prove of vital importance.

The news of Oriskany, with its implication that Fort Stanwix would soon be captured, was welcome to Burgoyne at Fort Edward. For despite his success, he had much cause for anxiety. Of the 1,400 horses contracted for in June in Canada, only 500 had arrived. Many of his wagons had been constructed hurriedly with unseasoned timber and were already breaking up. He needed to transport his flatboats from Lake George to the Hudson, as well as his equipment and his cannon. Gradually, with his limited haulage capacity—he had even commandeered some oxen—he was making progress, but it was far too slow.

And every day Schuyler's force at Saratoga was increasing. He still only had 4,500 men, nearly all from the militia, but the British margin of superiority was being continually narrowed. Burgoyne had just heard from Carleton, who refused his request to garrison Fort Ticonderoga, since his orders, which Burgoyne had helped frame, specifically limited his operational area to within the borders of Canada. This meant that the British general would have to leave at Ticonderoga men he suspected he was going to need, as, indeed, he was going to need St. Leger's force.

In addition, Schuyler's scorched earth policy was giving Burgoyne foraging problems, though he tried to shrug them off bravely. "The perseverance of the enemy in driving both people and cattle before them as they retreat," he wrote Germain, "seems to me an act of desperation or folly. The only purpose is to retard me for a time, which it certainly does. But it cannot finally injure me."

But time was now of the essence. Because of the delays, the junction with Howe at Albany, which in Canada and even at Skenesborough had not seemed overly vital, had now become an absolute necessity. "I have no news of Sir William Howe," Burgoyne wrote Germain anxiously on July 30. "I have employed the most enterprising characters and offered very promising rewards but, of ten messengers sent at different times and by different routes, not one is returned to me. . . ."

He did not have to wait much longer. Three days later an express arrived from Howe, but the news it contained disturbed Burgoyne so much he did not even mention it to Von Riedesel, who commanded half his army. Now there was no question any longer of Germain's canceling Howe's plans to go to Philadelphia. He was already on his way. No British troops would be at Albany to meet Burgoyne—unless Washington marched there with the main rebel army. "If he goes to the northward . . . ," wrote Howe, "be assured I will soon be after him to relieve you . . . success be ever with you."

By August 3, when Burgoyne read the letter in his headquarters near Fort Edward, Howe's army had been aboard a fleet of more than 260 vessels, sailing south, for two weeks.

14

OFF CAPE HENRY, VIRGINIA, August 12, 1777

"Could smell the land," wrote Engineering Captain John Montresor in his journal,[1] "the fragrance of the pines in particular at 6:30 this morning. The ships of war hoisted their colors, supposed for seeing the land. . . . A small flock of sand larks passed. . . . At 5:00 p.m. could observe the land from the deck. . . ."

It was a welcome sight, for it had been a terrible voyage. Three weeks ago the fleet had weighed anchor at Sandy Hook, its assembly point just outside New York Harbor, on a journey that under normal conditions should have taken seven or eight days. Repeatedly they had been lashed by summer storms. Masts had been struck by lightning, sails ripped. Collisions had been a daily occurrence between the 266 heaving vessels whose masters knew how easily they could lose the convoy and fall victim to the rebel privateers.

Then came the calms—sultry, windless days with temperatures way up in the eighties followed by breathless nights—and progress had stopped completely. By the twelfth, food and water were becoming scarce, especially for the horses, which suffered acutely from rough weather because they could not vomit. For five days, when the water was calm enough, the masters of the animal transports had been sending boats about the fleet trying to collect forage; daily carcasses of dead horses had been thrown overboard.

And as they sailed up the 200-mile-long Chesapeake Bay with rebels on the banks, there would still be at least another week before they could obtain fresh provisions.

Originally, when Howe first proposed to Germain that he should drive for Philadelphia, he had planned to march through Jersey. Throughout June, he had tried to maneuver the rebel army into a position for attack and almost succeeded. But although Washington shifted his ground to contest the road to Pennsylvania, he never completely relinquished the relative safety of the Jersey heights.

With the Continental Army poised to raid his extended lines of communications, Howe had to abandon the plan to go by land, and by the end of July he was withdrawing his combat troops from Jersey and embarking them on the ships moored off Staten Island in New York Harbor.

He delayed his departure only until his reinforcements, which he regarded as completely inadequate, and Clinton had arrived from Europe. Clinton, dubbed Sir Henry during his stay in London in an effort to soothe his ever-ruffled feelings, was to command in New York in his absence. Then, on July 22, the *Eagle* with the two Howe brothers aboard passed through the Narrows to head out to sea with the fleet waiting anchored at Sandy Hook.

In going by sea Howe was taking a risk, for it put him out of touch with Washington's movements. With Ticonderoga taken and Burgoyne advancing, there was always a slim chance that the rebel commander might leave Philadelphia undefended and march north, and that would demand a very fast response. Clearly the general should get back onto land as soon as possible.

From a fairly early stage, control of the Chesapeake had been central to Howe's planning; this would enable him to cut off the rebel army from the southern provinces that provided so much of its supplies. In fact, his prisoner General Lee, who, still facing the threat of execution as a deserter, was desperately playing with both sides, had urged that the waterway was the key to ending the revolt.

But the Delaware was nearer than the Chesapeake, thus requiring less time out of touch at sea, and the landing points on its banks were closer to the target city. So on July 30 the fleet sailed into Delaware Bay, where it was greeted by the saluting guns of the *Roebuck*, the British frigate on station.

In conference on board the *Eagle*, Sir Charles Hammond, the *Roebuck*'s captain, warned the Howes of the difficulties of taking the fleet up the river: underwater obstructions, shoals, waiting fire ships, guns on the banks. Possibly more important was his news that the rebel army had crossed the Delaware and was waiting at Wilmington. Now no matter where the British landed on the river, they could not break Washington's communications with the south. So the fleet went about and made for its original destination—and appalling weather conditions that were to cause it great havoc.

Early in the morning of August 16 the fleet started up Chesapeake Bay, anchoring during the ebb tide and going on again under the flood. The weather was still excessively hot, "the pitch," as Montresor recorded, "melting off the seams of the vessel." During the three days it had taken them to tack up into the bay, they had heard the signal guns, and on the evening of the fourteenth, "a large smoke made on the shore," carrying the news of their arrival to the rebel commander.

By the eighteenth, they were past the wide mouth of the Potowmack (Potomac) River, where a lone galley suddenly ran up the striped rebel flag and opened fire before it was chased off by a frigate, and heading for the Hooper Islands where fires were signaling their approach. The weather was wildly erratic, raging thundery squalls, which made navigation difficult in confined waters of variable depth, suddenly replacing calm.

Three days later, they had reached Annapolis; as the *Eagle* passed, two gun batteries ran up the rebel colors, but wasted no ammunition on so massive a target as the hundreds of ships that were passing within gunshot.

On the night of the twenty-second in pouring rain they anchored off Turkey Point between the mouths of the Elk and Susquehanna rivers where the channel narrowed. For two days, under the guns of an armed schooner, the fleet longboats sounded the Elk. Then, early on Sunday morning, two frigates sailed up the shallow river ahead of the transports, their bottoms cutting a channel in the soft mud. By nine thirty, covered by the two warships, the flatboats had started landing troops opposite Cecil Courthouse a few miles upstream.

For once Howe was in a hurry; Wilmington—and the rebel army—was not far away. Washington had avoided a major battle in Jersey but, so reasoned the British general, would now be forced to defend Philadelphia.

By September 8 Howe's preparations were completed for the advance on Philadelphia—and for what he hoped would be the final battle of the Revolution. The rebel army was waiting on his direct route to the city, carefully posted on the west of the

Brandywine Creek between the two Delaware river towns of Wilmington and Newport.

All the British intelligence indicated that Washington planned to make a stand there, but Howe was an artful strategist and did not choose to comply with what Washington had in mind.

The next morning, two hours before daylight, the army was on the move, marching in the usual two columns, one on the road with the cannon and the wagons and one in the country. It swung north through Newark into the Society Hills, camping eventually at Kennett Square on the highway from Nottingham to Philadelphia.

Washington responded, as he had to if he was to avoid being outflanked, by marching north to counter the British movement. He crossed the Brandywine Creek, which flowed south through western Pennsylvania into the Delaware at Wilmington, and established a two-and-a-half-mile line on the steep hills parallel with the water. From there he could dominate most of the fords through the stream where the British were likely to attempt a crossing in their drive for Philadelphia. But he put his main concentration at Chadd's Ford, on the main road to the city from Howe's camp.

Meanwhile, at Kennett Square Howe studied the reports of the rebel positions. He planned an assault scheme that was almost identical with the tactics he had employed so successfully in the Battle of Long Island: a large feint at the front to concentrate the enemy's attention while the troops for the main attack took a roundabout route to a position in the rear.

Von Knyphausen would advance in force along the Philadelphia road to Chadd's Ford—as Washington appeared to expect—where he would set up his guns, open fire, position his troops for the assault but wait for the sound of gunfire to the north before ordering the attack.

By then, if the plan were successful, a division of 7,000 men led by Cornwallis and accompanied by Howe himself would have marched north, crossed the Brandywine high upstream of the rebel line, then turned south on a road that led behind the hills on which Washington's troops were now posted. The two attacks, from front and rear, would then be launched simultaneously.

It was typical of Howe strategy, but it had worked before. And astonishingly it would work again.

* * *

At first, thick fog lay in the valley, and Von Knyphausen's men, marching through the cold dank air along the seven-mile stretch of road from Kennett Square to Chadd's Ford, could see only a few ranks ahead. But as the sun rose, the mist began to clear, lying in patches on the steep timbered hills that framed the highway.

At the head of the column and spread out on the flanks on either side of the road, an advance party of fifteen dragoons walked their horses, their eyes scanning the slopes for any movements that might indicate rebel gunmen. Behind them marched the Queen's Rangers, a Loyalist unit of carefully selected men, trained for special operations, and a new corps of riflemen each armed with a new weapon that loaded at the breach. Captain Patrick Ferguson, their commander, who had invented the gun, astonished senior officers at Woolwich to whom he demonstrated it by firing at six rounds a minute—twice the normal firing rate. Now it was about to be tested in action.

Following the mobile forward units came the long column of infantry that made up most of Von Knyphausen's force of 5,000—the British brigades in scarlet, the Hessians in blue—marching easily ahead of the cavalry and the artillery train, the smaller guns drawn by six horses, the heavier guns by bigger teams. Farther back up the road ambled the provision and baggage wagons and the cattle, protected on the flanks and at the rear by a strong rear guard of Scottish Highlanders.

An hour earlier, at 4 a.m., Cornwallis' division had started out along the same road. It contained many more combat troops than Von Knyphausen's column, including the storming units, the light infantry and the grenadiers, but it was unencumbered by baggage wagons or cattle. Speed was essential. The men had a long way to go, at least 17 miles before they went into action—provided Howe's circuiting plan worked without discovery.

As the long ranks of soldiers marched through the moist darkness, the jaegers, some on horses, some on foot, moved on ahead and, two miles toward Chadd's Ford, led the column off the Philadelphia highway onto the Great Valley Road, which ran parallel with the Brandywine.

The first shots broke the quiet of the early morning as Von Knyphausen's column approached Welch's Tavern, about three miles down the road from Kennett Square. The rebel marksmen, about 300, according to the general's formal report, were shooting from the cover of a wood on a hill behind the tavern; the rangers and the riflemen raced past the tavern, breaking off the road into the wood.

There were not enough rebels thrown forward to make much of a stand, and they retreated as soon as they were attacked, holding ground, firing for a few minutes, then relinquishing it.

Von Knyphausen, watching the skirmishing in and out of the trees on the hillsides ahead, did not even halt the column—at least, not for several miles until it neared the Brandywine when he had to, for the rebels had pushed troops in strength across the creek to challenge him.

They had chosen their position well. Near the creek, the narrow valley, which had so far contained the road in a defile, opened up into a fairly wide stretch of flat swampland surrounded by wooded hills before it joined the meadows that bordered the Brandywine. The swamp was central to the rebels' defense position, for it would keep Von Knyphausen's men from spreading out, forcing them to stay bunched on the road, easy targets for concentrated fire from troops posted all around.

As soon as the advance guard met the first burst of heavy shooting from the woods and the hills on the far side, Von Knyphausen halted the column and gave his orders quickly. The rangers charged up through the trees on the left to drive off the nearest enemy units covering the approach to the swamp.

Meanwhile, aides were galloping back along the road with instructions for the infantry columns to wheel off the highway onto the hills on both sides of the valley. Four guns were moved out from the artillery train and hauled up onto high ground on the right.

The approach to the marsh was cleared quickly. Now Von Knyphausen had to get his men across it under lethal attack.

His four guns opened up, plastering the far hills with solid shot and grape. Then Ferguson and his riflemen raced across the swamp through a blaze of shooting and made for cover at the foot of the hills on the right. Highly vulnerable, being so few, forced back by the pressure of the rebel firing to the edge of the marsh, they desperately searched for a new position they could hold temporarily until Von Knyphausen could reinforce them. They found it in a house.

As they opened up from the windows with their fast-firing rifles,

Von Knyphausen sent a corps of support troops across the marsh to back them—100 Hessians, who took up positions near the house. Then the rangers went over, running into the woods on the hill on the left under orders to attack fast with the bayonet.

Gradually, in this way, Von Knyphausen got more and more men across the swamp, and as he built up his attack forces, who were pushing up the hills on both sides, using bayonets when they could, the concentration of fire on the road was eased.

Rebel reinforcements came across the creek to support the men who were constantly giving ground, but now that the road over the swamp was safer, Von Knyphausen was able to send up his brigades in strength, as well as his artillery. By nine o'clock the rebels were being forced down through the woods onto the meadows that lay beside the Brandywine. A rebel battery of four cannon and a howitzer set up just the other side of Chadd's Ford was pounding metal onto the lower levels of the hill to cover the American retreat.

By now Colonel Samuel Cleaveland, who was commanding the artillery, had brought up his cannon onto the hills that overlooked the creek; the guns were firing continuously, crashing grape into the ranks of the rebels in the meadows as they dropped back toward the water. By half past ten the last of the American units had been driven across the ford, and the rebel commanders must have thought the assault through the creek imminent. The British and Hessian light troops were forming near the banks, Cleaveland's horse teams were rushing guns to new positions chosen to cover the crossing, but the general gave no orders to advance.

The mist had disappeared, and the sun was now burning down from a cloudless sky. Von Knyphausen's soldiers, sweating as always in their thick uniforms, could see the left wing of the main rebel line far up on a high hill on the other side of the Brandywine: long ranks of men stretching north along the parallel of the stream.

The hours went by slowly. Every now and then the general ordered a feint; the cannon would open up furiously for a few minutes, but the cannonades were followed by no infantry. Once both sides were rocked by an enormous explosion as one of the rebel ammunition wagons blew up. Soon after two o'clock it became obvious to the general that the enemy knew why he had delayed his attack. "Great movements were observed in the enemy's position on the opposite side of the creek," he reported.

* * *

Not long before this sudden spate of activity, Cornwallis' column some 12 miles to the north was splashing through Jefferies' Ford on the east branch of the Brandywine. They had been on the march for ten hours, but the movement had been brilliantly successful. It was now too late for Washington to use the creek as an obstacle.

Soon after they had passed through the ford, the jaegers in the vanguard turned off onto a road that led through the village of Sconnelstown. All morning they had been marching north. Now they were advancing south, in the opposite direction, on a country lane that led to Chester and on beyond it to Philadelphia. The column had become extended and ragged on the march, and at Sconnelstown the forward troops were halted to allow the rest to catch up. Then they all moved off again upward through thick woodland and into open country at the top of Osborne's Hill.

They were behind the rebel lines—two miles from Washington's extreme northern outposts and only four miles from Chadd's Ford, where the moment they opened up with the cannon, Von Knyphausen would order his men through the creek.

Across the valley that lay before them—a patchwork of farmland, orchards, plow and pasture—they could see the hamlet of Birmingham, dominated by a meetinghouse. Rebel troops were forming on the hill near it, and Howe must have been tempted to order an immediate attack before they had time to prepare themselves for the impact. But his men had been on the move since four in the morning; they were tired and hungry, hardly the ideal condition in which to mount an attack, and he gave orders for them to break ranks and rest.

It was probably wise of Howe to let his men relax, even though it meant losing some initiative and giving Washington time to reorganize his defense. As the British commander watched, rebel troops were gathering on the hill opposite, and guns were being brought up into position. But Howe was never a general to act precipitately. He liked to prepare his battles carefully, to advance in controlled order with his cannon properly placed, and situated as he was to attack simultaneously on two fronts, he had an enormous advantage. The only thing he lacked as usual was time. There were not many hours until darkness, but as usual this did not seem to worry him.

Not until an hour after the column had marched through the

woods onto the summit of Osborne's Hill were his troops formed
in battle order. By then the rebels, whom Howe estimated in his
report at 10,000, had formed on the opposite hill in a position
that Montresor described "as remarkably strong, having a large
body advanced, small bodies still further advanced and their rear
covered by a wood wherein their main body was posted." There
were woods, too, on their flanks. Sitting on his horse watching the
enemy movements, Cornwallis was overheard to say: "The damn
rebels form well."

Howe's troops were ranged waiting in three well-spaced columns
—the jaegers and the light infantry on the left, the grenadiers in
the center and the guards[2] on the right. The cannon were already
set up on the hill, their crews waiting for the orders to put down
the barrage ahead of the advancing men.

It was to be a set-piece battle, the kind the British often fought
in Europe. There were no fortifications, no redoubts for the rebel
marksmen to use as cover, as they had at Bunker Hill or even at
Long Island. It was to be man against man—or, rather, rank against
rank—the type of conflict in which rigid drill discipline inevitably
paid off.

The bands struck up; the order to advance was given. To the
thumping of the drums, the three thick, long columns marched
steadily and unhurriedly down the hill toward their enemy.

At the foot of the hill was a lane the British would have to cross
before they could move up toward the waiting rebel ranks. As
they approached, a sudden burst of shooting came from an
orchard on the left, but it did nothing to check the movement of
the three marching columns. The jaegers, who were nearest, moved
forward fast, crossed the lane and leaped onto the bank at the far
side. Resting their rifles on the rail fence at the side of the
orchard, they opened fire.

On the hill behind them, the gunners began firing shot over the
heads of the advancing troops. The British crossed the lane, then
deployed in long ranks. With bayonets lowered, they moved
steadily up the incline toward the rebels and broke into a run.

The Americans were much better drilled to withstand attack
than they had been at the Battle of Long Island, but they were
still ill equipped to stand up to trained, precision bayoneting by
veteran troops. Repeatedly they fired at the long lines of ap-

proaching British. Two cannon were shooting continuously, bursting flying metal at the nearing rows of scarlet.

Gaps appeared in the ranks and were promptly filled. There was no return shooting, except on the left, where the light infantry were slowed by a plowed field; neither the grenadiers in the center nor the guards on the right stopped to raise their muskets to their shoulders. They just charged on until the moment of bayonet impact—the moment for which their whole fighting technique was designed: thrust, twist, withdraw; thrust, twist, withdraw.

At Chadd's Ford, Von Knyphausen heard the cannonfire on Osborne's Hill and ordered the assault. Cleaveland's guns opened up firing as fast as they could reload to cover the crossing, and the assault units splashed through the shallow water of the ford, rushing the rebels' four-gun battery that had claimed many casualties during the morning.

They were storming an enemy who knew they were under strong attack in the rear, who could hear the ominous booming of distant artillery as well as sharp, deafening thunder crashes of the cannon across the stream. The rebels had moved forward in strength to support their gun positions and were shooting all the time as the British and Hessian support troops ran through the ford. For more than an hour under the onslaught of British and Hessian charges the rebels retained their form as they retreated gradually onto the heights. Then they realized that their front at Birmingham had given way. From the village of Dilworth, behind the hill on which Washington had ordered the stand against Howe and Cornwallis, groups of retreating Americans were hurrying in disorder toward Chester on the Philadelphia road.

The rebel commander had anticipated the possibility of retreat and posted men in force in a defile under General Nathanael Greene to hold the road to the south of Dilworth at the main line of retreat from Birmingham. He was no longer trying to win a battle but to save his army; this with great skill he did. For a while, in fact, for just too long, Cornwallis' pursuing soldiers were checked.

The defense on the other front against Von Knyphausen's force ended abruptly. Cornwallis' right wing had become entangled in a dense wood near the Brandywine, but at last they broke through to find themselves on the flank of the rebels still fighting stubbornly in the dusk against Von Knyphausen's troops. It was the climax. The Americans were unable to sustain attack from two directions and, like the others, gave way into retreat.

The end of the Battle of Brandywine, like the beginning, was a repeat of Long Island. Washington's force was shattered on every front. The totally disorganized rebel troops fled toward Chester; only the darkness saved them from annihilation or capture.

"The enemy's army escaped a total overthrow," Howe reported to Germain, "that must have been the consequence of an hour's more daylight."

Once again Howe's unhurried attitude had preserved Washington's army. As always, Howe's battlefield decisions left the impression he felt he could complete the operation tomorrow.

However, as they had at Long Island, the rebels displayed an astonishing resilience. The very next day, routed though they had been, they were on the march from Chester as an army. Presumably Washington wanted to get his men away from the immediate danger of a followup attack and give them a chance to recover.

He crossed the Schuylkill River and for a few days camped at Germantown just north of Philadelphia. Meanwhile, Howe sent Cornwallis forward to Chester, detached a small force to occupy Wilmington and, with the rest of his army, marched north toward Valley Forge.

It was a game of tactics. Washington needed to station himself so that he could challenge a British advance on Philadelphia; at the same time he had to keep from being driven into the fork on which the city was sited, between the Schuylkill and Delaware rivers. Howe, on the other hand, was determined to get his army across the Schuylkill to the north to achieve that situation.

For a week the two armies feinted and parried as Washington kept changing his position, crossing and recrossing the Schuylkill, so that he retained sufficient maneuverability to dart south to protect the city or north to check a flanking movement.

Then on September 22, Howe outwitted him. The British were near Valley Forge; the rebels on the east of the Schuylkill. Suddenly, Howe marched north in the direction of the American magazines at Reading, and Washington quickly moved north, too, on the other side of the river to counter him. As Howe had hoped, he overreacted and went too far. That night after darkness the British turned about and made a quick movement south. In the moonlight, before the rebels had time to challenge them, Howe's soldiers crossed the Schuylkill by two fords.

Now that Howe was between the Continental Army and Philadelphia, there was nothing Washington could do for the time being to save the city, which Congress had evacuated four days earlier to its usual retreat position at Lancaster.

At ten o'clock on September 26 British troops led by Lord Cornwallis marched through the streets of Philadelphia "amidst the acclamation," according to Montresor, "of some thousands of inhabitants." It was the home of many Quakers, who were strongly Loyalist. In taking possession of the biggest city in America, Howe had achieved at least part of his objective. He had not yet inflicted the essential final defeat on Washington and his army, but he had captured the nearest place the rebels had to a capital. As soon as the navy controlled the Delaware, he would be well positioned for further operations—for subduing New Jersey and Maryland and Delaware and Virginia. As he had always intended, he could act against the rebel supply lines from the south.

On the sunny day that Cornwallis rode past Philadelphia's City Hall, where the provincial delegates had voted in favor of so many rebellious resolutions against their King, Burgoyne was still camped by the Hudson, waiting for news of a movement of troops up the river from New York. But his situation had undergone a drastic change.

For a start, he was no longer in supply communication with Canada, meaning he would have to reach Albany before his food stocks were exhausted. And his army, which in July had been twice as large as the rebels who opposed him, was now greatly outnumbered by a force of 11,000 men.

15

UPPER HUDSON RIVER, August 20, 1777

From the big house where Burgoyne had set up British headquarters some nine miles south of Fort Edward, he could see the Hudson running fast and high, swollen by the storms of the past week.[1] The river was central to the critical decision he had to take, especially since the rushing waters had just swept away the bridge of log rafts that his engineers had constructed.

Burgoyne's triumphant advance had just been badly marred and yet even in retrospect, as he wrote to Germain that day, his bold attempt to solve his problems in one sudden strike seemed fully justified.

Two weeks before, when he was camped at Fort Edward, he realized he must advance fast. The enemy was still smaller in numbers than Burgoyne's army of professional soldiers, but once St. Leger had reduced Fort Stanwix—only a matter of time, since he was employing the zigzag trench technique to approach and blow up the walls—they would soon be threatened on their flank. If Burgoyne could attack during the next few days, the rebels would be forced to fight a battle against a superior force or retreat to Albany or New England. But he was frustrated by his lack of land transport and could not order the advance. Worse, "exceeding heavy rains," as he wrote to Germain, had softened the road from Lake George to the river so that "it was often necessary to employ ten or twelve oxen upon a single bateau." Even by August twentieth, when his luck had clearly turned, he only had four days' provisions and ten boats on the Hudson.

Von Riedesel had first suggested raiding rebel sources for supplies when he was camped at Castleton—merely a cautious probe from the main British line—but Burgoyne had rejected the proposal because he was moving his whole army forward. Then halfway through August, tormented by his inability to act, he had

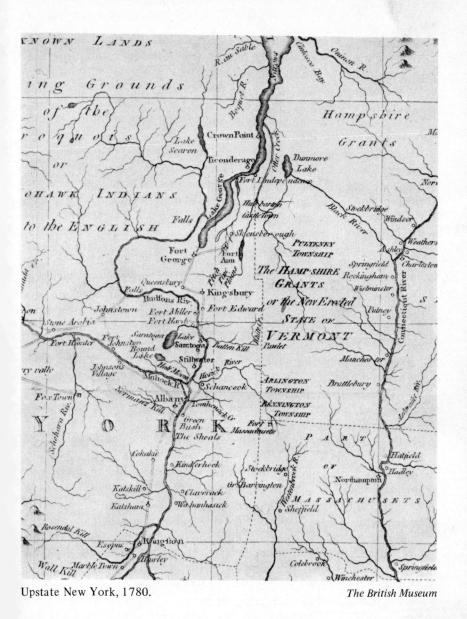

Upstate New York, 1780.

The British Museum

planned a far more hazardous move that stemmed from Von Riedesel's thinking: a strike northeast at the rebel supply dumps at Bennington in South Vermont that would also gather up horses, cattle and wagons. It was dangerous because the detachment would be exposed to attack from the rebel Colonel Warner at Arlington not far to the north and possibly from militia groups from other parts of New England.

Von Riedesel opposed the plan, and Burgoyne, fully aware of the risk decided that the detachment was to be large—nearly 1,000 men, including his ace corps of marksmen that always formed the advance guard for the army, as well as a strong party of Indians. He warned the veteran Hessian Colonel Friedrich Baum, who was to command it, to move his main body with great care "while the light troops felt their way" and to avoid being surrounded and cut off.

On the morning of August 16 Baum's column had left for Bennington, and the whole army had advanced on both banks of the river to the Batten Kill, a creek that flowed into the Hudson from the hills on Baum's route, to support the colonel if necessary and to act fast after his return.

Before daylight the next morning Burgoyne had been awakened by a messenger from Baum. The colonel was facing more opposition than he expected. In fact, he was in even greater danger than he realized, for he had allowed what he thought were Loyalists because of the white cockades they wore in their hats to camp on his flanks; but despite their hats, they were rebels—just waiting for the signal to attack him.

Burgoyne ordered out a relief force under the command of another veteran Hessian officer, Colonel Heinrich Breymann, who, so camp rumor had it, was in a state of constant dispute with Baum. This feuding was blamed by some of the British for the slow progress of the relief column, though a more important cause was the teeming rain that created enormous obstacles for the cannon on the steep hill roads.

By the time Breymann reached Bennington he was too late. Except for a few who managed to escape, Baum's entire force had been killed or captured, and Baum himself was dead. Only by immediate retreat and leaving his guns behind was Breymann able to extricate most of the support corps.

For Burgoyne, who had ridden out personally to meet Breymann and his tired men as they splashed back to camp through the Batten Kill, it was a disaster. He had lost 800 men he could not spare; worse, it had boosted the rebel morale. Baum's Indians who as usual had been impossible to control had capped the tragic story of Jane McCrea which the rebels had been using to inflame the inhabitants of the New England townships.

As Washington had discovered in New Jersey, the militia was often nervous of supporting a rebel army when the odds were against it. Now Bennington had provided the complete victory it needed for assurance, and as the news spread, they streamed into Schuyler's camp at Stillwater until they outnumbered the British by a substantial margin.

It shattered Burgoyne's own men, too. Most of his Indians, many of whom, including the "Grand Chief," had died at Bennington, decided to leave him. "On their first joining his army," Lieutenant Digby wrote in his journal, describing the Indian leaders' explanation to the general, "the sun arose bright and in its full glory; . . . but then that great luminary was surrounded and almost obscured by dark and gloomy clouds. . . ." Many of Burgoyne's Tories left him too, possibly because those captured at Bennington had been humiliated, killed callously in the act of surrender and, according to one report, branded with a red-hot iron.

Desertions among the regular troops had soared. Burgoyne, who prided himself on his humanity to his men, grasped at the traditional cruel methods to control them. Two men were sentenced to 1,000 lashes, another was executed. The few Indians who remained in camp were used to hunt down any soldiers who were found missing from their tents. In his general orders Burgoyne offered his scouts and sentries "twenty dollars for every deserter they bring in," directing further that if they "should be killed in the pursuit, their scalps are to be brought off." It was a drastic policy for a general who had urged his officers not to swear at the men and to treat them as "thinking beings."

In only a few days Bennington had crystallized all the adverse changes that had been gradually transforming Burgoyne's situation and forced him to decide the vital question: Should he stay where he was or even drop back nearer Lake George, where his communications and lines of retreat could be sustained, or drive on for Albany?

Albany lay on the west side of the river, and if he went on, he would have to cross the Hudson with his baggage wagons that in a limited way linked him to Lake George and the water route north. Since there would be no troops remaining on the east shore of the river to stop them, "I must expect a large body of the enemy . . . will take post behind me." He would be cut off from supply communication from Canada, so his army would have to carry all its provisions and ammunition and get through to Albany before the stocks ran out.

Obviously an advance with so many imponderables would be a colossal gamble; the militia, which had been discounted to some extent in the planning of the operation, was now roused and hostile on a big scale. "Wherever the King's forces point," he wrote that day to Germain, "militia to the amount of three or four thousand assemble in twenty-four hours."

Information had now come in that General Horatio Gates, who had taken over the rebel command the day before from Schuyler, was newly equipped with French cannon landed recently at Boston. And Putnam had sent up 2,000 men from the New York highlands; he had been able to do this, Burgoyne pointed out bitterly, because "no operation, My Lord, has yet been undertaken in my favor; the highlands have not been threatened."

He still did not know if they would be or even if any of his dispatches urging this had reached Howe. Two of his messengers had been intercepted on their way south and hanged, and it was possible the others had been captured, too.

There was no doubt Burgoyne should have stayed on the east bank of the Hudson until he had set up contact with the British in the south. And, as he wrote to Germain, this is what he would have done if there had been any "latitude" in his instructions. As it was, he took the astonishing view that he had no alternative but to advance. "My orders being positive to force a junction with Sir William Howe," he wrote, "I apprehend I am not at liberty to remain inactive." Yet, only two weeks before, he had heard from Sir William, and it was the second letter saying this, that he would not be there.

Burgoyne was an operator who had attained his high position through a certain natural cunning, a great deal of charm and a degree of ability. He may have been weak on his attention to detail, such as the organization of his land transport system which was the basic cause of most of his problems, but he was not a complete fool. There can only be one explanation why he took the decision he did on August 20. Appalled at the adverse impact he knew a retreat would make at St. James's, he had become temporarily unbalanced.[2]

He was a gambler, of course, and he was now making the wildest play of his life—with thousands of men as the stake.

Having made his desperate decision, Burgoyne delayed only until provisions for twenty-five days could be brought up. To take charge of the transport operation, he had ordered the efficient Von Riedesel back toward Lake George, where the German general had been joined by the Fridericke, the Baroness von Riedesel, his pretty blue-eyed wife, and their three children, one of whom was only eighteen months old. She was one of a number of officers' wives who had now come up Lake George by boat and before long were to be involved in war almost as closely as their husbands.

On August 28, eight days after Burgoyne had decided to advance, an Indian arrived at his headquarters with yet more bad news. A rebel detachment under Arnold had relieved the rebel garrison of Fort Stanwix without firing a shot. St. Leger's Indians, discomforted by their lack of blankets, raided during the Oriskany ambush and, scared on by the reported size of Arnold's corps, forced the British colonel to retreat. Burgoyne had to face the grim fact that not only was there no longer any threat to the rebel flank from the Mohawk, but he would not have St. Leger's force of nearly 2,000 men he so badly needed.

Even this new development did not change his plan to cross the Hudson. By now, providing further evidence that his mind was strained, his view of himself as a martyr general was beginning to form. "The expedition which I commanded . . . ," he wrote later, "was evidently intended to be hazarded." For if he retreated to Canada, it would leave "at liberty such an Army as General Gates' to operate against Sir William Howe."

Whitehall was capable of big blunders, but if Burgoyne had been thinking clearly, he could never have believed that even the British administration could have intended deliberately to sacrifice—to "hazard"—an army. No military objective could possibly have justified it, especially since, as Burgoyne well knew, such a decision must have enormous political repercussions in Europe.

* * *

On September 13 the British army was ready to move and crossed the Hudson over a bridge of boats.

A few days before, the rebels had moved north from Stillwater— where they had been forced to remain during the threat from the Mohawk and which was open country well suited to the British fighting techniques—to high and wooded ground where the British lines could not form easily, where targets for the cannon could not be seen clearly, where riflemen could find plenty of cover.

Slowly, with drums beating and colors flying, the British army moved south through the gorge-creased hills parallel with the river, while another column, with the boats, the wagons and most of the cannon, proceeded along the flats that bordered the water.

Progress was slow because the rebels had broken down all the bridges across the ravines, but the army did not have far to go. The rebel force was only 10 miles away.

The British waded the Fishkill Creek, just south of Saratoga, passed Philip Schuyler's great mansion and harvested his wheat, which surprisingly, despite his exhortations to everyone else, he had left undestroyed.

By the seventeenth the British were only four miles to the north of the rebel position on Bemis Heights, their lines stretching from the hills to the river where their main provisions were still in the boats. That morning they heard the rebel drums beating the men to arms.

Bemis Heights was a high plateau that sloped upward to the west from the river. It could be approached only by a steep ascent mostly through thick woods, which concealed it from reconnaissance except at very close quarters. The camp had been thoroughly fortified for siege, almost completely surrounded by long, wide walls of earth and felled trees, and all around were steep hills, crisscrossed with ravines.

The battle was imminent. Although Burgoyne wanted time to prepare the ground for his approach and his engineers were repairing bridges under the protective cover of no fewer than 2,000 men, he knew that the rebels might attack him instead of just waiting for an assault. There was continual skirmishing near the working parties and at the outposts. A foraging team was shot to death digging up potatoes in a field. In his general orders Burgoyne coldly pointed out that the men had no right to put themselves in jeopardy—"The life of the soldier is the property of the King"—and warned that "the first soldier caught beyond the advance sentries of the army will be instantly hanged."

For two tense days the army waited. They slept in the open, their tents still loaded on the wagons and in the boats. "We were very watchful," recorded Lieutenant Digby, "and remained under arms." They were only too conscious that badly outnumbered though they were and since retreat would now be problematical, they must win the battle or face the prospect of being starved into surrender. Already General Phillips had warned the artillery officers to save as much ammunition as they could and to remonstrate with the commanders they served if they believed their firing orders wasteful.

The morning of the nineteenth, though fine, was cool; fall was near, and a hoar frost whitened the grass. By nine o'clock Burgoyne's army was advancing to attack the rebels on Bemis Heights in three divisions, which, owing to the woods, were out of sight of one another much of the time. Phillips and Von Riedesel were with the left column moving along the riverside, led by a party of "shabbily mounted" Hessian dragoons, who were covering the baggage in the boats.

Burgoyne himself was with the center, which, under the immediate command of General James Hamilton, was approaching through the hills.

Brigadier General Simon Fraser, in charge of the right wing made up primarily of the advance corps, was moving through the woods in a wide circuit to assault the rebel lines from the west.

The terrain was difficult and, as Burgoyne had realized, several hours were required before the three columns could get across ravines and through woods to their starting positions for the attack. Carefully the center division moved down into the "Great Ravine," which lay in front of the rebel camp, crossed a bridge over the stream at the bottom and halted around noon. For an hour the troops waited until Burgoyne received a message from Fraser that his column had at last reached the high ground to the west—to the right of the main buildings of Freeman's Farm, which was his springboard for the assault.

Freeman's Farm, a cluster of log cabins set in a few acres of open ground axed out of the forest, lay directly between the center column and Bemis Heights, about a mile and a half away. When Burgoyne reached the farm, the British line would be formed as

Army positions after the Battle of Freeman's Farm, on September 20, 1777.
The British Museum. A Royal United Services Institution map

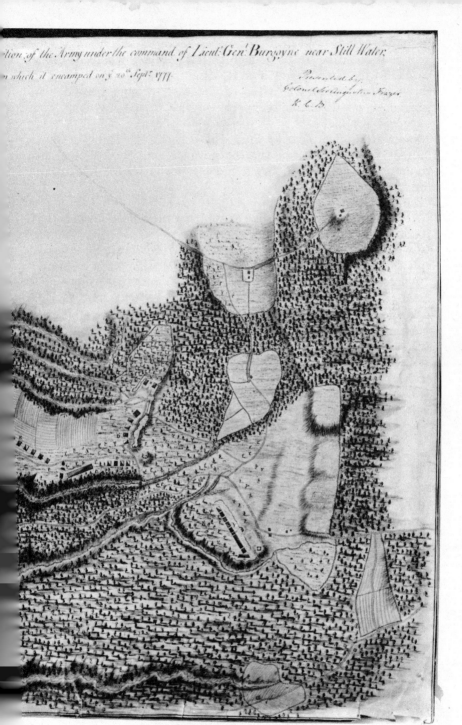

...tion of the Army under the command of Lieut: Gen.l Burgoyne near Still Water,
...n which it encamped on y.e 20.th Sept.r 1777.

Presented by
Colonel Sackingwater Frazer
R. L. B.

well as it could be in such rough country. Fraser would be in the woods to the west of him. Von Riedesel would be attacking uphill through trees from the river to the east, though the German general seems to have been very unsure of exactly what was expected of him.

Soon after one o'clock, Burgoyne ordered the firing of three musket shots, the signal for the advance on the fort, and his column with its cannon began moving slowly up the hill toward the farm.

At daybreak, intelligence had arrived at British headquarters that Daniel Morgan[3] and his celebrated corps of "Virginian" riflemen, now complemented with men from other provinces, were posted in the woods in front of the rebel camp. Morgan was well known to detest the British; once during service with the army under General Braddock in the French and Indian War, he had punched an officer who had struck him with the flat of his sword. He had been taken prisoner in the assault on Quebec, and Carleton had offered him a colonelcy if he would defect; but indignantly he had refused. He was a highly individual but brilliant natural commander. Instead of using drums to control his men, who were all expert shots, he sounded a decoy call that was designed for luring wild turkeys.

Fraser's advance troops on the right were the first British units to encounter Morgan's men. From high branches of the trees where the riflemen were perched came lethally accurate shots— aimed as always at the men who wore braid epaulets. Immediately the pickets fell back to Fraser's advancing line, "every officer," according to Lieutenant Digby, "being killed or wounded."

Fraser sent forward his light infantry and grenadiers, and under the blaze of drilled and coordinated shooting by ranks, Morgan's men were forced back. "About half past one, the fire seemed to slacken a little," reported Digby, "but it was only to come on with double force. . . ."

The rebels attacked again, this time supported in strength by troops commanded by Arnold, and the fighting became desperate. "From the situation of the ground and their being perfectly acquainted with it," wrote Digby, "the whole of our troops could not be brought to engage together . . . such an explosion of fire I never had any idea of before, and the heavy artillery joining in concert like great peals of thunder, assisted by the echoes of the woods, almost deafened us with noise."

Fraser's column bore the brunt of the defense at the early stages of the battle, but it was in the center that the key action was soon to be fought.

As the center column approached the farm through the woods on the hill, General Hamilton sent forward an advance unit of 100 men. They, too, met Morgan's riflemen, for he had posted them strung out in a long irregular line waiting in the log farm buildings, as well as in the trees.

The probing British companies met the same precision shooting that dropped so many men in Fraser's forward pickets on the right. And again casualties, especially among the officers, were high. Worse still, because of a stretch of open ground, they could not retreat and were pinned to cover.

Fraser, on their right, heard the shooting, realized the situation and ordered his light infantry to rescue them by swinging left and attacking. Under the blast of fire, the rebels fell back, and for a very short while, there was a lull in the fighting.

Hamilton's advance guard, after having been rescued by Fraser's light infantry, had dropped back to the main body of the center division. Now the general ordered an advance in strength, halting his men as they came to the edge of the woods that fringed the land surrounding the buildings of Freeman's Farm. His gunners put a couple of 6-pound shot into the log cabins from which Morgan's men had attacked his vanguard, but it induced no response; the rebels apparently had vacated the farm and dropped back into the woods beyond.

The infantry rushed across the clearing—under a blast of fire from the trees—and took cover behind the log cabins. As soon as they were stationed, the four cannon were galloped after them, the teams unhitched and the guns set up in pairs on both wings.

In the heavy fighting that Digby recorded, Arnold had been trying to push his troops around Fraser's right wing so that he could attack him from the rear. Now he had switched his tactics and had withdrawn his men and was now making a drive between Fraser's right wing and Hamilton's center to separate them. In response Hamilton regrouped his regiments in the form of a V—a salient—in front of the farm.

For three hours they fought it out, moving backward and forward across the field between the farm and the woods. "To an unconcerned spectator," commented Digby, "it must have had the most awful and glorious appearance, the different battalions moving to relieve each other, some being pressed and almost broke by their [the rebels'] superior numbers."

Repeatedly the British guns were captured and then recaptured in bayonet charges. The casualties were terrible, especially among the Sixty-second Regiment, which was posted at the point of the British salient and under attack from an arc of fire.

Lieutenant James Hadden, in charge of two guns on a hill at the left of the salient at the farm, had nineteen of his twenty-two men killed or wounded. Unable to fire either of his guns, he rushed to General Hamilton and asked for infantrymen to help him get the cannon back into action, but the general could not spare any men and referred him to General Phillips, who had ridden over from the left wing by the river to find out what was happening.

Immediately Phillips ordered Captain Thomas Jones, Hadden's brigade commander, to transfer the crew from a gun on the right of the salient to get one of Hadden's cannon firing again. When Hadden returned to his guns with his new crew, he found the line of the Sixty-second in confusion. Because the cannon had stopped firing, the rebels had stepped up the pressure on this front, and to counter them, the regiment had charged with the bayonet, and the troops had gone too far into the wood. Rebels concealed among the trees closed from the sides and captured twenty-five men from a corps that certainly could not spare them; half the men and more than half the officers had already been killed or wounded.

As soon as they got to the guns, Jones and Hadden opened fire, and immediately Morgan's snipers in the treetops concentrated on the artillery crews. Almost at once Jones was shot; all the gunners that Hadden had brought up were wounded. Once more his cannon were silent.

The line dropped back on the farm, but Hadden was forced to leave his guns on the hill. He carried his bleeding commander, Captain Jones, "into one of the huts which was filled with wounded" and, only with difficulty, found "a place to lay him in."

Von Riedesel on the riverbank could hear the fighting but was uncertain how to interpret his orders, for he was responsible for the boats and wagons. He sent an officer to Burgoyne for guidance, and the captain returned with instructions that the general leave a strong party to protect the baggage and to join the battle. Von Riedesel ordered the advance.[4]

When Hadden returned to the fighting from the hospital hut where he had left his dying brigade commander, the Sixty-second Regiment was still under terrible pressure.

General Phillips, seeing how desperate the situation was becoming, had already sent for some support cannon from the British artillery with Von Riedesel's column. Then he had galloped off to the left where another regiment, the Twentieth, was posted on the far side of the field. The moment his cannon were rushed toward the advancing rebels and set up, he brought up the infantry, which charged the American flanks behind salvos of grape and forced them back into the woods.

But again the rebels counterattacked. When, with their drums pounding, the Hessians advanced from the river up a steep timbered hill, manhandling their cannon, the British were again dropping back to the farm. The Germans charged through the trees, their guns firing at "pistol shot distance."

At the same time, Fraser on the right ordered his grenadiers forward in a determined strike. Relieved by this support, with both his wings assaulting the rebel flanks, Hamilton re-formed his shattered center and advanced.

Under this massive three-pronged drive the Americans dropped back to their lines at Bemis Heights. Burgoyne considered an assault on the fortifications; but it was late in the afternoon, and the light was fading. Fighting was becoming impractical. As it was, Fraser's grenadiers opened fire on the blue-uniformed Hessians, mistaking them for rebels in the dusk. After its mauling, Burgoyne's army was in no state to storm the stout, high walls of the enemy camp.

The British had held their ground, but already seriously outnumbered, they had suffered nearly 600 casualties, many of whom were still lying wounded in the woods within earshot of the troops who spent the freezing night where they had fought. "Though we heard the groans of our wounded and dying at a small distance . . . ," reported Digby, "[we] could not assist them till morning, not knowing the position of the enemy, and expecting the action would be renewed at daybreak."

Although the soldiers waited tensely for daylight, there was no action. The morning light revealed the usual heavy mist that marked the beginning of each day. Search parties went out to bury the dead and bring in the wounded who had survived. "Some of them begged they might lie and die," wrote Anburey, who was in charge of one of the units, "some upon the least movement were put in the most horrid tortures, and all had near a mile to be conveyed to the hospitals."

Meanwhile, Burgoyne went ahead with plans for an immediate attack on the rebel camp, and the troops were mustered when, according to General Phillips, Fraser urged the commander in chief to postpone the assault until the following day. His light infantry, who were to be the spearhead, were just too exhausted after the long action of the previous day and a sleepless night and needed rest.

Reluctantly, Burgoyne agreed. He used the opportunity to reposition his army so that his line was not so extended, shuffling it left so that his boats and his wagons by the river were better protected. That night, since only half of them were on duty at a time, the soldiers got some sleep. As they changed the watch in the darkness, they could hear the rebels felling trees to strengthen their defenses.

Before daylight a long-awaited messenger slipped into camp from New York with a letter containing only three lines in cipher from Clinton: "You know my poverty [in soldiers]; but if with 2,000 men, which is all I can spare from this important post, I can do anything to facilitate your operations, I will make an attack upon Fort Montgomery, if you will let me know your wishes."

Montgomery was one of two river forts that provided the nucleus of the rebels' defense system in the Hudson highlands. Clinton's proposal was not in the same category as a "junction with Sir William" at Albany, but at that desperate time anything seemed better to Burgoyne than nothing.

"An attack or menace of an attack upon Montgomery must be of great use," he wrote in reply, "as it will draw away a part of this force and I will follow them close. Do it, my dear friend, directly."

As soon as it was dark the next night, an officer in disguise left the British camp in an attempt to get through to New York. In case he was captured, as was very likely, the next day two other officers, carrying copies of the same letter, followed him, each taking a different route.

* * *

Clinton had only 7,000 troops to defend New York. When Howe had sailed south, he had been alarmed and astonished, mainly because the move left the city exposed to rebel attack. There were in fact two small strikes by rebel detachments, but by September 12, when Clinton sent his small offer of help to Burgoyne, he knew that Howe had landed and Washington was south of the Delaware. Also, he was "in hourly hopes" of the arrival of reinforcements from England.

Clinton's message decided Burgoyne to postpone his plans to attack the rebel camp. Again it was a gamble. Of the twenty-five days for which the army had brought provisions across the Hudson, only two weeks remained. Possibly with the limited extra produce brought in by the foraging parties and the fewer mouths to feed they could survive a little longer, but the time available for the breakthrough to Albany was getting very short. On the other hand, since Gates' army was so much bigger than Burgoyne's, it made sense to wait until he was threatened in the rear.

Instead of mounting an assault, the British entrenched. Massive working parties felled all the trees within 100 yards of their line to give the cannon free play and to strip away all cover. Then they built a long wall of earth and timber behind a deep ditch, and beyond it an abatis of trees, laid side by side, with their branches jutting toward the enemy.

For tense, precious days, they waited—both for news of Clinton's attack on the highlands and for an assault by the rebels. The two camps were only a mile apart. In each, the men could hear the challenges of the other's sentries. The British slept in their clothes, their weapons beside them.

On the twenty-first they heard the rebels cheering. In a *feu de joie* a gun was fired thirteen times, one shot for each of the thirteen rebellious provinces. It puzzled the listening men until a few days later when a Hessian officer, captured at Bennington, was sent over by the rebels with news that Skenesborough had been occupied and Ticonderoga attacked. The fort had held out, but the rebels now controlled the entrance to Lake George and had captured all the British boats.

From the moment Burgoyne had ordered the army across the Hudson, he knew his communications would be severed. But in the taut, tired atmosphere of the British camp, it was unnerving now that it had happened.

Every day and most nights there was shooting at the outposts. "We are now become so habituated to firing," remarked Anburey, "that the soldiers seem to be indifferent to it, and eat and sleep when it is very near them."

Then came the wolves.. At first, according to Anburey, the British thought the night howling came from dogs. "It was imagined the enemy set it up to deceive us, while they were meditating some attack." Then the noise was attributed to "dogs belonging to the officers and an order was given for the dogs to be confined within the tents. . . ."

The next night the howling grew louder, and a party was sent out to reconnoiter. They discovered the truth—and the attraction: the lightly buried dead. "They were similar to a pack of hounds, for one setting up a cry, they all joined and, when they approached a corpse, their noise was hideous until they had scratched it up."

Desertion was a continuing problem. On the twenty-third a man was sentenced to 1,000 lashes. A few days later, because of a mass defection by the civilian Canadians who drove the wagons, Burgoyne ordered all the drivers to be assembled and warned that seven of the deserters had already been scalped and the Indians were still searching for the rest.

By the twenty-seventh no further news had come into camp from Clinton, but Digby recorded a report that a messenger from him had been taken by the rebels with a letter concealed in a silver bullet.[5] The man had swallowed it as soon as he was captured, but the plan had not worked. "A severe tartar emetic was given him which brought up the ball."

The same day a copy of the rebel general orders was being circulated among the British. It did not make encouraging reading. "By the account of the enemy; by their embarrassed circumstances; by the desperate situation of their affairs, it is evident that they must endeavour by one rash stroke to regain all they have lost, that failing, their utter ruin is inevitable."

It was a fair comment on the British situation which only an imminent attack by Clinton could change. Of Burgoyne's original twenty-five days, now only nine remained; after that there would be a food crisis. The horses were already dying, for they had now cropped all the grass within the camp and forage was in very short supply.

The next day Burgoyne sent another message to Clinton—this

one far more desperate in its wording and containing a significant new feature: a request for Clinton's orders "as to whether I should attack or retreat to the lakes." Clinton, as he well knew, had no powers to give him orders—only Howe could do that—but Burgoyne was hoping to shift some of the blame by sharing the responsibility for what, short of a miracle, was clearly going to be a monumental disaster.

By the fourth Burgoyne was facing crisis. Nothing further had come from New York; the troops were now on half rations. That day, for the first time, he called his senior officers to his tent to consider what the army should do. He told them he was planning to leave 800 men to protect the magazines and supplies at the riverside and throw the rest of the army into a strike at the enemy's left in an attempt to "turn his rear." Vigorously Von Riedesel opposed the proposal; because of the woods they had been unable to get any reconnaissance parties near enough to assess the targets. They would be attacking blind. Also, the rear guard, protecting the baggage, would be hopelessly vulnerable to rebel attack.

Troubled, Burgoyne postponed a decision for twenty-four hours, and the next day they met again. Von Riedesel urged strongly that they should cross the Hudson and drop back to their earlier camp on the Batten Kill until they heard from Clinton. Fraser supported the German. Burgoyne hated the idea of retreat, but there was no arguing the blunt fact that no one had yet seen the left of the rebel lines, which he had selected as the assault point. He came to a decision: They would reconnoiter in force, foraging at the same time. If there were a weakness in the lines, they would attack at once; if not, he would adopt Von Riedesel's advice: On October 11, unless there was news of the anticipated attack from the south, he would order the army to retire.

Two days later, at one o'clock in the afternoon, Burgoyne rode out of the camp with all his senior generals at the head of 1,500 of his best fighting troops and ten cannon. They headed southwest in a circuit of the rebel camp and halted after about three-quarters of a mile in an uncut cornfield on a hill. The troops formed in a line 1,000 yards long at the back of the field to cover the foragers as they harvested. From the roof of a log cabin, Burgoyne and his officers trained their eyeglasses on the rebel lines, but the woods blocked their view of the fortifications.

In any case, their problem was shortly to become academic.

Shortly after half past two the Americans attacked both British flanks in the woods.

The battle lasted only fifty minutes, but it was a complete disaster for Burgoyne. The British were routed; they abandoned their guns, since most of the horses had been shot, and retreated— "which was pretty regular," according to Digby, "considering how hard we were pressed by the enemy"—to the lines. General Simon Fraser, spectacular on a gray horse riding up and down the ranks urging on his men, was an obvious target for the riflemen. The first shot went through the crupper behind his saddle; the second sliced his horse's mane. One of his aides urged him to ride out of the line of fire since a rebel was clearly trying to kill him, but the general refused. There was another puff of smoke. This time the man was on target, and Fraser, shot in the stomach, flopped forward on the saddle. He was the only wounded man the British took with them from the field.

The foragers reached the camp first, galloping back on their horses, having jettisoned their corn—all except one old soldier who came into the lines sitting on the forage, loading and shooting at his pursuers as he rode. "I'd sooner lose my life," he told an angry officer, "than my poor horses should starve."

"The troops came pouring back to camp," reported Anburey, who was in command of a guard. "It is impossible to describe the anxiousness depicted in the countenance of General Burgoyne," who immediately rode up to the quarter guards. "Sir," he told Anburey, "you must defend this post to the very last man."

Almost as he spoke, the guns on the right blasted loudly into action: The rebels were attacking the camp. Again and again the cannon fired, deafening overlapping explosions, spraying metal across the open space that had been cleared in front of the camp. The light infantry, posted on the walls at the point of the assault, were also shooting fast.

The rebels penetrated the abatis of trees—the first line of defense, designed as a check on attackers—only to encounter much too concentrated fire, so they checked and fell back, great holes carved in their line.

Then to the astonishment of the watching British troops,[6] a horseman picked his way through the branches of the abatis, probably through a narrow gap left for patrols. They recognized a bulky, black-haired figure astride a brown horse—Arnold, the rebel general.

He leaned forward in his saddle and galloped parallel with the fortifications right across the line of fire. The continual blasts of grapeshot and bullets from hundreds of muskets made it a certain death ride. Every man expected to see the horse crumple under him, but neither Arnold nor his mount were hurt.

He rode on past the end of the main British lines where there were a couple of log cabins and beyond them a redoubt, positioned on high ground to cover the British flank and manned by Colonel Breymann and 200 Hessians. One column of rebels was approaching from the west, where the battle had been fought earlier; Arnold rode up to them, yelled an order to follow him, swung his horse around and rode for the log cabins, which were defended by Canadian irregulars who put up little resistance as the rebels swarmed in.

Urging on the men, Arnold galloped around Colonel Breymann's redoubt under a continual blaze of shooting and entered through a sally port at the rear.[7]

The rebel general's sudden strategy was overwhelmingly successful. The rebels took the redoubt *and* held off a counterattack. But Arnold's incredible luck could not last forever. Under a burst of fire at closer range, his horse dropped under him, and he himself was shot in the leg, according to one unofficial report, by a German lying wounded on the ground. "Don't hurt him," Arnold is said to have shouted. "He's a fine fellow. He only did his duty."

By nightfall the issue was no longer in question. The rebels were in possession of the redoubt, and Colonel Breymann was mortally wounded.

The capture faced Burgoyne with yet another crisis on this disastrous day. For the redoubt overlooked the British lines, making them utterly vulnerable to its artillery; it was vital that he move the army before daybreak.

Ironically, so the British learned later, because of a running feud between the generals, Gates had stripped Arnold of his command and ruled that he should take no part in the action. Burgoyne had been forced to abandon his camp by a man who was disobeying orders.

That night the British evacuated their lines at Freeman's Farm, went through the ravine they had crossed in their advance on September 19 and camped on the heights of the next hill. "It was done with silence," Digby recorded, "and fires were kept lighted to cause them not to suspect we had retired from our works."

There was no doubt that the hasty move was necessary; as they marched in column in the darkness, Lieutenant Anburey "heard the enemy bring up their artillery, no doubt, with a view to attack us at daybreak."

From their new position, they were well placed to fight off the assault they expected during the day and could also protect the hospital tents and supply base that were still where they had been for more than two weeks, in the meadows by the river.

While the British column was moving in the darkness to its new position, Baroness von Riedesel was still awake in the house she had taken over near the river. She had planned to give a dinner party for the generals the previous evening and, although the crisis of the afternoon had canceled it, the table was still laid, "when they brought me upon a litter poor General Fraser (one of my expected guests), mortally wounded. Our dining table . . . was taken away and in its place they fixed up a bed for the general. I sat in a corner of the room trembling . . . the thought that they might bring in my husband in the same manner . . . tormented me incessantly."

"Do not conceal anything from me. Must I die?" Fraser asked the surgeon, who told him that there was nothing he could do. The ball had passed through his intestines.

"I heard him often amidst his groans, exclaim . . . 'poor General Burgoyne! My poor wife!' " wrote the baroness. ". . . I knew no longer which way to turn. The whole entry and other rooms were filled with the sick. . . . Finally, I saw my husband coming . . . and thanked God that he had spared him to me. . . .

"We had been told that we had gained an advantage over the enemy, but the sorrowful and downcast faces which I beheld, bore witness to the contrary and, before my husband again went away, he drew me to one side and told me . . . that I must keep myself in constant readiness for departure.

"I spent the night . . . looking after my children whom I had put to bed. As for myself, I could not go to sleep, as I had General Fraser and all the other gentlemen in my room, and was constantly afraid that my children would wake up and cry and thus disturb the poor dying man, who often sent to beg my pardon for making me so much trouble.

"About three o'clock in the morning, they told me he could not last much longer. . . . I accordingly wrapped up the children in the bed coverings and went with them into the entry [of the house]."

Fraser died in the morning at eight o'clock, when from his post in a gun battery in the new British position on a hill Lieutenant Digby was watching "the enemy marching from their camp in great numbers, blackening the fields with their dark clothing. By the height of the work and by the help of our glasses, we could distinguish them quite plain. They brought up some cannon and attempted to throw up a work for them, but our guns soon demolished what they had executed."

Burgoyne's plan was to hold off the rebels with his cannon until darkness, when he would attempt a retreat across the Hudson. Later he wrote of hoping to bring them to battle near the river where the open ground would suit his soldiers, but this was ultra-optimistic, for their morale was suffering badly.

Time had almost run out for him. The troops were on very limited rations, and there was only enough food even at this reduced level for a very few days.

Already the rebels were acting to cut off a British escape to the north. Their troops were moving up the far bank of the river, presumably to take possession of the heights at Fort Edward.

At one period during the morning the rebels formed as though they were going to attack. "Several brigades," recalled Anburey, "drew up in line of battle, with artillery and began to cannonade us."

In response a howitzer fired, and the high-angled shell fell short. The rebels cheered. "The next time the howitzer was so elevated that the shell fell into the very center of a large column and immediately burst, which so dismayed them that they fled off into the woods."

Although they did not form again, their guns kept firing. At midday they opened up on the hospital tents, "taking them," so Digby presumed, "for the general's quarters." Orders were given for the wounded to be moved out of range—"a most shocking scene—some poor wretches dying in the attempt, being so very severely wounded."

Had Burgoyne's men only known that during those desperate hours in which they moved the hospital tents under shell fire British troops were already in Fort Montgomery, their morale would have soared. Certainly the general might have changed his plan to retreat.

* * *

That morning in Fort Montgomery—from which he could survey the Hudson below—Sir Henry Clinton considered with some satisfaction the results of his assault. It had achieved far more than he had hoped originally. Although he had used more men than he had intended, he now controlled the highlands. He had stormed the two major forts and occupied minor positions. He had broken the boom the rebels had constructed across the river and burned all their vessels. "Nous y voici," he wrote to Burgoyne in a note that never reached him, "and nothing now between us and Gates."

He did not press on immediately to Albany, as Burgoyne had asked, but since he had now been offered reinforcements from Rhode Island, such a plan was forming in his mind.

At sunset Fraser was buried on the hill by the gun battery where Digby was posted, a spot he had specially requested. He had asked for no "parade" other than "the soldiers of his own corps."

The procession carrying the corpse went up the steep slope in full view of both armies, and as it passed Generals Burgoyne, Phillips and Von Riedesel, "they were struck at the plain simplicity of the parade, being only attended by the officers of the suite . . . and joined the procession."

The rebels, seeing the gathering of men by the gun battery, opened fire as the funeral service was conducted by the chaplain. "The incessant cannonade during the solemnity," Burgoyne wrote later, "the steady attitude and unaltered voice with which the chaplain officiated, though frequently covered with dust which the shots threw up on all sides of him; the mute and expressive mixture of sensibility and indignation upon every countenance; these objects will remain to the last of life upon the mind of every man who was present."

The Baroness von Riedesel was watching from a distance. "Many cannon balls also flew not far from me, but I had eyes fixed upon the hill, where I distinctly saw my husband in the midst of the enemy's fire."

"Suddenly the irregular firing ceased," wrote Benson Lossing, the historian. The rebels had at last realized the reason for the gathering. "The solemn voice of a single cannon, at measured intervals, boomed along the valley. . . . It was a minute-gun fired by the Americans in honor of the gallant dead."[8]

The funeral and the dying light of dusk were all that had delayed the retreat. "The horses," recalled the baroness, "were already harnessed to our calashes." As on the previous night, the march was to be as quiet as possible. "Fires had been kindled in every direction; and many tents left standing to make the enemy believe that the camp was still there." It was impossible to move the wounded, so Burgoyne planned to leave them under a flag of truce with a letter to Gates, requesting his mercy.

At nine o'clock the column started moving off in the darkness. Von Riedesel had taken over command of the advance troops, now that Fraser was dead. In her calash, just ahead of the quietly moving column, the baroness tried to keep her children quiet. "Little Frederica was afraid and would often begin to cry. I was, therefore, obliged to hold a pocket handkerchief over her mouth, lest our whereabouts should be discovered."

Anburey was with the rear guard, which did not leave the camp until eleven. "For near an hour," he wrote, "we every moment expected to be attacked, for the enemy had formed on the same spot as in the morning; we could discern this by the lanterns that the officers had in their hands and their riding about in front of their line, but though the Americans put their army in motion, they did not pursue us. . . ." Before dawn Burgoyne sent forward an order for the army to halt to allow the provision boats to catch up; meager rations were distributed and the men encouraged to rest.

By the afternoon, when the British continued their retreat, it was raining heavily, turning the roads into thick mud. The baggage wagons bogged down, and Burgoyne gave instructions for them to be abandoned, along with the tents for the weary soldiers.

Not until after dark on the evening of the ninth did the head of the column wade across the ford of the Fishkill Creek, which flowed into the Hudson from the west. Just behind it were the heights of Saratoga and the fortifications that the army had constructed when they had camped there in September. Since he had not yet been able to push his men across the river because the rebels were posted in strength on the opposite bank, Burgoyne had decided to reoccupy his old camp; it was a good defense position, high up and overlooking open ground which would give good scope to his guns.

Burgoyne and his staff officers spent the night in Philip Schuyler's mansion by the Fishkill and evidently helped themselves to his cellar, much to the disgust of the Baroness von Riedesel, who indignantly described how the house "rang with singing, laughter and the jingling of glasses. There Burgoyne was sitting with some merry companions at a dainty supper while the Champagne was flowing. Near him sat . . . his mistress."

The general did not escape reality long. At daylight, with the rear end of the column still passing through the Fishkill, Burgoyne withdrew to the camp on the heights and, since Schuyler's house would provide cover for the rebels, gave orders for the artillery to destroy it.

Gates' army came in sight in the late afternoon and set up their line just the other side of the Fishkill. There was another strong force across the Hudson, as well as Morgan and his riflemen who had taken a wide circuit and were now posted to the west. Only the road immediately to the north along the west bank of the Hudson was still open.

Early the next day, under the cover of a morning mist, the rebels tried to block this escape route. A large force crossed the Fishkill and struck north along the river road; but the fog lifted, and the British cannon were able to check them.

Again Burgoyne held a council with his senior generals to decide what to do. And again Von Riedesel had a plan. They should abandon their baggage and strike north in darkness, on the chance that they could drive across the river at a ford four miles above Fort Edward. From there the road led to Fort George at the tip of the lake. Since their boats had now been captured, their position would be better by only a margin, but at least they would not be surrounded as they were now.

As he had before, Burgoyne postponed a decision for twenty-four hours, then, the following afternoon, gave his approval; the army would march that night. At ten o'clock, Von Riedesel who was commanding the vanguard sent a message to his commander in chief that he was ready to start. But by then a scout had brought intelligence that "the enemy's position on the right was such . . . that it would be impossible to move without being immediately discovered." Burgoyne canceled the breakout attempt.

By the following day, the twelfth, it was no longer practical; in the night a big rebel detachment had crossed the Hudson from the east and set up batteries.

The British were now completely surrounded and under constant fire. "Every hour," recorded Von Riedesel, "the position of the army grew more critical. . . . There was no place of safety for the baggage and the ground was covered with dead horses that had either been killed by the enemy's bullets or by exhaustion, as there had been no forage for several days. . . . Even for the wounded, no spot could be found which afforded them a safe shelter—not even, indeed, for so long a time as might suffice for a surgeon to bind up their ghastly wounds. The whole camp was now a scene of constant fighting. No soldier could lay down his arms day or night, except to exchange his gun for the spade when new entrenchments were thrown up."

The baroness and the children had taken over the cellar of a house which she shared with some wounded officers, one of whom found he could stop Frederica from crying by imitating the bellowing of a calf. In the room above their heads, the surgeons were operating under exceptionally difficult conditions; during the course of just one day, Madame von Riedesel reported, eleven cannonballs went through the house. One man, whose leg was about to be amputated, had the other taken off by a shot.

By morning the cellar always stank, and the baroness would fumigate it by pouring vinegar over hot coals. Water, however, was the main problem, for whenever any of Burgoyne's men approached the river, the rebels opened fire. The shortage was even more acute in the baroness' shot-battered house because of the needs of the wounded. At last, one of the soldier's wives offered to take the buckets down to the water, insisting the rebels would not kill a woman. With great courage, she walked to the river, but she was right—they did not open fire on her.

Repeatedly the general begged his wife to allow him to send her and the children over to the Americans. Already one wife whose husband had been taken prisoner had gone to them and been treated with great courtesy by Gates. But the baroness would not hear of it. She had made her own arrangements for the children. Each of three wounded officers in the cellar had agreed to take one child on his horse.

By October twelfth the position of the British was clearly hopeless. No news had reached the camp of an attack by Clinton. Burgoyne held a meeting—not just with his generals but with all his senior officers—and for the first time he mentioned the dread word "capitulation," which "he had reason to believe had been in the contemplation of some, perhaps of all, who knew the real situation of things."

He put two questions: Was an army of 3,500 men, "well

provided with artillery," ever justified in surrender? If so, did their present circumstances provide sufficient reason?

The answer to both questions was a unanimous yes, though it might not have been had they known that at that very moment a fleet was sailing up the Hudson through the highlands toward them. It was carrying only 2,000 troops, but Major General Vaughan, its commander, had orders to "feel his way to Burgoyne . . . and even join him if required."

But Burgoyne, still starved of any information from the south, at last took the inevitable decision and sent a message to Gates under a flag of truce suggesting a meeting between staff officers "to negotiate matters of high importance to both armies."

The following morning Major Robert Kingston left the British lines on the heights, was met by the rebel Colonel James Wilkinson, who blindfolded him and led him to the tent of General Gates.

The blindfold was removed, and Kingston, as Wilkinson recorded, took the outstretched hand of the rebel commander. Burgoyne, Kingston told him, realized that because of the "superiority of your numbers," Gates could "render his retreat a scene of carnage on both sides." He was "impelled by humanity . . . to spare the lives of brave men upon honourable terms."

"To my utter astonishment," wrote Wilkinson later, since it was normal for the defeated side to make proposals, "General Gates put his hand to his side pocket, pulled out a paper, and presented it to Kingston, observing: 'There, Sir, are the terms on which General Burgoyne must surrender.' "

The demand was in effect for unconditional surrender, and when Kingston took it back to his commander, Burgoyne rejected it, insisting that unless some of its terms were altered, "this army . . . will rush on the enemy determined to take no quarter."

Meanwhile, by agreement during the negotiations, hostilities had been suspended, and the guns were silent. "We walked out of our lines into the plain by the river," remarked Digby.

Burgoyne proposed his own terms to Gates, insisting that the troops should march out of their camp with the full honors of war, retain their baggage and, instead of being imprisoned, be permitted to return to Britain on condition that they did not serve in North America again during the present contest.

These were arrogant demands for a defeated army to make, but to Burgoyne's surprise and growing suspicion, Gates agreed to them. His messenger who arrived early in the morning brought only one condition: The formal surrender should take place at two o'clock that day.

There were already rumors that Clinton was approaching. The Baroness von Riedesel even quotes a deserter as coming through the lines with news that the British with a fleet had reached Esopus, 45 miles south of Albany, on October 8—though it is hard to believe that anyone would have deserted to the British during those critical hours.

But it provided Burgoyne with a flicker of hope, and immediately he began to play for time. He asked for the surrender ceremony to be postponed and sent over a request for the word "capitulation" in the document to be changed to "convention." He sought permission, which was refused, for a staff officer to view the rebel troops to assure himself that Gates' army truly was three to four times the size of his own, which he suggested somewhat speciously, was the reason for the surrender.

For Burgoyne the timing was tragically narrow. The strange deserter, quoted by the baroness, was right on all his facts—except the date. Only on that afternoon while the general's negotiating officers were arguing points with their rebel opposites were the British ships off Esopus slowly working upstream against an adverse wind.

There were signs of an active defense. Although the British were still out of range, the rebels were manning batteries. Major General Vaughan landed the troops and set the town on fire. It was there that he was told that a messenger had arrived the previous night with the news that Burgoyne had surrendered. This was enough for the general. His soldiers went back aboard the ships and the fleet headed back to New York.

At Saratoga, Burgoyne was still doing what he could to drag out the negotiations. He even consulted his officers on whether he could honorably withdraw from the agreement his negotiators had signed but still awaited his ratification. There was disagreement on this, but Von Riedesel was adamant that, honor apart, it would be utterly foolish to risk such excellent surrender terms for an unconfirmed report that could be wrong.

Gates ended the dithering. He sent a blunt note to the British camp: Unless Burgoyne signed the agreement within two hours, he would reopen hostilities. Reluctantly Burgoyne signed.

At ten o'clock the following morning, with its bands playing, the army marched from its lines on Saratoga Heights. "But the drums have lost their former inspiriting sounds," commented Digby glumly, "and, though we beat the Grenadiers March, which not long before was so animating, yet then it seemed by its last feeble effort as if almost ashamed to be heard on such an occasion."

Across the Fishkill, in the American camp, another band was playing "Yankee Doodle Dandy," the song that had been transformed from a British taunt to a rousing rebel anthem.

It was the only action that was in the least provocative. Gates had done his utmost to reduce the humiliation of the surrender. He had ordered those troops who had crossed the Fishkill to return within their lines, so that as the British piled their arms in the riverside meadow, they did not do so under the gaze of the enemy that had defeated them.

Burgoyne's soldiers were impressed, too, as they marched on through the rebel camp by the demeanor of Gates' men. "I must say," said Digby, "their decent behaviour during the time (to us so greatly fallen) merited the utmost approbation and praise."

"Not one of them was properly uniformed," remarked a Hessian officer, "but they stood like soldiers, erect with a military bearing. . . . There was not a man among them who showed the slightest sign of mockery. . . . It seemed rather as if they wished to do us honor."

Burgoyne and his general had gone across the Fishkill earlier to dine with Gates. The meal had been surprisingly cordial. The British commander had proposed the toast of George Washington, and the American general had responded by raising his glass to King George III.

It is not entirely strange that later, when Burgoyne tried to comfort the Baroness von Riedesel with the words "You may now dismiss all your apprehensions, for your sufferings are at an end," she responded acidly: "I would certainly be acting very wrongly to have any more anxiety when our chief has none—especially when I see him on such a friendly footing with General Gates."

By then the surrender ceremony had been completed. The British troops had been halted near Gates' large tent, and as the two commanders emerged from it, the American general "paid Burgoyne almost as much respect as if he was the conqueror," recorded Digby. "Indeed his noble air, though prisoner, seemed to command attention."

The two men faced each other. Burgoyne drew his sword and handed it to Gates, who received it with a bow and returned it, and the northern army began its long march on the road to Boston.

In Philadelphia, five days later, Howe heard reports of the surrender and wrote Germain his opinion that they were "totally false." The success of his own army was by no means complete. Earlier in the month the rebels had attacked his camp at Germantown, the site of the main British encampment, and although he had driven them off, the move was clear evidence that Washington was not beaten yet.

Meanwhile, the Delaware was not open to the British fleet. The garrisons of rebel forts on the islands downriver had not surrendered. Only the day before Howe wrote to Germain, a Hessian attack on one of them had been driven off with enormous casualties, and two British ships had been set on fire.

It took Howe more than a month to take the islands. Although it was getting late in the season for campaigning, on December 4 he made one last attempt to destroy the rebel army with a sudden attack on its camp in the hills at White Marsh, but Washington had chosen his position too well. There were actions, and one of Howe's copybook flanking movements, and the Americans even retreated at one stage; but at last it became clear to the British general that success, even if he achieved it, would be costly. He withdrew his army and returned to Philadelphia for the winter.

The Continental Army, as always at the end of the year, was ragged and ill equipped. This time it was short of food as well. Washington led it to the barren hillside of Valley Forge on the west bank of the Schuylkill to spend the cold bleak months until the spring.

But then it would no longer be fighting the same kind of conflict. Burgoyne's surrender was to cause a drastic change in the character of the Revolution and the attempts to subdue it. Until then the battles had been events in what was essentially a domestic affair within the British Empire. Now the revolt of the American colonies against their king was to become a world war.

Two days before the British army marched from Philadelphia on its way to the hills at White Marsh, the first report of Saratoga reached Europe.

16

LONDON, December 3, 1777

That night, the House of Commons was crowded, as it always was at times of growing crisis.[1] All day rumors had been circulating London that disastrous news had arrived of Burgoyne's army. At the morning's levee at St. James's the King, "to disguise his concern, had affected to laugh," so Horace Walpole sneered, "and to be so indecently merry that Lord North endeavoured to stop him."

By the evening London was tensed. It was the second day of a new attack on the government in the House of Commons by the antiwar opposition, which had acquired a more virile dynamic. The night before, Fox, who had recently been ejected from a London dinner party for proposing a toast to George Washington, had opened the assault by demanding a debate on "the state of the nation."

Now other Whigs were following his lead, challenging government statements. Colonel Isaac Barré, a voluble critic of the administration, was on his feet haranguing Lord George Germain for misleading the House on the numbers of Howe's troops. The tall cool Colonial Secretary sat listening impassively on the government front bench.

His evident calm, which always infuriated the opposition, must have irritated the bellicose colonel to a point at which he could control himself no longer. Suddenly he changed the subject completely and challenged Germain angrily "to declare upon his honour what has become of General Burgoyne and his brave troops?" Was it not true that expresses had arrived from Quebec with news of his surrender?

It was one of those dramatic moments in parliamentary history that artists are prompted to paint. The allegation was true enough, though the expresses from Carleton to the King at Queen's House the previous evening had only contained unconfirmed reports, and certainly it was no surprise. Even in October, when the news of Saratoga could not possibly have reached Europe, Walpole had been reporting "more accounts of Burgoyne being defeated by Arnold with 2500 men . . . in the utmost distress and likely to be starved into a surrender."

Even so, since unconfirmed information was so often wrong as indeed was Walpole's,[2] the King had hoped to keep the news quiet until he had the official account. But it was too sensational to conceal for long from a hostile opposition that saw it as a complete justification of its peace policies.

Slowly, in answer to Barré's challenge, the lugubrious Germain had risen to his feet and calmly conceded that "though the recital must give me pain, I know it is my duty to inform the House that I have indeed received expresses from Quebec." But the news of the surrender and of the rebel agreement to send the army home came only from reports from deserters who had come into the fort at Ticonderoga.

His brief announcement, in which he pleaded for "judgment on the conduct of the general and the minister" to be "suspended," sparked off a vicious onslaught on him by critics who were almost more angered by "his cool and easy manner" than they were by his revelation.

"Does the Noble Lord know the extent of his criminality?" demanded Barré.

"A whole army compelled to lay down their arms and receive laws from their enemies," declared Burke, "is a matter so new that I doubt if such another instance can be found in the annals of our history."

"The obstinate wilful ignorance and incapacity of the Noble Lord calls loudly for vengeance," asserted Fox, demanding an official inquiry. "The disgrace" of "the gallant general" that resulted from "the direction of a blunderer . . . is too shocking a sight for humanity to bear unmoved."

Poor Germain must have wondered that night if he had been wise to move back into public life, for in truth the shadow of his court-martial for cowardice in the Battle of Minden always lay very near the surface in the opposition attacks on him. It was not to be long before he was to challenge one member to a duel for speaking too blatantly of the need for a "second trial."

That night the opposition fully exploited the opportunity given it by the surrender. The ministers were displayed as brutal military despots, the Americans as noble patriots, magnanimous in victory. "We employed the savages to butcher them, their wives, their aged parents and their children," declared Burke, "and yet, generous to the last degree, they gave our men leave to depart on parole" —words that were soon to seem hollow, for Congress, supported implicitly by Washington, reneged outrageously on Gates' surrender agreement and imprisoned all of Burgoyne's men.

Lord North, with his great jowls wobbling, stood up to calm the row. In a careful reasoned speech he defended government policy, declared that he was sure that Germain would welcome an inquiry at which he would "acquit himself," and he himself offered to resign from a place to which he had been "dragged . . . against his will."

He knew he could control the House by vote, but although he did not state this from the floor, he believed the crisis demanded changes at the top and even a coalition. In private letters to the King he even suggested a Cabinet post for Fox of all people and urged the recall of the famous Chatham to take his own place.

The King, as always, was cool and unshaken by the news and assured his Premier warmly that "the manly, firm and dignified part you took, brought the House to see the present misfortune in its true light as very serious but not without remedy."

Just how serious it was would depend on the reaction to the news at Versailles. Would it inspire the French to escalate their assistance to the rebels to a point of war?

Persistently in Paris, Lord Stormont tried to sense the intentions of the French government. "This unhappy event," he reported, "has greatly elated all our secret enemies here and they break out in the most intemperate joy." The ministers, however, were "decent and guarded" and had given orders that the Paris *Gazette* was to make no reference to the surrender until it was announced through official channels. And they were being very careful, for the suspicious ambassador could discern no change in their "tone and manner" toward him. "My language to them," he assured Weymouth, "was . . . suitable to the post allotted me here as having the honor to represent a nation that is not to be bowed down by a casual reverse of fortune."

Stormont knew very well that a treaty with the rebels was in draft. The spy, Dr. Bancroft, was still working for the American negotiating team— though now, with the approval of London, he was acting as a double agent.

Bancroft reported to London the exact details of the treaty, but for more than a year now, the British had distrusted him. His facts always needed confirmation.

Paul Wentworth, the main London contact for the British agents in France, was in Paris at the time under urgent instructions from Lord North to explore the possibilities of a peace deal with the rebels. This had produced a delicate and complex situation, for the rebels had long trailed tempting hints of negotiation in front of the Paris embassy, but Stormont had repeatedly criticized them as nothing more than attempts to get leverage in their negotiations with the French. Now, over dinner with Silas Deane, Wentworth received the same treatment. As always, nothing tangible developed.

In the last weeks of December even Bancroft was believed when he reported that he had orders to "fend off" Wentworth until dispatches about the treaty were well on their way to Congress.

At the minister-ambassador level, the French were still behaving as though Saratoga had made no difference to their relationship with either the British or the rebels. Even so, the skeptical Stormont made frequent visits to Versailles to sniff out the rumors and attempt to assess what was going on in the Council. There was constant talk of war.

On Christmas Eve he paid a seemingly routine call on Vergennes in his search for indications of the French intentions. As he rose to leave, the minister asked him casually if he "had anything new."

"Nothing from England, Sir," answered Stormont, "but if one half of the news of Paris is true, it seems to me very doubtful whether I will have an opportunity of wishing Your Excellency a happy new year."

Vergennes "seemed surprised and begged me to tell him what I alluded to: 'You,' said he, 'live in the world. I lead the life of a hermit and scarce ever stir out of my closet.' "[3]

Even allowing for the diplomatic veneer, this was a bit rich for Stormont to stomach, but skilled negotiator that he was, he behaved as though Vergennes were speaking with sincerity. He talked of the persistent rumors of the French treaty with the rebels.

Vergennes looked pained. He despaired of the gossips of Paris; he had been at "both councils and could assure me on his honor that no mention had been made of North America or of anything relating to it."

For all their protestations, Stormont did not believe the French. He suspected that they were just gaining time while they completed their preparations and warned French ships on foreign stations to keep their distance from British men-of-war. He wrote home that both France and Spain "feed the American war in hopes that it will exhaust our strength and that out of it some occasion will arise for them to strike a sudden and unexpected blow"—probably in the West Indies, where both countries had ships and troops.

By February the experienced old diplomat sensed that the strike he had forecast was imminent. "There is a sort of fermentation here in the moment such as I never remember to have seen," he reported. "Your Lordship will scarce believe it but they are preparing against an invasion." Troops were marching to Brest and the Channel port towns.

In London, the opposition, which always regarded defense against the Bourbons as far more important than subduing the rebels, campaigned energetically for the unconditional withdrawal of all troops from America. There was not so much difference now between the policies they were urging and those of the government; with France showing dangerous signs of more aggressive assistance, despite the smooth talk of its ministers, it was obvious that peace with the rebels was now highly desirable.

The King had already approved the dispatch to America of a new negotiating commission with a wide brief. They were empowered to offer almost everything the rebels had ever demanded—except complete independence, and although they kept it secret since it was a negotiating card, they even had orders to refer home any requests for this. But before the commissioners could leave, Parliament had to give its authority.

While the debates were in progress in London, Lord Stormont in Paris was living in an uncomfortable limbo on the brink of war. It was soon to end. On March 13, 1778, Emmanuel-Marie, Marquis de Noailles, French ambassador in London, called on Lord Weymouth in Whitehall with a note that was phrased with belligerent defiance. It declared that King Louis had signed a treaty of commerce and amity with the independent states of America and warned that should that commerce be "interrupted," France would "support the dignity of the flag."

Technically the note was not quite a declaration of war, but it was so close that it made little practical difference. Clearly before long, French and British ships would be once more blasting broadsides at each other. That night a messenger left London for Paris with instructions to Lord Stormont to quit the French capital "without taking leave" of the perfidious court at Versailles.

At a Cabinet meeting the next day at Lord Weymouth's house the ministers framed their policy for the crisis. For the time being the Revolution was to lose its priority. Britain would retrench; ships and troops would be stripped from the forces in America for deployment in the West Indies, where it now seemed the action would center, and at bases in Florida, Newfoundland and Canada — and, of course, at home, where the danger might well be greatest. In Britain the militia would be called out, the Channel ports garrisoned and the army positioned strategically to resist invasion. It was a classic danger, and there were classic plans for countering it.

In America Sir William Howe had asked the royal permission to resign his command, because, he complained, no one seemed to take any notice of his recommendations in London. At last Clinton was to have a chance to prove that he could do better than the general he was always criticizing. Not that he wanted the post under the present conditions. "No officer who had the least regard for his professional fame," he commented gloomily, "would court a charge so hopeless as this now appeared likely to be."

On March 21 Germain sent Clinton orders to take over the command in America from Howe and, so that he spare the detachments needed in the new theaters, to evacuate Philadelphia. All remaining soldiers were to be shipped to New York, which the British were to hold as their main HQ. Major offensive operations were to be suspended for the time being while the Peace Commission negotiated with Congress and Franco-Spanish intentions were gauged. Later, if it was still necessary, a campaign might be initiated in the South.

The change in Britain's situation since 1776, when the Howes took a major army into New York Harbor to discipline their rebellious colonials, was almost unbelievable. Now it was on the defensive against powerful enemies who had long been awaiting their opportunity to strike. Hurriedly it was closing its ranks in preparation for the first blow.

In St. James's and Whitehall a painful reappraisal of the govern-

ment was in progress. Lord North, from the start always a
reluctant Premier, was trying to resign in favor of Lord Chatham,
who, as William Pitt, had been the strong leader who had steered
Britain to such spectacular victory in the Seven Years' War.
Though old now, he was the ideal leader for international crisis,
especially since he would carry with him the support of the whole
country.

But petulantly the King refused even to talk to his old enemy,
Chatham, and would only agree to his inclusion in a Cabinet
headed by North. "I would rather lose the crown I now wear," he
told him, "than bear the ignominy of possessing it under their [the
Whigs'] shackles."

Ever conscious of the bitter precedent of the executed Charles I,
the King always regarded his power in Parliament as having
priority over anything else, including war with France and Spain.
He paid off Lord North's heavy debts, to ease his personal worries,
and persuaded him to stay at his post. Even Germain, who was on
the point of being dismissed, kept his job because the King could
trust him in the Commons. Finally, after all the talk, the only big
change involved Lord Jeffrey Amherst, who had refused to take
the command in America in 1775, but since the French were now
the main enemy, joined the Cabinet as military supremo.

The King had achieved his object: He still had ministers he could
rely on to execute his policies. They might not be the best
ministers, but they were under his control.

By the end of March most of the arguments were over, the new
policies were settled, and orders had gone to all commanders. Now
London waited tautly to see what France and Spain were going to
do.

It was at sea that the most important battles were likely to be
fought in the immediate future, and it was there that Britain
would probably have its greatest scope for action. It was there,
too, that it was most vulnerable.

For although Lord Sandwich had always declared his policy of
keeping the British navy superior in strength to the combined
fleets of France and Spain, just at this moment—despite a rush
building program in the dockyards—it was smaller. But there was
still time to remedy the situation. Spain had not yet entered the
conflict. If Britain could defeat France soundly in a quick sea
battle and destroy many of its ships, it could regain the naval
supremacy. Also, if the British admirals could achieve victory, the

rich West Indian islands, which provided France with no less than a third of its total world trade, would open up the scope, not merely for defense, but for a highly lucrative series of attacks.

 Despite the crisis and the narrow margins in which the ministers were working, the situation that faced them was not completely black. And at that moment a naval clash was clearly imminent.

 The French had two big fleets in preparation—at the Channel port of Brest and in the Mediterranean harbor of Toulon, where the Comte Jean d'Estaing had been hurrying to take command just before Lord Stormont left Paris.

 To counter these forces, two British fleets were fitting out in south coast ports. They were to be led by Admiral Augustus Keppel, a Whig who earlier had refused naval command in America, and Vice Admiral John Byron, who was known as "Foul Weather Jack" because he always seemed to attract storms. Keppel's target was the French Channel Fleet. Byron was to challenge D'Estaing wherever he went; the intelligence reports were uncertain, but his destination was assumed to be America.

 On April 27 news reached London that D'Estaing had sailed on the eleventh with a fleet that included eleven ships of the line. It was provisioned for nine months, supporting the theory that it was on its way across the Atlantic.

 Byron's ships were still not ready for sea, and in the first week of May, the King went personally to stay at Portsmouth in the hope that the royal presence would persuade the fitters to hurry.

 By the time the fleet's sailing preparations were completed there was some doubt about where D'Estaing was headed. At one moment he was reported to be at Cádiz, which could mean he was routed toward England; then another sighting showed that he was still in the Mediterranean. Byron was ordered to wait. Not until June 2 did a British frigate that had been shadowing the French admiral come into Portsmouth under full canvas with the hard news that D'Estaing was through the Strait of Gibraltar and heading southwest. Byron was ordered to sail for New York.

 It was inevitable that "Foul Weather Jack" would run into a near-cyclone size gale that scattered his ships across the ocean.

 A few weeks after Byron sailed west in pursuit of D'Estaing, Keppel's big fleet of thirty ships clashed with the French Channel force under Admiral d'Orvilliers. For three days after the two admirals sighted each other 66 miles west of Ushant on July 23 the sixty ships maneuvered for position. Then suddenly the wind veered in favor of the British. Keppel ordered his fleet into the attack, and D'Orvilliers turned to meet him. The two fleets met, fired their enormous broadsides—and passed. Night stopped the action, and the French used the darkness as cover to retreat.

Technically the British had won—and their casualties were only half those of the enemy—but Keppel had sustained so much damage he had to limp back to port for repairs. Certainly it was not the overwhelming victory Britain needed before Spain joined its ally, but it had shown that for the time being the Home Fleet was strong enough to withstand invasion.

The crisis lost some of the tautness that had marked it until then. The immediate danger seemed past. The King and his ministers could breathe again, at least for a while, and consider their position in America.

By the time the news of Keppel's action reached London Clinton had just evacuated Philadelphia, but it had not been the simple operation the Cabinet had intended. There were not enough ships to transport in one movement all the troops and the thousands of the city's Tories, and a two-stage evacuation was impractical, exposing to attack as it would those who remained after the first convoy had left. Also the reported approach of D'Estaing's battle fleet would present a clearly unacceptable danger to the army at sea.

So Clinton decided to march the 90 miles across New Jersey to New York: with more than 14,000 men, with a baggage train of 1,500 wagons, with many of the army's women—and with Washington poised at Valley Forge to swoop on him across the Jersey heights.

17

ALLENTOWN, NEW JERSEY, June 25, 1778

It was still dark when the advance guard marched, but already the dawn air was warm, warning of yet another sweltering summer day with temperatures up in the nineties.[1] For the first time, the position of the column of the baggage train, 12 miles of wagons and cattle and women, had been changed. Until this morning, while the army had been moving north, it had been kept at the rear; but now that the troops had swung east and the main point of danger had changed, most of the men were waiting at the roadside as the creaking carts lumbered past, with the women walking beside them.

The women had caused Clinton a good deal of trouble. Always the source of problems to commanders, these were immeasurably increased in a retreat when they could not be left in a rear base. When he had first planned the evacuation, Clinton had decreed that only two women per company could accompany the army—provided they were "known to be good marchers, as no carriages will be allowed for them or their baggage." The others would go by ship. Repeatedly he changed their position in the column and tightened the supervision of them. They were not keen on traveling by sea—probably because the scope for plundering was so limited—for five days after the army had started marching, Clinton complained in his daily orders that, "many [women] . . . who had been sent on board the transports at Philadelphia were at present with the army."

Clinton's decision to take this long and motley column to New York by land involved enormous risk—but a risk only marginally smaller than alternative ways of evacuating the city. Before the British left Philadelphia, the main rebel army with about 14,000 combat troops was still at Valley Forge, only 25 miles away to the northwest. Gates with another 4,000 men was on the Hudson. If the militia was rallied, the British could find themselves as outnumbered as Burgoyne had been; moreover, no matter what route Clinton took to reach New York, his enormous column would have to pass through "several strong defiles" in New Jersey's hills, where he would be dangerously exposed to attack.

Clinton's emotions were mixed, as his notes and writings make clear. His overriding purpose, as he put it, was "unquestionably retreat," but after the humiliation of Saratoga he was yearning for a battle. If he could only tempt Washington to attack him—and could then defeat him—the personal reward for him as the commander in chief would be enormous. In national terms, it could well make France think again and act as a curb on Spain.

Given the opportunity, his chances of a victory were higher than they seemed. After three years' campaigning, Clinton's army was probably the finest in the world. "I had little doubt respecting the issue of a general and decisive action with them."

On the other hand, in addition to his superior numbers, the initiative was with Washington. He could choose his battleground —and New Jersey with its craggy hills and woods seemed ideal— and he could march light, without the encumbrance of a vast baggage train.

But, Clinton pondered, why should Washington risk any kind of confrontation? The Peace Commission had now arrived from England and had sent a message to Congress indicating they were keen to negotiate and, as the rebels knew, empowered to be generous. Freedom from taxes, representation in Parliament, removal of the British army and many other of the factors that had caused the rebellion were now to be offered to the Americans.

Congress, however, refused adamantly to discuss anything until its independence had been acknowledged or until all British soldiers had left American soil—leaving the negotiators waiting with nothing to do until they received further instructions from London.

Certainly the evacuation of Philadelphia did not strengthen their negotiating position. Nor did it give Washington any incentive to expose his men to danger. But there were other considerations. Clinton's vulnerable column was certain to be an attractive target for the rebel commander—especially its baggage train badly needed by his underequipped army that had endured a very hard winter at Valley Forge. Also, another victory over the British would be important politically to the Americans in their new relationship with France.

For these reasons, Clinton prepared to withdraw the army from Philadelphia in an atmosphere of dangerous uncertainty. Would Washington attack? Would he try to grab the British baggage train? And if he *were* going to attack, would he strike at the very beginning of the evacuation when the British were most vulnerable, as the army was crossing the Delaware?

The rebels made no challenge at this stage. All day on June 17, under the cover of the guns of the warships, the baggage was pushed across the water to a well-defended bridgehead that had been set up on the Jersey bank. That night in darkness, the main body of the troops followed it in flatboats. Then the big transports, with the rest of the baggage, a regiment of Hessians whom Clinton did not trust and the Tory wives and daughters, dropped downriver to Delaware Bay to be ready for the quick dash in convoy for New York.

As soon as the river crossing was complete, the army began marching, leaving Philadelphia open to the rebels.

The British met little in the way of opposition to start with. There were obstacles: The bridges were all down, trees had been felled here and there to block the road; but there was no real challenge.

Clinton left the baggage train at Haddonfield, only seven miles from the river, while the engineers cleared the road ahead. Also, he expected trouble in the pass through the hills at Mount Holly, and had prepared a flanking plan to meet it. He wanted to clear the heights before he brought up his hundreds of wagons.

Strangely, the pass was not contested. Rebel militia were posted there, but they retreated as the British advance corps approached and on June 21 Clinton sent orders back to Von Knyphausen, who commanded the troops in charge of the baggage, to join him.

Even though the march had been relatively easy so far, Clinton was now fairly certain that Washington was going to challenge him. For two days, his agents reported, the rebel army from Valley Forge had been crossing the Delaware at Coryell's Ferry some 50 miles to the north. Its headquarters had been set up at Hopewell not far from Princeton, but forward units were probing south. Also, Gates was reported to be on the march toward them from the Hudson.

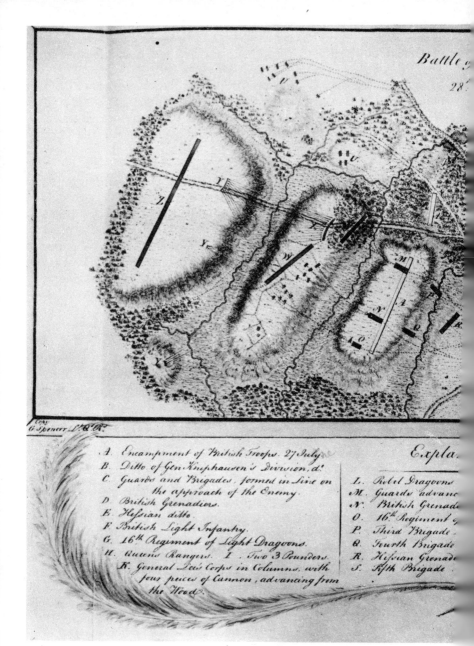

Battle
28

Expla

A. Encampment of British Troops. 27 July.
B. Ditto of Gen. Kniphausen's Division, d.
C. Guards and Brigades, formed in Line on
 the approach of the Enemy.
D. British Grenadiers.
E. Hessian ditto.
F. British Light Infantry.
G. 16th Regiment of Light Dragoons.
H. Queens Rangers. I. Two 3 Pounders.
K. General Lee's Corps in Columns, with
 four pieces of Cannon, advancing from
 the Wood.

L. Rebel Dragoons
M. Guards advanc
N. British Grenad
O. 16th Regiment o
P. Third Brigade
Q. Fourth Brigade
R. Hessian Grenad
S. Fifth Brigade

The Battle of Monmouth, June 28, 1778.

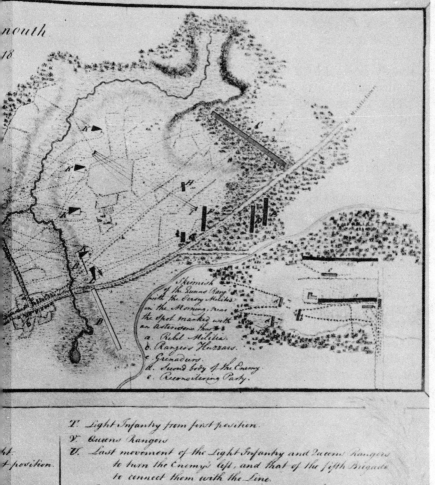

nouth
18

Skirmish
of the Queens Rang[er]
with the Jersey Militia
on the Morning, near
the Spot marked with
an Asterism thus **
a. Rebel Militia.
b. Rangers Huzzars.
c. Grenadiers.
d. Second body of the Enemy.
e. Reconnoitering Party.

T. Light Infantry from first position.
V. Queens Rangers
U. Last movement of the Light Infantry and Queens Rangers
 to turn the Enemy's left, and that of the fifth Brigade
 to connect them with the Line.
W. Position to which General Lee retreated thro' the Woods, on the
 advance of the British Army, who drove him from it,
 and Occupied it, during the remainder of the Day.
X. British Artillery.
Y. Rebel Artillery.
Z. Washington's Army.

Journal of Operations of the Queen's Rangers by John Simcoe, 1787

Slowly the British army with its wagon train proceeded north toward the rebel forces that so substantially outnumbered it. Another column, commanded by Cornwallis, was advancing cautiously along a road farther west, nearer the river, to provide cover against sudden attack.

The weather had been changing drastically—torrential rains interspersed with spells of intense and overwhelming sunshine—but by Wednesday the twenty-fourth, the storms had stopped. The soldiers marched under a fierce sun through thick hot sand on the road that glared the heat back at them.

The skirmishes had grown more serious, too. Several times Lieutenant Colonel John Simcoe, with the huzzars of his Loyalist Queen's Rangers in their green uniforms, had charged sniping parties, and the noise of light guns employed to clear small groups of rebels from the cover of trees and houses had been heard all day along the column.

That day they reached Allentown. Until then, while marching north along the line of the Delaware, Clinton had been able to keep his options open regarding his exact route to New York. Now, he had to decide how he was going to cross New Jersey—*and* to reveal it to Washington. He could aim straight north for the Hudson or northeast for Staten Island at the mouth of the Raritan or, as he now planned, swing farther east still and make for Sandy Hook, where the fleet could pick him up and ferry the army through the Narrows to New York. This road, via Freehold and Middleton in Jersey's Monmouth County, ran through country that was fairly open, and Clinton hoped that Washington "might possibly be induced to commit himself some distance from the strong [hilly] grounds of Princeton, along which he had hitherto marched." And to his surprise he was right, for he found that the terrain was not favorable to the rebels.

At 4 a.m. the next morning, the twenty-fifth, when the British wheeled to the east, the baggage train took the lead behind the advance corps. The new route, with the wagons at the front, eased some of Clinton's anxieties. Until that morning he had been marching toward the enemy; now with the change of direction, the rebel army was behind him. As a result, the closer his baggage moved to the coast, the easier it would be to protect. His strong rear guard, consisting of the "elite" of his troops commanded by Cornwallis, had a freedom of movement for aggressive action that it had lacked before because of the need to protect the long line of carts.

The column progressed slowly toward Freehold as the sun burned down from a cloudless sky; by midday the temperatures had passed the hundred mark. Swarms of mosquitoes raided the streaming skins of the thousands of sweating men and women. Soldiers fainted; some even died.

The rebels were getting close now. Minor attacks were in motion all day, and it was rumored in the column that among their assailants was Morgan and his riflemen, who had been so effective against Burgoyne's troops in the woods at Freeman's Farm.

Often Cornwallis kept his cavalry hidden in the woods at the rear of the column in the hope of cutting off attackers, but he was never able to bring them into action.

That night the advance corps halted about four miles from Freehold. The next morning they entered the village, and Clinton decided to "halt there for a day and look about me." The general had good strategical reasons for a pause, for he was exceptionally well positioned. Freehold, a little cluster of some forty clapboard houses ranged around the steepled, slate-roofed Monmouth County Courthouse, was at a right-angled junction of the main route from Allentown, along which the British had approached, and the road from Cranbury, where Clinton's scouts had located the "gross" of the rebel army.

It was Clinton's last chance of an action, and the dangers that faced him were fewer now than at any time since he had evacuated Philadelphia. The safety of the high ground at Middletown, which adjoined the coast at Sandy Hook, was only 12 miles away. Freehold itself, where his tents were now pitched, was a very strong defense position set on a high ridge of hills with woods all around it.

However, when Clinton and his escort rode up the Cranbury road, which the rebels would presumably advance along, his hopes of "a decisive action" faded. For in the last mile to Freehold, the route cut through country crisscrossed by ravines and surrounded by marsh and woodland. The road itself crossed three of these ravines before reaching Freehold. Clinton could not believe that Washington would risk pushing his advance troops through the first ravine because the restrictions of the terrain would keep him from rushing support if the British attacked in force. Equally, any forward movement would be limited in those defiles with fast retreat impossible.

So Clinton rode back to his headquarters in the Monmouth Courthouse convinced that, since he "could not entertain so bad an opinion of Mr. Washington's military abilities" as to think he would take either risk, there would be no major battle here. But on the march to Middletown, his baggage train would still be highly vulnerable to serious raiding, especially when the road reached downhill from Freehold between high ridges, and he knew the rebels were considering an attack at this point because all day on Saturday, the twenty-seventh, the British had clashed with their reconnaissance parties examining the ground.

At dawn on Sunday morning Von Knyphausen and his hundreds of wagons started off down the steep hill road toward Middletown. Clinton wanted to move the column past those dangerous ridges as early as possible, but because he knew the rebel "gross" was now at Englishtown, only five miles away along the Cranbury road, and he could not be certain of Washington's intentions, he held back Cornwallis and the rear guard at Freehold under orders not to march until several hours after the wagons were on the move.

Meanwhile, his mounted scouting troops were on the alert around the village for any signs of enemy activity. The rebels were there all right—and in some force. While the main body of the army was marching out of the village at eight o'clock in the heat of an already scorching sun, Lieutenant Colonel Simcoe with forty huzzars of the Loyalist Queen's Rangers clashed with a large group of the enemy in the woods to the northeast of the courthouse.

The enemy movement was puzzling to Cornwallis, who did not order the rear guard to move off from the village until ten o'clock. By then they were gathering in some force on the edge of woods across open ground on a hill overlooking the Middletown road. Uncertain of their purpose, the general ordered measures to keep them at their distance. Guns were unlimbered at the rear of the column and opened fire. "A few cannon shot," recorded John André, "put the infantry back in the wood. Only the cavalry continued to follow."

Then, a few minutes later, a large rebel column appeared far back on the Cranbury road, and wheeled to join the other troops high up in the open ground. Now in their new strength, the rebels began to advance, following the marching British troops under the cover of their guns. Cannon shot began dropping into the rear of Cornwallis' column.

Clinton was riding some distance ahead in the column as it moved down the hill when the reports of the enemy's actions began to reach him. Aides from Von Knyphausen had ridden back to warn him that the rebels were attacking on both flanks of the baggage train. Also, another big detachment had been sighted approaching from the north.

By now Clinton had heard the cannon fire from the rear, and a staff officer galloped up from Cornwallis with the news that the enemy had begun "to appear in force on the heights of Freehold that he had just quitted." Clinton turned his horse and hurried back to the rear. He was delighted, and surprised, by the new events because it meant that Washington had taken the decision he had been certain he would avoid. He had pushed his advance guard across the ravines and, in doing so, had severed it effectively from the main part of his army.

Now it seemed Clinton might get the battle he hankered for under conditions that were exceptionally favorable.

For the road was leveling out onto a "small plain" nearly three miles long. He had open country, an enemy that was limited in numbers—they were about 4,000—and the barrier of the defiles to prevent Washington sending up support on any scale. In addition, by attacking, he could relieve the pressure on his baggage train. He planned to strike so hard that General Lee, who was in command of the rebel vanguard, would have "to call back his detachments from my flanks to its assistance."

It happened just like that and much more easily than Clinton expected. While his long line of wagons continued slowly toward the heights of Middletown, 2,000 men in the British rear guard, supported by 4,000 other troops in the column, turned about and started marching back toward Freehold.

Seeing the danger of the open country, the rebels dropped back onto the hill that overlooked the Middletown road and formed in front of the wood. The enemy cavalry, commanded by the young Marquis de Lafayette, advanced from the rebel right wing as though to attack, but the experienced Clinton could see that he was not too sure of his tactics, "seeming to be in the air."

He ordered the dragoons to attack. But as the cavalry with sabers pointed galloped at the rebel horsemen, "they did not wait the shock, but fell back in confusion upon their own infantry." The British trumpets sounded the retreat, and the dragoons reined in their horses.

This precipitate withdrawal evidently shook rebel morale. When the thousands of British infantry formed and with drums beating, advanced in line, they retreated. "Nor was a shot fired," sneered André, "until we had crossed the Cranbury Road."

Unlike some of his officers, Clinton believed that this was the only action open to Lee. He felt that the whole rebel movement, which exposed the vanguard, was a grave tactical mistake—one which he was now planning to exploit. Washington, however, it was learned afterward, was so angered by the retreat that he assumed personal command of the troops and a few days later ordered his general's court-martial for disobeying orders.[2]

As the British line moved forward steadily, leaving the Monmouth Courthouse and Freehold Village on its left, the rebels streamed back along the Cranbury road; since it was too narrow to provide an escape route for the entire force, they fanned out to the south through woods that bordered the road. Still roughly formed, they slithered down the steep sides of the first and most easterly of the three ravines they would have to get through to reach the main body of the army.

Clinton had foreseen the rebels' inevitable dilemma once they started retreating. Although the rebels could scramble through the first two ravines, he knew that they could not easily cross the third defile because it was far deeper, with high, steep sides; they would have to cross it the same way they had advanced that morning—by the road, over a bridge. And because of their numbers, that would take time. Temporarily they would be trapped against the big gorge.

Clinton was grimly confident. If he was careful he might even turn the action into a rout.

He watched the long red ranks of his elite corps, the guards and the grenadiers, sweep across the Cranbury road and check before the first ravine. And on their left was his cavalry, the Sixteenth Light Dragoons; approaching behind, in line like the British, were the blue-uniformed Hessians, their bands throbbing out the step. Already they had their orders: They were to hold the heights by the first ravine, so that the attacking troops could drop back to their protection should this prove necessary.

Meanwhile, the light infantry were advancing in a different direction. Hidden by the woods, they were moving up the northerly route toward Amboy, which formed a junction with the Cranbury road; when they broke from cover, they would be able to fall suddenly on the rebel left flank.

The drums were beating as the lines of sweating men advanced to the first ravine and clambered down the incline. The dragoons pressed their horses, which sank to their hocks in the swamp on each side of the stream.

Their passing of this ravine was not contested; by the time they were across it and the line was formed again and moving forward on the other side most of the rebels were through the second ravine. But by now, even though they were still in full retreat, some guns had been set up.

As the guards and the grenadiers slithered down the sides of the second ravine the white flashes of the cannon marked the new position of the battery. The explosions, deafening in the confines of the gorge, numbed the ears of the soldiers as they wallowed through the marshy bottom. Grapeshot rained on them. Leaving their dead and wounded in the mud for the surgeons, they clambered up the far side of the gorge.

Now that they were across the two obstacles of the ravines, Clinton ordered the classic technique for promoting panic in retreating men. The dragoons with sabers swinging rode down the rebel infantry as the retreating men desperately tried to escape the slashing of sharp steel.

Avid for success, Clinton saw in the situation all the early signs of the rout he wanted so badly. But his cavalry were suddenly checked, completely halted and forced back by a unit ranged behind a fence that would have formed an absolute barrier to a charge. The rebels were "throwing in upon us a very heavy fire through their own troops"; the shooting "galled" the dragoons "so much as to oblige us," as Clinton put it, "to retreat with precipitation upon our infantry."

Meanwhile, the American retreat was suddenly slowed by the personal intervention, so Clinton later discovered, of Washington himself. Some of the American troops turned off the road and formed on hills on both sides with their backs to the ravine.

Like the artillery that had raked the British as they had crossed the middle gorge, it was obviously a holding operation—a hurried move to stem pursuit to the bridge and cover an orderly retreat across the ravine. Also, it enabled Washington to set up a drop-back line in strength on the other side of this gorge, using both the retreating troops and reinforcements he was bringing up from the main army.

The British formed for attack in two long ranks to the left of the road. Guns were brought up to cover the assault. The heat was now appalling. Even in the shade the temperature was as high as 96; but most of the combat was fought in the fierce glare of the sun.

Along the whole front the British advanced, their cannon firing. The cavalry, now repositioned on the right, were closely formed, the width of a horse between each man, walking at first to keep pace with the infantry, who were moving forward with their muskets at the hip, bayonets pointed forward, drums beating. The rebel guns, set up on a hill on the left, were firing, too. Men dropped in the ranks. One single cannonball, slicing down the line, knocked the muskets out of the hands of a whole platoon.

As always the ranks did not break. The gaps were filled; there was no check.

The ranks of cavalry with standards carried in the center of each unit moved into the trot. Always officers had to be careful not to take them too fast too early, so that the horses were not tiring as they struck the enemy. They began to canter, sabers still resting scabbard down on their thighs, points up. The trumpets sounded the charge. The dragoons spurred their horses, leveled their sabers and galloped across the road at the waiting lines of rebels.

The volley came late, at short range. Men slipped from their saddles; horses crumpled. But the others went on riding hard onto their target, easing their weight back onto their buttocks as they struck. They broke the line, sending the rebels reeling back toward the gorge, and captured Colonel Nathaniel Ramsay, one of their commanders.

It was not so easy for the infantry on the other side of the road. They charged the rebel line behind the fence and were fought back. They charged again with the bayonet, and again. At last, they broke them and forced them, too, back to the ravine, but the stand had achieved its object: Washington's lines were established behind the gorge.

At this stage, when all the rebels had been driven from the territory between the ravines, Clinton "had no intention of pushing the matter further." Clearly it would be unwise for him to take on the whole Continental Army, supported by militia, with 6,000 men. Within the limits of the gorges, the battle had been practical, as his men had proved, because Washington could not use his superior numbers.

So the British general planned a withdrawal to the heights on the Freehold side of the ravine behind them, and to cover this move, he had of course left the Hessian troops there posted in strength. But unfortunately—and "impetuously"—the light infantry had advanced far too far on the right and were attacking the left wing of the main rebel army. Clinton ordered them back, but their retreat would have to be covered if they were not to be isolated.

This did not appear too much of a problem. The British were in possession of the whole east side of the ravine, and a row of guns had been set up to counter a rebel battery just across the gorge. Clinton gave instructions for the British positions to be held until the light infantry had dropped back, when the whole withdrawal movement could be put into operation, and rode back to his headquarters that once again had been set up in the Monmouth Courthouse.

So far as the general was concerned, the battle was over, and since he had driven the rebels in retreat before him, he regarded it with some logic as a success. Anyway, "the heat of the sun was by this time so intolerable that neither army could possibly stand it much longer."

But the battle was not over. Very shortly Clinton had to return. "From my intentions not being properly understood," his troops had left the covering ground, "and the enemy began to repass the bridge in great force." At the same time the rebel guns were firing continuously.

Clinton, who was still trying to organize a withdrawal, found himself drawn back into battle on this sweltering afternoon. To cover the retreat of his light infantry, who were pinned down by the rebels' new positions, he had to order another attack.

Despite the heat the fiercest fighting of the day began and continued, with the guns of both sides firing continuously and a series of bayonet charges by the infantry, until dusk when at last Clinton was able to pull back his army to the heights of Freehold.[3]

Considering the limited military objectives, it had been an expensive action in casualties for both sides, and enemy fire was not the only killer. Nearly sixty of the British troops died of sunstroke.

Clinton did not give his men much time to recover. The rebels had advanced to the ravine near the village, and their sentries were only a quarter of a mile from the British lines. Washington was planning to attack the next morning.

Fortunately the moon that night was only in the sky for a few hours; before eleven it was dark. At midnight Clinton's soldiers started marching— in silence, stealthily, one battalion at a time. By daylight the next morning the only British who lay between the rebels and Freehold Village were the wounded, left there with a surgeon under a flag of truce. And the dead. And fifteen American prisoners.

By then the troops had caught up with Von Knyphausen and the baggage train, and at ten o'clock had reached the safety of the high ground at Middletown.

The next day the army reached Sandy Hook; and the ships of the fleet, which had sailed up the coast from Philadelphia, began the ferrying operation through the Narrows to New York. By July 5 the operation was complete—but only just in time. For that day, the Comte d'Estaing and his battle fleet arrived off the coast of Virginia. On the eleventh, with twelve ships of the line and six frigates—as well as 4,000 French troops—he threatened New York.

It was the crisis that had been inevitable ever since the French had recognized American independence. The Cabinet had foreseen it and taken what measures they could to meet it; but none of Admiral "Foul Weather Jack" Byron's storm-battered ships had yet appeared in coastal waters, and Lord Howe's little fleet was badly outgunned. He had three ships of the line and three frigates less than D'Estaing—only 534 cannon against the 834 that the French could deploy.

Meanwhile, Washington was marching the Continental Army to the Hudson; together with Gates' troops he had some 20,000 men. During those few days in July, the future of the British in New York seemed very bleak.

In a straight sea battle, Howe would probably have lost any conflict with D'Estaing. But he was stanced for defense just outside New York Harbor in restricted waters featured by a shallow sandbar that, as the British captains knew from experience, was hazardous to big ships.

Howe adopted a classic plan. A small advanced squadron was

positioned to fire at the enemy as they felt their way over the sandbar. The remainder were anchored in line in the channel, so that as the French ships approached the Narrows, they would have to run the gauntlet of multiple broadsides.

For eleven days the two fleets lay anchored in sight of each other. Then, on July 22, with a following wind and a high spring tide, the French weighed anchor and began their approach to the harbor. But on closer investigation, D'Estaing's pilots advised against attempting the bar with the bigger ships. The French admiral hesitated, then called off the attack; his fleet went about and made out to sea.

During the next few days, four British warships arrived in New York from various directions—including the first of Admiral Byron's unhappy fleet. Howe guessed that D'Estaing had sailed for Rhode Island, where the rebel General Sullivan was threatening the British garrison. With his new reinforcements, even though he was still marginally outgunned, the admiral felt strong enough now to challenge the French in open waters.

He arrived off Rhode Island on August 8 just as the French ships had entered the passage to Newport. D'Estaing, nervous of being blockaded, made a run to sea under a north wind, and for two days the two fleets maneuvered, until a gale scattered them. As the weather eased, several independent actions were fought between individual ships with inconclusive results.

Both admirals gathered their ships and assessed the damage. Howe returned to New York, D'Estaing made for Boston—robbing General Sullivan of the support he needed for his attack on Rhode Island—but by then British transports were approaching up the internal waters of Long Island Sound with Clinton and a relief force. To avoid being cut off, the rebels were forced to withdraw to the mainland. For the time being Rhode Island had been saved.

Howe followed the French to Boston but arrived there to find D'Estaing's ships lying safely under the unassailable cover of the guns of the town.

The British fleet returned to New York, where the morose admiral, "Black Dick," gave up his command to sail to England. For this he was criticized; but the Howe family reputation was at stake, and his presence as its senior member was much needed.

His brother had not been welcomed home as the winner of battles—for they had not achieved their object—and in the bitter aftermath of Saratoga, the court and the government were cool. Anonymous writers, both in the press and in pamphlets, were sniping at him constantly, lampooning his delays, his failure to follow through his battles and, inevitably, his decision to go south instead of north up the Hudson to meet Burgoyne. Soon he was pressing for a court of inquiry so that he could present his defense, but the government was not keen to stir muddy waters that would inevitably present the opposition with more ammunition.

Meanwhile, in New York, tension was easing. The mood was similar to that of London after the recent confrontation of the French and British Channel fleets. The challenge of the rebels' new and powerful ally had been met. It would come again, but for the moment the point of crisis was past. There was time for preparation.

Clinton had carried out the main part of his orders from Germain; he had retrenched in New York. Plans had either been executed or were in hand for reinforcing Florida, Canada, Newfoundland and Nova Scotia. Very carefully, the British once more moved onto the offensive in a minor way.

In November two troop convoys sailed south under fleet escorts with orders to attack. One, under the command of General Grant, was steering for the West Indies, which the Cabinet in London believed would be the main center of action on the American side of the Atlantic.

The other, under Lieutenant Colonel Archibald Campbell, was carrying a force to invade Georgia—the last of the American provinces to send delegates to the rebel Congress and a possible springboard for a future campaign to recover the South, a possibility always being discussed optimistically in London.

Both missions were completely successful. By January the British had taken the strategically important French island of St. Lucia—and fought off a determined attempt by D'Estaing to recover it—and had driven the rebel opposition out of Georgia.

The news fed the new temporary mood of optimism in St. James's and Whitehall. Following the King's demand for "activity, decision and zeal," Germain bombarded Clinton with letters that infuriated him urging offensive operations. To the general, London was being completely unrealistic; he was expected to conduct the war with the kind of aggressive planning that Howe had been able to display, and yet his force had been stripped by detachments.

For a man like Clinton, with his erratic moods that varied from deep pessimism to occasional jaunty optimism, it was too much. Repeatedly, like Lord North, he asked permission to resign, and, like those of the Premier, the requests were refused.

In fact, Clinton was just as keen as Germain to be ambitious in his campaign planning. The success in holding off D'Estaing had, he believed, soured the rebel view of their new allies and created an opportunity for Britain. Many Americans were tired of the conflict that had now been in progress for so long. "One vigorous campaign," he wrote, "tout sera dit." But for this he needed many more men. It was the same old cry that Howe had made so persistently; though with his reduced forces, Clinton had more reason for complaint than his predecessor.

In flattering letters Germain tried to soothe his prickly general, but he still could not help nit-picking and interfering. Clinton exploded. "I am on the spot," he wrote home angrily at one moment. "The earliest and most exact intelligence on every point ought naturally, from my situation, to reach me. . . . For God's sake, My Lord, if you wish me to do anything, leave me to myself and let me adapt my effects to the hourly change of circumstances."

And he was not doing badly. Apart from the military aspects, his secret agents were digging away at the foundations of the rebel army. To William Smith, New York's chief justice, he confided that he expected to be "presented soon with the heads of some of the Rebel leaders." He was in direct touch with at least two of them who were smarting under heavy-handed treatment by Congress—Philip Schuyler and Benedict Arnold.

Also, under prodding from London, he was at last promoting the recruitment of Loyalists with a degree of enthusiasm. Although some American units such as Simcoe's Queen's Rangers had fought extremely well, the British had always been lukewarm about the Loyalists. But now, short as they were of troops, they began to tap this enormous source of bitter manpower.

For the first time Loyalist officers were put on the same pay scales and rank hierarchy as the British regulars. Some effort was made to exploit the Americans' countries of origin. An Irish unit was established, and a Scottish group and a Roman Catholic corps. A whole Loyalist regiment comprising both infantry and dragoons was set up around the nucleus of the Queen's Rangers under the title the British Legion. Wearing green uniforms, its colonel was nominally Lord Cathcart, but its active commander was a ruthless but spectacular lieutenant colonel of cavalry who was only twenty-three, Banastre Tarleton. Tarleton's Legion and in particular his Green Dragoons were to play an important and even brilliant part in the fighting that lay ahead. As a highly mobile assault unit, it was especially formidable because, unlike the British and the Hessians, its troops hated their rebel enemies with a fierce intensity.

The early persecution of the Tories had grown far more vicious. At Bennington surrender had been refused to many who were killed in cold blood. After the evacuation of Philadelphia two Loyalists had been hanged. During the fighting in Georgia, several loyalist American prisoners had been executed summarily by the rebel troops; this, in turn, had provoked retaliation in kind by Tory commanders. Branding on the hand was an accepted punishment meted out by rebel courts. Responding to Clinton's desperate need for men, the Tories were to contribute a great deal statistically to his forces. The province of New York alone was responsible for 15,000 men in both the army and navy. In Georgia more than half the British force was American. In addition, the British were now encouraging Loyalist privateering, and they met a strong response. For apart from the opportunity for fighting the rebels, there was prize money to be made. Advertising posters throughout New York City urged recruits to join the crews of the ships that were fitting out. One of these was the *Fair American*, the commissioning of which was financed by the "Loyal Ladies of New York."

In fact, the enthusiasm for privateering was so great that the navy soon complained it was obstructing manning and provisioning the fleet. Eventually, it took over the whole operation, working with a board of directors consisting of the leading Loyalists from each province. The British fitted out the ships while the board supplied the officers and crews. The fleet of Associated Loyalists was soon harrying the New England coast.

Through much of 1779, Clinton put his Loyalists to full use—though he found them hard to control. Shadowed as it was by the new developments in Europe, it was a year of small operations, of raids and counterraids.

In the North the two men who had run the ambush at Oriskany, Colonel John Butler and Thayendanegea, the Mohawk chief, swooped through Wyoming and upper New York with mixed forces of Tories and Indians displaying a level of brutality that was to be a great embarrassment to the government in London. The rebels soon retaliated; within months General Sullivan was leading an expedition in revenge against the Six Nations of the Iroquois League, of which Thayendanegea was a leading chief, deploying methods that were hardly less brutal.

From New York Governor Tryon led a series of raids on the seaport towns that provided the bases for the rebel privateers. The regulars went raiding, too. So, for that matter, did Washington; his men recaptured the Hudson fort at Stony Point, taken by the British, and seized the garrison of Paulus Hook just across the river from Manhattan.

For the most part the clashes were not too serious. It was, in fact, a period of pause while the effect of the French Alliance and the imminent entry of the Spanish into the war was assessed.

The first winter months of 1779 had been hard, and the Hudson had frozen, which caused Clinton to expect a rebel attack on New York across the ice. The Continental Army was very close—at Morristown in the Jersey hills where it had spent the cold months after Princeton in 1777—but no assault came. Washington, too, was doing his assessing and certainly, surmised Clinton, could not have been too encouraged by the first French efforts.

The sense of euphoria that marked the British in both London and New York in the spring of 1779 did not last long. In June they faced crisis again on both sides of the Atlantic. The Spanish ambassador in London handed Lord Weymouth a belligerent note that, like the French action the year before, was the equivalent of a declaration of war. By the end of July an invasion fleet of ships of both nations had sailed for Britain from Corunna in northern Spain, while at the two French ports of Le Havre and St.-Malo an army of 31,000 men was assembled waiting to be ferried across the Channel under the guns of the warships.

By halfway through August the enemy vessels were anchored in the Channel off Plymouth. So far they had been unchallenged by the British Home Fleet, which was far to the west under the command of Sir Charles Hardy. Poised ready to block the way to Ireland, the expected assault point, it had been borne out into the Atlantic by an east wind.

The fact that they did not know the position of the British fleet made the enemy commanders nervous, and they weighed anchor and went looking for it. By the time they made contact, Hardy's ships were in the Channel heading for Portsmouth—between the enemy and Britain. The invasion had been hurriedly organized. There had been delays at Corunna; many of the ships needed revictualing. The French and Spanish commanders decided on postponement and returned to their home ports. Britain had survived yet another threat.

Across the Atlantic, however, a French offensive had produced a new crisis. St. Vincent and Grenada, one of the richest of the sugar islands, had been taken, and the fleet was assembling at Santo Domingo in obvious preparation for a strike at Jamaica.

As soon as Clinton heard the news, he sent Cornwallis with 4,000 troops to reinforce the island's garrison. On the way the earl learned that D'Estaing and the French fleet had left Santo Domingo—but not on course for Jamaica; they were steering north. New York could again be the target, so the troop convoy turned about and made back to British headquarters. But D'Estaing was not aiming for New York, at least not immediately, but for Savannah, Georgia. On board his ships he had 6,000 French troops ready to cooperate with the rebel General Benjamin Lincoln who was marching on the town overland from Charleston in South Carolina.

Outnumbered as the British garrison was by two to one, its prospects were very poor. For six weeks Savannah lay under siege. The town was bombarded by D'Estaing's guns and eventually stormed at dawn on October 9. But the British fought off the attack, inflicting heavy losses, until the French admiral, fearful of the seasonal gales, reembarked his troops and withdrew. Lincoln and his rebels had no alternative but to march back to Charleston.

To Clinton in New York it was the signal for Britain to move once more onto a major offensive to break the Revolution. By calling off the siege of Savannah, D'Estaing had left him the base that was vital to further operations in the South. "I think this is the greatest event that has happened the whole war," Clinton wrote in one of his moments of enthusiasm that interspersed his periods of gloom.

The timing was right. Admiral Marriott Arbuthnot, an irascible seventy-year-old who had arrived with a new fleet to take over the naval command, had brought reinforcements. Sooner or later Georgia would surely be retaken unless he could support it; this meant occupying neighboring South Carolina.

But Washington appeared to be anticipating his thinking. The defenses of Charleston, the seaport capital of the province, were being strengthened, and Clinton's agents reported that the rebel commander was planning to send down a reinforcement of 2,000 men. So the British general decided to act quickly before the rebel arrangements were complete. He made hurried plans to attack the port with every man he could spare.

Since Saratoga, british policymaking in Whitehall had been centered on the South. The concept of military subjugation had now been replaced with the long-term plan of returning as large an area as possible to civil government with each province supplying delegates to what (eventually) would be a kind of Loyalist congress. The aim was to copy Washington's successful technique, deployed brilliantly before Saratoga, of employing local militia to operate in their own territories in times of crisis, with support when necessary from a small full-time army. London hoped this would help deflate the Revolution, which, to judge from what Clinton and others had reported home, already seemed to be occurring.

The focus of the new thinking was centered on the Southern colonies whose wealthy plantation families tended toward Loyalism. They had been slower than the Northern provinces to join the revolt, and although they had been a large source of supplies to the rebel army, Florida's Governor Patrick Tonyn had reported that now the British naval blockade of their coast was making them "sick of the opposition of Government." Also, they were in no mood to fight. "I am certain," wrote Tonyn, "the four southern provinces are incapable of making any very formidable resistance; they are not prepared for a scene of war."

Clinton's plans to put this statement to the test involved a risk that had existed in no other campaign in America since Lexington. He would have to supply the army by water; until Saratoga Britain had always retained command of the sea. Now with a permanent threat from French and Spanish warships, this was no longer so certain. But both New York and London saw it as a calculated speculation.

Clinton gave the final orders, and an army of 8,000 men was embarked.

At noon in brilliant sunshine on Christmas Day, Clinton and Cornwallis boarded a ship and ran out through the Narrows filled with drifting ice. The fleet, already waiting at Sandy Hook, weighed anchor and sailed south for Charleston.

18

BEFORE CHARLESTON, April 13, 1780

At ten oclock in the morning, the batteries of big 24-pounders set up in front of the siege lines opened fire on the town.[1] The rebels had fortified well; from the other side of two abatis of felled trees, enormously thick walls and a wide canal stretching across the isthmus from river to river, eighty cannon responded.

Then the British gunners, using 10-inch mortars, lobbed in some fire carcasses, and flames leaped skyward from houses in three parts of the city.

Clinton was furious. He had already had trouble reasoning with the navy, which with its unsubtle broadside mentality had urged the destruction of the town, jocularly suggesting that it should "send some twenty-four pound shot into the stomachs of the women to see how they will deliver them."

Clinton had condemned this whole thinking as pointless, insisting it was "absurd, impolitic and inhuman to burn a town you mean to occupy." Now much to the amusement of the naval captains, his own artillery had done it—though the fires were small and controllable. He ordered his gunners to select their targets, laying the cannon to smash the fortifications and enemy guns, not the homes of people he hoped to pacify.

At every level from military strategy to psychology Clinton was being ultracautious. Charleston had been the scene of the one big failure of his career, the humiliating defeat in 1776 when the rebel guns on Sullivan's Island had fought him off and crippled several British ships; this time he was determined that there should be no mistakes. For the first time in two years he was in charge of a major initiative that could, if handled properly, give him control of "the southern provinces and perhaps much more."

Two months had already passed since his troops had gone ashore near Charleston. Though there was no opposition they had carefully crossed the islands that, like the encircling mainland arms that protected Boston, covered the harbor waters from the Atlantic winds.

With equal caution Admiral Arbuthnot had pushed his frigates, their armament removed to lighten them, across the shallow sandbar at the entrance to the harbor. He anchored them out of range of the guns on Sullivan's Island which they would have to pass to approach the town.

Then Clinton decided to wait, even though he could view his target across the waters of the harbor from the British position on James Island. It was an elegant town—more than 1,000 houses, well spaced out on wide avenues—that filled the base of the isthmus formed by the Ashley and the Cooper rivers, flowing down from the north.

Clinton's earlier intelligence that Washington had decided to deploy all the resources he could spare to defend the city was now confirmed. The 2,000 Continental troops that his agents had predicted would be marching south to swell the garrison were on their way, and other detachments would be following.

The rebel attitude to the South Carolina capital made it even more vital that the British assault should be successful. Clinton was leaving nothing to chance. Impressed by the fortifications, he delayed the attack and sent to New York for another 3,000 men. He ordered the garrison at Savannah to join him as well.

Clinton was very clear on his objective and how to achieve it. He needed more than just the occupation of the town, although this was vital strategically as a supply point; he wanted a surrender. When Washington's reinforcements reached the town, General Lincoln would have roughly the same number of men that Burgoyne had marched across the Fishkill into Gates' camp in 1777.

Clinton, in other words, wanted a Saratoga—with all the psychological impact that this would have throughout the thirteen American provinces.

Temperamentally the general was suited to siege warfare with its methodical and well-established techniques of envelopment, and was less concerned by the waiting than by fear of misjudgment. When his impatient officers urged action, he curbed them. "If we proceed cautiously," he said, "we should take the place in the manner we wished. If we hurried it, we might be affronted."

The waiting did nothing to ease the tensions in his personal

The siege of Charleston

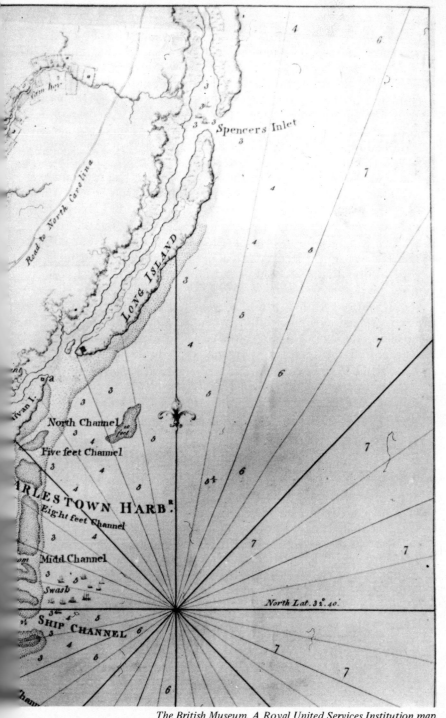

The British Museum. A Royal United Services Institution map.

relationships that were to become a vital factor in the events he was now initiating. When he had been second-in-command to Howe, he had been a carping critic. Now that he was in charge of the army, he was just as prickly, though it took the form of suspicion of the top-ranking officers and doubts about the personal loyalty of the junior men. He was too cold and remote to be a popular commander, and this bitter knowledge rankled him.

He had quarreled with two of his favorite staff officers, who had now left his headquarters, and unlike the close cooperation that had always existed between the Howe brothers, he was barely on speaking terms with the crusty Admiral Arbuthnot. Clinton brooded in his camp on land while the elderly admiral kept to his quarters on his flagship. In fact, he would have tried the patience of any general, for he vacillated constantly and, even when he made a decision, often changed his mind. Clinton had no direct control over him; he could do no more than request his cooperation.

His relations with Cornwallis were not much better. They had been strained ever since 1776, when, in a moment of frustration, he had ranted about Howe to the earl. Cornwallis had mischievously reported the remarks to Howe, who was deeply offended and reminded Clinton of them.

Nevertheless, Clinton had great respect for Cornwallis as a general. When he learned he was returning to America to become second-in-command, Clinton renewed his request to London for permission to resign, suggesting Cornwallis would be an excellent commander in chief.

Cornwallis had not been enthusiastic to start with, but as time went by, the idea of taking over the command had begun to appeal to him. Since both men assumed the King would agree, Clinton had developed his campaign policies in full consultation with the man he assumed would be executing them.

There was little secret about it; Cornwallis had begun to receive the "homage" at headquarters staff officers always gave the commanding general, while Clinton, whom they presumed would soon have little influence over their destinies, began to receive less attention—a change he resented.

Halfway through March, with the army camped near Charleston waiting for reinforcements, the shocking answer to Clinton's latest resignation request arrived from London. The King did not

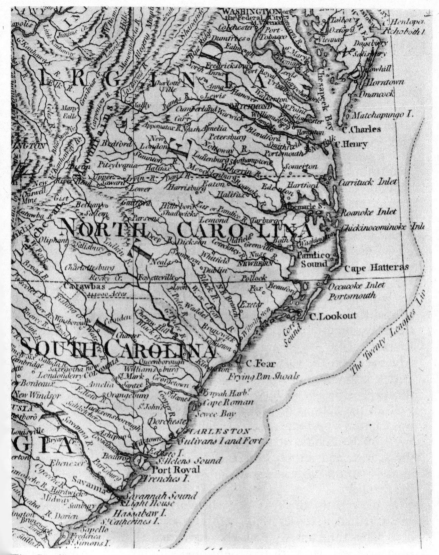

The Carolinas.   *The British Museum.* Engraved by William Faden, 1792

approve it; he was "too well satisfied with your conduct to wish to see the command of his forces in any other hands."

Understandably Cornwallis was deeply offended. Though he could scarcely blame his chief, he made the highly unusual request no longer to be consulted on plans and suggested he be given the independent command of a detachment.

So Clinton was opening a big and vitally important new campaign on the worst of terms both with the admiral who was supposed to cooperate with him and with the second-in-command who was expected to support him.

Surprisingly, despite this, he was extremely successful. On the night of March 28 the army crossed the Ashley River onto the Charleston isthmus in flatboats sent up past the town in darkness and began marching south toward the port that had been prepared for siege with the help of an army of slaves.

Two nights later the British "broke ground" 800 yards from the walls of the town and started work during darkness on the first parallel—a trench, cut across the isthmus to give the siege troops cover from defenders' guns. The working parties were still digging all night when, on the seventh, the last of the rebel reinforcements from Washington's army in the north went down the Cooper River.

In the town the garrison rang the church bells and fired a *feu de joie*. Clinton, too, was pleased; the more troops in town, the more spectacular the surrender.

Of all the actions in which he took part the siege of Charleston was Clinton's personal design. He applied a system of rigid control. Even in the middle of the night he stalked the trenches checking the works, and although as a general he should not have risked himself within range, he was almost killed by bursting shells from the rebel guns.

By the eighth, the first parallel two miles long was completed, and fortified batteries were being thrown up in front of it. Two days later the guns were nearly ready, and Clinton sent a flag of truce to the town with the traditional summons to surrender and received the traditional defiant answer from General Lincoln.

Clinton began to tighten his grip. At dawn on the eighth Arbuthnot's frigates had made a run past the guns of Sullivan's Island and with the exception of one vessel that had run aground had sealed the southern approaches to the port. Now the general planned to close Lincoln's communications that were still open along the Cooper and from the segment of country to the northwest of town.

On the twelfth he sent Lieutenant Colonel James Webster with 1,500 men to take over control of the upper reaches of the Cooper. The advance guard consisted of Banastre Tarleton and his dragoons and Major Patrick Ferguson with his fast-firing riflemen armed, as they were at Brandywine, with his novel breech-loading weapons.

Tarleton had already clashed unsuccessfully a few days before with a unit of enemy dragoons commanded by Colonel Washington. Now the rebel colonel had joined Brigadier General Isaac Huger and Count Casimir Pulaski, and Tarleton was to have better luck. His men stopped a Negro on the road and discovered he was carrying a message from Huger to the garrison in Charleston which divulged the exact disposition of the rebel troops, straddled across the Cooper River by Biggin Bridge. Tarleton took his troops forward with great caution and in darkness, in the early hours of the fourteenth, attacked. The surprise assault was overwhelming; those rebels who were not sabered fled to the nearby swamps.

With Tarleton's horsemen covering the bridge, the British infantry crossed the river, to be joined a few days later by more regiments to block Charleston's supply lines from the northwest. More important from Clinton's viewpoint, since he had never hoped to starve the garrison, was that these had been potential escape routes, and the general's one great fear, which would have destroyed his whole grand conception, had been a mass retreat by Lincoln and his thousands of men. Now that the town was completely invested, this was impossible.

Clinton had given Cornwallis the independent command he had requested—responsibility for all troops east of the Cooper. But as early as April 26 the suspicious general was wondering if he had been wise. "He will play me false, I fear," he noted.

Meanwhile, on the isthmus his engineers had been deploying the classic techniques that had been evolved over centuries to take towns: From the first parallel, the working parties had been carving trenches forward and had then dug sideways to form the second parallel only 450 yards from the town, again reaching almost from river to river. And the whole complex of batteries had been moved forward.

By the twenty-fifth most of the third parallel, close to the canal that formed the outer rim of the town's defenses, was complete.

The jaegers were now in the forward trenches "within point-blank shot . . . so that they [the rebels] could not open their embrasures on the left without loss."

Even though the trenches were dug in zigzag to provide cover against oblique shooting from more distant points on the walls, the working parties were far more vulnerable at such close range. The rebels lit fires between their two abatis of felled trees to provide illumination for their gunners during the darkness; lethal bursts of grapeshot caused a sharp increase in British and Hessian casualties.

But as Clinton built up his forward power, it was only a question of time. "The enemy could touch off but one gun in the course of the day, for they could not load them on account of our rifles," crowed Hessian Captain Johann Hinrichs on the twenty-seventh "They tried to mask the embrasures with cowhides; however, as soon as a hide moved, the bullets of the Jagers, who were posted with cocked and levelled rifles, struck into the embrasure . . . we chased the enemy away even from behind the sandbags of the ramparts."

The rebels repositioned some of their guns out of the jaegers' line of fire, and by the thirtieth they were once more putting down a barrage, though it was far more limited than it had been before. By then, too, the engineers had tunneled through to the canal and were draining it.

All the time the British were moving closer; small trenches and works were now nudging the rebel defenses. During the first days of May Clinton was completing his final preparations to assault the town, though he wanted to avoid "the cruel extremities of a storm" if he could. The fire capacity he was building up on the base of his third parallel would be overwhelming. It took several days and nights to set up the 24-pounder batteries and supporting communication to the magazines, but once they were established, the town was doomed.

On May 8 the artillery commander reported to Clinton that his guns were "ready to open" at point-blank range. The admiral made one of his rare visits to the shore to discuss arrangements for the bombardment by the ships, although even then he still had not decided to what extent he would risk his ships within range of the town's guns, and jointly they sent in a last summons to surrender.

Clinton was not at all certain what the answer would be. Two days earlier he had written Cornwallis that "I begin to think these people will be blockheads enough to await the assault. Je m'en lave les mains."

Lincoln's position was desperate, but he tried to negotiate terms, insisting that the militia should not be regarded as prisoners of war and demanding the right to march out of the town with colors unfurled to the music of a British or American tune. But unlike Gates at Saratoga, the British commanders were in no fear of a relief force. Curtly they rejected his offer, and since he still refused to hand over the town, the next morning "our guns and Howitzers opened a murderous fire."

The rebels endured it for two days, during which the troops crossed the canal and made final plans for the storm. Clinton, still anxious to avoid opening the town to his "exasperated soldiery," decided on a careful use of flames to increase the pressure on the American general. Early in the morning of the eleventh, recorded the Hessian Captain Johann Ewald, "the batteries were ordered to fire hot shot into the city, which set fire to seven houses in the suburbs . . . the generous Commander in Chief ordered the batteries to be silent while they burned to give this stubborn people time to think it over."

His "generosity" was rewarded. At two in the afternoon a white flag fluttered from the ramparts. By that night General Lincoln had agreed to the British terms.

The next day the British commanders rode into the city at the head of two companies of grenadiers. They were met at the gate by Major General Lincoln on horseback, who formally surrendered the town. "The moment the British Grenadiers came under the gate," recalled the watching Hinrichs, "the oboists played 'God Save the King.' " Then "the garrison came out. They were permitted to march off with drums beating and trumpets sounding, but their colors had to be cased. Since they were not allowed to play an English march, they played the 'Turk's March.' "

The rebels piled their arms near the gate, and two British regiments entered the city with colors flying. The royal standard was hoisted and a salute of twenty-two guns fired.

Clinton's careful planning had bloomed into the biggest British victory of the war. Of the 6,000 rebels who marched out of the town, nearly 5,500 were soldiers of the Continental Army. In addition, he took four frigates, several other armed vessels and 400 guns.

Although the operation had lasted nearly four months, it had provided a good demonstration of humane military efficiency to the bellicose naval men: On each side there had been fewer than 300 casualties.

The impact in Europe of this Saratoga-sized rebel defeat was resounding. Since the early days of Concord and Bunker Hill, the successes and defeats of King George's American rebels had had their most critical reactions in the capitals of Europe. America had become a lever in a bigger struggle; indeed, the rebellion depended entirely on its value to the Bourbons, for without their support there is little doubt it would have collapsed.

Now, however, there was a change in the European situation. Events across the Atlantic were being watched closely in courts other than those of the two great power allies, Versailles and Madrid, for the balance of power was in issue. A British defeat might make the Bourbons too powerful, an eventuality that would not be in the interest of the Hapsburgs, despite Marie Antoinette, or even of the Romanovs. For currently Catherine of Russia was vigorously promoting her influence in Western Europe.

As a result, the fiercely fought capture of what by European standards was a hot sleepy little seaport in the American South was now a matter for serious consideration by cabinets in St. Petersburg and Vienna and The Hague.

The situation in Europe was constantly changing, and Charleston had given Lord George Germain a valuable weapon in another campaign he was conducting carefully. The Spanish were reluctant belligerents, as they had been in the last war, but because of the size of their navy they were highly dangerous. Within months of their hostile note amounting to a declaration of war the British were trying to negotiate a separate peace, offering Gibraltar as the price they might be prepared to pay. By the end of 1779 Father Hussey, an Irish priest known to the British as a Spanish secret agent, had left for Madrid with a letter from Germain inviting approaches. Another diplomatic channel had also been opened: the King of Naples, the brother of Charles of Spain, who maintained an ambassador in London.

But diplomacy took time, especially when conducted with an enemy; and the British Cabinet followed the policy of combining delicate peace feelers with vigorous attacks on Spanish possessions on the west of the Atlantic in hopes of making them seem costly when contrasted with the offer of Gibraltar—even though the Rock citadel was then under siege.

Soon after Spain had entered the war, the British had seized the tiny port of Omoa, in Spanish-owned Honduras in the narrow portion of Central America. From there and from Jamaica attacks were being planned on other Spanish possessions—the islands of the Spanish Main and New Orleans. And in Madrid this danger seemed heightened after D'Estaing's humiliation in his attempt to take Savannah.

Now the capture of Charleston, the first of the dramatic victories in the South, would help Germain tighten the pressure at the diplomatic level. The vigorous and successful presence of the British in strength in Georgia and the Carolinas would make a deep impression in Madrid.

Charleston of course was only a start. While Clinton returned to New York, Cornwallis remained in South Carolina in command of 8,000 troops and prepared hastily to extend British control throughout the province. Also, there were pockets of rebel troops that still required action. Three detachments forked out from Charleston with orders to set up a chain of outposts.

In mid-May Cornwallis himself marched with 2,500 men for Camden, which had been selected as the main base in the interior of the province. It was not far from North Carolina, the next area intended for British occupation, and reports had come in that retreating ahead of him was a regiment of Continental troops commanded by Colonel Abraham Buford—all that remained in the province of Washington's soldiers.

Buford had been 40 miles from Charleston on the Santee River when the city fell. Now he was making for the safety of the North Carolina border. Cornwallis soon realized that the rebel force ten days' march in front of him had too big a lead to overtake with infantry, so he ordered Tarleton to pursue them on horseback. It was the type of challenging assignment for which the young cavalry colonel was highly suited.

Banastre Tarleton was regarded by Cornwallis, as he was to soon write to Germain, as the most brilliant cavalry commander he had ever seen in action. Clinton, too, had enormous respect for him. Neither of them appeared to regard his operations as exceptionally brutal, although they came to cause intense hatred from the rebels.

Certainly his progress since he had arrived in America as a cornet

just before the Battle of Long Island had been astounding. Now
only four years later, he was a lieutenant colonel and one of the
most celebrated officers in the army. Very shortly Germain was to
send out the King's personal commendation of him.

Still only twenty-five, cruel, brave and greatly admired by his
troops, he was exceptionally good-looking—"with a face," as one
observer put it, "almost femininely beautiful" and "a form that
was a perfect model of manly strength and vigor."

"Tarleton boasts of having butchered more men and lain with
more women than anybody else in the Army," Horace Walpole
was to report later—a comment that was to provoke a bitter retort
from Richard Sheridan, who had known him as a student. "Lain
with!" the playwright echoed. "He should have said ravished!
Rapes are the relaxation of murderers."

Evidently there was no shortage of women willing to be raped.
While still a cornet when the army was in Philadelphia, he was
discovered in bed with the mistress of one of his senior officers,
and the duel challenge that followed caused a scandal that was
even reported across the Atlantic in the London press. It merely
enhanced his reputation as a hell-raising, hard-living young officer
who was excellent company in the mess.

In actions his success was fantastic—usually against very superior
forces. His techniques were almost always pitched on speed,
surprise and impact. He was merciless—not only with his enemies
but also with himself and his men—but then he was highly able.

He was, for example, a brilliant rider, though characteristically
his methods of control were harsh and probably ruinous. One of
Cornwallis' messengers reported watching him mount for the first
time a "magnificent" black horse that had been declared "altogether unmanageable." The animal's "progress was one continual
bound, at times swinging the grooms clear from the earth as
though they were tassels hung on his huge spanish bit," but
Tarleton, armed only with "spurs of immense size" and a "heavy
scourge with shot well twisted onto its knotted lash," was
determined to force it into submission.

Plying "the whip and rowel like a fiend," he stayed on the horse's
back despite wild leaps, bucking and rearing until "the horse was
completely subdued and at the word of command followed him
around like a dog . . . from his laboring and mangled sides the
mingled blood and foam poured in a thick and clotted stream."

This, one suspects, was typical of Tarleton: He was a skillful successful soldier, but he was unsubtle to the point of stupidity. In the contest he had achieved his objective—personal domination—but the methods he had chosen had almost certainly spoiled the horse.

This was the brash young colonel who now chased Buford and his rebels, displaying the mobility and attack sense that always won the admiration of his commanders. He took 40 English regular dragoons and 250 men from his Loyalist British Legion, 100 of whom were infantrymen who rode two up behind a cavalryman.

Tarleton and his detachment left Cornwallis' army on May 27, hurried across the Santee Hills and through the swamps of the Wateree River. Several horses died in the heat, to be replaced promptly by other mounts purloined from local residents, and by the next afternoon they had ridden the 60 miles to Camden, where Tarleton learned that, two days before, Buford had been 12 miles north of the town.

The colonel ordered his men on, and by early the next morning he knew Buford was only 20 miles ahead of him. At three o'clock on the twenty-ninth his advance corps came within sight of the rebels at Waxhaw near the North Carolina border. In only fifty-four hours, Tarleton and his men had covered 105 miles.

Tarleton sent forward a flag to Buford with a message, warning him that he was "almost encompassed by a corps of seven hundred"—more than double the number he truly had—and demanding his surrender. "To prevent the effusion of human blood," he wrote, "I make offers which can never be repeated. . . . If you are rash enough to reject them, the blood be upon your head."

Buford sent back the flag with the defiant assertion that he would defend himself "to the last extremity."

This was normal language. Traditionally, if surrender offers were rejected, slaughter was permissible—if only for the reason that troops storming a town could never be controlled. The words were rarely interpreted literally. But Tarleton meant what he said.

By the time his messenger returned with Buford's rejection, the cavalry of his advance guard was formed ready in line. As soon as Tarleton read the message, the trumpets sounded, and they charged the rebel rear guard. Astonished by the speed of the assault, the rebel Americans were overwhelmed by the vicious sabering by Loyalist Americans.

Hurriedly Buford formed the main part of his force for defense in an open wood. With nearly 400 infantry as well as some cavalry he outnumbered Tarleton's troops by a considerable margin. But apparently he did not understand the basic principles of fighting mounted troops—unless he thought the widely spaced trees would check them. Instead of ranging his men behind the barrier of his wagons, which would have made a cavalry charge impractical, he formed his infantry in open line.

Three hundred yards away, Tarleton ranged his men for the attack: "two hundred and seventy cavalry and infantry blended." He himself with thirty selected dragoons, mostly Americans, and some legion infantry formed the left wing. Just before he ordered the assault, he heard the enemy officers warning their men in traditional rebel style to hold their fire until the dragoons were within ten paces. Tarleton then knew he would win. For this was not Bunker Hill with troops advancing on foot: A horse could cover 10 yards in a second.

Again Tarleton's trumpets sounded, and the line of horsemen charged through the trees toward the ranks of waiting men. Tarleton and his left wing raced for the flank. He passed the end of the rebel line, galloped for the standard-bearer in the center at the rear and cut him down with a slash of his saber. Almost immediately another rebel shot the colonel's horse—and it collapsed under him.

By that time the battle had become a massacre. Repeatedly the dragoons swept through the rebel infantry, slicing with their sabers; the legion men on foot plunged after them with jabbing twisting bayonets. According to one rebel report, the wounded lay in piles, and Tarleton's men, after stabbing those that lay on top, used their bayonets to drag the bodies aside so that they could reach those underneath.

The rebels later claimed that Buford's attempts to surrender with a white flag early in the fight were ignored and asserted that many of his men were killed after they had thrown down their weapons. Unhorsed as he was, Tarleton may have found it hard to control his soldiers or may have used his situation as an excuse not to curb them. In any case, he did not feel that Buford was entitled to much protection since his surrender offer had been "positively rejected."

"I summoned the corps," he wrote in a brief note to Cornwallis.

"They refused my terms, I have cut a hundred and seventy officers and men to pieces." He also took fifty-three prisoners.

After this Tarleton was a marked man by the rebels; in the Continental Army, "Tarleton's Quarter" became the synonym for killing men who offered to surrender. Cornwallis, however, saw nothing especially brutal about his behavior. "I can only add the highest encomiums on the conduct of Lieutenant Colonel Tarleton," he wrote to Clinton. In England, as soon as the news was published in the London *Gazette* on the orders of an impressed Germain, Tarleton became a celebrity.

Tarleton's action at Waxhaw appeared to seal the British occupation of South Carolina. For a few weeks it seemed the Cabinet's new policy of placing the emphasis on civil government, supported by loyal American troops, might be effective. Cornwallis established the outposts he had planned, soldiered mainly by Loyalists, and formed seven battalions of militia, amounting to more than 4,000 men, though these would only operate in their immediately local areas.

Across the border the Tories of North Carolina were eager for action, but the earl "gave them positive directions to attend to their harvests and to remain quiet until I could march to their relief." He wanted to wait until the cool of the fall before he struck north.

"Everything wearing the face of tranquility and submission," as he wrote to Germain on June 21, Cornwallis left Camden under the command of young Lord Rawdon and returned to Charleston, "where I had much business to do . . . regulating the civil and commercial affairs of the town and country."

"The face of tranquility" did not last long. Cornwallis had hardly reached the capital when he heard that the rebel Major General Johann Baron de Kalb had entered North Carolina with 2,000 Continental troops determined to set up a base at Hillsboro in the north of the province.

The news did not alarm him. Even the three big rebel militia groups, who would obviously operate with De Kalb, were a long way off. No offensive was likely until North Carolina's harvest was in.

But the fact of the Continentals' presence precipitated trouble. Despite Cornwallis' orders, there were two Loyalist uprisings in North Carolina—"driven to it, as they said, by the most barbarous persecution." Then the rebel General Thomas Sumter, "an active and daring man," crossed the border at Catawba in the west and rallied 1,000 men. The British called out the militia to support their outposts.

Still Cornwallis did not consider it very serious. "I was very unwilling to put the troops in motion . . . during the intense heat of the Summer." Through most of July there were skirmishes along the border "but none of any material consequences." More disturbing was the undercover activity. "The enemy had . . . filled this province with their emissaries and in all the eastern part of it were planning a general revolt." At the same time, purges of Loyalists in North Carolina were causing nervousness south of the border. Several of "our friends" had been executed. Many others had been "confined in dungeons, loaded with irons."

During the last week of July Cornwallis received news that General Horatio Gates, the victor of Saratoga, had arrived in North Carolina to take over command of the army. There were signs that the attack might come sooner than the British commander had expected. The pressure on the outposts was continually growing. Sumter assaulted the British position at Rocky Mount in the west and was only barely fought off with heavy casualties. Rawdon had had to abandon another post at Cheraw Hill near the border, after the supposedly Loyalist militia had mutinied.

In early August an express reached Charleston with news that Gates was marching south with his army. Lord Rawdon withdrew all the men he could from the outposts in an attempt to defend Camden. By August 9 the rebels were across the border; according to intelligence, they totaled 6,000 men, excluding Sumter's 1,000 who were still deployed in the country.

By the time Cornwallis rode into Camden on the evening of the thirteenth he found Rawdon with his soldiers formed on a hill just outside the town, awaiting attack at any moment by the rebels, who were only 12 miles away. His force was completely inadequate; against Gates' 6,000 men, he had only 1,400 regular and American regimental troops, plus 500 militia, who under the circumstances might not be too reliable. In the hospital in Camden were another 800—most of them stricken with fevers caused by the Carolina summer.

"I now had my option to make," Cornwallis explained to Germain, "either to retire or to attack the enemy; for the position at Camden was a bad one to be attacked in."

At that stage he could have retreated fairly easily to Charleston, but although he would still possess the city, it would mean giving up South Carolina, at least for the time being. Since he had left the port fully garrisoned and stanced for siege, the earl decided that there was "little to lose by a defeat and much to gain by a victory." But outnumbered as he was, he would have to make his plans with extreme care.

For two days he "took great pains to procure good information of their movements and position." Scouting parties and Tories provided him with an exact picture of the enemy encampment.

On August 15 Cornwallis gave orders that the troops would march that night. His aim was to approach the enemy in darkness and to attack at daylight, but he was not able to execute the attack as planned. The evening before the troops marched, Tarleton and a reconnaissance unit of legion cavalry captured three American soldiers, who under questioning explained that General Gates had given orders for his troops to move, to attack the British camp next morning near Camden.

The rebels, it seemed, had the same plan as the British: The two armies would be marching toward each other in the darkness. Cornwallis did not alter his orders. Perhaps he mistrusted the soldiers, but Camden was a bad defense position—he could not stay where he was.

On a humid, sultry night the British column marched north. As usual, well ahead of the main body rode twenty dragoons as scouts, fanned out and alert for any signs of the rebels. Immediately behind them marched a forward party of legion infantry.

For four hours there were no incidents, and the column moved steadily forward in the darkness. It was not until two thirty, when the British scouting cavalry were nine miles out of Camden, that, far ahead along the road, they detected horsemen against the background of scattered pines. They were their opposite numbers—the advance dragoons of Gates' army.

Quickly the British cavalry formed and charged the Americans. The advance legion infantry followed up along the road at the run behind the galloping horses.

Surprised by the fast attack, the rebel dragoons fell back on their main column, and immediately the American infantry started shooting—deploying as they did so off the road on both sides.

As happened so often to attacking cavalry, the dragoons were

suddenly exposed to great danger—under heavy fire on their flank
as well as the front. As the bullets whistled, one of which
wounded their commander, they wheeled and galloped back down
the road. The legionnaires on foot kept shooting, but there were
only twenty of them, and they, too, were quickly forced back to a
British line that was already formed waiting across the road.

Farther back in the column, Cornwallis made his plans. From the
local Tories who were with him he knew that the position of the
British was very good for a force that was smaller than the enemy.
The ground was "narrowed by swamps on the right and left,"
while between the marshes it widened to the rear of the rebels,
meaning that if the British could force them to relinquish
territory, there would be scope for a flank action. Cornwallis
waited until daylight. "At the dawn I made my last disposition,
forming the British infantry on the right and the Loyalist American Regiments, the Legion and two new North Carolina Regiments, on the left." Tarleton with his Green Dragoons was
waiting in column at the rear under orders "to seize any opportunity that might offer to break the enemy's line. . . ."

The morning was hazy as the sun rose: another scorching day.
The ground between the swamps was halved by the road from
Camden; on either side were pine trees, well spaced.

Although Cornwallis had originally intended to make his main
push against the Continentals, his formation, planned in the early
dawnlight when his intelligence of the enemy arrangement was
probably limited, had ranged his British regulars on the right
against Gates' militia.

Just before the battle as he sat on his horse studying the enemy
line, it was this rebel wing that attracted the general's attention.
"Observing a movement on their left which I supposed to be with
an intention to make some alterations to their order," he directed
Webster to attack quickly. "In a few minutes the action was
general along the whole front."

The British let out a cheer and advanced. They halted, raised
their muskets to their shoulders and fired a volley. Then, with
weapons at their hips and bayonets pointed forward, they charged
the militiamen.

The battle-experienced militia of Massachusetts or New Jersey or
New York might have withstood a bayonet charge by British
regulars *on confined ground*, although it is doubtful, for under
these conditions British professionals were at their most terrifying.

But this was the first time a battle of any size had been fought in the South, and the sight of the fast-approaching line of sharpened steel was clearly too much for the unseasoned farm men.

In panic the whole rebel left wing broke. "At least two thirds of the Army fled without firing a shot," was the disgusted comment later of the rebel Colonel Otho H. Williams, who tried to rally them.

Watching from behind his advancing troops, Cornwallis could make out little of what was happening. With the American left wing in flight, the flank of Gates' Continental troops was opened. Webster did not bother to pursue the fleeing militia; it was not going to be a long battle and there was plenty of time for that. He wheeled his men and launched an immediate attack on the side of the rebel right wing that was already struggling against the frontal onslaught of Cornwallis' American troops.

The Continentals fought desperately, but their position was hopeless. "After an obstinate resistance for three quarters of an hour," Cornwallis reported, the enemy was in "total confusion. . . . At this instant, I ordered the cavalry to complete the rout."

There were two charges by the dragoons—the first led by Major George Hanger, Tarleton's friend and number two in the legion, the second by Tarleton himself. The legion's charging horses and swinging sabers ended the battle. "The Continentals, the state troops and the militia," wrote Tarleton, "abandoned their arms, their colors and their cannon to seek protection in flight."

It was still early in the morning. No parliamentary inquiry was to criticize Cornwallis for failing to follow up his victory, as Howe had been criticized. Gates had fled, having ridden 90 miles without stopping, and was finished as an officer, unlike Washington, who had been on the march the morning after Brandywine.

Throughout the intense heat of that summer day Tarleton and his dragoons pursued the fleeing rebels, riding saber charges at terrified men. By the time the cavalrymen halted at last, they were more than 20 miles from the battlefield.

The British, according to Cornwallis, had killed 800 to 900 rebels and had taken 1,000 prisoners. Among these was the mortally wounded Baron de Kalb, a professional whose loss would be keenly felt by Washington.

The British general was still not satisfied, as Howe would probably have been. He sent messengers into North Carolina urging the Loyalists to rise immediately, to seize the leading rebels in the province as well as their magazines and to attack the stragglers of Gates' army. On the same day he ordered Tarleton to find General Sumter and his big militia detachment that had not taken part in the battle.

With 350 men Tarleton moved swiftly up the Wateree River, which flowed south past Camden, and by that night had found the Americans—camped on the other side of the river near Rocky Mount. He ordered his men to spend the night in silence without lighting fires, but for once the British colonel, with his incredible mobility and sense of strategy, awoke to find his enemy had slipped away in the night.

Tarleton was after him very fast. His dragoons swam their horses across the river, hanging onto their tails and controlling them by undoing one side of the bridles so that the reins reached to the rear. His infantry were ferried across in boats.

The legion picked up Sumter's fresh tracks easily enough and pushed on after him all morning in intense heat. By noon many of the infantry were too exhausted to continue, but Tarleton was not stopping now that he was so close. He went on with 100 dragoons and 60 of his foot troops mounted behind them. Five miles farther on, he found the rebels resting in the heat of the early afternoon beside the waters of Fishing Creek with arms stacked, cooking, even bathing—completely unaware of their danger.

It was a typical Tarleton situation, and despite his limited numbers of only 160, he exploited it with his usual efficiency. The Green Dragoons charged on the astonished rebels, killed 150 of them and took 300 prisoners, as well as forty-four wagons. The triumph was marred only by the fact that they did not get Sumter, who escaped by leaping on a horse that was grazing nearby and galloping off without a saddle.

As usual Cornwallis was delighted. His cavalry colonel may have been a bit brutal, but he certainly achieved fantastic results. "The action is too brilliant to need any comment of mine," he wrote Germain.

If there were a few doubts after the surrender of Charleston that the British had established a proper grip on South Carolina, these were now dispelled. And Cornwallis was not going to repeat the mistake that Howe had made so often before in the hope of winning the civilian population. He had seen enough Americans sign the oath of allegiance to the King and then use this as cover to attack his troops. "I shall give directions," he wrote, "to inflict exemplary punishment on some of the most guilty, in hopes to deter others in future from sporting with allegiance, with oaths and with the lenity and generosity of the British Government."

The two spectacular victories, Charleston and Camden, caused the repercussions that Clinton had always anticipated would result from big success in the Carolinas. They shook the Revolution as had no other events with the possible exception of the chase of Washington through Jersey in December, 1776.

One reason for this was their timing. The rebellion had been in progress for five long years. The British had made all the concessions that Samuel Adams and the militants had originally demanded. The efforts of the French, from whom the rebels had expected so much, had been a deep disappointment. The Spanish had displayed an equal lack of vigor. Both big powers were for less interested in America than they were in the rich islands of the West Indies, and even there the British Admiral Sir George Rodney had recently clashed with the French Admiral Comte Luc Urbain de Bouexic de Guichen and forced him to run for the cover of the shore guns of Martinique with twenty-two ships of the line.

Even worse, Congress had become hopelessly topheavy and inefficient. Its currency policy was in crisis, threatened by rampant inflation. Many of Washington's troops had not been paid for months and were moving angrily toward mutiny.

It was at this moment, when the morale of the rebels was so low, that Clinton was preparing to activate a brilliant move he had been planning for more than a year. Added to the big British successes in the South, it could only widen sharply the cracks that were already evident in the revolt. Even if the psychological impact were inadequate to achieve this object—and the optimism of British generals had often been proved to be excessive—the military gain would be enormous.

Clinton was just completing a deal he had negotiated with one of most celebrated generals in the rebel army. It would give him the Hudson highlands, from which he could harry the rebel communication with New England and the Northern provinces, as well as 3,000 men and a vast quantity of Washington's stores.

Clinton had arranged nothing less than the purchase of West Point and the related forts in the highland complex—for £20,000.

19

OFF TELLER'S POINT, Hudson River, September 22, 1780

The night air was cold, as the boat pushed off from the British sloop. In the clear sky the high wooded banks of the river were barely visible as the two rowers heaved on their oars; muffled with sheepskins, they made no noise in the rowlocks.[1]

In the stern sat Major John André, huddled inside a heavy blue watch cloak that he wore over his uniform. He was heading for a predawn meeting that would send into action up the Hudson a force of 5,000 British troops waiting poised at New York under the cover story that they were destined for the Chesapeake.

For André it would be the climax of eighteen months of planning since the May day last year when Joseph Stansbury, a Tory from Philadelphia, had first called at British headquarters with a fantastic proposition: Benedict Arnold had decided that the best way he could "serve his country," as he was to write later, was by "accelerating the termination of this unhappy contest." Arnold of all people! The almost legendary rebel leader who had led his men on the incredible expedition up the Kennebec to the St. Lawrence; the man who with homemade ships had held off Carleton at Valcour; the general whose brilliant attack on the Hessian redoubt at Freeman's Farm had forced Burgoyne to abandon the British lines.

Stansbury indicated that the outright rejection of the British peace proposals after Saratoga and the alliance with the Catholic France had led Arnold to question whether Congress was still acting in the interests of the American people.

Twenty-eight years old, good-looking and highly talented—a writer and artist as well as an officer—André was adjutant general of the British army and responsible for running the headquarters staff. One of his duties was to control the network of British spies, but none of his agents was in a top position such as that occupied by Arnold. André reported immediately to Clinton that the possibilities were endless—a fact Arnold had already recognized, for he was demanding a guarantee, whether his efforts were successful or not, of £10,000.

Clinton did not mind paying for results and on some scale, as he was soon to demonstrate, but he was not committing himself until he knew what he was getting for his money. It was a sensible precaution since suddenly Arnold's position had become precarious. He was facing a court-martial on charges that he had used his position as commander of Philadelphia, a nonfield appointment resulting from his leg wound at Freeman's Farm, for commercial exploitation—an allegation that had been made against him before in regard to his activities in Canada in 1776.

For months, while he negotiated with the British about more spectacular plans, Arnold supplied information to André through a series of go-betweens, writing always under the cover name of "Gustavus" or "Monk." In his replies, the young adjutant general adapted his own name to "John Anderson."

At one stage, negotiations between Arnold and the British broke down over the issue of the guaranteed payment to the general. When contact was renewed a few months later, there had been two important new developments. First, Arnold had been acquitted of the main charges in his court-martial, though reprimanded on minor counts, and thus was no longer suspended from army command. Second, Charleston was going to fall to the British at a time when, as Arnold pointed out, the Revolution was coming under great stress. Thus any major strike against the rebel army he could engineer in collaboration with the British would be doubly catastrophic.

Clinton was now clear what form this collaboration should take. In 1777 Howe had forced him to evacuate the forts in the Hudson highlands that had fallen to him so easily just before Saratoga. He wanted them back. Overlooking the river from their craggy heights, they were always the key to the control of the upper Hudson and in British hands could divide America. Now their strategical value was even greater because at West Point, a little downstream of Fort Montgomery, the rebels had established their main Northern supply base. The capture of the highlands, following on the shattering effect of the surrender of Charleston, would be certain to have traumatic repercussions.

Moving with great care, Arnold sought the command of West

Point, an appointment which included responsibility for the whole area. It took him several months to achieve his object. At one stage, in fact, Washington offered him the left wing of the Continental Army, expecting him to grasp eagerly at this opportunity of getting back into action. He was a little surprised when Arnold pleaded his leg was still giving him trouble and repeated his request for West Point. Eventually, the rebel commander agreed, and the general took up his new post in early August.

By then there were other reasons Clinton wanted to launch his spectacular assault plan. The expected French fleet had arrived in America in July, and even though Arnold had alerted André to the important fact that its destination was Rhode Island, which the British had evacuated last year because they did not have the ships or troops to hold it, Arbuthnot ignored Clinton's suggestion that he should challenge the enemy ships.

Rhode Island had thus become a French base occupied by Lieutenant General Comte de Rochambeau and 6,000 troops brought to America by the fleet. Unlike D'Estaing's instructions before him, Rochambeau's orders were to place himself under the command of Washington. It was the beginning of a new French initiative—and a fairly desperate one at that. The court at Versailles was beginning to question whether the high cost of their two-and-a-half-year-old alliance with the Americans was merited by the limited results. Under these circumstances, the dramatic British capture of the highlands, coupled with the equally dramatic defection of one of the rebels' most brilliant generals, was certain to make a deep impression on the French. Just how rotten, they might ask, was the rebel army that they were now supporting in some strength? To what extent could its leaders be trusted? If so celebrated a man as Arnold had returned to the royal allegiance, what other generals were also in touch with British headquarters?

As Clinton saw it, there was no time to waste. Quite apart from the generally demoralized state of the rebel army, Washington and Rochambeau—as he knew from Arnold—were preparing an attack on New York. His own plan to make a fast strike at Rhode Island in July had failed in mid-execution because Arbuthnot suddenly went to sea with all his ships, thus removing the vital naval cover for the assault. The admiral's strange explanation was that he believed the French were about to sail and wanted to position his ships to challenge them.

Clinton's bitter conflict with Arbuthnot was to prove expensive to the British. Had the attack on Rhode Island been successful it could well have altered drastically the course of events that were now in motion.

Ironically, and certainly unwittingly, Arnold was already predicting the pattern that these would take in a warning to André that another fleet would soon be on its way from Brest with 2,500 more troops. "If this division should arrive soon," he wrote, "they will probably make the French fleet nearly equal, perhaps superior to the British and there is some expectation of a reinforcement from the West Indies." Because of this the rebel "affairs, which do not wear a pleasing aspect at present, may soon be greatly changed."

This did not strike Clinton as too serious a danger at the moment. Admiral Thomas Graves had just arrived with some new ships of the line from England, and Sir George Rodney had brought his fleet into New York from the West Indies. But without question the strike at West Point should be made before the French reinforcements arrived.

By the end of August Clinton was pressing hard for action. There seemed little reason for further delay; Arnold was now in command at West Point, and the British had agreed to his full price of £20,000. Already he had weakened the highland defenses under the pretext of having them strengthened. He had made gaps in the walls of several forts—a preliminary to rebuilding. Most important, on the grounds that the heavy chain boom that stretched across the river as a barrier to attacking ships needed repair, Arnold had ordered the removal of one of the 240-pound links for examination, bridging the gap only by a piece of rope that would part the moment it was struck by a ship under way.

All that remained to transform the plan into action was a meeting between Arnold and a British officer to settle the final details of the assault and to tie up the last unsettled aspect of the financial arrangement. For although Clinton had agreed to the price for the successful capture of West Point, he still refused to be committed on a firm payment in the event of failure—and on this Arnold was determined. Also, Clinton, wary of espionage, wanted to make certain he was not being hoaxed into a clever trap by the rebels and that André's contact was truly Arnold.

The arrangements to meet seem to have been made more complicated than necessary. Arnold strongly resisted the suggestion that he meet André as a British officer, while Clinton was adamant that André should wear his army uniform, was not to go within the rebel lines and was to receive no documents.

After several abortive attempts to meet Arnold lower down the river, on Wednesday, September 20, André went aboard the British sloop *Vulture*, which was anchored upstream off Teller's Point, not far from the town of Haverstraw and only 18 miles below West Point. This stretch of the river, like the country on either side, was a kind of neutral territory between the British and American lines and, as a result, was the scene of constant skirmishing between regular patrols and Loyalist and rebel militia.

André alerted Arnold to the fact that he was on board the sloop by signing the words "John Anderson, Secretary" to a formal complaint by the *Vulture*'s captain that one of his boats had been fired on while carrying a flag of truce. It produced the required result. Soon after midnight on Friday, a boat came alongside the sloop with a man named Joshua Smith, who bore a note from Arnold saying he would conduct André to a "place of safety."

Although he would have preferred to have met Arnold on the ship, André went with Smith to a landing place a little upriver on the west bank of the Hudson in Haverstraw Bay, where he met Arnold "hid," as Smith was to testify later, "among the firs."

There is no official record—no reports by André or Arnold—of what plan was agreed to at that meeting in darkness, although both François de Barbe-Marbois, secretary to the French legation in Philadelphia, and Lieutenant George Mathew[2] of the Coldstream Guards, both of whom could have had special knowledge, wrote dogmatic assertions of the arrangements. The British would attack simultaneously by land and water. Arnold would weaken the defense forces at the assault points by sending detachments to other parts of the highlands where they could be surprised by British units. The fortifications had already been opened up, and the chain boom was no longer a barrier to the ships. When the British were three miles from West Point, two of Clinton's officers, in American uniforms, were to ride ahead to Arnold at full gallop to obtain his final instructions.

One part of the plan, according to Lieutenant Mathew, was that Arnold should rig a fake resistance at one of the forts and send a desperate message to the army for reinforcements. Because of the importance of the highlands, Washington would almost certainly command the relief force in person and might be captured in the ambush.

The attack would begin in four days' time—during the early hours of Tuesday, September 26. From the British point of view, it was a brilliant plan. All that was necessary to launch it into action was for André to return to New York. Arnold had brought with him some papers, mainly details of the West Point defenses written in his own handwriting, and at his urging André placed them between his stockings and the soles of his feet.

It was now nearly daylight, but when the two men returned to the waiting boat, the oarsmen complained that they were too tired to row against the flood tide back to the *Vulture*. So Arnold decided that André should spend the day in hiding at Smith's house, a couple of miles up the riverbank, riding there on a spare horse he had with him.

On the way they were challenged by a rebel sentry, who let them pass as soon as he recognized Arnold, but André was alarmed, for he knew he was now within the rebel lines.

From the house during the day, they heard the sound of guns as rebel artillery, brought up by some keen militiamen on the east bank of the Hudson, bombarded the *Vulture*. Arnold and Smith decided it would be safer for André to go back to New York by land, rather than attempt a return by boat to the ship, which might well be under surveillance by rebel patrols. To do this dressed as a British officer with his scarlet regimentals under the blue watch cloak would make discovery highly probable; so apprehensively—for as long as he was in uniform, he could not be accused of spying—André agreed to replace his jacket with a civilian coat supplied by Smith. He also took some papers with details of West Point, most of which were written in Arnold's handwriting.

He had now disobeyed all three of Clinton's orders.

That night he started on his journey accompanied by Smith. They had a pass signed by Arnold, ordering the guards at King's Ferry to let them through.

They crossed the Hudson without incident, and in the morning Smith, who had been warned the Loyalist militia was active in the area, left André to continue the journey alone.

On the road André did meet three militiamen, but they were not Loyalists, a fact he unwisely failed to determine before revealing his association with the "lower party" (*i.e.*, downriver). They grabbed him, searched him, found Arnold's papers in his stockings and took him to the nearest rebel army outpost at North Castle.

* * *

Meanwhile, the *Vulture*, damaged by the rebel guns, was still anchored near Teller's Point. André had been gone for forty-eight hours, and her officers had now become very anxious. They were not left in doubt much longer. The next day Arnold's barge, flying a flag of truce, bore down swiftly on the sloop. In the stern was the general, a pistol in each hand.

The news of André's capture had reached Arnold that morning at his house while he waited for Washington to join him for breakfast. His escape from arrest for treason on a spectacular scale had been narrow.

Clinton abandoned his assault plan, though Arnold pressed him not to, assuring him, according to Rodney, that he would "answer with his head" if the forts were not "taken in ten days."

Clinton must have been tempted, for a fast strike would have seemed practical. The troops were embarked on the assault ships; the physical defenses of the forts were still weak; the chain boom across the river was still faulty. But Washington's troops in the area were double the number of Clinton's attack force, excluding militia, and since failure "would be death to our cause in the present stage of the war," he decided the risk was too great. "The impropriety of the measure under such circumstances," he told the complaining Germain acidly, "must be obvious to Your Lordship."

The troops, who should have taken the highlands, sailed south toward Cornwallis. And Clinton devoted all his energies to trying to save his young adjutant general, whose capture plagued him with bitter self-doubts whether his orders had been explicit enough. Both he and Arnold wrote to Washington insisting that André had left the *Vulture* under a flag of truce sent by the commanding officer of West Point, which, as Arnold asserted, he was within his rights to dispatch. Under these circumstances, he could not be regarded as a spy. They warned that if he were executed, they would retaliate by carrying out death sentences on forty South Carolinians who were under arrest for breaking their oaths of allegiance to the King.

The arguments had little effect. Rebel officers negotiating with Clinton's representatives indicated that André, already found guilty on spying charges by a hastily convened army board, would be freed on only one condition: the return of Arnold to face trial.

It was an impossible proposition for Clinton. Had he agreed, it would have ended any hope of further high-level defections, and he was in touch, as he told Chief Justice William Smith, with other rebel generals. Even more important, it would have done immeasurable damage to the Secret Service. It was vital that spies could trust in British sanctuary if they sought it as Arnold had.

So André, standing on a wagon as a drop, was hanged on a hill just outside Tappan Village.

Despite the failure of the plan, Clinton rewarded Arnold well. He was made a brigadier general in the British army and given £6,315 in cash for the property he had lost; his wife and sons were awarded income for life.

Having changed sides, Arnold grasped the royal cause with almost as much enthusiasm as he had opposed it in storming Quebec. In an address to the "Inhabitants of America," he denounced "the impolicy, tryanny and injustice [of Congress] which, with sovereign contempt of the people of America, studiously neglected to take their collective sentiments of the British proposals of peace." He mocked that France was "too feeble to establish your independency which was, so perilous to her distant dominions [because it might be infectious], the enemy of the Protestant Faith." He issued a call to those "officers and soldiers of the Continental Army who . . . are determined to be no longer the tools and dupes of Congress or of France" to join a corps he was forming on the same service conditions enjoyed by British troops.

At another level, he wrote long memorandums to Clinton and Germain suggesting ways of bringing wholesale defections in Washington's army, including the ingenious suggestion that the British should offer them land as an inducement, with the acreage depending on rank. "Money," he wrote, "will go further than arms in America."

In strategic terms, the arrival in New York of Arnold could not be compared with the capture of West Point, but because of his reputation, its impact on the already weakened morale of the rebel army was enormous. And this was an area of warfare which Clinton was studying very closely, deploying every technique he could apply to the widening of the internal fissures that might cause its collapse.

On January 3, 1781, news arrived in New York that suggested the crash was in motion. On New Year's Day, the Pennsylvania

Line—an entire corps of 2,500 of Washington's best troops, commanded by General Anthony Wayne—had mutinied at Morristown. With a battery of complaints, including arrears of pay, poor food, inadequate clothing and technicalities about their term of service, they had marched to Trenton under the leadership of a committee of sergeants to demand justice from Congress.

Even the crusty old Admiral Arbuthnot shared the optimism of the general he disliked so much that "the crisis of the Rebellion was coming."

Promptly Clinton reinforced his army on Staten Island at the mouth of the Raritan River and sent messengers to the mutineers offering British protection and the immediate payment of all money due them from Congress. There were no strings to the offer, though they could join the army if they wished, other than "laying down their arms and returning to their allegiance."

For nearly two weeks Clinton heard nothing; then he learned that two of his messengers had been hanged at a crossroads just across the Delaware from Trenton. Sadly Clinton wrote Germain that "the malcontents had wanted chiefly to be out of military service—not at all to change sides." But many of the Pennsylvanians were permitted to leave the Continental Army.

By then the New Jersey regiments had mutinied, too. Again Clinton, moving much more cautiously, tried to exploit the situation, but this time Washington realized the danger of contagion and treated the mutiny harshly. He promptly executed the leaders and asked Congress to permit him to increase his flogging sentences to 500 lashes. The Americans, too, it seems were becoming "bloodybacks."

Although the results of the mutinies were disappointing to Clinton, the discontent they reflected was encouraging. Also, the general had great hopes that negotiations with Ethan Allen, whose attempt to set up Vermont as a fourteenth American province had been deflected and shelved by Congress, would bring him the support of the tough men of the Green Mountains in return for royal recognition of the state.

That January while Clinton was trying to exploit the natural erosion in Washington's army, the British were campaigning again, and the commander in chief had wasted no time in using his new general. Arnold's reputation for fast and brilliant maneuvers would, he hoped, have a great impact on the Americans once these qualities were employed against them. Halfway through December, Arnold sailed from New York with nearly 2,000 men for Portsmouth, the Virginia port at the mouth of the James River near the entrance to the Chesapeake.

Clinton had good reasons for sending him there. If Arnold could destroy the rebels' magazines and cannon foundry on the James River, the main source of their armament, he would provide a diversion in the South to help Cornwallis, as well as give him a base on the Chesapeake for future actions.

Despite his brilliant victory at Camden, Cornwallis needed a diversion. He had learned the bitter truth that while there was a nucleus of Continental troops in the South, the territory under his control would be racked constantly by revolt.

After Camden, he had advanced into North Carolina to Charlotte but had not been able to press on farther, as he had intended. Throughout the fall, the border country had been the scene of constant battles, raids and counterraids. Tarleton and the Loyalists had been in regular and very bloody skirmishes—some of them involving large numbers—with the rebel guerrilla leaders such as Sumter, Marion and Colonel Elijah Clark.

Then in October had come the trauma of King's Mountain when Major Patrick Ferguson and 1,000 Loyalists had been surrounded by frontiersmen from Black Mountain in the west. Yelling "Tarleton's Quarter," they had killed him and massacred many of his men and later hanged some of the prisoners their officers had eventually persuaded them to take, treating the remainder with what Cornwallis complained formally was "an inhumanity scarcely credible."

The Black Mountain men came from Indian country into which the white Americans were encroaching constantly, and temporarily Cornwallis forced them home by rousing the tribes to attack their home farms. But the effect of King's Mountain was disastrous to the British. "No sooner had the news of it spread through the country," Clinton related, "than multitudes of disaffected flew to arms from all parts and menaced every British post on both frontiers."

Immediately Cornwallis dropped back over the border to Winnsboro while he completed his plans for a new offensive. Months ago he had reached the conclusion that the only way to calm the Carolinas was to strike north at Virginia. This would force the

Continentals to drop back to counter his move and thus make the activities of the rebel militia easier to contain.

Cornwallis had been unable to march until January because he did not have enough men or transport, since Clinton had taken many of the army's wagons back to New York when he sailed from Charleston. But in December reinforcements under General Leslie had arrived at Charleston, and a message had come from Clinton that Arnold was on his way to Portsmouth, Virginia.

The time for his big forward movement had arrived. It coincided with the return from London of Major Alexander Ross, Cornwallis' aide-de-camp, whom he had sent home to report in person on the news of Camden, the normal practice with big battles. Ross told him he was regarded with warm enthusiasm in Whitehall and St. James's, while official attitudes to Clinton were growing cool. Just as Burgoyne at the end of 1776 had seemed the active hard-hitting general Britain needed, in contrast with the cautious Carleton, now Cornwallis was seen as a man of dynamism compared to a wearying and overcareful Clinton.

Throughout the war, both for international and domestic imperial reasons, there had been an urgent need for a quick ending of the Revolution. Now in the autumn of 1780, the crisis that faced the King and his ministers was more serious than any that they had yet faced.

Britain itself was marked by great unrest. In the spring the religion-motivated Gordon Riots had produced a state of civil war in London that the troops had put down only with considerable killing. In the House of Commons Lord North had barely succeeded in fending off an opposition move to strip away the royal right to dissolve Parliament, and there were so many waverers in the ministry that the King had taken the rare step of summoning the Cabinet to his presence in order to stiffen their resolve. The British national debt had nearly doubled since the outbreak of the rebellion, and despite the lowering of physical standards and raising recruitment bounties, the sources of new troops were nearly exhausted.

Far more serious was the growing threat of Russian participation. In May the Empress Catherine had astonished the King—who again, as in 1775, had been led by his ambassador to believe that he could expect military assistance—by issuing a declaration of "Armed Neutrality" that in effect contested the blockade right of British cruisers. At the same time she was promoting the idea of a

league of the northern neutral powers. This would make her an
ally of Holland, with whom Britain was locked in a serious quarrel
over the issue of supplying the King's enemies with naval stores,
especially copper; there had already been some incidents when
British blockade cruisers boarded and searched Dutch transports in
the Channel.

If Russia entered the conflict with Holland on the side of France
and Spain, the result could only be catastrophic for Britain.
Against this ominous background it became imperative to crush
finally the Revolution in America—a goal that did not now seem
too remote in London. For both the rebels' powerful European
supporters were known to be tiring of a war in which the gains had
not yet matched the enormous cost; in fact, Spain had responded
well to the peace feelers.

For Germain the most tantalizing aspect of his post as the
director of the war in America was that the Revolution seemed so
often to be at the point of collapse—as, in truth, it was. One major
effort was all that seemed necessary to produce the desired result,
but always the Colonial Secretary was frustrated by commanders
in chief who complained constantly about the shortage of troops
and such mundane details as communications and transport.
However, Cornwallis with his brilliant Tarleton had shown what
could be done when well-trained troops were properly used against
very superior numbers of rebels.

After Saratoga, when he had become so vulnerable to opposition
attacks, Germain's impatience had driven him to become ever
more strident and dogmatic. Now with Britain faced by these new
threats he became increasingly dictatorial. He had always tended
to interfere, but now he moved very close to an attempt to
exercise direct control from London over a war 3,500 miles away.
He was one of the architects of a tragedy whose roots were to lie
in the conflict of personalities.

Clinton, who, unlike Germain, realized that he could not
supervise personally a campaign so far from New York as the
Carolinas, had agreed to permit Cornwallis to report direct to
London. He had also given him freedom of action but laid down
the overall policy that whatever his junior general did, he was not
to risk losing Charleston or South Carolina.

It was heady news that Ross brought back from London to
Cornwallis. Clearly he was soon to be commander in chief under
especially glorious circumstances. In fact, Germain sent a message

to Clinton that if he could not "remain in good humor," his resignation would now be acceptable, but Clinton did not then act on the suggestion. His friends reported that there were press attacks on him at home; all the signs indicated that he was being shouldered out. If he left his post now, it would be under conditions of cold criticism, so he ignored Germain's hint.

Buoyed up by the new confidence in London, Cornwallis completed his plans for his big strike north. As soon as Leslie brought up the reinforcement from Charleston, he would have an army of 4,000 men. Since General Nathanael Greene, who had now replaced Gates as rebel commander in the South, had barely 3,000, many of them unreliable militia, the British would be a far superior force.

Greene was a highly able general, *and* he had Daniel Morgan, who, as the British had already discovered, was probably, after Arnold, the most brilliant of the rebel field officers. Greene could not risk a straight confrontation but he could threaten Cornwallis' offensive. This he did by splitting his army, normally regarded as bad tactics in traditional warfare, and placing the two sections on the British flanks where already he had militia guerrillas operating.

If Cornwallis moved forward, he would be in danger from both sides. If he tried to solve the problem by striking at either rebel force, the other would be free to sweep through South Carolina. Daniel Morgan commanded one unit of 1,000 men high up the Broad River, far to the west of the British camp at Winnsboro. Greene himself was with his main army, commanded by General Huger, which now moved to the Pee Dee River to the east of Cornwallis' position.

If Cornwallis was to advance, he had to destroy one of them, and the force he chose for his target was Morgan. On January 7, having heard that Leslie had marched from Charleston, Cornwallis put his troops in motion slowly and very carefully, moving northwest between the Broad and Catawba rivers, keeping a wary eye on Greene, who was now in his rear.

Believing that Greene's scope for action would be temporarily curbed by the approach of Leslie from the southeast, he left a strong garrison at Camden and sent Tarleton with a big detachment up the west side of the Broad River to find Morgan. His orders were to defeat him or to drive him across the Broad River, where Cornwallis could pounce on him.

That was the theory. In fact, Morgan was on the Pacolet River much farther west than Cornwallis had expected. Also, it was not the weather for campaigning in Carolina. Because of the heavy rains, the many rivers that flowed down from the Appalachians had flooded over their banks and turned normally passable swamps into lakes. By January 12 Tarleton knew where Morgan was—or, rather, where he had been, for he was on the move all the time. But he could not attack him because the fast swollen waters of the Enoree were impassable. Impatiently, while his scouts ranged up the river searching for a crossing place, he lay camped on a plantation waiting for the flood levels to subside.

20

BROAD RIVER, SOUTH CAROLINA,
January 12, 1781

"The rains," wrote Cornwallis, "have put a total stop to Tarleton, and Leslie and I do not think it right to advance too far with a large train of provision waggons and so small a corps."[1]

He had moved from Winnsboro–but only just. He had now heard that just as Tarleton was held up by the Enoree, Leslie and his big column of reinforcements was checked by the floodwaters of the Santee not far out of Charleston. Until he knew that Leslie had a clear road to join him, he dared not go ahead with his plan to cooperate with Tarleton.

For the moment Tarleton was on his own. Furthermore, just now when close communication was vital, contact was hard to maintain since the messengers had great difficulty riding through the flooded country.

By the fourteenth, a week after he had marched, Cornwallis was still only 30 miles from Winnsboro. Two days later, the water levels had eased, and Leslie got through the swamps of the Santee and was on the move again toward him. But the waiting Cornwallis suspected it was too late. "I fear Morgan has too much start of you," he wrote to Tarleton.

He need not have worried, at least not for that reason, for by then Tarleton was closing on Morgan. He had crossed the Enoree by a ford several miles upstream only to face the obstacle of the swollen Tyger. On the fifteenth, he solved this by swimming his horses across the river and making log rafts for his infantry and baggage. That night he learned that the rebels were only a few miles ahead of him across the Pacolet with heavy concentrations of troops at every ford.

Tarleton had been with the army in Pennsylvania and repeated the trick maneuver that Howe had used to cross the Schuylkill. He marched north up the west side of the Pacolet and camped without fires. As the rebels, searching for him, went past on the other bank, he moved swiftly south again, and his men crossed the river by a now-unguarded ford.

Immediately his scouts were out searching for Morgan's main force. "Early in the night," he wrote, "the patrols reported that General Morgan had struck into the byways tending towards Thickelle Creek."

Reveille in the British camp was at two in the morning. An hour later the column was in motion, and before dawn the advance dragoons had clashed with an enemy patrol.

By seven o'clock the British were formed only 400 yards in front of Morgan's force, and Tarleton was feeling confident. Often at this stage before an action he was faced with an enemy who outnumbered him; this time both sides were roughly equal numerically, but the British had much greater quality—more cavalry and two 3-pound guns, known as grasshoppers because they were set up on legs instead of carriages.

Morgan had drawn up his main line on a ridge at the top of a slope of grazing land, known locally as the Cowpens. Forward ranks of rebels stood waiting for the British attack lower down the hill among well-spaced oaks and chestnuts.

Six miles behind the rebel position, curving around from its left flank, was the Broad River. Tarleton noted with satisfaction that technically Morgan's position was a bad one, for he was fighting with a barrier behind him which clearly limited his scope for retreat. Only later did Tarleton discover that he had chosen it deliberately so that his militiamen had no way of escaping from the battlefield; they *had* to fight. So in retrospect Morgan's disposition did not seem so careless.

If anyone was careless, it was Tarleton. He was so sure of victory that he did not rest his troops even though they had been on the move since two in the morning. Impatiently he advanced to disaster.

He was given a taste of it early. With Morgan's forward pickets interrupting his surveillance of the ground, he sent a troop of dragoons in at the gallop to clear them. But the pickets consisted of the expert riflemen who had done so much damage to Burgoyne at Freeman's Farm; they stopped the cavalry in mid-charge, dropping fifteen men from their saddles in the first volley.

Tarleton reacted as British officers always reacted in this situation—and properly. He ordered the advance of the line in strength under the covering barrage of his cannon. Steadily, with their drums beating, they moved up the slope of the Cowpens—ranks of Loyalist green and British scarlet—under very heavy fire. It was the scene that formed the beginning of almost every battle. As men fell, their places were filled; formation of the rank was everything. Then they charged with the bayonet.

The forward rebel units did not even wait to receive it. They dropped back immediately toward the main line on the ridge, consisting of Morgan's Continental Army troops. Quickly Tarleton ordered the dragoons on his right wing to charge the retreating men. They met very heaving shooting from the Continentals—and a charge by Morgan's cavalry, whom the rebel leader had kept hidden behind the ridge. The British horsemen dropped back to the line which was still advancing.

Tarleton had kept some Highlanders in his reserve and now sent them forward with their screaming pipes and pounding drums under orders to attempt to outflank the rebel right.

Tarleton watched carefully as Morgan's right wing fell back in response to this threat. It was the start of a retreat of his whole line. They marched down the hill away from the British.

Tarleton should have been on his guard; the rebels were formed and moving back under disciplined control. Unwisely the young British commander allowed his men to charge. Yelling, they ran down the hill in open ragged order after the retreating men.

Then, just as they were closing on them, the Continentals stopped suddenly, whipped around—and fired, as they did so, from the hip. Without question it was a brilliant move; at so short a range the damage of that sudden blast of musket shot was immense. Tarleton never did understand how his success was changed so suddenly to terrible failure. Years later he was still speculating on how "some unforeseen event" could "throw terror into the most disciplined soldiers." Now, however, "an unaccountable panic extended itself along the whole line."

The rebels followed up their paralyzing blow with a fast bayonet attack. A saber charge by their cavalry created even more chaos. Most of Tarleton's infantry just turned and ran. His Highlanders threw down their muskets and surrendered. Desperately, in the hope of checking the rout, he ordered his dragoons to charge, but, as he wrote bitterly, "they did not comply with the order. . . . About two hundred dragoons forsook their leader and left the field of battle."

His artillerymen kept the two grasshopper guns firing until they were captured in a rebel charge. Fifty English cavalry rallied to Tarleton, who, because his own mount was shot, was now on a surgeon's horse. They clashed once with the rebel cavalry—a defiant fighting retreat—and rode off to burn their baggage before escaping from the area.

It was a defeat of appalling proportions—"the most serious calamity since Saratoga," as Ross, Cornwallis' aide, put it. At Turkey Creek, 25 miles to the south, the earl had to digest the fact that his losses "did not fall short of 600 men"—nearly a sixth of his whole army.

Almost worse was the fact that the effect of the Battle of Cowpens on the South was very similar to the impact of Bennington on the North. It dampened the spirits of the Tory countrymen and encouraged the rebel sympathizers to rally to Greene. The true battle for America was always fought in the elusive realm of confidence. Now, like Gates' army on the Hudson, Greene's force was to grow, and Cornwallis' was to become smaller.

The general was fully conscious of his changed situation. Ordering Leslie to join him from Camden, he struck north fast to intercept Morgan before he crossed the two forks of the Catawba. But the American general was too quick; by the time the British reached the south fork of the river at Ramsour's Mills, having been checked by "the swelling of numberless creeks," Morgan was two days' march ahead of him.

Speed was now vital, and Cornwallis ordered the destruction of all "superfluous baggage and all my waggons except those loaded with hospital stores, salt and ammunition and four reserved empty in readiness for sick or wounded."

Meanwhile, as the general soon learned, Greene was riding hard to join Morgan, having ordered Huger to march north after him with the rest of the army as fast as possible. At the same time a rush operation was in motion to challenge the British crossing of the wide waters of the north fork of the Catawba. For 40 miles along the river the fords were guarded in strength by the rebel militia and some of Morgan's men.

At one o'clock in the "dark and rainy" morning of February 1 the British broke camp and marched for the river under orders to blast their way across. At dawn Lieutenant Colonel Webster made a feint with guns at one ford while the Coldstream Guards prepared to cross through another.

When he saw from the campfires how strong the enemy was, Cornwallis had second thoughts. The ford was "500 yards wide, in many places up to their [the men's] middle, with a rocky bottom and strong current," but he "knew that the rain then falling would soon render the river again impassable," so he ordered "them to march on . . . but not to fire until they gained the opposite bank."

Under a blaze of rebel shooting, the guards fought their way through the foaming icy water, advancing in tight platoons as a brace against the force of the current. It was too much for some of the horses, which were swept over and carried struggling downstream. "The Light Infantry [of the guards], landing first, immediately formed," reported Cornwallis, "and in a few minutes killed or dispersed everything that appeared before them." He did not mention that he, too, was soaked through, for his horse was shot from under him as he rode through the ford.

The British pressed on quickly after Morgan "in the hopes to intercept him between the rivers." Some 70 miles ahead, beyond Salisbury in North Carolina, lay the Yadkin—in full flood, like the Catawba, and often an uncrossable torrent after heavy rain. With the rain streaming down the faces of the marching soldiers, the chances of Morgan's being checked were high. Urgently Cornwallis drove his men along the muddy roads and through the floods of swollen creeks. To increase the speed of his column, he burned more of his wagons so that he could double up the horse teams.

Two days later, in the afternoon, the advance troops entered Salisbury, and Cornwallis learned that Morgan was only seven miles ahead of him at the trading ford of the Yadkin. As soon as he received the intelligence, he sent on Tarleton with his dragoons, as well as some mounted guards. "Owing to the rain, darkness and bad roads," Tarleton wrote, "the troops did not arrive at the Yadkin till near midnight."

By then the rebel infantry had crossed the river in boats. The cavalry and most of Morgan's wagons had gone through the ford, and the waters had risen, making the ford impassable. The guards attacked the militia who were stationed to protect all that remained of Morgan's wagon train. It was not much consolation, for Cornwallis needed no wagons.

For two days the British were checked; with so little transport, they needed the provisions they could obtain at Salisbury. Then they crossed the Yadkin at a shallow ford upriver, which involved a detour of 50 miles. By that time, "our friends," as Cornwallis always described the Tories, had reported that Morgan was pressing on to Guilford on the Haw River, where he was to rendezvous with the rest of Greene's army which Huger was bringing up from the Pee Dee. To reach Guilford, yet another big swollen river, the Deep, would have to be passed. Beyond it lay the broad rushing waters of the Dan—and, of course, Virginia.

Cornwallis was convinced that Greene "not having had time to collect the North Carolina militia . . . would do everything in his power to avoid an action on the south side of the Dan." The British general hoped to force him to fight by cutting off his retreat through the upper fords of the river, which, he was informed, was the only way Greene could get his army to safety. The lower fords were impassable at that season of the year, and there were not enough boats at the ferries.

Cornwallis was completely correct in his assumption that Greene would avoid action, but as he learned later, the rebel general believed that the farther north he could lead the British, the more vulnerable they would be. While the American magazines were close by in Virginia, the British supply lines were now very extended. Cornwallis had ordered a sea base to be opened at Wilmington on the North Carolina coast, but even this would be 200 miles from the Dan River.

By February 9 the British were at Salem, 25 miles west of Guilford, where Huger had that day joined Morgan and Greene. The two armies raced for the Dan. The continuous heavy rain alternated with snowstorms. The red clay of the roads, which froze into deep ruts at night, softened during the daytime, clinging to the soldiers' feet, clogging the wagon wheels and the horses' hooves. Creek after creek, with the freezing waters running high and the bridges broken down, had to be waded.

Nevertheless, Cornwallis allowed no respite. On the thirteenth the British marched 40 miles in twenty-four hours—a fantastic distance under normal conditions and close to miraculous with the terrain in the state it was.

And all the "exertions," as Cornwallis reported to Germain, "were in vain." His intelligence about the possibility of crossing the river lower down was "exceedingly defective," for that, as the British learned too late, was Greene's intention. By the fourteenth, when Tarleton and his advance patrols, now properly informed, rode up to Boyd's Ferry, the rebels were across the river on the Virginia bank. So were all their boats.

* * *

Cornwallis knew he could not pursue the rebels any farther. Virginia was "too powerful a province," and his troops were too exhausted. He moved by easy marches to Hillsboro, where he raised the royal standard and called on all loyal Americans to assist him in restoring "order and constitutional Government."

There, nine days later on February 23, he got the news that Greene had recrossed the Dan with large reinforcements. Others were on their way. Soon his army would be well over double the size of the British force. The same day 200 Loyalists assembling near the Deep River were attacked by rebel cavalry. Many of them, according to Cornwallis, "were inhumanely butchered, when begging for quarter." It did not raise the morale of "our friends."

Cornwallis was in a critical situation that compared in many ways with that of Burgoyne on the Hudson. As a result of Cowpens and other wastage, his army, according to his own assessment, was now only 1,600 strong and very short of supplies. By contrast, Greene's force, which intelligence put as high as 10,000 men, was growing daily.

It was vital that the British set up communications with the new base at Wilmington, selected by the general because it lay at the mouth of the east-flowing Cape Fear River, which he had planned to use as a traffic route.

At the same time he was obsessed, as Burgoyne had been, with the psychological battle for the loyalties of Americans and knew there was no hope of rallying the North Carolina Loyalists "whilst a doubt remained on their minds of the superiority of our arms." Despite his absurdly small numbers, he was determined to challenge Greene.

For three weeks the two forces maneuvered for position, with detachments clashing regularly. Cornwallis dropped down onto the Deep River, all the time edging southeastward toward the Cape Fear River, which would link him with Wilmington. On March 14 he was warned by his agents that the rebel army "was marching to attack the British troops." Later that day he heard that they were camped only 12 miles away at Guilford.

Even though the majority of the rebels were militia, Cornwallis' plan to attack was almost suicidal. What is more, he launched it without any proper intelligence of the enemy's position. He was relying on finding Greene and using his bayonets, which he did.

At dawn the next morning the army marched to Guilford and soon after midday met the advanced rebel troops in thick woods and drove them back quickly to their main lines, formed in long ranks across fenced open fields in front of Guilford Courthouse.

The battle was short—only an hour and a half—but it was fantastically, even fatally, expensive. The British advanced under cover, and under the attack, of heavy artillery fire. Then it was Bunker Hill all over again: repeated bayonet charges despite appalling casualties; great holes carved by rebel shooting in the ranks; orderly withdrawals for re-forming; then into the attack again over the bodies of the dead.

At a crucial moment the advancing Coldstream Guards were attacked by rebel cavalry. According to one account, which does not actually conflict with Cornwallis' report, the general gave orders for his cannon to open fire with grape on the enemy dragoons, even though they were in close combat with the elite regiment of his infantry.

The colonel of the guards, wounded earlier and near the earl, begged him to countermand the order—since the British guns would be killing his men as well as the rebel horsemen—but Cornwallis, convinced it was vital at that moment to throw back the cavalry, refused to change his orders. The gunners opened fire, spraying metal into the melee of men and screaming horses.

Cornwallis gained a technical victory—the rebels were fought into flight and their guns captured—but the price was more than 500 British casualties, nearly 1 in 3 of Cornwallis' already depleted force. It was far too dear. Because of "the care of our wounded and the total want of provisions in an exhausted country," Cornwallis wrote, the British could not even pursue Greene's troops, who dropped back 18 miles to Troublesome Creek.

It was the end of the North Carolina campaign, the accounting of the race for the Dan. By slow marches, the army—now, apart from the sick, barely 1,000 men—moved to the Cape Fear River only to find that no stores could travel up it because the high banks were manned by rebel militia. Meanwhile, Greene followed at a distance as Cornwallis' column of weary and wounded men progressed toward the coast.

Without question, Cornwallis, behaving with Germain's encouragement as though he were an independent commander, had disobeyed Clinton's orders to preserve Charleston and South Carolina. As soon as Clinton discovered that the glorious victory at

Guilford had lost the province, he took the view that the earl should have stopped at the Yadkin, when he could still have withdrawn to South Carolina.

This possibility was still open to him, and soon after he arrived at Wilmington a message came in from the commander at Charleston. Georgetown, a rebellious port between them, was temporarily under British control; boats were available on the Waccammaw River, which reached most of the way there from Wilmington.

But Greene, after shadowing the retreating British column toward the coast, was now marching south. Deciding that the risk to his small and battered army from a hostile country would be too great, Cornwallis did not pursue him, just sending a warning message—which never arrived—to Lord Rawdon, the commander at Camden.

In this one decision, Cornwallis threw away the South. He relinquished control of all of South Carolina, except for parts of the coast. Patently his effort to dominate North Carolina had been unsuccessful; even Georgia was now placed at risk.

It was a critical choice in time for the earl, for in the major capitals events had been moving fast and the diplomatic balance was very fine. In London, on a morning in January, seven years to the day since the news had arrived of the Boston Tea Party, a new crisis had caused the King to cancel the levee and to summon the Cabinet.

France was preparing to sell out the rebels, leaving Britain in possession of large parts of America. Spain was grasping for the bait of Gibraltar. But paradoxically, the rebels' two main allies were not the main items of discussion that day. The prime urgent reason for the meeting was the imminent, potentially catastrophic danger presented by the unpredictable Empress of Russia.

21

LONDON, January 19, 1781

It was rare for any Cabinet minister to be seated in the presence of the monarch, but the King dispensed with the usual formality and for the first time in his reign permitted his ministers to sit with him around a conference table.[1]

Even Samual Adams could scarcely have predicted that his "Mohawk" raid on the tea ships in Boston Harbor could have led to a confrontation between Britain and Russia, yet the key question at that meeting was: Would Catherine enter the war against the British, or could they buy her off with Minorca? With its fine, deep natural harbor and its strategic position in the western Mediterranean, the island would be ideal as a Russian base. Furthermore, Prince Gregory Potemkin, the czarina's politically powerful lover, had assured the British ambassador in a private talk that the Empress would go to great lengths for it.

In a brash spate of bold diplomacy the King and his ministers had taken an enormous risk. In December they had declared war on Holland—a move that they *knew* would antagonize Catherine, a move, moreover, that would spread a conflict that had already stretched British resources to the extreme. For Dutch-owned Ceylon would provide a base for the French to support their militant sympathizer, the Sultan Hyder Ali, in fighting the British in Madras. And Dutch-owned South Africa, which included the Cape of Good Hope, must become a serious threat to the sea routes to India.

In addition, it would immediately increase the enemy naval force by twenty ships of the line.

In St. James's and Whitehall the risks had been finely calculated. It was brinkmanship on the grand scale, but it was decided it was absolutely vital. The Dutch government had ignored all diplomatic efforts to stop it from breaking the British blockade in the

Atlantic. In the English Channel their ships were running into French harbors with the copper that was vital to King Louis' fleet. St. Eustatius, the Holland-owned island in the Caribbean, was a supply base for both the rebels and the two enemy powers. From the cover of Amsterdam and other ports, John Paul Jones, the rebel privateer, was executing daring raids on British shipping.

To the British government the naval blockade was an issue of top policy priority, for the shortage it created kept enemy ships out of action in the dockyards—critically important with the narrow balance of naval power. The stubborn attitude of the Dutch government gave the British two alternatives: submission on the blockade issue or war, which would give the royal cruisers freedom of action and was more important than the new dangers presented by the Dutch navy.

So the decision was made for war, but the timing was extremely delicate. Holland was planning to join the armed neutrality alliance designed to protect neutral shipping that was being promoted by Russia; as soon as the Dutch government signed, Catherine would be committed to support Holland with armed force.

It was vital, therefore, that Britain should be at war with Holland *before* she signed, before she became a technical ally. And its reason for the declaration of hostilities must having nothing provocative to do with the issue of neutral shipping.

As the early autumn winds churned the English Channel, Lord Stormont, now Secretary of State for the Northern Department, searched for an adequate excuse. In September he found one. The Amsterdam authorities were negotiating with Congress to supply the rebels with funds, an unfriendly act permitted by a theoretically friendly government. A patrolling British frigate searched a ship on which Henry Laurens, a Congressional delegate, was traveling to Holland. As the cruiser bore down, he saw the danger and threw his papers overboard, but did not put enough weight in the packet. A sailor on one of the frigate's longboats fished it out of the water before it sank and gave Stormont the proof he needed. After a formal complaint, he issued an ultimatum to the Dutch government. But alerted by news from Holland, he had to act even before his ultimatum expired: Barely hours before the Dutch signed the alliance, the British ambassador was ordered to leave The Hague, and a ship was on its way to the Caribbean with orders to Admiral Sir George Rodney to attack St. Eustatius.

For an administration that was often dilatory it was high-speed action, and it was certainly open to criticism. A state of war existed between Britain and Holland, but during the last days of December the men in St. James's and Whitehall waited tensely for Catherine's reaction.

On January 19 the Russian ambassador called on Lord Stormont and handed him a very hostile memorandum from an angry Empress—and the King summoned his Cabinet. This was the crisis, and a great deal depended on how the British reacted to it. Just how much they were gambling was underlined vividly by Lord Sandwich at that tense and anxious meeting. The First Lord of the Admiralty, as he indicated later, was in no doubt what would happen if Russia entered the conflict against Britain. "We shall never again figure as a leading power in Europe," he declared, "but think ourselves happy if we can drag on for some years a contemptible existence as a commercial state."

In an attempt to appease the Empress, the government decided to offer her Minorca, which would tempt her, if she "would use her influence . . . to secure peace for Britain" in the war with France and Spain. She did not take the bait, but it removed some of the heat from the crisis, and the Armed Neutrality League decided not to back Holland by force.

In fact, even before Catherine knew about the British declaration of war on Holland, she had already offered formally through her ambassadors to mediate in the main conflict *and* had been accepted by all three combatants, as was Britain's request that Austria, which had previously made the same offer, should act as co-mediator.

While Cornwallis' soldiers were racing Greene's troops through the mud of Carolina toward the Dan and dying in the fields by Guilford Courthouse, peace plans were being thrashed out in the capitals of Europe. Despite the angry realization of John Adams, then in Paris, that the rebel cause was in danger of being jettisoned, Congress was being pressured by Versailles to compromise.

France made it clear that it was prepared to withdraw its forces from America and for the time being even leave Britain in possession of the territory it already held, provided it evacuated New York—so strongly did the French want to end the war.

All the same, the peace moves did not prevent the departure from Brest of another big fleet in March, this time under the command of the Comte François de Grasse.

In May the ambassadors of the mediators delivered their proposals to the courts of the three combatants. As a starting base
they proposed an armistice for a year and a peace conference in
Vienna. They conceded the right of Britain to negotiate separately
with its American colonies, but—and for the King, who regarded
his colonies as a domestic matter, it was an enormous "but"—insisted that any settlement with the rebels should be signed
conjointly with the peace agreements with the other powers.

By now the mood in London was once more surging with
optimism. The obvious eagerness of France to pull out of the
conflict and all the reports of its economic pressures were noted
enthusiastically in Whitehall. France was known to be deeply
disillusioned by the low morale of Washington's army, by the
mutinies and defections; certainly without it, the British government assumed, the rebel force would disintegrate—a view with
which Washington himself agreed. "We're at the end of our
tether," he was to write in April, 1781. So what was the point in
the British negotiating?

"This war, like the last, will prove one of credit," commented
the King jauntily. With the start of the Austro-Russian mediation,
the British had ended the separate peace negotiation with Spain,
even though Madrid had agreed in principle to the British offer.
But now the way things were going, there seemed little point in
sacrificing Gibraltar.

At last, in June the British decided to exploit France's obvious
economic difficulties and declined to attend any mediation conference at which their American rebels were present. Heady with the
success of the courageous diplomacy of the past few months, the
King and his ministers had now grown too bold. It was to be an
irony of history, for the American Revolution might have turned
out very differently if the proposed peace conference at Vienna
had ever been held.

Meanwhile, Germain was pressing Clinton hard for the victory
that was now necessary to complete the rosy view of the conflict
that was forming in London. In January at the height of the crisis,
he had emphasized to him the seriousness of the fact that "our
enemies are increased and the states of Holland are to be
numbered amongst them. Every exertion must be made to bring
the American war to a conclusion . . . the circumstances of this
country cannot support a protracted war."

By May when he still did not know the full extent of the situation in the South, victory through diplomacy and arms seemed very close. Vermont, he believed, was just about to abandon the revolt. "The private accounts I have seen of Ethan Allen's transactions give me hopes that he is acting under General Haldimand's directions [from Canada] and that when the season admits of the general's sending up a body of troops into Vermont, the inhabitants will declare for the King which, with the reduction of the southern provinces must give the death wound to the Rebellion, notwithstanding any assistance the French may be able to give it; and, if that were the case, a general peace would soon follow. . . . As so much depends on our success in America, you cannot be surprised that the eyes of the people of England are turned upon you."

From Germain's point of view everything was set for the final climax. With France and Spain weakening, with the Russian threat receding, the situation in America seemed more favorable than it had appeared at any time since 1776. Despite setbacks such as King's Mountain and Cowpens, the South seemed in London to be near submission. Americans in the King's service, as Germain had pointed out in March, were "more in number than the whole of the enlisted troops in the service of Congress."

The one big problem was Clinton, who was not displaying the activity or enthusiasm for the Cabinet's policy of conquering the South that was evident in Cornwallis' aggressive campaigning. Germain found himself supporting the views of an active junior general against his wearying commander in chief as he underlined the British American war policy to Clinton with cold clarity. "I am commanded by His Majesty," he wrote, "to acquaint you that the pushing of our conquests from south to north is to be considered as the chief and principal object of all the forces under your command."

As always he was months out of date. Since Cornwallis had decided not to chase Greene to South Carolina, there were not many conquests left in the South; but there *were* troops, and how to use them now became the key point of a conflict between Clinton and Cornwallis that was to prove critical, one of the factors that transformed a situation basically highly favorable to the British into disaster.

* * *

At the end of March, as his battered army dressed its wounds and repaired its equipment at Wilmington, North Carolina, Cornwallis rethought his policy. Despite his failure to set up British control in the Carolinas, his letters reveal a strangely buoyant confidence—a result of Germain's reassuring letters, a flattering memorial from the House of Commons and the obvious fact that Clinton had lost the confidence of the government. Cornwallis himself was clearly the key general in America and the man who would hand the King the victory he needed.

The method now seemed clear to him. He realized he could never control the South without more support from "our friends." And since they had now learned how dangerous it could be to display their loyalty if there were an avenging army within reach, as would always be the case while the rebels controlled Virginia, it became obvious to the earl that he must take this province—and quickly, before the summer heat became too intense.

In Virginia he already had an army waiting to help him with what he now saw with a resurging enthusiasm was the key plan to the final crushing of the Revolution. At Portsmouth, just inside the Chesapeake, Benedict Arnold's small raiding force had been strengthened with heavy reinforcements under Major General William Phillips, now exchanged after his capture at Saratoga.

Washington, avid to capture Arnold, had sent in Lafayette with a small strike force backed by French ships from Rhode Island. But for once old Admiral Arbuthnot had displayed a surprising agility. He had chased the French and had driven them from the Chesapeake. Stripped of his naval cover Lafayette had been forced to keep his distance, though he was still hovering not far away near Richmond.

At Portsmouth, therefore, there were 3,500 British troops with an additional 1,500 soon due to leave from New York. If these men were added to those at Wilmington, Cornwallis would have a force big enough for aggressive operations in Virginia. Early in April he took the first moves to mount his new offensive.

On April 10 the frigate *Amphititre* sailed from Wilmington with letters for Phillips at Portsmouth and Clinton in New York.

"Now my dear friend," the earl told Phillips, as though this point had occurred to no one else, "we must have a plan. Without one, we cannot succeed." His plan was to abandon New York and to concentrate the whole British weight on the Chesapeake, a plan that ignored Canada and the negotiations in Vermont and the whole strategic value of the Hudson. It was thus seen by Clinton as just a little wild.

"I am very anxious to receive Your Excellency's commands," Cornwallis wrote Clinton, "being as yet totally in the dark as to the intended operations of the summer." Until now Clinton, too, had been totally in the dark, for it was hard for him to settle campaign plans until he knew the results of the earl's lunge into North Carolina.

Cornwallis did not wait to receive the C in C's commands. At the end of April, after ordering Phillips to bring his force to Petersburg just to the south of the James River below Richmond, he marched to Virginia.

As the news from the South reached New York, Clinton became increasingly horrified.

At first he had been delighted by the news of the Battle of Guilford; even the normally distorted rebel accounts, which arrived before the British versions, suggested that the action had given Cornwallis control of North Carolina. Then he began to learn the truth. He heard that Greene, no longer checked by Cornwallis, was threatening Camden, and although Lord Rawdon had marched out to meet him and forced the rebels back in a very well-fought action at Hobkirk's Hill, it could be only a matter of time before the town fell to the rebels. The British troops in South Carolina were spread thinly through the province in outposts, raising the truly vital question whether they could fall back on Charleston and save the port. Then Clinton received news that the rebels had struck as far south as Georgia: Augusta was under siege.

That Cornwallis had turned his back on this chaos in the South seemed incredible to Clinton. "I shall dread what may be the consequence of Your Lordship's move," he wrote, adding that if the earl had mentioned his plan to join Phillips in his first letter from Wilmington, "I should certainly have endeavoured to have stopped you."

The commander in chief was in an unhappy situation. Remembering his own experience on detachments, he had deliberately left Cornwallis scope to take what actions the local situation demanded. Cornwallis would never be able to claim, as Burgoyne had claimed, that his orders were too rigid. All the same, Clinton strongly felt he had no right to march to Virginia—or to abandon South Carolina, which he had been specifically ordered not to put at risk—without consultation with his senior general. But even now he still left him leeway and ultimate control of Phillips' force. "What is done cannot now be altered," he said and made the best of it.

On May 20 Cornwallis' column of troops, tired from marching more than three weeks from Wilmington, entered Petersburg. There Phillips' force—now under the control of Arnold, since Phillips had just died of a fever (although Arnold too, was soon to fall ill and to return to New York)—was camped waiting for him.

Cornwallis assumed command of the combined army and, four days later, put the troops in motion with a purpose that would be contested by no one: an attack on Lafayette, then at Richmond, who had to be destroyed before any serious campaigning could be launched.

The marquis with a much smaller force than Cornwallis' army backed away and moved toward Maryland—the province from which General Wayne would soon be marching to join him with what remained of the mutinous Pennsylvania Line. It became the same kind of game that Howe had played with Washington after Brandywine. Lafayette did not want to be too far from the British, hoping to harry them and possibly catch them by some surprise attack if they became exposed; but he could not risk a formal action, and he had to stop Cornwallis from getting between him and Wayne—which was now the earl's aim.

Cornwallis put his army across the James River, striking north swiftly. Lafayette went north, too, keeping his army 20 miles away, marching parallel until he reached the Rapidan River when he turned west to join Wayne and, after a few days, veered south.

All the time, Cornwallis chased him hard but never quite caught him. Tarleton and his dragoons came in sight of the rebels at one moment, but without the army their scope for action was very limited. At last the earl abandoned the pursuit and dropped down to Williamsburg—as he had told Clinton he would—to wait until he had "the satisfaction of hearing" from the commander in chief.

On June 26, the day after he reached Williamsburg, he heard from Clinton. New York was threatened with a siege by joint rebel and French forces. Cornwallis was, therefore, to "take a defensive station in any healthy situation you choose, be it Williamsburg or Yorktown" and to send to Manhattan "in succession as soon as you can spare them" some 3,000 troops.

This, as it turned out, was a crucial letter. Unlike the previous correspondence, when the differences between the two men had been displayed at a level of suggestions and opinions, Clinton was giving firm orders—orders with which Cornwallis disagreed. For this reason, either deliberately or subconsciously, he misinterpreted them.

As he now saw it, the British should either concentrate on the Chesapeake, as he had suggested, or forget the whole area. He could see no point in holding "a sickly defensive post in this bay, which will always be exposed to a sudden French attack." Sullenly, he wrote to New York asking permission to return to Charleston and gave orders for the immediate evacuation of the Williamsburg peninsula.

The next day after a brief but inconclusive clash with Lafayette, who attacked in the belief that most of the British troops were on the far bank of the river, the army crossed the James and marched toward Portsmouth, where Cornwallis planned to embark the troops for New York on board the transports.

He had not been marching long before an appalled letter arrived from Clinton, rebuking him strongly for leaving the strategic Williamsburg peninsula. There was no question of the British abandoning the Chesapeake, Clinton insisted. Cornwallis was to establish a base for ships of the line, and the anchorage the admiral had chosen was Old Point Comfort near Portsmouth. Since he would need working parties of soldiers to do this, he could keep the troops destined for New York until the project was completed.

But Cornwallis' engineers condemned Old Point Comfort as useless for the purpose. Instead, Cornwallis informed Clinton coldly, "in obedience to the spirit of Your Excellency's orders," he proposed to seize and fortify Yorktown and Gloucester, which, from both banks, dominated the mouth of the York River. This was "the only harbor in which we can hope to give effectual protection to line of battle ships."

At the beginning of August transports sailed up the Chesapeake and started landing the army on the banks of the York River, but Cornwallis was obeying orders he believed misguided from a commander in chief he expected soon to replace. The weather, as always in Virginia in high summer, was excessively hot. The earl's lack of enthusiasm, coupled with the high temperatures, made the progress of the working parties slow—fatally slow.

22

NEW YORK, August 28, 1781

It was a beautiful August day.[1] The wind was light, and the sun burned down from a cloudless sky. If there was a faint uneasiness at British headquarters on Broadway because the purpose of Washington's latest movements was unclear, there was no sense of the crisis that would soon face the staff officers. "A signal early this morning," Frederick Mackenzie was to note cheerfully in his journal, "for a fleet of men of war"—the sails had been sighted from Staten Island of Rear Admiral Sir Samuel Hood's fourteen ships of the line from the West Indies. In the harbor, the battle squadron of Rear Admiral Sir Thomas Graves,[2] who had now taken over the flag from Arbuthnot, lay at anchor.

That afternoon the wind freshened from the south, and by evening Hood's men-of-war were swinging on their cables at Sandy Hook and the admiral was on his way by boat for a meeting with Clinton and Graves on Long Island.

"If chance has really any influence over the affairs of men . . . ." Clinton was to ruminate in his retirement, "the tide of fortune with respect to the British interests in America was now very evidently beginning to turn against us." It was not too evident that day. The news from the South, of course, was bad—the Spanish had taken the small British post in West Florida, and all that remained under British control in Georgia and the Carolinas were the two ports of Charleston and Savannah—but the overall picture was encouraging.

In July Washington's army had crossed the Hudson to Westchester, where it was joined by the 6,000 French troops under Rochambeau that had been based on Rhode Island. It came as no surprise. Four weeks earlier a British patrol had captured a courier on his way to Pennsylvania; in his pouch were letters from

Washington to Congress and from Rochambeau to the French legation in Philadelphia. They detailed the plans for a joint attack on New York, but even more important, they contained "an intimation from the Court of France," as Clinton put it, "that this was the last campaign in which the Americans were to expect assistance of either troops or ships from that nation,"[3] which, of course, the ministers in London already assumed.

This suggested to Clinton that the obvious British policy should be to avoid "all risks as much as possible"; as long as they did not suffer any serious defeats during the next few months, "time alone would soon bring about every success we could wish." To the general, therefore—despite Germain's urging—there was no point in mounting big offensives, which might fail. The key was a strong defense.

Clearly the assault on New York was to be the last big effort before Versailles abandoned its collaboration with the American rebels. And Clinton was determined that it should fail.

He had some reason for optimism. He was severely outnumbered, of course. The enemy lines that stretched across Westchester from the Hudson to Long Island Sound contained 11,000 French and American Continental troops, and Washington could boost this overnight to nearly double this figure by merely calling in the local New York and New Jersey militia. The British had fewer than 10,000, but Manhattan Island with its heights and surrounding rivers was suited to strategic defense.

Also, its narrow, shallow harbor entrance was easy to hold against approach from the sea—as Howe had demonstrated in the face of D'Estaing's threat in 1778—for Washington's army was not the most important factor that Clinton had to assess: In April the large French fleet of twenty-six ships of the line under the Comte de Grasse had arrived in the West Indies.

From a very early stage in its preparation in Brest, the fleet had been watched closely by British spies. Soon after it sailed, Germain assured Clinton that De Grasse had no plans for North America. But Clinton, who had now experienced two summers since the French had entered the war, did not believe him. He expected it on the coast in August, and by June, apart from the indications in captured letters, he had proof: A frigate had left Rhode Island for the West Indies with American pilots. Even by mid-August, Washington had made no serious move to strike at New York, for all the display of troops on Westchester; Clinton assumed he was waiting to combine his operation with the arrival of De Grasse.

The ominous shadow of the French admiral loomed over the whole strategic situation. Even so, it was not overwhelmingly critical. Rodney was in the West Indies with a British fleet watching the French "like a lynx"; if they sailed for America he would be in close pursuit. But unlike the other concentrations of enemy ships and troops on which Clinton's spies were continually reporting, De Grasse was unpredictable. He could swoop suddenly from the distant south, and Clinton could not be sure what point of America he would strike.

Apart from the uncertain threat of De Grasse, nevertheless, in August, as Clinton surveyed the war theater under his command, he was not too anxious. He believed he could hold New York and was soon to receive reinforcements from Europe. A squadron of French warships under the newly arrived Admiral Louis, Comte de Barras was at Rhode Island, but this was exactly counterbalanced by the British ships, now commanded by Admiral Thomas Graves, who was then cruising off Boston searching for an expected enemy convoy.

On the Chesapeake, Cornwallis' army of nearly 8,000 men was still being ferried daily to his new station on the York River and was considerably larger than Lafayette's force now camped on the Pamunkey high up the Williamsburg peninsula.

And so the summer weeks went by with no movement on either side. In fact, Clinton was having more trouble with Germain and his complaining letters than from Washington.

It was not until mid-August that there were signs of enemy movement. A letter from Rodney warned that De Grasse was sailing for America. Sir Samuel Hood would be on his way with a fleet to cover him, making first for the capes at the entrance to the Chesapeake and then scouring the coast up to New York.

By the time Hood arrived at Sandy Hook on the evening of the twenty-eighth, his frigates had probed the Chesapeake and Delaware Bay. But there had been no sign of De Grasse, he assured Clinton and Graves at their Long Island meeting. This was good news. For the two commanders had been waiting only for Hood's arrival before launching a quick raid on Rhode Island to destroy De Barras' ships. All day, in fact, the troops had been going aboard the transports. But by ten o'clock that night, Clinton abruptly canceled the plan. A messenger had ridden in from East Hampton high up the Long Island coast to say that three nights before, on the twenty-fifth, De Barras and his squadron had sailed from Rhode Island.

The question facing the three men was where was he sailing? It was not the only query. For some days Clinton had been puzzled by Washington's movements.

On the twentieth the rebel troops camped in Westchester had started crossing the Hudson. By the twenty-seventh, the day before Hood had arrived at Sandy Hook, Clinton had written to Cornwallis that the rebels had taken a position at Chatham in New Jersey "that seemed to threaten Staten Island."

"I cannot well understand Mr. Washington's real intentions. . . ," he told the earl. "It is possible he means for the present to suspend his offensive operations against this post and to take a defensive position at the old post of Morristown, from which he may detach to the southward."

Three days later he was still trying to fathom the rebel plans. "Mr. Washington's force still remains in the neighbourhood of Chatham," he wrote. But in fact by then it was on the move to the south, as Clinton was to learn in a very few hours. A tiny scrap of paper had come into British HQ, concealed in a button, with the brief message: "The Chesapeake is the object—all in motion—August 29th—Squibb."

Several spies had suggested rebel intentions to the southward, which was probably why Clinton had speculated on the possibility of detachments; but "Squibb" was the cover name for a trusted British agent, and the shock element in his note was the word "all." It was not a detachment; the whole army was on the march.

Immediately it put De Barras' departure from Rhode Island in a new context. The Chesapeake must be his destination, too, and that obviously was where De Grasse would be heading—if he had not already arrived.

That night Graves' squadron passed the bar to join Hood's vessels at Sandy Hook. As senior admiral, Graves on board the *London* assumed command and the combined fleet of nineteen ships of the line sailed for the Chesapeake.

Even then, there was no sense of truly serious crisis either in New York or in the flagship. Hood, who had been shadowing the French in the West Indies, was convinced that the combined British naval force was equal to any fleet the enemy could muster when De Barras joined De Grasse. Besides, he and Rodney had assumed that the French must leave some ships on the West Indies station. But Hood and Rodney were wrong. It was to be some time before the British commanders realized quite how wrong, but by the time the British fleet had started sailing south, Cornwallis at least had some suspicions about the naval strength of the French.

YORKTOWN, August 31

A British naval lieutenant from the frigate *Charon* was the first to discover the truth, for the entrance to the Chesapeake could not be seen from Yorktown. He was transporting some dragoons to Old Point Comfort near Portsmouth to act as an escort, though to whom is not recorded, when by Cape Henry he saw the French fleet, dominated by De Grasse's massive 104-gun flagship *Ville de Paris*.

Cornwallis' urgent message to Clinton in cipher was brief: "There are between thirty and forty sail within the capes, mostly ships of war and some of them very large."

By that night, as Cornwallis reported to New York, a French ship of the line and two frigates lay anchored at the mouth of the York River. He was under blockade.

The earl was not ready for the crisis. Just over a week before he had written to Clinton that although "the works at Gloucester" were ready for defense against "sudden attack," he was only just about to start fortifying Yorktown across the river. Owing to the "difficulty of constructing works in this warm season," he would need at least "six weeks to put the intended works into a tolerable state of defense."

Now he would not have that much time. Only two days after De Grasse had arrived in the Chesapeake, he reported, "Forty boats with troops went up the James River." These were French soldiers under General Claude, Marquis de St. Simon that De Grasse had brought with him, and as Cornwallis soon learned from Tarleton's patrols, they were stationed on James Island to check any British attempt at a breakthrough to North Carolina.[4] At the same time Lafayette had moved to Williamsburg in line with James Island, 12 miles north of Yorktown.

It is doubtful if the French and rebel troops could have stopped a British escape at this stage. Cornwallis, as Clinton later noted bitterly, "could have marched out 5,500 as good troops as any in the world." Both Lafayette and St. Simon "had not altogether 5,000⁵ exclusive of militia."

But it was early for drastic measures. Unless he could "annihilate" Lafayette and the French, Cornwallis would only be able to get his combat troops away, leaving the remainder in a weak post to be taken prisoner. On the other hand, if he were defeated in the battle, it would mean the "immediate loss" of Yorktown, and, as he said later, he would have been "exposed to public execration" for not waiting for relief from New York.

As was so often the case in British affairs in America, it was a matter of critical timing. He had provisions, he had men by the thousand for fighting and for fortifying, so the British dug in. Under pressure, the enormous working parties labored long hours to strengthen the defenses of the town, and the army set up a strong position in front, with a chain of redoubts.

Late in the afternoon of the fifth, the soldiers in Yorktown, sweating over their shovels in the summer heat, heard the distant thuds of the salvos at sea.

OFF CAPE CHARLES, VIRGINIA, September 5

The fleet was running for the capes under a following sea, the waves building behind them at times as the wind blew up suddenly for a few minutes in short squalls. On the starboard beam was the coast of Delaware—territory Clinton had planned to take a few months ago and which now might have been under British control if Cornwallis had not followed his own plans and marched to Virginia.

. At ten o'clock from HMS *Barfleur*, Hood, who commanded the van, saw the signal flags shake out from the masthead of the scouting frigate, standing far ahead of the fleet. Its captain had sighted a fleet.

The Chesapeake was still some distance away, dark contours in the distance; there was plenty of time and Graves was not hurried. Another half hour passed before "Prepare for action" was flying from the masthead of the *London*, precipitating the same spate of activity on every ship in the fleet: the opening of the ports; the running out of the cannon; the assembling of the starting ammunition on the gundecks.

"We cleared" was the brief comment in the log of the *Shrewsbury*, then stationed in the rear of the fleet but soon to be fighting a crucial part of the action. "Clearing for battle" was a literal phrase; the sides of the ship were opened as fully as possible so that the enemy shot could pass right through, since anything the cannonballs struck would be shattered. The overriding principle was not to provide cover for the crews but to preserve as much of the ship as possible from the massive destruction of a broadside.

At eleven o'clock the *London* was signaling "line of battle," and the eighteen line ships slowly took up station behind each other, heading for the southern end of the 10-mile gap between the capes. This was where the main channel led into Chesapeake Bay, limited by Middle Ground shoal 3 miles north of Cape Henry.

Guessing that the French would sail out of the bay, Graves was forming his line so that he would be running parallel to the windward of them as they ran out to meet him. They were still "at anchor about Cape Henry," as Hood recorded, but "their topsail yards [were] hoisted aloft as a signal for getting under sail."

In fact, to save the time-wasting process of weighing anchor the French slipped their cables and "came out in line of battle ahead but by no means regular and connected."

As he watched them from the *Barfleur*, Hood, who had been so sure of British naval equality, must have been disturbed, for there were twenty-four ships of the line tacking out of the bay, bending under the northeast wind—five more than the British were taking into battle against them, more than 300 extra guns. And still Hood did not know the full extent of his mistake.

Advancing as they were on a superior enemy, the British would need the initiative of wind advantage. But the French often fought defensively, even relinquishing the wind sometimes when they could take it: For, with the wind pressure heeling them away from the enemy, they could open their lowest ports without fear of taking in water. And this was where the biggest caliber guns were mounted.[6]

The two fleets ran on toward each other. By the end of the morning the van ships were nearly in line some three miles apart. Graves' plan was to keep on his present course until the center ships were opposite each other and then to turn into the attack. But the squally weather with its changing wind pressures was not ideal for an action. As he watched the enemy ships streaming out of the Chesapeake, the admiral was sending signals all the time to his ships to get on station, and high up in their rigging their crews were reefing sails if they were coming on too fast or opening up more canvas if they were dropping back.

By two o'clock, as the two fleets ran on opposite courses, the center ships were still not in line. But Graves knew he would have to "wear" his ships soon, for his lead vessel was approaching the shallow water of the Middle Ground shoal, as the French well knew. Their line, formed in such a hurry, was still very ragged, and their van ships were too far ahead of their main fleet and, thus, vulnerable to attack. Realizing this, they leaned eastward to increase their distance from the British and, as Graves reported, "to enable their center to support them or they would have been cut up."

And they *should* have been cut up, according to Hood watching impatiently from the *Barfleur* in the van. The admiral waited for the *London* to signal the rear ships to fall down, running fast before the wind as they would be onto the exposed French vessels, but all he saw at the *London*'s masthead were the flags warning the whole fleet: "Prepare to veer."

"It was a glorious opportunity," he wrote later, "but it was not embraced." Graves was older than Hood and more rigid in his thinking. He seemed to like to use his fleet as a single fighting machine, uncomplicated by detachments. Also, as Hood was to demonstrate later, he did not have the same flair.

At two fifteen because of the shoal ahead, the fleet went about. Each ship turned heavily, her sails loosening, heeling to starboard as once more they scooped the wind, and headed east—until Graves halted the whole line to allow the French to catch up.

But De Grasse was not waiting to challenge the British. His ships kept on running out to sea. Graves tried to maneuver his fleet to close.

Under these conditions, with the squally weather and the French van leading away, it was a complex operation. Now that the British had turned, their rear ships were in the lead. The *Shrewsbury*, with its seventy-four guns, headed the line and, under the orders flying from *London*'s mast, was on a collision course with the front French ship. The two lines of ships, therefore, formed an angle, the points of which were closing all the time—but not very fast. Nearly two hours were to pass from the time the fleet went about before the battle started, two hours during which the *London* was flying repeated signals to the *Shrewsbury* to lead farther to starboard and to other ships to keep station.

For the conditions in which Graves was operating, his commanding seems to have been far too inflexible for so crucial an action. As long as the "line of battle" signal flew, no vessel could deviate from its course behind the lead ship. Later Hood claimed that the signal was never struck, thus causing misunderstandings when Graves ordered close action, and even the *London*'s log shows that it was hoisted several times during the battle. Certainly, because of the wide angle of approach, the rear division never came close enough to the enemy to engage.[7] The lead ships, however, were soon involved in a very fiercely fought action.

Just before four o'clock, Graves ordered his fleet to "close to one cable," and a few minutes later the red flag at the fore-topgallant signaled "engage the enemy."

The *London*, according to her log, "filled the main top sails and bore down" on the French. More than forty starboard guns crashed out a massive explosion of smoke and flame.

At the head of the line the *Shrewsbury* was "within musket shot" of the French lead ship. As Captain Mark Robinson saw the *London* fire her opening broadside at long range, he was closing "with our opposite to pistol shot" distance. At four thirty his starboard guns were firing, and his enemy ship was answering with great effect. Cannonballs and grape raked his rigging. Only a quarter of an hour after the battle had started, "our fore topsail came down." With the guns crashing out repeated salvos, seamen fought to clear the sails and masts from a deck clouded with smoke. Then "the main and mizzen top sail yards came down also."

Behind the *Shrewsbury* in the line, the *Intrepid*, the *Montagu*, the *Princesa* all were furiously engaged, their guns firing constantly. Farther back the *Terrible* was in trouble. She had been leaking badly for a couple of days, and all her pumps had been in operation before she went into action. Now she was taking in water fast, and her sails were slashed by shot. Near her, the *Ajax* had lost her top gallant, and her crew was hoisting another under blasts of grape, while below them the gunners were fighting the ship, salvo after salvo shaking the masts.

In the center there was chaos. As the *London* bore down on the enemy, she overran the two ships ahead of her in the line. Now they could not fire their guns for fear of hitting the flagship. In an attempt to create order, Graves flew the signal for "line of battle."

By five o'clock the *Shrewsbury* at the head of the line was taking terrible punishment. She had lost much of her top rigging, and now her "lower masts were much damaged." Soon afterward the captain lost his leg and the first lieutenant was killed. The captain of the *Intrepid* hailed her and "desired us to cease firing so that he might . . . take our place. At this time, we had not a brace bowling or hardly a fore main shroud standing."

The *Intrepid* had already forced the ship she was fighting "to turn her stern." Now she put on sail, passing the stricken *Shrewsbury*, "keeping her fire well up and closing with the enemy's van."

At last the French bore away, and soon after six, Graves ordered the cease-fire so that he could assess the condition of his ships. The action had lasted only an hour and a half—and truly achieved nothing—but some of his vessels were badly damaged. Just how badly he did not fully discover until darkness, when he sent frigates up and down the line. The reports were not encouraging: His three lead ships were so battered they were unable to keep the line. Two others were leaking dangerously. Yet a third—the *Princesa*, which carried the flag of Rear Admiral Francis Drake— was "in momentous apprehension of the main top mast going over the side."

Fortunately the weather the next day was calm, and the French stayed well away, engaged like the British repairing their damage. Graves summoned his two junior admirals to a conference on the *London*. He had sent two frigates into the Chesapeake to reconnoiter; in the bay they had sighted five enemy vessels, four of which were big enough to be ships of the line.

Hood was in no doubt what they should do. He urged his senior admiral to take the whole fleet into the Chesapeake to the "succour of Lord Cornwallis."

But Graves was worried by the danger of being blocked in and anxious about his crippled ships—with some reason. Two nights

later, when the weather blew up, the *Terrible* made a distress
signal and had to be attended by frigates, and the *Intrepid* sent a
warning message that her main topmast had gone and she expected
her foreyard to go at any moment.

For eight days, to Hood's growing anger, the British admiral
took no decision at all. The fleet just drifted. Sometimes the
French were in sight and sometimes not. For two days, De Grasse
had the wind, but he did not take his opportunity to attack;
indeed, he had little to gain by it. Repeatedly, at conferences, and
at one stage by letter, Hood pleaded with Graves that the fleet
"should get off the Chesapeake before him [De Grasse]. It
appeared to me a measure of the utmost importance to keep the
French out."

Graves, however, decided against it. The next day the enemy
fleet was no longer in sight. Eventually, on the thirteenth, Graves
sent a message to Hood that the scouting frigate *Medea* had
signaled that De Grasse was back in the Chesapeake. What action
did he now suggest? "Sir Samuel," Hood replied tautly, "would
like to send an opinion but he really knows not what to say in the
truly lamentable state we have brought ourselves."

There seemed no point in staying inactive where they were.
Several of the ships were so damaged that they needed dockyard
attention; the *Terrible* had deteriorated to the point that the
admiral had ordered her destruction.

So the fleet, its mission failed completely, headed north for New
York.

NEW YORK, September 13

It was raining as the *Pegasus* frigate, heeling under the northeast
wind, ran in to Sandy Hook and let go her anchor. Four days had
passed since she had left the semicrippled fleet, waiting uncertain-
ly off the Chesapeake while the admiral tried to make up his mind
what to do.

That night Clinton read Graves' gloomy letter and called a
council of war for the morning to decide on action. "The enemy
have so great a naval force on the Chesapeake," Graves had
written, "that they are absolute masters of its navigation. . . . In
this ticklish state of things Your Excellency will see the little

probability of anything getting into York River but by night and of the infinite risk to any supplies sent by water."

The failure of the navy to open the Chesapeake was an enormous setback, but there was still time for new plans. From the returns of Cornwallis' commissaries it was clear that he had fairly ample provisions. "The post of York," the minutes of the next day's war council recorded, "may be defended with its present garrison against 20,000 assailants for at least three weeks." This gave some scope either for another naval strike or for a movement by land to cooperate with a breakout.

Despite the report from Graves, the best hope still lay with a seaborne relief effort. For three more ships of the line, bringing Admiral Robert Digby from England to take over naval command from Graves, were expected in New York at any moment. The *Terrible* had been sunk, but the new arrivals would reduce the French superiority to only three major fighting vessels—or so Clinton, like Graves and his admirals, thought, for all the commanders were assuming that the fleet that had fought them on the fifth included De Barras' squadron from Rhode Island. But in fact by the day of the battle the ships from Rhode Island had not reached the Chesapeake.

When the council of war met in British headquarters on the tenth, there were 5,000 assault troops already embarked waiting on transports in the harbor. But it seemed wise to wait until Digby arrived with his extra men-of-war.

Three days later a letter arrived from Cornwallis by an armed galley—"built like a whaleboat . . . quite open"[8] with fourteen oars and two sails—that had slipped under the guns of the French guard ships. His dispatch, written on the eighth, seemed to confirm that the war council's decision had been sound.

The earl appeared confident. "I am now working hard at the redoubts of the place. The army is not very sickly. Provisions for six weeks. I will be very careful of it."

On the nineteenth the flags on the mast at Staten Island signaled the sighting of Graves' fleet, limping home for repairs, but when he anchored at Sandy Hook two days later, he was no consolation to Clinton. "The injuries received by the Fleet in the action. . . ," he wrote, "makes it quite uncertain how soon the Fleet can be got to sea."

During the impotent days that followed, Clinton must have cursed the bar at Sandy Hook, even though it had probably saved

New York from D'Estaing in 1778, for it took the best part of a week to get the ships up into the harbor and the biggest of them still had to wait for the spring tides. By then the crisis had soared to a new peak, and the commander in chief knew that unless he could pressure the navy into hurrying, there would be a disaster at Yorktown even greater than at Saratoga.

On the twenty-third two letters came in from Cornwallis. One was calm; he did not propose "so desperate" an expedient as a breakout since "as you say Admiral Digby is hourly expected and promise every exertion to help me." But the other, written a few hours later when he had received new information, was taut with alarm. Now that De Barras had joined De Grasse, he reported, there were no less than thirty-six French ships of the line in the Chesapeake—most of them anchored abreast across the entrance to the channel.

De Grasse had taken an enormous gamble. Both Rodney and Hood had assumed that he would send a squadron to America,[9] but he had left the West Indies without protection and taken his whole fleet. As Cornwallis was fully aware, even if Digby did arrive in time the French superiority could still be as much as fourteen line of battle ships—possibly 1,000 guns more than that the British could deploy. "This place is in no state of defense," he wrote. "If you cannot relieve me very soon, you must be prepared to hear the worst."

Clinton reacted to the news by demanding an immediate conference with the naval chiefs. The next day, the twenty-fourth, Graves stepped ashore onto the New York quay as the guns of the battery boomed in formal salute.

Tensely when Clinton emphasized "that Lord Cornwallis' situation" required "the most speedy assistance," the admirals agreed to his relief plan: The fleet, with 5,000 troops under Clinton's personal command, would blast its way through the French line at the entrance to the Chesapeake and form a defensive ring at the entrance of the York and James rivers.

This was not as wild a plan as it seemed. When the tide was running, the sea gushed through the Chesapeake Channel very fast, building up a "great swell." It ran too strongly, according to the naval advisers, for the French ships to swing around on their cables to "bear" with their broadsides on "ships approaching them."

If the British got through the line, the fleet could anchor in the restricted, calmer waters nearer Yorktown that were "better calculated for its smaller number and . . . our ships could resist the attack of the enemy by having free use of their springs." Meanwhile, they could land the troops on either river and put them into action wherever they could be most effective.

That night Clinton wrote to Cornwallis that "there is every reason to hope we shall start from hence the 5th of October"—in ten days' time. Meanwhile, his staff was working on the plan. More letters went off by fast open boat: Would Cornwallis send someone to both capes around October 7 so that the fleet could have up-to-date information about the enemy positions before it went into action? At the sound of gunfire the earl was asked to make "three separate smokes" if all was well "and, if you possess the post of Gloucester, four."

The navy was doing its best to rush the refitting of the damaged ships. In the dockyard the men were working from daylight until ten at night. For once the interservice rivalries were forgotten, and the army offered the navy any materials it wanted.

The day after the war council had met Admiral Digby arrived in New York with his ships of the line, but in view of the crisis, he left the command with Graves.

Despite all the activity, Clinton soon suspected that the fleet would not be ready by the October 5 start date. In council he considered other plans that might be launched more quickly—such as a strike by land through New Jersey at Philadelphia, which would force Washington to divert troops from Yorktown—but the idea was rejected because the preparation might delay the "principal object," the breakthrough from the sea.

By the thirtieth there was no longer any possibility of the navy's being ready by the scheduled date. "From the assurances given me this day by Admiral Graves . . . ," Clinton wrote Cornwallis sadly, "we may pass the bar by the 12th October if the winds permit and no unforeseen accident happens. This, however, is subject to disappointment."

Once more he was considering an attack across Jersey which now seemed more attractive: "I shall persist in my idea of a direct move [by sea] even to the middle of November, should it be your Lordship's opinion that you can hold out so long; but if, when I hear from you, you tell me that you cannot . . . I will immediately make an attempt upon Philadelphia by land. . . . If this should draw any part of Washington's force from you, it may possibly give you an opportunity of doing something to save your army. . . ."

But even as Clinton was writing to him, the chances of escape had been sharply reduced, for Washington and the French were now stationed around Yorktown in a tight ring.

YORKTOWN, September 28

They came at last, shortly before noon with the sun glinting on their bayonets, along the main road from Williamsburg that reached down the peninsula near the river—the beginning of a seemingly endless column of more than 16,000 men. The first British to see them through the trees in the distance were light infantrymen, manning a forward picket by the road; they dropped back, alerting Tarleton.

The legion dragoons mounted and formed—and watched as the American Continental troops filed off the road toward Wormley Creek, which hooked up around the town from the river below. The white-uniformed French who followed them in the column carrying white silk standards set up their line across the road, extending left to the water above the port. Yorktown was invested.

So was Gloucester by that time. A patrolling troop of huzzars of Simcoe's Queen's Rangers saw them approaching—300 French cavalry and à long column of infantry, supported by American militia. Like the picket across the river, they retreated immediately behind the cover of the British lines.

In a way it was a relief to Cornwallis, for he had been expecting the appearance of the soldiers ever since he had heard four days before that the Hudson troops had joined Lafayette. Some of the despair that had marked his last message to Clinton when he knew the true size of the French fleet seemed to have gone. "There was but one wish throughout the whole army," he wrote to New York the next night, "which was that the enemy would advance."

Yorktown was a small tobacco port of some seventy houses, set on a low hill near the York River. During the weeks since the French had sailed into the bay, the British had worked hard to prepare it against attack. Earthworks, with redoubts and batteries for sixty-five guns, surrounded all parts of the town that did not overlook the water, where a barrier had been formed with sunken vessels. There two frigates, the *Charon* and the *Guadeloupe,* lay anchored to serve as extra armament.

Also, the British had set up a strong outer defense. Two creeks which flowed into the York formed protective arms to both the north and the south of the town. Across the half mile strip of land between the creeks the army had built fortifications of felled trees with batteries in redoubts at the most vulnerable points.

On the night of September 29, the day after Washington had surrounded the town, the galley that seemed able to slip past the French warships in the Chesapeake with an astonishing skill arrived at Yorktown with Clinton's message that the relief fleet would sail on October 5. Conscious that his outer defense line could be cut off, Cornwallis immediately called the troops back into the town and abandoned the works.

As the days went by, the earl watched from the big house on the fringe of the town that he had chosen as his HQ as Washington prepared his siege—with the same deliberate care that Clinton had displayed at Charleston. His men, who had occupied the position the British had abandoned, were building redoubts and assembling the materials for digging the parallels. So far the enemy guns had hardly fired at all, but it would not be long before they opened up.

At Gloucester there was more activity. Cavalry were not likely to be much use in Yorktown, so Cornwallis had sent Tarleton across the river with his dragoons.

Simcoe, who was ill in bed, suggested an idea to him. The Duc de Lauzun, who commanded the French horse there, had seen how few mounted rangers he had at the post but would not know that Tarleton had crossed the river with the Green Dragoons. Why not, he proposed according to his journal, send out the Ranger huzzars as a decoy, which the duke would be bound to attack, and set up the legion cavalry in ambush?

Early the next morning a large foraging force went out of the British lines. Tarleton rode with them but kept his dragoons out of sight in woods.[10] On this side of the river where the country was rougher, the enemy lines were farther away—four miles from Gloucester—and the foragers were not disturbed as they harvested Indian corn. It was not until they were on their way back that the Duc de Lauzun and his uhlans charged on them along a lane.

The siege of Yorktown

the SIEGE *of*

YORK TOWN

in

VIRGINIA.

Engraved for Stedmans Hiſtory of the American War.

REFERENCES.

A. *Redoubt taken by assault on the 14.ᵗʰ Oct.ᵗ at Night by the Americans.*

B. *Redoubt taken by assault on the 14.ᵗʰ Oct.ᵗ at Night by the French.*

The History of the Origins of the American War by Charles Stedman, 1794

A legion scouting officer galloped the warning, and the dragoons formed to meet the approaching French cavalry. "Tarleton picked me out," recorded the Duc de Lauzun in his memoirs, "and came to me with his pistol raised. We were going to fight between our respective troops."

They never did, for at that instant a French uhlan thrust his lance into the mount of a dragoon next to the British cavalry colonel. The stricken animal plunged sideways, toppling Tarleton's black horse and pinning him beneath it.

Promptly, the duke leaped from his saddle and ran forward to take him prisoner, but "a company of English dragoons threw itself between us and protected his retreat."

Tarleton, though badly hurt by his fall, mounted another horse and ordered his men to retire and re-formed them under the cover of his infantry. The French cavalry charged again, but as so often happened, the controlled musket fire checked them.

Now Tarleton ordered his legion dragoons into the attack, but they, too, were stopped by well-formed infantry.

Reluctantly they turned and followed the forage back to Gloucester. There, because of reports that Tarleton had been defeated, the garrison were stood to at their posts, expecting immediate attack by the French. Simcoe, who was so ill he could not walk, had been carried on a stretcher to his horse so that he could command his rangers. But the French did not follow. There was no point, for the focus of the siege was across the river.

On the night of October 6, low clouds hid the moon. The men on duty on the newly constructed walls of Yorktown peered through light rain into the blackness. All night the British guns were firing from one point or another along the ramparts whenever their officers suspected enemy activity.[11] On the north by the riverbank, a forward redoubt, manned by the Welch Fusiliers, was attacked by the French, but the British fought it off. It was unlikely they would hold the redoubt for long, for it was one of several forward positions that were clearly vulnerable although valuable for flank firing in the assaults that would surely come.

Just how imminent these were became obvious as the daylight slowly revealed the country outside the town. For in the night the enemy had started work on the first parallel—only 600 yards from the walls. They had made good progress, too. Already the trench was deep enough for musketmen *and* for the working parties to continue digging by day.

British shells were soon exploding near the parallel, but it meant, as Cornwallis knew only too well, that time was getting very short. "I can see no means of forming a junction with us but by the York River," he had written to Clinton, "and I do not think that any diversion [such as the suggested attack by land on Philadelphia] would be of any use to us. . . . I see little chance of my being able to send persons to wait for you at the Capes, but I will if possible."

By the ninth, three days later, the siege batteries had been set up. The attack began slowly. Early in the afternoon the French guns near the river to the north opened up on the town. The cannon were only 12-pounders, though the French also had some howitzers, and did little damage, but they forced the *Guadeloupe* frigate to shift its station, moving farther off across the river.

Two hours later, the first of the American batteries started firing on the south of the town with 18- and 24-pounders. Shot crashed into the buildings of the port. In one house some British officers were having dinner when the walls caved in; one man died, and three were badly wounded. Cornwallis, too, was forced to evacuate British headquarters because the house was too conspicuous and singled out as a prime target.

That night Major Cochrane arrived from New York to explain Clinton's relief plan in detail. He did not survive long. Two days later he went onto the walls with Cornwallis and sighted one of the guns. After it fired, he peered over the parapet to see what damage it had done, and his head was shot off.

By then the *Charon* frigate had been set on fire by hot shot from the French guns, and the British situation was becoming critical. All the enemy batteries along the first parallel were now completed, and forty guns "mostly heavy" and sixteen mortars were firing on the town "without intermission."

"We have lost about seventy men . . . and many of our works are considerably damaged," Cornwallis wrote to Clinton at midday on the eleventh. "We cannot hope to make a very long resistance." By five o'clock in the afternoon, as he added in a postscript, he had lost another thirty. By midnight the enemy had started on their second parallel only 300 yards from the town. "We continue to lose men very fast."

Helpless, Cornwallis watched as the enemy worked on the second trench, relentlessly closing their grip on him. If only the fleet had sailed on schedule from New York on October 5, it would have arrived by now, and British ships might have been ranged defensively around the mouth of the York and the James. Even if it had left on the twelfth, it could have still just reached him in time. But once the enemy set up the batteries of the big caliber guns on the second parallel and opened up at a range of only 300 yards, it would be over—just as it had been at Charleston, even though the walls of that town were much stronger than the still damp earthworks that were all that protected Yorktown. General Benjamin Lincoln, who had surrendered Charleston, was in a more fortunate position now; he was among the generals commanding the besieging force.

Two nights later, on the fourteenth, the enemy stormed two advanced British redoubts just to the south of the town and incorporated them in their second parallel. The margin of time that still remained for Clinton and the fleet to arrive was now almost nonexistent. The only way Cornwallis could buy a few hours was by taking drastic action to postpone the moment when the guns by the new trench blasted into fire at what would be virtually point-blank range. So he ordered a sortie for the next night.

It was a desperate move. He chose his best troops—350 men selected from the guards, the grenadiers and the light infantry. Not long before dawn, they charged out of the town onto the nearly completed batteries, fighting their way with bayonets into the redoubts that protected the guns. They killed and wounded 100 of the French and spiked eleven cannon.

But apparently they did not have proper spikes, for, as Cornwallis reported, the guns "were soon rendered fit for service again and, before dark, the whole parallel and batteries appeared to be nearly complete."

That day Cornwallis was facing the ultimate crisis. Even now, before the second parallel batteries opened up, he could not use his guns. His ammunition was almost gone, and every time his gun crews ran forward a cannon anywhere on the walls the intensity of the attacking fire was so heavy it made survival impossible.

The alternatives were a surrender or a breakout, and Cornwallis decided on the latter, planning to go north from Gloucester where the enemy were fewer. He had already written to Clinton urging that, "because the safety of the place is so precarious . . . I cannot recommend that the fleet and army should run great risk in endeavouring to save us." One boat had taken the warning to New York; others, with copies, had been ordered to wait on the coast near the Chesapeake.

That night at ten o'clock, the boats started ferrying the troops across the mile-wide York River to Gloucester. But Cornwallis' luck was out. All evening the weather had been calm, but near midnight, when several boatloads of his men had been landed on the far shore, a sudden storm broke. Rain gushed down in torrents. A high wind screamed down the York River, carrying the boats away downstream.

It was the end of the escape attempt. "In this situation, with my little force divided," wrote Cornwallis, "the enemy's batteries opened at daybreak."

During the morning, as the enemy's guns broke down the Yorktown defenses, Cornwallis' troops were brought back across the river in the boats that had been recovered. But even after a few hours of the new bombardment, "the walls were in many places assailable. . . . By the continuance of the same fire for a few hours longer, they would be in such a state as to render it desperate with our numbers to attempt to maintain them."

At last, deciding that "it would have been wanton and inhuman . . . to sacrifice the lives of this small body of gallant soldiers," Cornwallis ordered a drummer—accompanied by an officer with a flag of truce—to mount the parapet and beat to "parley."

According to rebel sources, the drumming could not be heard because of the incessant crashing of the guns; but the rebel commanders understood the purpose, and the guns suddenly ceased firing. In the quiet that followed, the boy—beating his drum—and the man—bearing the proposal to suspend hostilities—walked out of the town toward the enemy lines.

Cornwallis, remembering Saratoga, proposed that the army should be permitted to return to England on the condition that they would not take up arms against America or France. Washington, remembering Charleston, insisted that the terms should be the same as those given to General Lincoln at that capitulation.[12]

Simcoe asked Cornwallis permission to escape, since all his rangers were Loyalists and could expect harsh treatment. He planned to cross the Chesapeake in boats and make for Maryland, but the earl insisted that "the whole of the Army must share one fate."

He tried to obtain a guarantee that Loyalists would "not be punished for having joined the British army," but Washington refused to agree to this since it was "altogether of civil resort." All that Cornwallis could obtain in the way of concession was the American commander's consent that one ship could sail unexamined for New York. It provided an escape for the most "obnoxious" of the Americans in his army.

At two o'clock in the afternoon of the nineteenth the British, with their drums beating, marched out of Yorktown along the road toward Hampton to the south. For nearly a mile they passed between the ranks of the enemy—the Americans to the right and the French to their left.

Because Cornwallis was ill, General Charles O'Hara carried the earl's sword. But when he approached Washington, the American commander, either because of his rank or because of Charleston, referred him to General Lincoln.

Formally Lincoln accepted the sword—and handed it back. And the British marched on down the road to lay down their arms in a field within a circle of French huzzars. The tune their bands played, according to some accounts, was an old British marching song: "The World Turned Upside Down:"

> If ponies rode men and if grass ate the cows,
> And cats should be chased into holes by the mouse. . . .
> If summer were spring and the other way round,
> Then all the world would be upside down.

NEW YORK, October 19

"The fleet were all over the bar this morning," recorded Mackenzie, "and at 4 this afternoon were under way, stretching to the Eastward"—twenty-five ships of the line and eleven smaller men of war on their way to rescue an army that was at that moment piling its arms under the eyes of a ring of French huzzars.

It had taken more than two days to get the fleet down to Sandy Hook from the harbor, and even Admiral Graves was becoming exasperated by the holdups. "I should have explained to your Excellency," he wrote in a note to Clinton on the seventeenth, "that all this show of signals and topsails were . . . to push forward the lazy and supine. And I am sorry to find that difficulties go on increasing and that nothing can turn the current but being actually at sea."

After they had sailed, Cornwallis' last letter—written just before his escape attempt, urging that there was nothing now that a relief force could do—arrived at New York and was sent after the fleet by a fast sloop. But Clinton and Graves on board the *London* decided to sail on; there might be some action still open to them. Early in the morning of the twenty-fourth, when the capes at last were in sight, the scope for this seemed very small. An open boat came alongside the flagship; in it were three men, presumably Loyalists, who said that they had left Yorktown on the eighteenth, the day after Cornwallis had sued for surrender.

Clinton and Graves sent boats in to the shore to obtain confirmation. At last, forced to face the fact that they truly were too late, the admiral once more turned his fleet about and headed back to New York.

For all practical purposes, the American Revolution—and the long British attempt to suppress it—was over. The British retrenched in New York for the time being, and no more serious fighting took place. Because the revolt was now entwined in a complex international conflict, it was to be some time before the realities were recognized officially. Nearly four years, in fact, were to pass before the final formality took place in London.

23

LONDON, June 1, 1785

It was early in the afternoon—and damp, for there had been a thunderstorm[1]—as the coach drove between the heavy oak gates of St. James's Palace and drew up in the courtyard. From it stepped two men: the Marquess of Carmarthen, the British Secretary of State for the Southern Department, and John Adams, the first ambassador of the United States to be appointed to London.

They entered the old red-brick Tudor palace where, ten years before, the King and his ministers had considered the shocking news of the harrying of British troops on the Concord road, and climbed the wide, red-carpeted staircase to the first floor. Slowly they walked beneath the crystal chandeliers, between the liveried footmen, through the series of anterooms that formed a corridor to the State Apartments.

A great deal had happened since Yorktown. The government had fallen; the Whigs had taken power. Lord George Germain, now Lord Sackville, had retired from office to his big estate in the country. Rodney had routed De Grasse in the West Indies and even taken him prisoner. Gibraltar had withstood four years of siege, though Minorca had been taken. At last, after months of bargaining with their island colonies as counters, the European powers had negotiated the peace they had started seeking in early 1781.

By then the British had withdrawn their troops from America and acknowledged its independence. Even so, the visit of the American that afternoon was an occasion marked by irony. The King, who at one stage after Yorktown had threatened to abdicate rather than change his American policy, was now to receive the man who had campaigned in Congress against him so bitterly—a man who, as his letters reveal, resented the formal and almost obsequious behavior that was now expected of him. "My first thought and inclination had been to deliver my credentials silently and retire," he wrote, but he had been persuaded by friendly ambassadors that "it was indispensable that I should make a speech . . . and as complimentary as possible." It was only with an effort that he had decided to take their advice, for he was no friend of the British and least of all of the King.

Adams was asked to wait in the Levee Room with its big windows overlooking St. James's Park, and filled "with ministers of state, lords and bishops and all sorts of courtiers." Then Lord Carmarthen returned and asked him to go with him to the King's Closet.

George III was now in his mid-forties. He was still a stubborn and dogmatic man with a complete belief in the divine right of kings, but he ruled a nation that for all its imperfections was leaning toward democracy. John Adams was in his palace only because Parliament—the British people—had demanded that he should recognize the independence of the American provinces.

The meeting, therefore, was between a monarch who had been forced against vehement personal convictions to acknowledge America as a sovereign state and an ambassador who was tensed for any kind of slight, alert for signs that his new country was not classed at the court of St. James's as an equal of other nations.

Despite these combustible elements, the confrontation deeply moved both men. Conforming somewhat reluctantly with the custom of the European courts, Adams bowed three times on entering the Closet—"one at the door, another about half way, and a third before the presence."

"The appointment of a minister from the United States to Your Majesty's Court," he said, "will form an epoch in the history of England and America. . . . I shall esteem myself the happiest of men if I can be instrumental in recommending my country more and more to Your Majesty's benevolence and of restoring . . . the old good humor between people who, though separated by an ocean and under different governments, have the same language, a similar religion and kindred blood."

From the lips of a revolutionary who had considered retiring in silence, this was generous. "The King listened to every word I said with dignity . . . ," Adams reported later. "Whether it was the nature of the interview or whether it was my visible agitation, for I felt more than I did or could express, that touched him I cannot say. But he was much affected and answered me with more tremor than I had spoken with."

"I will be frank with you," said the King, after acknowledging what Adams had said. "I was the last to consent to the separation; but the separation having been made, I have always said . . . that I would be the first to meet the friendship of the United States as an independent power. The moment I see such sentiments and language as yours prevail . . . let the circumstances of language, religion and blood have their natural and full effect."

Both men were perhaps a little overconscious that they were making history, but it was a fair start to a new relationship between an old power and a young nation that had been torn from it in six years of bitter conflict.

NOTES

CHAPTER 1

1. Thirteenth Parliament, since the Act of Union in 1707, when the Parliaments of England and Scotland were united under the title Great Britain.

2. The source material for this chapter has come primarily from the Colonial Office and State Papers in the Public Record Office in London, the Dartmouth manuscripts, the *Correspondence of George III* edited by Sir John Fortescue, various contemporary diaries, including Horace Walpole's *Last Journals*, the *Parliamentary History of England* and newspapers of the day. I have also used the *Memoirs and Life of Benjamin Franklin*.

3. Only a courtesy title like the titles of other lords in the House of Commons, because he was the son of a peer.

4. Sometimes known as the Secretary for America, since he was responsible only for colonies west of the Atlantic.

5. A rail was carried on the shoulders of two men, and the victim was placed astride it, held in position by people on each side and carried through the streets.

6. Formerly William Pitt, the man who directed Britain to victory in the Seven Years' War.

7. Hutchinson had in fact been frustrated by weak British administrations for years. This almost certainly explains his lack of vigor.

8. The officer was defended by John Adams, then on the radical fringe, and acquitted.

9. The British Prime Minister is today technically the First Lord of the Treasury, the Chancellor of the Exchequer being the Second Lord. This was not the rule in the eighteenth century. Pitt, for example, ran the Seven Years' War as the most senior Cabinet minister while Secretary of State for the Southern Department.

10. There was no formal opposition party, as there is today. Opposition consisted of members who disagreed with government policy. Edmund Burke tended to be the most dominant figure among opposition members because he was an orator of extraordinary talent.

CHAPTER 2

1. Sources: the copious correspondence between Lieutenant General Gage and Lords Dartmouth and Barrington, the Secretary for War, provide the main research. Admiral Samuel Graves' long and detailed story of the naval side in his *Conduct*, and the vivid letters written in diary form by Boston citizen John Andrews have provided important support. Wells' *Life of Samuel Adams*, local Boston newspapers and a range of secondary sources, including Belcher, Bancroft, Frothingham, Trevelyan, French and Ward, have also been consulted.

2. According to Trevelyan, who does not cite his source.

3. Massachusetts had two legislative houses: the Assembly, the lower house (of which Adams was clerk) that was elected by vote, and the Council, the executive body which ruled the province. The members of the Council were appointed by the Assembly, except for the governor and the lieutenant governor, who were, of course, appointed by the King.

There was, therefore, a strong democratic element to the government. This, however, could be controlled by the governor's power of veto. Parliament decided this was not enough in its growing sense of outrage as the result of the tea party and provided that all members of the Council would be nominated by the King for the time being.

4. The story of this attempt to bribe Adams does not appear in British sources to my knowledge, but it is told graphically by Wells in his life of Adams, as well as in other American sources. In the context of the situation, it seems likely it was true.

5. Andrew Oliver, lieutenant governor in the letters scandal involving Franklin, had now died.

6. John Andrews.

CHAPTER 3

1. Sources: Colonial Office Papers, domestic and foreign State Papers, Calendar of Home Office Papers in the PRO. The *Parliamentary History*, the *Memoirs and Life of Benjamin Franklin* and Walpole's *Last Journals* have also been used.

2. The speed of this crossing seems hardly possible. However, the departure date of September 9 is recorded on Gage's copy of the letter. It had reached London by October 17, when Dartmouth mentioned it in his reply as having arrived by the *Scarborough*.

But this reply was long and detailed and, since it laid down new policy, must have taken well over a week.

This brings us very close to October 3, when, from the Calendar of Home

Office Papers, we know a Cabinet meeting was held at 10 Downing Street, where it was decided to send the three ships of the line. This decision—and Gage is informed of this in Dartmouth's letter of October 17—must have been made after news from America. When the government's reaction to rebel accounts of Concord is recollected, it is unlikely that they would have made a major decision without an official report from Gage.

The prevailing winds at this time of the year were westerly, and I can only conclude that the *Scarborough* did make a very fast crossing.

3. Only the draft of this letter exists, but I am assuming it was sent.

4. As a plan, this was second best. The King had asked Sir Jeffrey Amherst, supreme commander of British and American troops in the Seven Years' War and much respected by the colonials, to take over as C in C, but Amherst asked leave to decline. He was not the only one: Several other men who were offered various appointments, including Admiral Augustus Keppel, also refused because of their opposition to the government's policy.

5. This incident involving Lord Sandwich is not reported in the *Parliamentary History of England*, which is an abridged version of what went on in Parliament, but Franklin covered it fully in his letters.

CHAPTER 4

1. The main sources of the pre-Lexington period described in this chapter are the Colonial Office Papers in the Public Record Office in London and Allen French's *General Gage's Informers*, based on the Clinton Papers. Most of the correspondence between Gage and London has been published *(Correspondence with Secretaries of State)*, but some of the enclosures, such as intelligence reports, captured letters and newspaper clippings, have not, although some of these are still in the London files. I have depended heavily on private and official accounts of British officers, notably: Lieutenant William Sutherland, Lieutenant Frederick Mackenzie, Lieutenant John Barker, Ensign Jeremy Lister, Major General Martin Hunter (then an ensign), Ensign Henry de Berniere, Lieutenant William G. Evelyn. Major John Pitcairn and Colonel Francis Smith.

I have also combed American sources for details of the terrain, concentrations of rebel gunfire and information not contained in the British reports, especially Paul Revere's versions of what happened during the night, which I have used to support brief British references. Among the books, French, Belcher, Trevelyan and Ward have proved useful, and in particular Frank W. Coburn's *Battle of April 19th* and Arthur B. Tourtellot's *William Diamond's Drum*.

Admiral Graves' *Conduct* provides interesting detail of some of the events that took place in the harbor.

2. At this time, a British infantry regiment usually consisted of 450 to 500 men divided into companies of 38 privates each. Each regiment usually had

two light guns attached to it, though these were often detached to the rest of the artillery for battle.

3. There is no reference to horses in any British reports of the April 19 conflict, but the custom at the time was for a 6-pounder gun to be drawn by six horses. Cleaveland, the artillery colonel, had written to London on April 17 saying that he had twenty horses, and under these circumstances, it is inconceivable that they would not have been used to draw guns on a march of at least 18 miles in hilly country, even though no eyewitness appears to have mentioned them. I have therefore taken the view that horses would have been used.

4. The figure is not clear in the manuscript. It is either 15,000 or 75,000—both impossible in the context. Because 1,500 would be too few, I have assumed 7,500 to be correct, although it sounds a bit high.

5. Although intelligence reports exist, there is, in fact, no proof that they came from Church. There is little doubt that Church was a British spy, and I am assuming that intelligence about the inner workings of Congress came from him; but it is probable that Gage had other informers.

6. Each British regiment had a company of grenadiers and a company of light infantry attached to it, both corps consisting of specially selected and trained men. For this operation, Gage had drawn them from the regiments to which they were normally attached and was using them as a single commando-type group.

7. Renamed Arlington.

8. Sutherland reported that Adair called out that the "two fellows were galloping express to alarm the country." But they were going the wrong way—*i.e.*, toward the marching troops. At that stage, Adair knew nothing about the famous ride of Paul Revere. Sutherland, it is assumed, got it a bit mixed up in hindsight.

9. This incident is reported by Sutherland. I am assuming Grant rode out with the artillery chaises the previous afternoon. He could have been one of the officers selected for lookout duty on the roads; but the artillery must have had an officer in charge of them, and Gage's orders indicate that the chaises were to meet up with Smith's column on the road.

10. It may seem strange that the troops would have marched this far with unloaded muskets, but the reports of both Sutherland and Pitcairn are clear on this.

11. This incident, timed as I have written it, was in both Sutherland's and Pitcairn's reports.

12. All the British reports, including Pitcairn's, suggest he gave this as a general direct order to the troops, but I cannot believe he did it this way. A column of 200 men would be 100 to 150 yards long—impossible to address adequately. He must have issued his orders through an officer of some kind, as I have indicated in the text.

13. Many American eyewitness reports state that Pitcairn fired the first shot with his pistol, though some of them concede that he might have done so

merely to frighten the militiamen into dropping their guns. They also assert
he urged his men to open fire. This is in complete contrast with Pitcairn's
own report and those of the other British officers and is unlikely. Pitcairn had
nothing to gain and everything to lose by allowing his men to open fire and
presumably kill some of the provincials. His account, which is virtually what I
have written, is completely credible in the context of the situation. The
American eyewitnesses were interrogated by Provincial Congress leaders
intent on painting the situation as blackly as possible so they could exploit it,
and it is probable that, following the drama of the day, imaginations ran a bit
wild.

14. According to Sutherland.

15. Although the British believed for a long time this was a scalping, and
Percy reported it formally as such, American sources have claimed that a farm
boy hit the soldier wounded from gunfire over the head with an ax as he tried
to get up off the ground. The wound he caused resembled a scalping.

16. It is uncertain what Percy referred to in his report, unless the cruelty
comment stemmed from the incident at the North Bridge in Concord, when
the soldier's head was opened in what the British believed was a scalping but
which the Americans claimed was an axing (see note 15). I have seen no other
incidents in the British records.

17. Sources for the Battle of Bunker Hill are copious and to some extent
contradictory. Howe's letters and orderly book and the Clinton papers,
Burgoyne's letters, accounts by Marine Adjutant Waller, Lieutenant John
Clark, Lieutenant Frederick Mackenzie, Gage, Colonel Samuel Cleaveland,
Admiral Graves in his *Conduct*, Dr. Grant, Lord Rawdon, Captain George
Harris, Ensign Martin Hunter and some unknown British officers have been
used. A few incidents, mainly anecdotal, have been taken from American
eyewitness sources. Samuel Drake's *Bunker Hill* and Harold Murdock's story
of the day have also been used, as well as Allen French's highly detailed
account in *The First Year of the American Revolution*.

18. No mention is made of drummers in any reports of the battle, either
British or American, that I have seen. However, the drum was the normal
method of passing orders in the field from the infantry commanders, as the
trumpet was for cavalry, and I am assuming that it was employed this time as
usual.

19. I have assumed the time when the light infantry moved to the beach
and the three lines became two lines since this is obscure in the reports.

20. Writers have made great play with the story that the guns could not
fire because 12-pound shot had been sent for 6-pound guns. This story does
not hold up as it has been represented. Four 12-pound cannon were among
the guns sent over from Boston and 12-pound shot were, of course, sent for
them. Cleaveland insisted later that he sent sixty-six rounds for each gun. It is
possible that only 6-pound guns, which would have been lighter to haul, were
sent forward from Moulton's Hill to support Howe. It is possible, too, that
boxes of 12-pound shot were taken forward in error from Moulton's instead

of 6-pound shot, but in this event the correct ammunition would not have been far away; it certainly would not have been in Boston, as the story suggests, since Howe reported the firing at the start of the advance. It may have been added to the holdup. There is some doubt if the guns shot ball, as well as grape, when they again came into action later.

21. The sources for this anecdote are two people who heard it from Small himself on separate occasions. However, the fact is that Small was a marine officer and should have been fighting on the left—not on the right where I have placed him. However, the anecdote could not have happened on the left. If Putnam had done what he did behind the walls of the redoubt, Small could never have seen him. There is no doubt that, during this stage of the battle, Putnam was behind the rail fence. I am therefore assuming Small was not with his own unit, as, indeed, Marine Major Pitcairn had not been at Lexington.

22. The question of whether there were rifles at Bunker Hill is controversial. Rifles manufactured in Pennsylvania were certainly in use in America by this date. The issue is whether or not they were employed in New England by the woodsmen. In view of their superior accuracy, although they took longer to load than muskets, it seems probable that they were.

CHAPTER 5

1. Most early press reports gave the number of rebels pursuing the British as 100 (the *Gazetteer* writer, in quoting 150, had not read his own newspaper properly), whereas, in fact, it was several thousand. This error was possibly a deliberate misrepresentation by the rebels, but it is more likely it originally referred to the number of provincials lined up at dawn on Lexington Green and was then misreported.

2. General sources of the chapter: As for earlier chapters on London scene, the *Correspondence of George III*, the Home Office Calendar and the Colonial Office Papers, the Dartmouth correspondence, contemporary newspapers, the *Parliamentary History of England* and Walpole's *Last Journals* have provided the main research structure.

3. Newspapers in London did not have political policies as such. Each carried editorials contributed by correspondents of widely differing viewpoints.

4. The casualty figure, of course, was wrong.

5. Prussia, Britain's ally in the Seven Years' War, had not been satisfied by treaty arrangements at the end of that conflict and now regarded Britain somewhat coldly.

6. Lord Germain's title, like so many others, was held by courtesy. He could, therefore, sit in the Commons.

7. Until the post of Secretary of State was created for the colonies, or for America, as it was sometimes known, there had only been two Secretaries of

State for foreign affairs: for the Northern and the Southern Departments. Both occupants of the traditional positions had fought the idea of the new secretaryship carrying the same status as theirs. Dartmouth had accepted this, but not Germain.

CHAPTER 6

1. My sources for the events that occurred in Canada in 1775-76 were reports to London by Governor Sir Guy Carleton and Lieutenant Governor Hector Cramahe; the diaries and accounts of officers living in Quebec, notably those of Thomas Ainsley, John Coffin, Colonel Caldwell, Captain Patrick Daly; and, to a lesser extent, several anonymous accounts accredited to British and militia officers in compilations of documents by Frederick C. Wurtele. An important additional source, which included the detailed story developed by Simon Sanguinet only a few months after the siege was over, was another set of documents collected for the Quebec centenary celebrations in 1875.

Very occasionally I have used rebel sources—notably John Henry, Abner Stocking and Major Meigs—when they have enhanced the British stories. British naval reports have also been employed.

2. Historians, writing from all perspectives, have made heavy emotional weather about the use of the Indians and the question of who first employed them. American writers, I notice, have tended to ignore this early letter of Ethan Allen (in the Colonial Office Papers at the PRO), which is a clear appeal for killing, and concentrated their arguments on the formal conference with Indian chiefs conducted by Schuyler a few months later, in which he urged them to stay out of the conflict altogether. Schuyler's reasons were not as humane as they sound, for he knew if the Indians were involved at all, more would be likely to side with the British, who had great influence through the Indian Department, than with the rebels.

Gage later recorded the fact that the rebels had used Indians at Bunker Hill—a civilized tribe, but technically Indians—as a complete justification. Possibly this was why Carleton was more willing to employ them in 1776 than he was now in 1775.

Indians had been employed by both sides in the Seven Years' War. Since then, however, continuing trouble with the Indians, Pontiac's uprising in particular, had made the issue especially sensitive.

3. According to Carleton, although other sources disagree.

4. By definition, a frigate was a warship with one tier of guns covered by a deck. A sloop had one tier of guns that were positioned on the upper deck and therefore uncovered.

5. The letter was actually addressed to John Manir, but since there was no one known of this name, it was assumed to be for John Mercier. Mercier, anyway, was imprisoned.

6. There is dispute whether Arnold's couriers joined Maclean in error or deliberately, as Kenneth Roberts, for one, has suggested. I have no evidence of the latter and have therefore assumed the former.

7. According to Carleton, it was a whaler, although other sources have suggested it was a skiff, propelled by paddles, and a canoe.

8. The approach of this ship was probably the source of the rumors of the planned attack on Arnold's rear that the rebel colonel referred to in his report as one of the reasons why he fell back to Pointe aux Trembles. There is no reference in the British records to any other vessel, certainly none with any soldiers on board, as Arnold believed.

9. There is some dispute about the weather. I have relied on Ainsley because he had a keen eye for detail and good descriptive powers.

10. The total number available to Montgomery is not known for certain. There were, it appears, just under 1,000 Americans, in addition to which there were Canadians. Some historians have questioned the presence of Canadians, but there is frequent reference to them in contemporary accounts by Quebec inmates and rebel leaders.

11. According to Ainsley, although some accounts have put the number of bodies lower.

12. Simon Sanguinet.

13. James Graham, *Life of General Daniel Morgan*.

14. Britain also still had a small post in Florida, though this was not one of the thirteen colonies, and the sea base of Halifax in Nova Scotia that was useful for the ships, but, remote as it was, not much help from the viewpoint of internal colonial control.

CHAPTER 7

1. Sources: Colonial Office correspondence, Clinton, and Sir William Howe's Orderly Book.

2. According to a note in his papers, Clinton told Howe it was his opinion that "they would attempt to burn the town on Dorchester side." Howe answered that he was sure they would not attempt it because they would not dare risk their mortars on Dorchester Heights; "If they did, we must get at it with our whole force." (*American Rebellion,* 23). I provide this note for the benefit of readers, though, for me, it does not begin to explain Howe's neglect. Why should they not risk their mortars?

CHAPTER 8

1. Sources: Colonial Office Papers and Admiralty Papers.

CHAPTER 9

1. Sources: Correspondence between General Howe and the Colonial Office and Lord Howe and the Admiralty (in the Public Record Office); the journals of Ambrose Serle and Captain Henry Duncan, respectively secretary and flag captain to Lord Howe; *The American Rebellion* by Sir Henry Clinton, which provides his personal account of the Battle of Long Island and the assault on Manhattan, supported by his notes from the Clinton Papers; the letters of Lord Rawdon in the Hastings MSS; the diaries of Lieutenant Frederick Mackenzie, Lieutenant Colonel Stephen Kemble, Captain John Montresor and the Hessian adjutant general, Major Carl Baurmeister; Max von Eelking's *German Allied Troops in the North American War of Independence*.

Thomas W. Field's *The Battle of Long Island*, Henry P. Johnston's *The Campaign of 1776* and Thomas Jones' *The History of New York During the Revolutionary War* have provided invaluable supporting material, especially since all three have big appendices of original documents. Alexander Flick's *Loyalism in New York During the American Revolution* and Carl Van Tyne's *Loyalists in the American Revolution* have also been helpful.

2. Also known as the North River.

3. The source material on Mrs. Loring is very unsatisfactory, although many writers have played up her role. Most of the colorful copy is anonymous, attributed to unnamed British officers, although Charles Stedman makes a reference to her. Stedman wrote a history of the war in 1794, but his comment is especially interesting because he claimed to have been an officer in the army in America at the time.

4. This ramp-equipped landing craft is a great surprise since, according to naval experts at the Royal Maritime Museum at Greenwich, they were not in general use until the First World War. However, Francis Hutcheson, who was present on Staten Island at the time, mentions the design specifically in a letter in the Haldimand Papers. He, too, was surprised.

5. One of the most difficult facts to establish is how horses, cannon and wagons were transported across water. The general methods are known, but surprisingly—since this must have created far more problems than carrying infantry—the systems employed in individual actions are rarely referred to. Hundreds of horses, batteries of cannon and scores of wagons appear as if by magic across what are sometimes large stretches of water. In this instance, I have made some assumptions based on the methods in current usage and the landing craft employed, the details of which are fully recorded, after consultation with historical experts at the Royal Naval Maritime Museum at Greenwich, England. The reference by Hutcheson (see Note 4) to ramp-fronted landing craft is made by no one else, to my knowledge, and I suspect the reason is that they were unsuccessful, probably letting in water at the joins. It would also explain why they did not pass into normal military usage.

In my description, I have thus assumed that the traditional landing barges were used in the assault, some of which, even if those of the new design were also employed, most certainly were.

6. It seems extremely unlikely that the British would have landed on an enemy beach without putting down any covering barrage. Nevertheless, the records suggest this is what happened. All British accounts say the ships "covered the landing"; this could imply that they fired or that they were merely ready to if necessary. However, on other occasions when barrages were put down, such as before Bunker Hill and at Kip's Bay later in this chapter, the personal accounts always make a feature of them. Field, relying mainly on American sources, though he does not cite them in this instance, suggests the assault craft fired single cannon mounted in the front of the boats. I have found no British records to support this, and it seems unlikely, since grape from the warships would be far more effective.

There *were* no enemy defending. In that flat terrain, the British could presumably see this.

7. Records indicate the Hessians traveled in this way a few days later when another contingent crossed from Staten Island. I am assuming the officers insisted on it on both occasions.

8. In the ever-changing rebel command situation, Sullivan, previously in command of all troops on Long Island, was now number two under General Putnam and, in this capacity, in charge of the Flatbush-Bedford sector.

9. Johnston quotes accounts from the captured rebel officers and apparently interviewed their relatives. But he gives no story of the actual capture; nor does Evelyn, the British officer in charge of the patrol, although several of his letters on other matters exist. Both Clinton and Howe say they were captured quietly, interrogated by Clinton himself and revealed that the pass was undefended.

10. Field.

11. According to a rebel source. By this time, the red-and-white-striped flag was in use, and it is strange that this was not flying above the redoubt. To my knowledge, no British records mention it. A red flag, such as the one described, was flown at Bunker Hill, but this was before a suitable design could be developed.

12. Both Franklin and Adams give highly detailed accounts of this meeting.

13. Mackenzie, watching from Long Island, says the rebels went to a point *up* the river, but Clinton was much closer, so I stay with his version.

14. Trumpets were not normally used by the infantry at this time, but several rebel accounts report this incident and even suggest it was partially responsible for Washington deciding to make some kind of move to repair the shattered morale of his men.

CHAPTER 10

1. Sources: letters to the Admiralty by naval officers, supported by the journals of Lieutenant James M. Hadden, Lieutenant William Digby, General von Riedesel and Captain Georg Pausch. A. T. Mahan's *Major Operations of the Navies in the American War of Independence* and C. H. Jones' *The History of the Campaign for the Conquest of Canada in 1776* have been helpful. I have also consulted the letters of Arnold and Burgoyne, the helpful. I have also consulted the letters of Arnold and Burgoyne, and the memoirs of General James Wilkinson.

Because the action of the Battle of Valcour Island was focused in a very limited area that everybody present could clearly see, there are few of the discrepancies between the various accounts that have faced me in previous battles, which by their nature were more complex, with several areas of action.

2. A schooner was a vessel whose sails were rigged fore and aft, like modern yachts, and not square-rigged across the main line of the ship as were the men-of-war.

3. Lake Champlain and the Richelieu River flowed north into the St. Lawrence. For this reason, Carleton's fleet traveled "up" the lake, even though it was proceeding south.

CHAPTER 11

1. Sources: The same as Chapter 9, since it forms part of the same campaign. In addition, for my description of the storming of Mount Washington I have used an article by Edward F. DeLancey in the *Magazine of American History*, February, 1877, which—although one or two of the facts are wrong, as has become clear from contemporary material since published— has been particularly useful because of its detailed study of the Manhattan terrain in the eighteenth century. I also referred to William Abbatt's *The Battle of Pell's Point.*

2. This maneuver by Cornwallis is mentioned only by Clinton and Von Baurmeister to my knowledge, but I have featured it since these must be regarded as prime sources.

3. Both the terrain on the rebel left and their movements before the main British attack on October 31, when they were found to have evacuated their lines, are subjects of dispute in various accounts. I rely on Clinton, for he was there and involved at the highest level.

4. Several historians put the attack time earlier, although both Robertson's and Howe's official report put it at noon, as I have.

5. There is no actual record that Cornwallis had dragoon patrols out looking for Lee at this stage, but this was an obvious move. A dragoon patrol actually captured Lee less than two weeks later.

CHAPTER 12

1. Sources: The action at Versailles is taken almost entirely from the long and vivid letters to London of Lord Stormont, the British ambassador. For the Bancroft material, I have used Edward Bancroft's *Narratives of the Objects and Proceedings of Silas Deane as Commissioner of the United States to France* (which includes the first of the spy's reports to London), Carl Van Doren's *Secret History of the American Revolution* and various secret documents in Steven's *Facsimiles of Mss. in European Archives*. For the London scenes, I have used Knox, Clinton, the *Correspondence of George III*, the Domestic State Papers and the correspondence between Germain and Howe. Piers Mackesy's *The War for America*, Alan Valentine's *Lord George Germain* and De Fonblanque's *Political and Military Episodes . . . of the Right Hon. John Burgoyne* have also served as guides.

2. Howe expressed his views at length in his examination before a parliamentary committee.

CHAPTER 13

1. Sources: Burgoyne's *Orderly Book, State of the Expedition* (and *Supplement*), *Letter to His Constituents*; correspondence with Germain, Howe and Lord Derby; his speeches in Parliament and the inquiry. Journals of Lieutenants James Hadden, Thomas Anburey, William Digby and Captain Georg Pausch; correspondence of Major General Baron von Riedesel and Baroness von Riedesel. De Fonblanque's *Political and Military Episodes . . . of the Right Hon. John Burgoyne*, Samuel Drake's *Burgoyne's Invasion of 1777*, Hoffman Nickerson's *Turning Point of the Revolution*, F. J. Huddlestone's *Gentleman Johnny Burgoyne* and the several books of W. L. Stone have been used as guides.

2. Reports vary whether Burgoyne was on the *Maria* or the *Royal George*, but the latter seems most likely.

3. Again, there is variation between reports on whether the advance took place on July 1 or June 30.

4. Reports conflict about whether the guns were actually on the summit by sunset or whether the rebel general assumed, when he saw men standing on the top of the hill, that the guns would soon be there. Lieutenant Digby reports the movement of the two 12-pounders past his picket in darkness on the night of the fifth. Other reports suggest the guns were on the hill but unassembled by nightfall. I find it difficult to accept that the rebels would have evacuated so quickly without the glint of a gun and have therefore assumed that Digby was possibly mistaken on his timing.

5. Some evidence has been produced that she was actually shot by rebels

and scalped by the Indians afterward, but since neither Burgoyne nor General Gates (who later exploited the incident) knew of this, it does not affect the story.

CHAPTER 14

1. Sources: reports by Howe and Von Knyphausen, journals of John Montresor, Stephen Kemble, Von Baurmeister, Major John André and Ambrose Serle.
2. The guards regiments, in this case the Coldstream Guards, were the elite regiments of the army that had developed from the sovereign's personal guards. Their officers ranked above equivalent officers of other regiments. They differed from those other elite units, the light infantry and the grenadiers (not the Grenadier Guards), in that these were not formed as a regiment (see Note 6, Chapter 4).

CHAPTER 15

1. Sources: The same as Chapter 13.
2. This is a more extreme view than that taken by most historians, many of whom have blamed Germain for the whole affair. I cannot accept this. Any orders to generals at that time were clearly intended to be altered, as Germain was to point out later, if the local situation made it necessary, as it certainly did on the upper Hudson. Other historians have blamed Howe, but Howe made it plain in plenty of time what he was going to do and gave his reasons.

The truth is—and it becomes obvious when the details of the actions are examined—that Burgoyne was a very poor general. His decision now was inexcusable and would never have been accepted by Howe, Clinton or Cornwallis. Leaving Canada before he had properly organized his means of communication caused all his trouble. Otherwise, he would now have been at Albany; nothing would have held up his advance against a much smaller force. His fighting of the two battles of Freeman's Farm indicates a clear weakness in both tactics and use of forces at his disposal.
3. Morgan had been returned to the continental army in one of the exchanges-of-prisoners that were under constant negotiation between the British and Americans.
4. Von Riedesel's doubts about what he should do are very strange, as is the time it took him to get his troops into action. By his own account, he sent an officer to Burgoyne for orders at two o'clock, fairly near the beginning of the battle, but even though the center was under terrible pressure, the Hessians were not engaged until near the end of the day.

Why did Burgoyne call them up so late? The same question could be asked about the disengaged Twentieth Regiment which General Phillips eventually brought into action.

By all contemporary accounts, Burgoyne was personally brave, but apparently he became very harassed under battle conditions.

5. Other sources have suggested it was one of Burgoyne's messengers to Clinton, not the other way around as Digby states, who was captured and swallowed the silver bullet. I merely report what Digby wrote in his journal on a specific date.

6. Strangely, none of the British sources available have referred to this famous story of Arnold's ride, although they have confirmed that its purpose was achieved: the capture of Colonel Breymann's redoubt. I have therefore used rebel sources for this incident.

7. Some historians, notably Stone, who specialized in this period of the war, have stated that he leaped his horse over the wall of the redoubt. This seems extremely unlikely: First, the wall would probably have been too high. Second, landing in a redoubt in which there were 200 hostile men would have been hazardous and, under the circumstances, pointless.

8. None of the British sources available refer to this minute gun described by Lossing, though one of them does suggest that the rebels may not have realized the purpose of the gathering. Baroness von Riedesel quotes Gates as saying after Saratoga that he ordered the guns to stop firing as soon as the true nature of the gathering was reported to him.

CHAPTER 16

1. Sources: the same as previous chapters on the London scene: *Parliamentary History*, Walpole, *Correspondence of George III*, Cabinet papers, State Papers, contemporary newspapers, etc. Also, the Auckland Papers in the British Museum.

2. Walpole's information seems to have been a mixture of the actions at Bennington and Fort Stanwix.

3. Vergennes had, in fact, discussed the main points of agreement with Franklin and Deane on December 12.

CHAPTER 17

1. Sources: Clinton; William B. Willcox's *Portrait of a General*; William S. Stryker's *Battle of Monmouth*; the *Journal* of Major John André, *Simcoe's Military Journal*; A. C. Flick's *Loyalism in New York*; C. Van Tyne's *Loyalists in the American Revolution*.

2. Historians agree that it is extremely difficult to establish exactly what happened at Monmouth. As in previous battles, I have selected Clinton whenever there is doubt, although his version conflicts with other sources. I

have also used André, who drew some very good and detailed sketches, and a highly detailed map drawn by Lieutenant Spencer of the Queen's Rangers.

3. Both the British and the rebels claimed a victory at Monmouth. If Clinton's version is accepted, the rebel claim must be regarded as specious; he had driven the rebel army back across three ravines, and was now withdrawing to continue retreat.

CHAPTER 18

1. Sources: Clinton's *American Rebellion*; Cornwallis' *Correspondence*; Colonial Office correspondence with commanders in chief; William B. Willcox's *Portrait of a General*; Bernhard A. Uhlendorf's *Siege of Charlestown*; Banastre Tarleton's *History of Campaigns in Virginia*; Robert D. Bass' *The Green Dragoon*; Hastings MSS (includes Cornwallis' long and vivid letter about the Battle of Camden), Archibald Robertson's *Diaries and Sketches in America.*

CHAPTER 19

1. Sources: Clinton; C. C. Van Doren's *Secret History of the American Revolution*, whose main sources are Clinton's British headquarters papers at Ann Arbor University; Winthrop Sargent's *Life and Career of Major John André, Adjutant General of the British Army in America*; Isaac N. Arnold's *Life of Benedict Arnold.*

2. Quoted by Sargent.

CHAPTER 20

1. Sources: Cornwallis; Clinton; Stopford-Sackville papers (Lord Germain); Tarleton; Simcoe; Robert D. Bass' *The Green Dragoon*; Charles Ross' *The Correspondence of Charles, First Marquis Cornwallis.*

CHAPTER 21

1. Sources: Colonial Office Papers; Clinton; Cornwallis; *Correspondence of George III;* S. F. Bemis' *Diplomacy of the American Revolution*; B. F. Stevens' *Campaign in Virginia.*

CHAPTER 22

1. Sources: Clinton, Cornwallis, Simcoe, Captain Henry Duncan, the Sandwich Papers (for Graves and Hood), the Hood Papers, logs of HM ships, *The Campaign in Virginia* edited by B. F. Stevens for exact dates of arrival of letters between Cornwallis and Clinton, Henry P. Johnston's *The Yorktown Campaign and the Surrender of Cornwallis*, William B. Willcox's "The British Road to Yorktown," Randolph G. Adams' "A View of Cornwallis' Surrender."

2. Not to be confused with Admiral Samuel Graves, in command at Boston in 1775.

3. According to William B. Willcox in *Portrait of a General*, Clinton misinterpreted the reference to French intentions, which were not worded so dogmatically in the captured letters.

The issue of the captured letters is something of a mystery, because Clinton had to send them to London for decoding, and the plain-language versions did not reach him in New York until August. A possible explanation is that his staff in New York succeeded in decoding parts of them—the vital parts. At any rate, the quote is taken from his own version of what happened in *The American Rebellion*.

4. Clinton notes in *The American Rebellion* that Tarleton told him after the war that on discovering St. Simon's troops, he pleaded with Cornwallis to make a breakout attempt but that Ross dissuaded the earl in view of Clinton's letters of the second and sixth promising relief. This cannot be completely correct because there was a time gap of some nine days between the day St. Simon went up the James and the arrival of Clinton's first letter on the thirteenth. By the time Clinton made this note, though, his quarrel with Cornwallis had become very bitter, and he was exploiting every fact he could to lay blame on him.

5. Cornwallis put it at 4,000 combat troops fit for duty, discounting sick and nonfighting personnel.

6. The French had relinquished the wind in the previous clash at the Chesapeake earlier in the year when Arbuthnot prevented enemy ships from blockading Arnold.

7. Aware of criticism by his junior admiral, Graves made a special point in his report that the "line of battle" signal was not flying all the time during the action, though the *London*'s log shows it was hoisted during the battle. In any case, Hood surely should have put his ships, now the rear guard, into action; he had two hours to do so. The point he made was that "engage" involved independent ship action while the "line" signal required the ships to keep station in the fleet. The two signals were therefore contradictory.

8. Mackenzie.

9. Some historians have suggested that Rodney's misjudgment of De Grasse's plans was partly due to the fact that Rodney was ill and was in fact on his way home to recover.

10. All sources do not agree with Simcoe's version of this in the *Journal of Operations of the Queen's Rangers*. According to some accounts, Tarleton was actually riding with the foragers when the French cavalry attacked, possibly because he thought the decoy had not worked.

11. It is strange that fire balls, such as those used by the defenders of Quebec in 1775, were not employed to provide illumination.

12. The point about the Charleston surrender was that the rebels were refused permission to march out with their colors unfurled. This was regarded as ignominious, and now the British would have to march out with their colors "cased."

CHAPTER 23

1. Sources: My main source for the meeting between the King and John Adams, and for the dialogue in particular, which he quotes, is taken from Adams' highly detailed letter to Jay in Congress. Most of the London dailies reported the occasion, indicating its importance, but gave no details beyond the presentation of credentials. The London *Chronicle* reported the thunderstorm, and I have taken a slight liberty in assuming that it occurred during the morning.

BIBLIOGRAPHY

MANUSCRIPTS AND ORIGINAL PRINTED SOURCES

(Note abbreviations: PRO = Public Record Office, London. HMC = Historical Manuscripts Commission, London, which has calendared many private collections of papers with generous excerpts and sometimes even full texts of letters. A set of HMC volumes is in the British Museum and other libraries.)

Admiralty Papers: Correspondence between Admiralty and naval commanders, including Admirals Sir Samuel Graves, Lord Howe, Thomas Graves, Marriot Arbuthnot, Sir Samuel Hood. PRO Series ADM 1 & 2 (for digests of in-letters, see ADM 10, 11, 12).

———: Logs of HM ships. Series ADM 51.
Amherst Papers: PRO.

Artillery: Correspondence between artillery officers and artillery HQ. PRO Series C05.

Auckland Papers: Mostly to and from William Eden, later Lord Auckland, who at one relevant time controlled the British Secret Service. Additional MSS, British Museum.

Cleaveland, Samuel: PRO War Office Papers. Series W055.

Colonial Office Papers: Correspondence between the Secretary of State and his staff with governors and commanders in chief in America, including Thomas Hutchinson, Generals Thomas Gage, Sir William Howe, Sir Henry Clinton, John Burgoyne, Lord Cornwallis. The files include enclosures such as relevant reports to the commanders from junior officers, intercepted enemy letters and local newspaper clippings. PRO Series C05.

———: Canada: military and civil correspondence to and from Sir Guy Carleton and his staff and from naval and military commanders operating in the province. PRO Series CO42.

Cornwallis Papers: PRO, London.

Dartmouth Papers: HMC, 1895 and 1896 (20). British Museum.

Duncan, Captain Henry, *Journal*. Miscellany, Navy Records Society, Empress House, London.

Eden, William: See Auckland Papers.

Eyre-Matcham Papers: HMC, Various 1909. British Museum.

Germain, Lord George: See Stopford-Sackville Papers.

Graves, Admiral Samuel, *Conduct* (journal). Additional MSS, British Museum.

Graves, Admiral Thomas: See Sandwich Papers.

Haldimand Papers: Additional MSS, British Museum.

Hastings (Lord Rawdon) Papers: HMC, 1934 (78).

Home Office: Calendar of Home Office Papers (George III) 1770-75. Cabinet minutes, interdepartmental correspondence, etc., mostly in Colonial Office and State Papers. PRO, London.

Hood, Admiral Sir Samuel: Navy Records Society, Empress House, London.

Howe, General Sir William: Evidence before committee of the House of Commons. PRO.

Hutcheson, Francis: See Haldimand Papers.

Jenkinson Papers: Additional MSS, British Museum.

Knox Papers: HMC, Various 1909.

Lothian, Marquess of: HMC, 1905.

Rawdon, Lord: See Hastings Papers.

Royal Institution: American MSS in the Royal Institution of Great Britain. HMC 1904-1909.

Sandwich Papers: Navy Records Society, Empress House, London.

State Papers (Domestic), George III: Cabinet minutes, interdepartmental correspondence, etc. PRO.

State Papers (Foreign) (France): Correspondence with ambassador. Series SP 78.

Stopford-Sackville (Lord George Germain) Papers: HMC, 1910 (49). British Museum.

Stormont, Lord: See State Papers (Foreign).

Tupper, Major: PRO. Admiralty Papers—see also Allen French's *The First Year of the American Revolution*.

War Office: Correspondence between commanders and their staffs with Secretary for War, etc., Series WO 1, 2, etc.

PRINTED DIARIES AND LETTERS WRITTEN BY PARTICIPANTS

British, Hessian and Canadians in America and Canada

Ainslie, Thomas: See Wurtele, Frederick C.

Anburey, Thomas, *With Burgoyne from Quebec*, 1963.

———, *Travels Through Interior parts of America*, 1789.

André, John, *Journal*, 1908.

Barker, John, *British in Boston*, 1924.

Baurmeister, Adjutant General Carl, *Revolution in America*, 1957.

Burgoyne, John, *Letters to His Constituents*, 1779.

———, *Orderly Book of Lieutenant General John Burgoyne*, 1860.

———, *State of the Expedition*, 1780.

———, *Substance of General Burgoyne's Speeches*, 1778.

———, *Supplement to the State of the Expedition*, 1780.

Caldwell, Colonel: See Wurtele, Frederick C.

Clarke, John, *Narrative of the Battle of Bunker Hill*, 1775.

Clinton, Sir Henry, *The American Rebellion*, 1954.

———, *Narrative of Lieutenant General Sir Henry Clinton*, 1783.

———, *Observations of Mr. Stedman's History*, 1794.

———, Correspondence: See B. F. Stevens' *Campaign in Virginia.*

Coffin, John: See Wurtele, Frederick C.

Cornwallis, Lord, *Correspondence of Lord Cornwallis,* ed. by Charles Ross, 1859.

———, Correspondence: See B. F. Stevens' *Campaign in Virginia.*

Daly, Patrick: See Wurtele, Frederick C.

De Berniere, Ensign, *Account* (Massachusetts Historical Society, Collections, Series 2, Vol. 4).

Digby, William, *British Invasion from the North*, 1887.

Evelyn, W. G., *Memoirs and Letters of W. G. Evelyn*, 1879.

Ewald, Johann: See Uhlendorf.

Gage, Thomas, *Account of the Battle Fought in America*, 1775.

———, *Correspondence with the Secretaries of State*. (Yale Historical Publications, Manuscript and edited texts no. 11), 1931.

Hadden, J. M., *Journals and Orderly Book*, 1963.

Hanger, George, *Life and Adventures of Colonel George Hanger*, 1801.

Hinrichs, Johann: See Uhlendorf.

Howe, Sir William, *Narrative in a Committee of the House of Commons, 1779*, 1780.

———, *Sir William Howe's Orderly Book*, ed. by B. F. Stevens, 1890.

Hunter, Sir Martin, *Journal of Sir Martin Hunter*, 1894.

Hutchinson, Thomas, *Diary and Letters of Thomas Hutchinson*, 1883-1886.

Kemble, Stephen, *The Kemble Papers* (New York Historical Society Collections, Publication Fund Series, Nos. 16 and 17), 1868.

Lamb, Roger, *Journal*, 1809.

———, *Memoir of His Own Life*, 1811.

Lister, Jeremy, *Concord Fight*, 1931.

Literary and Historical Society of Quebec, *Historical Documents,* Series 4, No. 4.

Montresor, John, *The Montresor Journals* (New York Historical Society Collections, 1882).

Murray, Sir James, *Letters from America*, 1951.

New York Historical Society Collections, *Journal of Occurrences in Quebec*, 1868.

Pausch, Georg, *Journal of Captain Pausch*, 1886 (Mansell's Historical Series, No. 14).

Percy, Hugh Earl, *Letters from Boston and New York,* 1902.

Pettengill, R. W., *Letters from America*, 1924.

Riedesel, Friedrich Adolf von, *Memoirs of General von Riedesel,* 1868.

Riedesel, Friderike, Charlotte Louise von, *Letters and Memoirs of Baroness von Riedesel,* 1827.

Robertson, Archibald, *His Diaries and Sketches in America,* 1930.

Sandwich, Earl of, *Private Papers of John, Earl of Sandwich, 1771-1782,* 1932.

Serle, Ambrose, *American Journal, 1776-1778*, 1940.

Simcoe, J. G., *The Journal of Operations of the Queen's Rangers*, 1787.

———, *Simcoe's Military Journal*, 1844.

Stedman, Charles: See General Works.

Stevens, B. F., *Campaign in Virginia, 1781*, 1888. (Letters of Clinton and Cornwallis.)

Stone, W.L., *Letters of Brunswick and Hessian Officers*. 1891.

Tarleton, Banastre, *A History of the Campaigns of 1780 and 1781*, 1787.

Uhlendorf, Bernhard A., *The Siege of Charlestown*, 1938 (University of Michigan Publications, Historical and Political Science, Vol. 12).

Von Huyn, J. C.: See Uhlendorf.

Waller, Marine Adjutant, *Orderly Book* (Massachusetts Historical Society). See also Allen French's *The First Year of the American Revolution*.

Wurtele, Frederick C., *Blockade of Quebec*, 1905 (Literary and Historical Society of Quebec, 7th Series of Historical Documents, 1905).

Americans and French in America

Allen, Ethan, *Narrative of the Capture of Ticonderoga*, 1849.

Andrews, John, *Letters of John Andrews*, 1866.

Cresswell, Nicholas, *Journal*, 1924.

Lafayette, Marquis de, *Memoirs*, 1825.

Lee, Charles, *Memoirs*, 1792.

Revere, Paul, "Letter to Dr. Belknap, Describing His Ride to Lexington, etc.," *Massachusetts Historical Society Proceedings for 1878*, published 1879.

Stocking, Abner, "An Interesting Journal," *Magazines of History* (Extra No. 75), 1921.

Sullivan, John, *Letters and Papers* (New Hampshire Historical Society Collections, Vols. 13-15), 1930.

Wilkinson, James, *Memoirs of My Own Times,* 1816.

Contemporary Journals, Reports etc., in London

Adams, John, *The Works of John Adams,* 1856.

Burney Collection of Newspapers, British Museum.

Franklin, Benjamin, *Memoirs and Life of Benjamin Franklin,* 1818.

Galloway, Joseph, *Examination of Joseph Galloway,* 1779.

George III, *Correspondence of George III,* ed. by Sir John Fortescue. 1967.

Gibbon, Edward, *Private Letters,* 1896.

Grafton, Duke of, *Autobiography and Correspondence of the 3rd Duke of Grafton,* 1898.

Harcourt, Elisabeth, *Mrs. Harcourt's Diary of the Court of King George III* (Miscellanies of the Philobiblon Society), 1854.

Jesse, J. H. *Memoirs of the Life etc., of George III,* 1867.

Newspapers, contemporary: See Burney Collection above.

Papendiak, Charles L. H., *The Court and Private Life at the Time of Queen Charlotte,* 1887.

Parliamentary History of England.

Walpole, Horace, *Last Journals.*

Wraxall, Sir Nathaniel, *Historical Memoirs,* 1836.

GENERAL WORKS

Abbatt, William, *The Battle of Pell's Point,* 1901.

Adams, C. F. and J. Q., *The Life of John Adams*, 1871.

Adams, Randolph G., "A View of Cornwallis' Surrender," *American Historical Review*, Vol. 37 (October-July, 1931-32).

Alden, J. B., *The Rise of the American Republic*, 1963.

Anderson, Troyer S., *The Command of the Howe Brothers During the American Revolution*, 1936.

Arnold, Isaac N., *The Life of Benedict Arnold*, 1880.

Aubrey-Fletcher, N. L., *The History of the Foot Guards to 1856*, 1927.

Bancroft, Edward, *Narrative of the Objects and Proceedings of Silas Deane as Commissioner of the United States to France* (Winnowings in American History Revolutionary Narrative No. 4), 1891.

Bancroft, George, *The History of the United States of America*, 1834-74.

Barrington, Shute, *The Political Life of Viscount Barrington*, 1814.

Bass, Robert D., *The Green Dragoon*, 1958.

Beirne, F. F., *Shout Treason*, 1959.

Belcher, Henry, *The First American Civil War*, 1911.

Bemis, S. F., *Diplomacy of the American Revolution*, 1935.

Bill, Alfred Hoyt, *The Campaign of Princeton (1776-1777)*, 1948.

Brayley, E. W., *Londiniana*, 1829.

Carter, William, *Detail of Engagements etc. 1775-1776*, 1784.

Carrington, H. B., *Battles of the American Revolution*, 1876.

Chalmers, Harvey, *Joseph Brant*, 1955.

Clara, Dora M., *British Opinion and the American Revolution*, 1930.

Clode, C. M., *Military Forces of the Crown*, 1869.

Coburn, Frank W., *Battle of April 19th*, 1912.

———, *Battle on Lexington Common*, 1921.

Cornwallis, Lord, *General Regulations*, etc., 1798.

Croly, George B. C., *The Political Life of Edmund Burke*, 1840.

Curtis, Edward E., *Organization of the British Army in the American Revolution* (Yale Historical Publication, Miscellany No. 19), 1926.

Davies, G., *Early History of the Coldstream Guards*, 1924.

Dawson, Henry B., *Battles of the United States*, 1858-60.

De Fonblanque, Edward B., *Political and Military Episodes . . . of the Right Hon. John Burgoyne*, 1876.

DeLancey, Edward F., "Mount Washington and Its Capture on 16th November 1776," *Magazine of American History*, Vol. 1, February, 1877.

De Peyster, J. W., *Life and Misfortunes etc. of Sir John Johnston*, 1882.

Doniol, Henri, *Histoire de la participation de la France à l'establissement des Etats-Unis*, 1886-99.

Drake, Samuel, *Bunker Hill,* 1875.

Duncan, Francis, *History of the Royal Regiment of Artillery*, 1872.

Dundas, Sir David, *Instructions for Formation and Movements of Cavalry*, 1799.

Edwards, Thomas J., *Standards, Guidons, Colours etc.,* 1953.

Eelking, Max von, *German Allied Troops in the North American War of Independence*, 1893.

Field, Thomas W., *The Battle of Long Island*, 1869.

Fleming, T. J., *Now We Are Enemies*, 1960.

Flick, A. G., *Loyalism in New York* (Studies in History, Economics and Public Law, Vol. 14, No. 8), 1901.

Forbes, Arthur, *History of the Army Ordnance Service*, 1929.

Force, Peter, *American Archives*, Fourth and Fifth Series, 1837-46, 1848-53.

Fortescue, Sir John, *History of the British Army*, 1899-1930.

French, Allen, *The First Year of the American Revolution*, 1934.

———, *General Gage's Informers*, 1932.

———, *Old Concord*, 1915.

———, *The Siege of Boston*, 1911.

———, *The Taking of Ticonderoga*, 1928.

Frothingham, Richard, *The History of the Siege of Boston*, 1849.

Fuller, John F. C., *Armament and History*, 1946.

———, *British Light Infantry in the 18th Century*, 1925.

George, Mary D., *London Life in the 18th Century*, 1925.

Gordon, William, *The History . . . of the United States of America*, 1788.

Gottschalk, L. R., *Lafayette and the Close of the American Revolution*, 1942.

———, *Lafayette Joins the American Army*, 1937.

Graham, Henry, *History of the 16th Queen's Light Dragoons*, 1912.

Graham, James, *Life of General Daniel Morgan*, 1856.

Greene, G. W., *Life of Nathanael Greene*, 1867.

Guttmacher, M.S., *America's Last King,* 1941.

Hargreaves, Reginald, *The Bloodybacks*, 1968.

Hatch, Louis Clinton, *Administration of the American Revolutionary Army*, 1904.

Hinde, Robert, *Discipline of the Light Horse*, 1778.

Hinkhouse, F. J., *Preliminaries of the American Revolution* (Columbia University Studies in History, Economics and Public Law, No. 276,) 1926.

Hudleston, Francis, *Gentleman Johnny Burgoyne,* 1927.

Hughes, B. P., *History of British Small Bore Artillery,* 1970.

James, C., *Regimental Companion,* 1803.

Jennings, Sir William, *The Queen's Government,* 1965.

Johnston, Henry P, *The Battle of Harlem Heights,* 1897.

———, *The Campaign of 1776* (Long Island Historical Society, Memoirs etc., Vol. 3), 1867.

———, *The Yorktown Campaign and the Surrender of Cornwallis,* 1881.

Jones, Charles H., *The History of the Campaign for the Conquest of Canada in 1776,* 1882.

Jones, Thomas, *The History of New York During the Revolutionary War,* 1879.

Lee, Henry, *Memoirs of the War in Southern Department,* 1812.

Lossing, B. J., *Pictorial Field Book of the American Revolution,* 1850.

Lowell, E. J., *The Hessians . . . in the Revolutionary War,* 1884.

Lucas, Reginald, *Lord North,* 1913.

Lundin, Charles Leonard, *Cockpit of the American Revolution,* 1940.

Lushington, S. R., *Life and Services of General Lord Harris,* 1840.

Mackesy, Piers, *The War for America,* 1775-83.

MacKinnen, Colonel, *Origin and Services of the Coldstream Guards,* 1833.

Mahan, Alfred T., *Major Operations of the Navies in the American War of Independence,* 1913.

Marlow, Louis, *Sackville* [Germain] *of Drayton*, 1948.

Martelli, George, *Jeremy Twitcher* [Lord Sandwich] , 1962.

Moore, Frank, *Songs and Ballads of the American Revolution*, 1856.

Moore, George H., *Treason of Charles Lee*, 1860.

Muller, John, *Treatise of Artillery*, 1768.

Mumby, F.A., *George III and the American Revolution,* 1924.

Murdock, Harold, *Earl Percy's Dinner Table*, 1907.

Neuman, G. C., *History of Weapons in the American Revolution*, 1967.

Nickerson, Hoffman, *Turning Point of the Revolution*, 1928.

Onderdonk, Henry, *Revolutionary Incidents of Suffolk and King's Counties*, 1849.

Pakenham-Walsh, R. P., *History of the Corps of Royal Engineers*, 1889-1958.

Pares, Richard, *George III and the Politicians,* 1953.

Partridge, Bellamy, *Sir Billy Howe*, 1932.

Pemberton, N. W. B., *Lord North*, 1938.

Peterson, H. L., *The Book of the Gun*, 1962.

Reid, Loren, *Charles James Fox*, 1932.

Rogers, F., and Beard, A., *Paul Revere: Patriot on Horseback,* 1943.

Sabine, Lorenzo, *American Loyalists*, 1847.

Sargent, Winthrop, *Life and Career of Major John André, Adjutant General of the British Army in America,* 1902.

Scott, Duncan S., *John Graves Simcoe*, 1926.

Scott, Sir James S. D., *British Army—Origin, Progress, etc.*, 1868.

Sheppard, J. E., *Memorials of St. James' Palace*, 1894.

Shy, John W., *Towards Lexington*, 1965.

Sparks, Jared, *Diplomatic Correspondence of the American Revolution*, 1853.

Spector, Margaret M., *American Department of the British Government*, 1768-82.

Stedman, Charles, *History of the Origins etc. of the American War*, 1794.

Stevens, B. F., *Facsimiles of Mss. in European Archives, 1773-83*, 1889-98.

Stone, W. L., *Campaign of Lieutenant General John Burgoyne*, 1877.

———, *Life of J. Brant-Thayendanegea*, 1864.

———, *Reminiscences of Saratoga*, 1880.

———, *Visits to Saratoga*, 1895.

Stryker, William S., *Battle of Monmouth*, 1927.

———, *Battles of Trenton and Princeton*, 1898.

Sweet, Samuel, *History of the Bunker Hill Battle*, 1827.

Tourtellot, Arthur B., *William Diamond's Drum*, 1960.

Treacy, M. F., *Prelude to Yorktown*, 1963.

Turner, Edward R., *The Cabinet Council of England in the 17th and 18th Centuries, 1622-1784*, 1930.

———, *Privy Council of England in 17th and 18th Centuries*, 1927.

Trevelyan, Sir George, *The American Revolution*, 1905.

Turberville, A. S., *The House of Lords in the 18th Century*, 1927.

Valentine, Alan, *Lord George Germain*, 1962.

———, *Lord North*, 1967.

Van Doren, C. C., *Mutiny in January*, 1943.

———, *Secret History of the American Revolution*, 1941.

Van Tyne, C., *Loyalists in the American Revolution,* 1902.

Wallace, Willard M., *Appeal to Arms*, 1951.

———, *Traitorous Hero*, 1954.

Ward, Christopher, *War of the Revolution*, 1952.

Wells, W. V., *Life etc. of Samuel Adams*, 1866.

Wilkins, W. H., *Some British Soldiers in America*, 1914.

Willcox, William B., "The British Road to Yorktown," *American Historical Review*, Vol. 52 (October-July, 1946).

———, *Portrait of a General* [Sir Henry Clinton], 1964.

Wright, J. W., *Notes on the Siege of Yorktown,* 1932.

Zweig, Stefan, *Marie Antoinette,* 1933.

Index